Midterms and Mandates

New Perspectives on the American Presidency
Series Editors: Michael Patrick Cullinane and Sylvia Ellis, University of Roehampton

Published titles

Constructing Presidential Legacy: How We Remember the American President
Edited by Michael Patrick Cullinane and Sylvia Ellis

Presidential Privilege and the Freedom of Information Act
Kevin M. Baron

Donald Trump and American Populism
Richard S. Conley

Trump's America: Political Culture and National Identity
Edited by Liam Kennedy

Obama v. Trump: The Politics of Rollback
Clodagh Harrington and Alex Waddan

Obama's Fractured Presidency: Policies and Politics
Edited by François Vergniolle de Chantal

The Republican Party and the War on Poverty: 1964–1981
Mark McLay

Midterms and Mandates: Electoral Reassessment of Presidents and Parties
Edited by Patrick Andelic, Mark McLay and Robert Mason

Forthcoming titles

Harry S. Truman and Higher Education
Rebecca Stone

Sports and the American Presidency: From Theodore Roosevelt to Donald Trump
Edited by Adam Burns and Rivers Gambrell

JFK's Grand Strategy: Breaking the Cold War Mould in the Kennedy White House
James Cooper and Ian Horwood

Series website: https://edinburghuniversitypress.com/new-perspectives-on-the-american-presidency.html

MIDTERMS AND MANDATES

Electoral Reassessment of Presidents and Parties

Edited by Patrick Andelic, Mark McLay and Robert Mason

EDINBURGH
University Press

Edinburgh University Press is one of the leading university presses in the UK. We publish academic books and journals in our selected subject areas across the humanities and social sciences, combining cutting-edge scholarship with high editorial and production values to produce academic works of lasting importance. For more information visit our website: edinburghuniversitypress.com

Edinburgh University Press Ltd
The Tun – Holyrood Road
12(2f) Jackson's Entry
Edinburgh EH8 8PJ

First published in hardback by Edinburgh University Press 2022

Typeset in 11/13 Sabon by
Cheshire Typesetting Ltd, Cuddington, Cheshire, and
printed and bound by CPI Group (UK) Ltd,
Croydon, CR0 4YY

A CIP record for this book is available from the British Library

ISBN 978-1-4744-7818-2 (hardback)
ISBN 978-1-4744-7819-9 (paperback)
ISBN 978-1-4744-7820-5 (webready PDF)
ISBN 978-1-4744-7821-2 (epub)

Contents

List of Figures and Tables

Figures

Tables

Acknowledgements

As editors, we express our thanks to the British Association for American Studies (BAAS) and the US Embassy in London, which provided financial support for our project. We are grateful, too, to the institutions which provided a home for the project's meetings – the National Library of Scotland (and especially Dora Petherbridge) and the Institute for Advanced Studies in the Humanities at the University of Edinburgh (and especially Donald Ferguson and Ben Fletcher Watson). That Edinburgh University Press is our project's longer-term home is a matter of similarly good fortune, and our gratitude extends to all at the press and particularly to Jenny Daly, Ersev Ersoy, and Sarah Foyle, as well as to our series editors, Michael Cullinane and Sylvia Ellis, and those who reviewed our work for the press.

Notes on Contributors

Patrick Andelic is Senior Lecturer in American History at Northumbria University. He is the author of *Donkey Work: Congressional Democrats in Conservative America, 1974–1994* (University Press of Kansas, 2019) and has contributed articles to *The Historical Journal*, the *Journal of Policy History*, and the *Journal of Arizona History*.

Julia R. Azari, who completed her PhD at Yale University in 2007, is professor of political science at Marquette University (PhD, Yale University, 2007). She is the author of *Delivering the People's Message: The Changing Politics of the Presidential Mandate* (Cornell University Press, 2014) and co-editor (with Lara Brown and Zim Zwokora) of *The Presidential Leadership Dilemma: Between the Constitution and a Political Party* (SUNY Press, 2013). Her work has also appeared in *FiveThirtyEight*, *Foreign Affairs*, and *Politico*, and she is a regular contributor at the political science blog *Mischiefs of Faction*.

Mark Eastwood holds a PhD in American History from the University of Nottingham. His research was funded by the Midlands3Cities doctoral training partnership (DTP) of the Arts and Humanities Research Council (AHRC), the British Association of American Studies, the European Association of American Studies, and Historians of the Twentieth Century United States. Previously, he was an AHRC International Placement Scheme fellow at the John W. Kluge Center at the Library of Congress and a postgraduate fellow at the Eccles Centre for American Studies at the British Library. Until 2021, he was an associate lecturer in history at De Montfort University. He now works in a professional role for the AHRC Midlands4Cities DTP at the University of Nottingham.

Nadia Hilliard teaches US politics and American political thought at the Institute of the Americas, University College London. The author of *The Accountability State: U.S. Federal Inspectors General and the Pursuit of Democratic Integrity* (University Press of Kansas, 2017), she has researched comparative immigration policy, public accountability in the US federal bureaucracy, and, most recently, the idea of political fraternity. Among other hobbies, she paints animals in her spare time.

Richard Johnson is Lecturer in US Politics and Policy at Queen Mary, University of London. He is the author of *The End of the Second Reconstruction: Obama, Trump, and the Crisis of Civil Rights* (Polity, 2020) and *US Foreign Policy: Domestic Roots and International Impact* (Bristol University Press, 2021).

Andrew Johnstone is an associate professor of American history at the University of Leicester. His publications include *Against Immediate Evil: American Internationalists and the Four Freedoms on the Eve of World War II* (Cornell University Press, 2014) and (as co-editor with Andrew Priest) *US Presidential Elections and Foreign Policy: Campaigns, Candidates and Global Politics from FDR to Bill Clinton* (University Press of Kentucky, 2017). His articles have appeared in *Diplomatic History*, the *Journal of Contemporary History*, the *Journal of Transatlantic Studies*, and the *Journal of American Studies*. His current book project examines the relationship between the rise of the American public relations industry and the rise of the United States as a world power.

Mark McLay is Lecturer in US Twentieth Century History at Lancaster University. His first book, *The Republican Party and the War on Poverty: 1964–1981*, was published by Edinburgh University Press in 2021. He has contributed to *Constructing Presidential Legacy: How We Remember the American President*, edited by Michael Patrick Cullinane and Sylvia Ellis (Edinburgh

University Press, 2018) and has published articles in the *Journal of Policy History* and the *Historical Journal.*

Robert Mason is a professor of history at the University of Edinburgh. He is the author of *Richard Nixon and the Quest for a New Majority* (University of North Carolina Press, 2004) and *The Republican Party and American Politics from Hoover to Reagan* (Cambridge University Press, 2012). With Iwan Morgan he is co-editor of *Seeking a New Majority: The Republican Party and American Politics, 1960–1980* (Vanderbilt University Press, 2013) and *The Liberal Consensus Reconsidered: American Politics and Society in the Postwar Era* (University Press of Florida, 2017).

Iwan Morgan is Emeritus Professor of US Studies at University College London and a specialist in US political history. His publications include: *Nixon* (Bloomsbury, 2001); *Seeking a New Majority: The Republican Party and American Politics, 1960–1980*, co-edited with Robert Mason (Vanderbilt University Press, 2012); and *Reagan: American Icon* (Tauris, 2016). His latest book is *FDR: Transforming the Presidency and Renewing America* (Bloomsbury, 2022).

Andrew Rudalevige is Thomas Brackett Reed Professor and chair of the Department of Government at Bowdoin College. A graduate of the University of Chicago and Harvard University, he is past president of the Presidents and Executive Politics section of the American Political Science Association. Rudalevige's books include *By Executive Order: Bureaucratic Managements and the Limits of Presidential Power* (Princeton University Press, 2021); *Managing the President's Program: Presidential Leadership and Legislative Policy Formulation* (Princeton University Press, 2002), which won the national Neustadt Prize; *The New Imperial Presidency: Renewing Presidential Power after Watergate* (University of Michigan Press, 2006); and the co-authored textbook *The Politics of the Presidency* (Sage, 2022). He writes frequently on executive power as a contributor to the *Washington Post*'s *The Monkey Cage* blog and is the creator of the PBS

LearningMedia video series 'Founding Principles' on American government and civics.

Joe Ryan-Hume is a senior researcher at the Scottish Parliament and a Mellon-Schlesinger fellow at Harvard University. He also recently held the Royal Society of Edinburgh–Fulbright fellowship at Boston University and worked in the US Congress as a Lantos congressional fellow. He completed his doctorate in US political history at the University of Glasgow in 2017 and holds an MLitt in American studies and an MA in history from the same institution.

Sarah Thelen lectures in US history at University College Cork and has published a number of articles on the Silent Majority and other aspects of the domestic debates over the war in Vietnam. She holds a PhD from American University in Washington, DC, and is writing a monograph on White House efforts to rally support for the US war in Vietnam. Her research also explores the changing nature of patriotism, nationalism, and American identity in the twentieth century.

Sarah Tiplady completed her PhD on presidential campaign strategy at Keele University in 2019. She was awarded the 2018 Richard E. Neustadt Postgraduate Paper Prize by the American Politics Group (APG), and a postdoctoral fellowship at Keele University in 2019. Her research predominantly focuses on presidential campaign strategy, investigating the element of 'the message' in campaign strategy through content analysis of the rhetoric in the form of campaign speeches.

Preface: Why Midterms Matter

Julia R. Azari

Elections do more than change who is in power. They also form the basis for narratives and stories about what is new in politics, and which political forces resist efforts to dislodge them. After the ballots are counted, politicians, the media and ordinary citizens begin to assign meaning to the results as a signal about where the nation is headed and what its voters have to say about it. Presidential elections lend themselves to this kind of analysis, but midterm elections have increasingly become subject to these larger narratives.

Perhaps the most obvious and prominent of these narratives is the idea of the 'referendum' on a presidential administration. The very phrase 'midterm elections' signals their connection to the president. While senators, representatives, governors and other officials are elected by their own constituencies, with distinct constitutional and governing prerogatives, their elections take place in the middle of a presidential term. From an election interpretation standpoint, the referendum view is a somewhat limited one, however. For one thing, the referendum is very rarely a positive one – the president's party, with a few exceptions, loses seats. It is hardly a meaningful referendum if we already know the results in advance. In addition, midterm elections carry substantive and symbolic significance all their own, and have lasting impacts on American politics well beyond the presidential term within which they occur.

Twenty-first-century midterm elections have proven significant and widely subject to interpretation. The 2010 midterms, famously interpreted by Obama as a 'shellacking', saw the rise of the Tea Party and a historic seat loss by House Democrats, as well as major losses at the state level.[1] These losses, and those of the 2014 midterms, form the basis of Obama's lacklustre legacy as a party leader. This legacy illustrates not only the challenges faced by Obama, but the broader phenomenon of his presidency – a popular, charismatic figure without the institutional resources or acumen to sustain a deeper movement. Taking the mediated, individualistic presidency to a new level, we saw Donald Trump win a surprise election in 2016 and enjoy Republican majorities for his first two years in office, only to have his party lose control of the House in the 'blue wave' of 2018. Two incredibly different presidents demonstrated a kind of structural similarity: command of media and personal brand could shape the partisan environment but not substitute for party organisation, and this tumultuous combination led to midterm election disasters that derailed their agendas and muddled their mandates.

However, this interpretation can be credibly contested. Perhaps the successes of the Republicans in 2010 were the result of a targeted and racist set of Astroturf campaigns against the nation's first African American president, exacerbated by structural advantages for Republicans in the Senate and redistricting in the House.[2] It is also possible that we can explain the 2018 outcome by considering that Trump did not win the popular vote in 2016, and as a result his agenda was not particularly popular, nor rewarded by voters in the 2018 elections. In both cases, the role of political organization and mobilisation likely mattered to the election outcome.[3] I raise these alternate explanations not because any of them are obviously correct, but because many interpretations are possible and the evidence is often ambivalent.

The stories of national election results are both complicated and simple, as I have noted in the past.[4] A few simple pieces of data allow us to make predictions about midterm outcomes: the president's party usually loses seats; more when the president is unpopular.[5] At the same time, these larger trends cover a variety of more complex situations: candidate recruitment, local dynamics and competition between party factions.

The midterms of the 2010s have shaped American politics in ways that go far beyond their significance for the Obama and Trump presidencies. The rise of the Tea Party in the 2010 and 2014 contests demonstrated that cultivating rage against political institutions and party leadership could constitute a political strategy on its own. This created the path for Trumpism and ultimately reshaped the direction of the Republican Party and the interpretation of conservative orthodoxy.

The 2018 elections may have also been a turning point, albeit a more complex and subtle one, for progressives in the Democratic Party. The midterms were not a clear victory for the progressive faction. As Meredith Conroy, Nathaniel Rakich, and Mai Nguyen note, the Democratic 'establishment' remained strong in 2018 – yet many of these candidates embraced progressive policy positions.[6] That year also saw the election of representatives like Alexandria Ocasio-Cortez (New York) and Ayanna Pressley (Massachusetts), who defeated long-term incumbents in surprising primary victories.[7] Rashida Tlaib (Michigan) and Ilhan Omar (Minnesota) were elected to be the first Muslim women in the US Congress. A historically diverse legislative class, with a few prominent primary defeats for establishment figures, lent itself to a narrative of a changing party – and country. While the Democratic caucus in Congress may still be a mix of progressive and moderate legislators, the national presence of figures like Ocasio-Cortez influences the perception of the Democratic Party and has contributed to its drift towards left positions on race, climate and economic issues.[8]

The impact of these recent contests illustrates the need to better understand modern midterm elections. Three major questions emerge with respect to midterms and mandates. First, how useful is the conventional wisdom that midterm elections are driven by 'thermostatic' politics, in which voters trend away from the party in power? This rule is one of the most reliable in American politics – yet the chapters in this volume offer a subtle challenge, suggesting that many factors can cause a midterm loss for the president's party. A closer look at twentieth-century midterm elections undermines the idea that electoral politics is driven mostly by a relationship between the president and the people. Instead, other factors also play a crucial role: electoral mobilisation of key geographic and demographic constituencies can shape election results, as can party leaders' choices about whom to mobilise and with what message. The chapters in this volume also explain how political conditions, such as the state of the economy and the presence or absence of war, can influence the midterm elections. These factors may not be closely tied with larger ideological movements or conflicts, yet they may drive results that are interpreted in those terms. Finally, it is a major irony of election interpretation that we look for major messages in elections whose results are so predictable.

The second major question deals with how midterm elections have shaped the major ideological movements of the twentieth century: New Deal liberalism and Reagan-style conservatism. New Deal liberalism transformed the Democratic Party into one guided by populist economic ideas and an active vision for government involvement in the economy, bolstered by a large, patchwork coalition.[9] A party agenda that embraced government action had to be carefully balanced with American concerns about socialism and excessive government intervention, a political tightrope that often constrained the party's agenda. Iwan Morgan describes in Chapter 4 how the 1934 and 1938 elections illustrated both the 'magnitude and limitations' of New Deal Democratic politics. The 1934 elections solidified the identity of the Democratic Party as a New Deal liberal project. But, a few years later, the losses for liberal Democrats in 1938, alongside the failure of Roosevelt's attempted 'purge' of conservative Democrats, solidified the 'conservative coalition' that would serve as a veto point for any leaders hoping to pass laws in the New Deal tradition. Robert Mason in Chapter 6 addresses the opportunities and limitations for conservatives challenging the post–New Deal Democratic Party in 1946 and 1950. The deliberate forging of a political strategy that equated liberal programmes with socialism and communism was not entirely new, but offered a politically feasible critique at a time when Republicans like Thomas Dewey were unsure about how to oppose the popular programmes of New Deal liberalism. This line of objection, however, proved effective in thwarting policy priorities and shaping the tenor of debate between the parties for many years to come.

The conservative movement arose long before Ronald Reagan won the presidency. Proponents of religious conservatism and free-market ideas gradually took control of the party, marginalising politicians who were more moderate on taxes, social programmes, social issues like abortion, and civil rights. Midterm elections also prove illuminating for the development of the conservative turn in the Republican Party. Not only can we trace its roots back to the 1950s through the struggles of the elections covered in Chapter 6, but we can also look at its earlier development during the Nixon years. The same debates about which issues to emphasise, and the struggles between moderates and conservatives, also shaped the administration's approach to the 1970 midterms. However, the context had shifted in two critical and related ways: the New Deal coalition had eroded in response to the strain of civil rights and the Vietnam War; and the changing meaning of identity politics meant new political opportunities and intra-party debates. The 1970 election rendered a mixed verdict on this approach and foreshadowed decades of struggles over how to expand the coalition while maximising political gain from white identity appeals. This dilemma has been a persistent one in modern Republican politics.[10] When the conservative movement was ascendant within the Republican Party, internal disagreements emerged that would influence how conservative ideology knit together different constituencies and perspectives. The Vietnam War context highlights the way in which modern conservatism merged patriotic appeals and identity politics. However, as with New Deal liberalism, the study of elections also shows us the limitations of these ideological currents. The account of the 1986 midterm elections in Chapter 12 highlights these limitations by complicating the narrative about an uninterrupted conservative ascendance in the 1980s. Once again, identity and cultural issues came into play, with liberals mobilising around women's issues and civil rights.

Analysis of midterm elections allows us to trace how two major ideological movements of the twentieth century were shaped by manoeuvring around inter- and intra-party clashes.

Groups within parties disagreed about how to take advantage of opposition opportunities and how to behave on the defensive when their parties controlled the White House. Midterm setbacks after successful presidential bids also outlined the limitations of ideological appeals, even as New Deal liberalism and the conservative movement defined their respective eras.

Finally, the study of midterm elections allows us to move into the more theoretical territory of what it means to be a party in opposition in the United States. Legitimate opposition had a rocky start in American politics, where party divisions were considered suspect at the founding.[11] The parties that eventually emerged were mutable coalitions of regional and ideological interests, conducive to internal fights. They also served as a vehicle for ambitious politicians who wanted to seek the presidency themselves. As a result of these two factors, presidents have often been constrained by opposition within their own parties, and only tenuously held any sort of leadership over them.[12]

The nationalisation of twentieth-century party politics has altered the relationship between presidents and parties. Midterms and mandates are relevant to this development. The phenomenon of the midterm election as a referendum on the president began to take hold in the New Deal era, as several of these essays describe. FDR's attempt to use the primary process to 'purge' his own party of New Deal opponents also illustrates the way in which presidents began to jockey for influence in a nationalised system. In the 1970 midterms, Nixon asked voters to deliver a Republican Congress who would support his agenda. Nixon's requests made explicit the claim that party, not institutional prerogative, would drive the relationship between the executive and legislative branches. The inverse was also true – electing the other party to a congressional majority came to stand in for a direct rebuke of the president's agenda. The sharpening of the ideological edges of party conflict – foreshadowing the hyperpolarisation of the twenty-first century – also became evident during the Nixon years.

Several subsequent developments have raised the stakes of midterm elections. As Frances Lee has observed, the competition for majority control has created incentives for parties in

Congress to eschew cooperation.[13] Looming midterms elections now have the potential to shape a president's first years and even months in office, as congressional co-partisans contemplate impending loss of power. Compounding this is a more fundamental stressor on American democracy in the twenty-first century: the declining sense of legitimate opposition. Arguably, the erosion of this key democratic value is asymmetrical, with congressional Republicans working to deny Barack Obama any policy victories and refusing to hold a vote on his Supreme Court appointment in 2016 (and later confirming a justice in 2020, weeks before the election). As writer Adam Serwer argued in 2021, Republicans are only willing to accept the legitimacy of votes for their own party.[14] At the same time, Democrats' reception of Donald Trump hardly affirmed his legitimacy, and focused (not without reason) on his violations of democratic norms and his attacks on various members of the political community. The shared sense between parties that the other has the right to govern and forms a *loyal* opposition has always been somewhat fragile. In the twenty-first century, it is at risk of disappearing altogether.

The combination of competitive elections, increasingly nationalised midterm contests, and the fraying concept of legitimate opposition means that understanding these elections and their history is all the more important. Midterm elections have long been viewed as referendums on the president; now that referendum is not just to slow the political agenda but to challenge the foundations of its legitimacy. These contests also help to determine what the new opposition party looks like, and whether it will be led by moderates or ideologues. The study of midterm elections can help to illustrate what legitimate opposition has meant in American government, and perhaps offer some lessons about how to revive the concept in contemporary politics.

Notes

1. Katie Sanders, 'Have Democrats Lost over 900 Seats in State Legislatures since Obama Has Been President?' *Politifact*, 25 Jan.

2015, https://www.politifact.com/factchecks/2015/jan/25/cokie-roberts/have-democrats-lost-900-seats-state-legislatures-o/, accessed 29 July 2021.

2. See, e.g., Clarence Y. H. Lo, 'Astroturf versus Grass Roots: Scenes from Early Tea Party Mobilization', in Lawrence Rosenthal and Christine Trost, eds, *Steep: The Precipitous Rise of the Tea Party* (Berkeley, CA: University of California Press, 2012), pp. 98–130.
3. Mobilisation efforts are widely credited with higher turnout in the 2018 midterm elections. See William Galston and Clara Hendrickson, 'The Democrats' Choice: The Midterm Elections and the Road to 2020', *brookings.edu*, 30 Jan. 2019, https://www.brookings.edu/research/the-democrats-choice-the-midterm-elections-and-the-road-to-2020/, accessed 29 July 2021.
4. Julia Azari, 'Narratives are Simple. Elections are Complicated', *Mischiefs of Faction on Vox.com*, 8 Nov. 2018, https://www.vox.com/mischiefs-of-faction/2018/11/8/18073998/narratives-are-simple-elections-are-complicated, accessed 29 July 2021.
5. James E. Campbell, 'Introduction: Forecasting the 2018 US Midterm Elections', *PS: Political Science & Politics* 51, S1 (Oct. 2018): pp. 1–3.
6. Meredith Conroy, Nathaniel Rakich, and Mai Nguyen, 'We Looked at Hundreds of Endorsements. Here's Who Democrats Are Listening To', *FiveThirtyEight.com*, 14 Aug. 2018, https://fivethirtyeight.com/features/the-establishment-is-beating-the-progressive-wing-in-democratic-primaries-so-far/, accessed 29 July 2021.
7. Shane Goldmacher and Jonathan Martin, 'Alexandria Ocasio-Cortez Defeats Joseph Crowley in Major Democratic House Upset', *New York Times*, 26 June 2018; Katharine Q. Seelye, 'Ayanna Pressley Upsets Capuano in Massachusetts House Race', *New York Times*, 4 Sept. 2018.
8. Alex Seitz-Wald, 'Progressives' Plans for Victory Just Took a Gut-punch. Now What Do They Do?' *NBC News*, 8 Nov. 2018, https://www.nbcnews.com/politics/elections/progressives-plan-victory-just-took-gut-punch-now-what-do-n933771, accessed 29 July 2021.
9. John Gerring, *Party Ideologies in America, 1828–1996* (New York: Cambridge University Press, 1998).
10. Shushannah Walshe, 'RNC Completes "Autopsy" on 2012 Loss, Calls for Inclusion Not Policy Change', *ABC News*, 18 Mar. 2013, https://abcnews.go.com/Politics/OTUS/rnc-completes-autopsy-2012-loss-calls-inclusion-policy/story?id=18755809, accessed 29 July 2021.

11. Richard Hofstadter, *The Idea of a Party System: The Rise of Legitimate Opposition in the United States, 1780–1840* (Berkeley, CA: University of California Press, 1969).
12. Daniel P. Klinghard, 'Grover Cleveland, William McKinley, and the Emergence of the President as Party Leader', *Presidential Studies Quarterly* 35 (2005): pp. 736–60.
13. Frances E. Lee, *Insecure Majorities: Congress and the Perpetual Campaign* (Chicago, IL: University of Chicago Press, 2016).
14. Adam Serwer, 'If You Didn't Vote for Trump, Your Vote is Fraudulent', *TheAtlantic.com*, 10 Dec. 2020, https://www.theatlantic.com/ideas/archive/2020/12/voter-fraud/617354/, accessed 29 July 2021.

Introduction: Midterms and Mandates, Presidents and Parties

Patrick Andelic, Mark McLay and Robert Mason

During the first century or so of US history, midterm elections were known simply as 'elections'.[1] They were not considered part of the rhythm of the presidential cycle, a barometer of public confidence in the president or their party. That changed over the course of the twentieth century. Where once midterms were relatively marginal and localised, they have become nationalised – that trend has mirrored both the development of the modern presidency and the professionalisation of political parties. Now they are a regular feature of America's political calendar – relatively unusual by international comparison – and one that is inextricably intertwined with the fate of the president in office. Even the collective name – 'midterm' – prioritises the relationship with the president. For the incumbents on the ballot, those elections represent the end of their terms, an opportunity for the public to pass judgement on whether they should continue in office or who their successors should be.

'Midterms' collectively refers to the hundreds of elections that take place on the Tuesday after the first Monday in November, two years following the most recent presidential election. They elect all 435 members of the House of Representatives and approximately one-third of the Senate (thirty-three or thirty-four senators in our day), as well as governorships, state legislatures, mayoralties and city councils, plus ballot initiatives and referendums. To discern, in those hundreds of events, clear trends or clean patterns is sometimes a fool's errand. National events jostle with local concerns, candidate effects and other factors to produce a multitude of outcomes. To paraphrase Bill Clinton, if the people speak through every election, it is not always clear what they have said.[2]

Midterm elections, according to Andrew E. Busch, 'have traditionally been the poor stepchild of American electoral studies in many respects'.[3] This collection brings together historians and political scientists to reflect on midterms on their own terms and in relationship with the presidency. The essays here focus principally on congressional elections (House of Representatives and Senate) and their relationship with the presidency. Perhaps even more so than presidential elections, midterms can provide insights into the relationship between the White House and Capitol Hill. Congressional politicians explicitly face re-election when the president does not but when presidential popularity is often a crucial factor. More often than not, the elected official uppermost in American voters' minds is not even on the ballot paper. The essays in this volume show how midterm elections offer a focus for White House–Capitol Hill and president–party interactions, which have significant implications for politics, party building and maintenance, and policymaking.

Surges and shellackings: the literature on midterms

The literature on midterms is not trivial, though most has been produced by political scientists. While the historiography of presidents and the presidency is extensive, few historians have engaged systematically with the midterms as an electoral phenomenon. Historians recognise that midterm results can be highly consequential for a president's agenda, but midterm campaigns remain overshadowed by presidential contests. Perhaps the best-known work on midterms is Andrew Busch's *Horses in Midstream*, which argues for the importance of midterms as 'an integral part of the system of checks and balances established by the Founders'.[4] He categorises midterm elections into four types: 'normal' midterms, in which the president's party loses seats but this does not imperil either the president or their party; 'preparatory' midterms, which herald and catalyse a lasting partisan shift in US politics; 'calibrating' midterms, which moderate a president's change agenda without derailing it entirely; and 'creative exceptions', in which the president's party sustains no losses and the executive gains 'all of the advantages for themselves which midterms usually confer on their opponents'.[5]

Most scholars who have engaged with midterms have concerned themselves with explaining one of its most consistent outcomes: that the president's party nearly always loses seats. This, for scholars and commentators, is something close to a law of political gravity in US elections. Indeed, since 1900, there have only been three midterms when the party of the White House incumbent has not lost seats in Congress (1934, 1998, and 2002). In those three cases, there were unusual factors that contributed to the exceptional outcomes – the beginnings of the New Deal, the Pyrrhic impeachment of Bill Clinton, and the aftermath of the 9/11 attacks, respectively.

As Andrew Rudalevige notes in his chapter, there are three prevailing interpretations of midterms in the political science literature: surge and decline; referendum voting; and balancing. Contributors in this volume engage with all three, but this volume does not subscribe to any as a definitive explanation for midterm change. 'Surge and decline' posits that midterm losses are simply the reversion to a political baseline after a successful presidential year; in winning the White House, a president helps other candidates of the same party to achieve election, too, in a surge of support, whereas two years later that 'coat-tail' effect is absent. 'Referendum voting' theories portray midterm results as voters passing judgement on the president's performance in office, and by extension the president's party. Finally, the 'balancing' theory is grounded in the idea that the average American voter is a moderate who seeks opportunities to limit a president's monopoly on power by supporting the opposition party. As Rudalevige shows, all of these theories are in some respects incomplete and none has become the prevailing orthodoxy among scholars.

The essays in this volume are less interested in *why* a president's party loses (or even occasionally gains) ground in Congress, than with the implications of those results. In particular, a unifying theme of this collection is the idea of 'mandate':

what is a mandate, who can lay claim to them within the US political system, and how can midterm elections produce new mandates and revise old ones? These essays reflect on whether and how midterm results can modify a president's mandate, either strengthening the political position of the president and the president's party or (more frequently) creating new challenges for them to navigate.

The trouble with 'mandates'

In early November 2020, with the Electoral College result uncertain but his popular vote lead growing, Democratic presidential nominee Joe Biden claimed that Americans had given him a 'mandate for action'.[6] Then the day before the Electoral College was due to meet in mid-December, Biden's campaign manager, Jen O'Malley Dillon, told journalists in a briefing that the president-elect had 'won decisively and has a clear mandate to lead this country'.[7] In these statements, Biden and his team were following a well-trodden path for incoming presidents: staking a claim to a 'mandate' and seeking to shape the political environment in a way that is favourable for new administrations.

As Julia Azari, one of the contributors to this volume, has suggested elsewhere, there are 'few concepts in American politics [that] have proved as controversial and yet as resonant as the presidential mandate'.[8] As generally understood, 'mandate' is the idea that an election victory confers upon an official the authority and legitimacy to pursue a specific policy agenda. It is also a concept that has become increasingly central not only to presidential rhetoric but to that of other political actors – from those who wish to displace the president's authority in general terms (such as the Speaker of a new majority in the House of Representatives for the out-party – the party not in control of the White House, that is) to those who seek to challenge the president in a limited and specific context (such as a governor opposing a president over a policy matter).

Scholars are divided on whether the mandate should be considered a real phenomenon or whether the idea of a mandate is fundamentally a myth. In the former camp is Patricia Heidotting Conley who describes mandate claims as 'both empirical statements about voters and strategic political calculations'.[9] Drawing on data about elections from 1828 through to the end of the twentieth century, and employing a range of case studies, she offers a schema that distinguishes between elections that produced clear 'popular mandates' (1952, 1964, and 1980), those that produced 'bargained mandates' (1948 and 1992), and those that produced 'victories but not mandates' (1960, 1976, and 1988).[10] By contrast, Charles O. Jones has suggested that the presidential mandate is 'a next-day convenience' for understanding election results and can 'become a kind of reality through its use in interpreting an election by media analysts, members of Congress, and presidents themselves'. It is 'a classic example of an illusion becoming reality in the context of power as persuasion', writes Jones.[11] The mandate can thus empower or constrain a president, depending on who is most successful at doing the persuading in the aftermath of an election.

Perhaps the most coruscating analysis has come from Robert A. Dahl, who has gone so far as to suggest that the presidential mandate represents 'the pseudodemocratization of the presidency'. By that 'cumbersome' term, Dahl writes, he means 'a change taken with the ostensible and perhaps even actual purpose of enhancing the democratic process that in practice retains the aura of its democratic justification and yet has the effect, intended or unintended, of weakening the democratic process'. That weakening of democracy, claims Dahl, takes two forms: the vanishing of congressional, popular, or other forms of restraint on the president; the weakening of democracy's deliberative qualities, which creates an enlightened citizenry.[12] A mandate allows a president to position themselves as a tribune of the popular will but this, suggests Dahl, comes at the expense of true democracy and accountability.

The essays in this volume do not make a definitive claim about the empirical reality of the presidential or congressional mandate. The contributors have not based their essays on a shared definition of the term. Mandate, however, is an abiding theme across the chapters here.

Chapter overview

The essays in this collection are collected into three parts. Part One takes a longer and more conceptual view, seeking to place midterm elections within wider institutional contexts that help to shed light on the commonalities and differences across various contests. The other two parts encompass ten case studies of midterm elections in the twentieth century, from the New Deal to the Reagan era. Part Two covers midterm elections that took place amid the rise and consolidation of the 'New Deal coalition' and the challenges that it faced during the mid-twentieth century. The third and final part explores the arrival of a conservative ascendancy during the latter third of the twentieth century, which involved challenges to the hegemony of the New Deal coalition.

Whatever the era, midterm elections have rarely been positive for the incumbent president. As Andrew Rudalevige charts, this seeming iron law of American politics has continued to hold firm throughout most of the post-Reagan era of partisan polarisation, during which time numerous presidents have experienced dramatic losses during midterm contests – with the notable exceptions of the 1998 and 2002 elections. Given the increased pull of partisanship on voter behaviour, Rudalevige cautions that such 'shellackings' are increasingly not a referendum on an incumbent president and, instead, offer mere reflections of party strength. Indeed, as Rudalevige notes, dramatic midterm losses have done little to predict whether or not the incumbent president would win re-election two years later, as seen with the contrasting outcomes for Bill Clinton, Barack Obama, and Donald Trump. Nonetheless, midterms remain focal points for presidential administrations, as demonstrated by the fact that Joe Biden's team were already plotting to avoid Democratic losses in 2022 prior to the 46th president's inauguration.

Continuing the theme of partisanship, Sarah Tiplady explores the extent to which presidents have utilised partisan rhetoric in their election and re-election campaigns. While scholars have focused on the candidate-centred nature of American politics, Tiplady's analysis finds that presidents have continued to stress partisan themes far more than usually acknowledged. Thus, these presidents have continued to show an understanding that it is not solely the desire to support a particular candidate that motivates voters, but instead it is crucial to appeal to the electorate's partisan instincts. Tiplady's work suggests that voters are therefore less likely to treat midterm elections as a referendum on the incumbent president, but instead an opportunity to either support their party or, perhaps more likely, punish the opposition party. Over time since the 1960s, she shows, presidential incumbents have tended to become more – not less – partisan while in office.

Nadia Hilliard demonstrates that in the contemporary era the outcomes of sub-federal elections during midterm years, including governors, state attorneys general, and mayors, can have a substantial impact upon a presidency. The victorious candidates for these offices, whom Hilliard collectively labels as encompassing a 'sub-federal accountability regime', carry into office their own midterm mandate to redirect the president's agenda. Through the various political levers at their disposal, Hilliard observes, such officeholders can radically reshape federal policy by either 'reinterpreting, refusing to implement, or directly challenging' such directives. In her exploration of the 2018 midterm elections and their consequences, Hilliard shows that victorious sub-federal candidates pursued more aggressive oversight of the Trump administration – thus frustrating Trump's own mandate.

The midterm elections that took place between 1934 and 1962 were shaped by the continued electoral appeal of New Deal liberalism. In this era, Democrats dominated both the White House and Congress. Iwan Morgan argues that it was not just the trend-bucking 1934 midterm elections – in which Franklin D. Roosevelt's party made significant gains – that should be viewed as a success, but that the substantial Democratic losses in 1938 also had a significant silver lining for the party of FDR. Taken as a pair, Morgan posits that the two midterm elections secured the realignment of the electorate in a fashion that benefited Democrats. In 1934, the substantial midterm gains for Roosevelt's party were the ultimate endorsement of New Deal liberalism. Fast-forward four years, and while Democrats endured their first poor election in a decade, Roosevelt's attempted purge of conservatives defined the Democratic Party as the liberal party in the United States – a label that proved electorally beneficial through to the 1960s.

Andrew Johnstone reassesses Roosevelt's third and final midterm, which took place during World War II – a contest that has received little scholarly attention. Johnstone contextualises the election in a similar manner to how historians understand the 1862 and 1864 elections that took place during the Civil War; events on the warfront were crucial in shaping the results. Had the elections taken place either a few months earlier or even days later, Johnstone suggests, the results would likely have been significantly different. The irony of this, Johnstone observes, is that Roosevelt's mandate to conduct foreign affairs was unaffected by Democratic losses. Instead, the ebb and flow of the war – and its impact on the midterm results – reinforced a conservative coalition in Congress that sought to reverse elements of the commander in chief's New Deal.

Even with Roosevelt's death in 1945, debates over New Deal liberalism continued to dominate midterm election contests in the post-war era. Surveying the four midterms that immediately followed the war, Robert Mason finds that the Republican Party used these contests to articulate a rebuttal to New Deal liberalism. Ultimately, Mason notes, with memories of the Great Depression looming large among the electorate, this continued campaign – across a series of elections – was unsuccessful in swaying voters to the Republican banner. Crucially, though, Republican efforts were not in vain. In consistently opposing New Deal liberalism, the Grand Old Party (GOP) was successful in checking the Democratic Party's commitment to the most liberal elements of that agenda. Thus, the cumulative impact of these midterm elections was to moderate the Democratic Party during its era of electoral dominance. As for the presidency, the midterm elections helped to stall Harry S. Truman's Fair Deal and ensure that President Dwight D. Eisenhower's vision for 'modern Republicanism' – more moderate than the agenda preferred by many Republicans – was unsuccessful.

Investigating John F. Kennedy's sole midterm election campaign as president, Mark Eastwood broadly agrees with the historiographical consensus that this was a success for the young president. But in his examination of voting patterns, Eastwood reveals a more complex and troubling picture for the Democrats. On one hand, Democrats could celebrate Kennedy's – and the party's – ability to win greater margins among Black Americans and 'peace' voters. Looking south, however, Eastwood notes that the Republicans made significant inroads into the Democratic Party's Dixie heartland. Indeed, while Eastwood argues that the 1962 contest had little impact on Kennedy's mandate, he posits that the electoral coalition that Richard Nixon would assemble six years later, in winning the presidency, first started to emerge in 1962.

The six midterm contests that took place between 1966 and 1986 show that the Republican resurgence trod a rocky path, with the GOP both enjoying promising victories and suffering devastating losses. Indeed, while the Republican Party came to dominate the presidency, midterm elections often served as reminders that the Democratic Party's hold on Congress was a puzzle for which the GOP did not yet have an answer. Even during the Republican revival in 1966, which saw the GOP recover from a streak of four poor election cycles, Mark McLay shows that the path to that revival involved embracing elements of President Lyndon B. Johnson's 'Great Society' – such as Medicare and federal aid to education – that would have been anathema to conservatives only a few years earlier. Still, in 1966, Republicans identified Johnson's increasingly unpopular 'War on Poverty' as a way to undermine Great Society liberalism more broadly. In attacking the antipoverty effort – associated in the public mind with helping poor Black Americans – the Republicans defined the terms on which Richard Nixon would successfully seek election in 1968.

While Nixon benefited from 1966, he was less successful as the incumbent president in 1970. As Sarah Thelen notes, Nixon made the then atypical choice to involve himself directly in the Republican campaign, spurred by the belief that he – and he alone – could activate 'Silent Majority' voters to turn out at the polls in support of his party, and perhaps even spur a realignment of the electorate. Thelen argues that the midterm contest was the first real test of whether the Silent Majority was a potent political force or merely a rhetorical weapon that was spent of ammunition. The disappointing Republican results suggested the latter, and Thelen writes that the elections spelt the end of the Silent Majority as an 'organising force in the administration'.

Nixon was no longer in the White House by the time of the 1974 midterm contest, but the Watergate scandal that ousted him from office ensured Republican disaster and ushered in a return of Democratic Party domination for the rest of the 1970s. In analysing both the 1974 and 1978 elections, Patrick Andelic sees both elections as the source of political challenges that Jimmy Carter encountered as president between 1977 and 1981. The resounding Democratic Party victory in 1974 saw Congress welcome a host of new representatives and senators, dubbed the 'Watergate babies', who sought to rein in what historian Arthur Schlesinger called 'the imperial presidency' and re-establish Congress as a co-equal – if not superior – branch of the federal government. These Democrats – who managed to maintain their dominant majorities through the 1978 elections – believed their mandate superseded that of Carter's. As such, Andelic suggests that Carter's legislative failings were not merely a reflection of the Georgian's inability to charm Capitol Hill.

In the penultimate essay, Richard Johnson examines the extent to which a 'ghost coat-tail effect' exists in midterm elections. Presidential candidates, it is well established, often receive a boost in support from their home state. Johnson dubs this phenomenon a 'favourite son effect' – updating a term previously associated with the politics of national conventions.[13] In his analysis, Johnson seeks to establish whether such an effect is present during midterm elections – does the president's party perform better in the incumbent's home state? While Johnson shows how Ronald Reagan's White House occupancy benefited Golden State Republicans in 1982, he also finds that the extent to which presidents have enjoyed a 'ghost coat-tail' has varied significantly in modern US history.

In assessing Reagan's second midterm, Joe Ryan-Hume finds that the Democratic Party's grassroots organising was effective in checking the Reagan Revolution. While scholars have previously focused on conservative triumph during the 1980s, Ryan-Hume shows that Reagan and the Republicans did not have it all their own way. Most notably, the 1986 midterm election results prevented 'The Gipper' from appointing arch-conservative Robert Bork to the Supreme Court and led to Reagan's success rate with legislative measures plummeting. Ryan-Hume argues that, while not quite able to end the Reagan Revolution, the midterm elections considerably dented Reagan's domestic mandate.

Although the outcome of the 1986 midterms was one of change, it also involved a reassertion of the status quo – of Democratic dominance on Capitol Hill even with a Republican at the White House – and thus, seen differently, a form of political stability. The elections of the near future seemed to provide confirmation of this stability. In 1988, Vice President George H. W. Bush managed to retain the White House for the Republicans while his party on Capitol Hill made no progress (suffering a net loss of two seats in the House and a net loss of one seat in the Senate). Two years later, stasis largely characterised Bush's midterms (with just one change in the Senate, because Democrat Paul Wellstone defeated Republican Rudy Boschwitz, the incumbent, in Minnesota, and with a net gain of seven seats for the Democrats in the House). And yet volatility soon displaced stability as the characteristic of the party balance that American elections created. Bush lost his re-election bid to Bill Clinton, and in 1994 the 'Republican revolution' that swept aside Democratic control initiated an era of more intense competition between the parties that would reshape the relationship between midterm elections and American politics. The role of midterms in the contemporary era, set in historical perspective, is Andrew Rudalevige's focus in the first chapter.

Notes

1. We are grateful to David Silkenat for this point. In the November coverage of the 1894 elections, for instance, in the *New York Times*, *Washington Post*, *Los Angeles Times* and *Chicago Tribune*, the only reference to 'midterm' or 'mid-term' came in a short item in the *Post* (and reprinted from the *Boston Herald*), which noted '[r]eversals of popular judgment are the regular thing in the middle of a Presidential term'. 'Mid-Term Disasters', *Washington Post*, 8 Nov. 1894.

2. In the days after the disputed presidential election of 2000, outgoing president Bill Clinton told the press that 'the American people have spoken, but it's going to take a little while to determine exactly what they said'. David E. Sanger and Marc Lacey, 'Clinton Tells of Talking with Gore after Vote', *New York Times*, 9 Nov. 2000.
3. Andrew E. Busch, *Horses in Midstream: U.S. Midterm Elections and Their Consequences, 1894–1998* (Pittsburgh, PA: University of Pittsburgh Press, 1999), p. 1.
4. Busch, *Horses in Midstream*, p. 6.
5. Busch prefers that his categories should be understood as 'descriptive in nature rather than analytically predictive'. Busch, *Horses in Midstream*, pp. 43–4.
6. Natasha Korecki, Christopher Cadelago, and Matthew Choi, 'Biden, Still Short of Outright Victory, Declares a "Mandate for Action"', *Politico*, 6 Nov. 2020, https://www.politico.com/news/2020/11/06/biden-vote-count-speech-434854, last accessed 25 Aug. 2021.
7. Jennifer Epstein, 'Biden Has "Clear Mandate," Aides Say as Electoral College Votes', *Bloomberg*, 14 Dec. 2020, https://www.bloomberg.com/news/articles/2020-12-14/biden-has-clear-mandate-aides-say-as-electoral-college-votes, accessed 25 Aug. 2021.
8. In her analysis of 1,467 presidential communications (speeches, statements, and other communications) between 1933 and 2009, Julia Azari argues that since 1969 presidents have made mandate claims more frequently. Julia R. Azari, 'Institutional Change and the Presidential Mandate', *Social Science History* 37 (2013): p. 484. See also Julia R. Azari, *Delivering the People's Message: The Changing Politics of the Presidential Mandate* (Ithaca, NY: Cornell University Press, 2014).
9. Patricia Heidotting Conley, *Presidential Mandates: How Elections Shape the National Agenda* (Chicago, IL: University of Chicago Press, 2001), p. 2.
10. As defined by Patricia Heidotting Conley, a president with 'strong popular support' and the apparent ability to mobilise a majority of voters can claim a 'popular mandate' and induce Congress to cooperate with their agenda. A 'bargained mandate' is the product of a president declaring a mandate with only 'moderate popular support' in the expectation of having to negotiate and even fight with Congress to realise that mandate. Finally, elections without mandates are the product of 'postelection climate[s] characterized

by a combination of low to moderate popular support and congressional hostility'. Conley, *Presidential Mandates*, pp. 20–1.

11. Charles O. Jones, *The Presidency in a Separated System* (Washington, DC: The Brookings Institution, 1994), p. 153.
12. Robert A. Dahl, 'Myth of the Presidential Mandate', *Political Science Quarterly* 105 (1990): pp. 370–1.
13. William Safire, *Safire's Political Dictionary*, updated and expanded edn (New York: Oxford University Press, 2008), pp. 237–8.

Part One

Midterm Elections in Institutional Context

1
Presidents and Midterm Loss

Andrew Rudalevige

'Well, we made history last night. Call it what you want: an earthquake, a tidal wave, a blowout. We got our butts kicked.' So said the chair of the Democratic National Committee on 9 November 1994, after his party lost its majorities in both chambers of the US Congress for the first time in forty years. 'A lot has changed since yesterday,' a stunned President Bill Clinton soon told reporters.[1]

A dozen years later, it was President George W. Bush's turn for chagrin after the Republican Party lost thirty seats in the House and six in the Senate to cede the GOP's majorities back to the Democrats. 'It was not too close,' he conceded. 'It was a thumping.'[2] Yet the thumping would get even louder in 2010. When Democrats lost more than *sixty* House seats that November, President Barack Obama was driven to the thesaurus. He settled on 'shellacking' – concluding that 'some election nights are more fun than others'.[3]

And in fact, for presidents, midterm elections rarely provide a fun evening. The 'midterm' refers to regularly scheduled congressional elections that occur at the halfway point of a presidential administration. Because a member of the US House of Representatives serves for two years, and a member of the Senate for six years, every election taking place at the president's midterm has all 435 House seats and one-third of the 100 Senate seats on the ballot. There are state and sometimes local races piggy-backed on that federal election as well: for governor, attorney general, treasurer, auditor, and the like, as well as statewide referendums and thousands of state legislative seats.

All this adds up to a high-stakes day for politicians at all levels – and one that has come to serve as a verdict of sorts on the sitting administration. And though some presidents are surely performing better than others at that point in their term, the president's party almost always gets a thumbs-down from the nation's voters. 'Historically, the president, you don't tend to do so well in the midterms,' President Donald Trump told a reporter in October 2018, a month before his own.[4] While Trump then predicted, 'I think we're gonna do well' – and after the fact asserted 'we did unbelievably well'[5] – the facts were, as usual, on history's side. While the GOP managed to keep its Senate majority, Republicans lost forty-one House seats and control of that chamber in November 2018.

This overall pattern of presidential punishment is so regular that it has been termed the 'iron law of midterm loss'.[6] Before the Civil War, there were only two instances (1814 and 1822) where the president's party wound up gaining House seats through midterm elections. And since the Union reunited for the 1870 midterms – a run of nearly forty elections through 2018 – the president's party has lost House seats in all but three cases.[7] Those three modern exceptions of 1934, 1998, and 2002 involve clear mitigating circumstances, and 2002 is the sole case where the percentage of the national two-party vote earned by the president's party rose from its level two years prior. Results in the Senate, with a smaller '*n*' reflecting incumbents elected six years prior and showcasing different geographies in different years, are more idiosyncratic. But here, too, the president's party has failed to gain seats in twenty-one of the twenty-seven Senate midterm elections since 1913, when direct election of senators commenced (replacing selection by state legislatures).[8] If not a 'law', then, midterm loss is at least a stern recommendation.

Any pattern predictable with even near-certainty in the political world must count as a puzzle. Political science giant V. O. Key said long ago that 'no logical explanation' could explain the regularity: 'the Founding Fathers, by the provision for midterm elections, built into the constitutional system a procedure whose strange consequences lack explanation in any theory that personifies the electorate as a rational god of vengeance and of reward.'[9] Still, in the five-plus decades since that observation, much scholarly attention has been devoted to restoring that god to the temple, for instance by seeking out systematic connections between electoral outcomes and economic conditions. Others stress presidents' centrality to the outcome – which, in fact, seems to have grown over time. Political scientist Gary Jacobson concluded in 2019 that midterms have become 'increasingly nationalized, partisan, and president centered'.[10] The 2018 elections exemplified the trend, as (perhaps not surprisingly) Trump was eager to make them all about himself. 'Pretend I'm on the ballot,' he told his rally crowds.[11]

In the end, the statistical anomaly is less crucial than its impact on presidential power. A few months after the 1994 midterms, Bill Clinton was effectively reduced to pleading for his own political existence. 'The Constitution gives me relevance,' he insisted. 'The power of our ideas gives me relevance. . . . The President is relevant here.'[12] But it could have been worse. In 1946, after Republicans won midterm majorities in both chambers, at least one leading Democrat urged Harry Truman to appoint a Republican secretary of state and then resign the presidency – the vice presidency being vacant and the secretary of state next in the line of succession at the time. Truman was asked about this proposal at a press conference a few days after the election. 'No comment,' he sighed.[13]

The remainder of this chapter tracks these topics. The next sections detail the history of midterm loss, then turn to the theories political scientists have used to explain the phenomenon. I then assess how well these theories fit the 2018 midterm election results before tracing the landscape of such referendums looking forward to 2022 and beyond. As noted, the national component of congressional elections generally, and midterms particularly, seems to have become more prominent in recent years. Given a trend towards increased polarisation – and perhaps towards increased participation and turnout as well – such elections may become less meaningful as specific referendums on individual presidents and more a reflection of simple partisan strength over time. Their implications for presidential power, or at least for presidents' political success, are perhaps less predictable. After all, both Clinton and Truman won re-election. Donald Trump did not.

Midterm loss, in brief

As noted, the scope of midterm elections goes well beyond the federal level. On 6 November 2018, for instance, thirty-six governors and dozens of other statewide elected officials, along with more than 6,000 state-level legislators, were before the voters. Further, thirty-seven states that allowed for referendum questions to be placed on the ballot asked their voters to decide more than 150 policies on issues ranging from taxes to abortion to legalising marijuana to expanding Medicaid to raising the minimum wage. Thus, while congressional elections are necessary to the proceedings, they are not always the most salient midterm political event in any given state.[14]

They are, however, the focus of most of the attention from reporters and 'Washingtonians' generally, given their potential to serve as a national bellwether close to halfway through a presidential term and the irresistible temptation for punditry this poses.[15] As summarised above, and detailed in Figure 1.1 below, the 'law of midterm loss' seems to govern their outcome. Since 1946, the president's party has on average lost twenty-seven House seats in the midterms. Therefore a good deal of scholarly attention has followed, too. Indeed, as early as the 1930s, one academic critic of divided government published an entire (short) book condemning the 'evil results of mid-term congressional elections'.[16]

Figure 1.1 shows that the thumpings and shellackings of recent presidencies – evil or not – have many forebears. Ulysses S. Grant's Republicans lost ninety-six House seats in 1874, and Grover Cleveland's Democrats suffered the worst drubbing in American congressional electoral history (125 seats lost) in 1890. Even Franklin Roosevelt was not immune: Democrats dropped more than seventy seats in 1938, though, given their huge House majority (they outnumbered Republicans 334–88 prior to the election), they retained control of the chamber nonetheless.

Those margins had been built, of course, through Roosevelt's landslides in 1932 and 1936, but also through a gain of nine

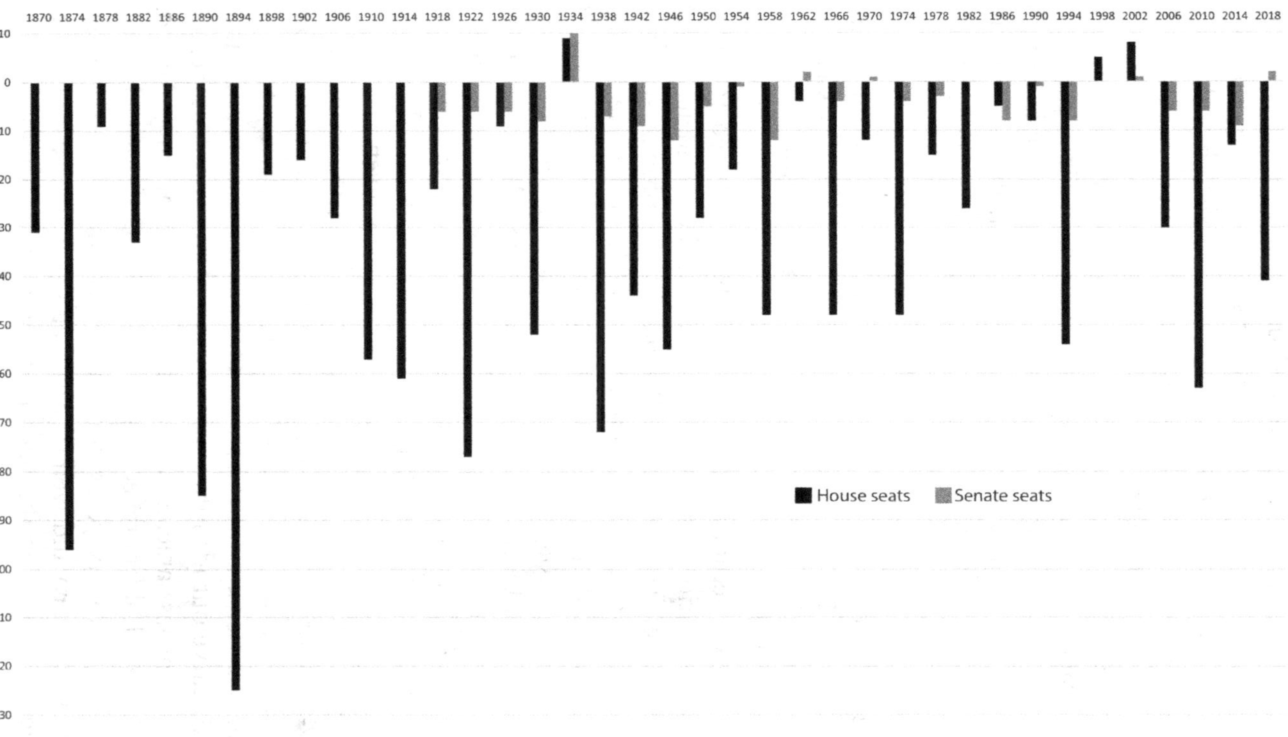

Figure 1.1 Midterm elections seat change for the president's party, 1870–2018

Source: *Vital Statistics on Congress*, **Table 2.4, as corrected**

House seats in 1934 when voters' desire to support the New Deal forged one of the rare violations of the law of midterm loss. The next exception was not until 1998, when Republicans' fervent efforts to impeach Bill Clinton backfired at the polls and Speaker Newt Gingrich's confident predictions of a thirty- to forty-seat GOP gain turned instead into five new Democratic House seats.[17] This was the first time since 1822 that a president had gained seats in the sixth, rather than the second, year of his term. The result cost Gingrich his job, but did not prevent Clinton's impeachment, which was approved along mostly party lines in December during a lame-duck legislative session. By contrast, after GOP gains in the 2002 midterms (eight seats in the House and two in the Senate) confirmed the post-9/11 popularity of George W. Bush, Democrats reversed course and passed the bill creating a new Department of Homeland Security that Bush had demanded.

In the two decades since, midterms have returned to form, with each iteration again yielding losses for the president's party in the House. The 2006, 2010, and 2018 elections switched majority control of that chamber. In 2006, the Senate flipped as well, as it did again in 2014 to give Republicans custody of both houses of Congress for the last two years of the Obama administration. Overall, as noted in this chapter's introduction, Senate outcomes are less predictable, with the president's party sometimes holding its ground and occasionally making slight gains. This can occur, as in 2018, even when results in the House are far more punishing. The Senate map in any given midterm is smaller, of course, given senators' six-year staggered terms – only thirty-three or thirty-four seats are contested[18] – and somewhat idiosyncratic, since senators (and Senate candidates) tend to be much better known than their House counterparts and more able to carve out identities independent of the president. Senate seats are far less amenable to partisan gerrymandering. And, of course, their holders reflect a partisan balance of power in their states lagged by six years, far earlier than the last presidential election. If a party did well six years ago, it will have more seats to defend, increasing the odds that some of its incumbents will fall short. However, research suggests that when the president's party is constant over that period – that is, at the time of the elections both two and six years ago – the Senate also consistently follows the law of midterm loss.[19]

The obvious question is why. Little of the limited literature on Senate results at the midterm veers towards theory, instead favouring forecasting models that identify the variables most highly correlated with actual outcomes using brute computing force.[20] In general, much seems to be explained simply by the number of seats being defended by the president's party and by the nationally polled 'generic ballot' which, shorn of candidate names, asks voters which party they prefer in their own district.[21] By contrast, there is significant research exploring and explaining the midterm loss phenomenon on the House side. Most of this work centres on midterms after World War II, since consistent demographic and economic data are much more readily available for that era.

Theories of midterm loss

Over several decades, scholars have sought to restore the omnipotence of Key's 'rational god of vengeance and reward' in midterm results.[22] There are three major theoretical categories: models of differential turnout, often termed 'surge and decline'; models positing a policy-based referendum; and models that see midterms as voters' desire to moderate and balance government, modulated by their 'surprise' at the results of the presidential election.

'Surge and decline'

As Figure 1.2 shows, American voter turnout at the midterm has been lower than during presidential elections since well before the Civil War. Political scientist Michael McDonald of the US Elections Project calculates that in the thirty pairs of elections from 1900 through 2018, average turnout of eligible voters (VEP) was 58.6 per cent in presidential elections and 42.6 per cent in midterms.[23] This gap has changed little over time: it is nearly identical if only considering elections after World War II (57.9 versus 42.1 per cent) or after the 1965 passage of the Voting

Figure 1.2 Voter turnout (eligible voters), in per cent, 1828–2020

Source: U.S. Elections Project, http://www.electproject.org

Rights Act (56.9–40.8 per cent). If anything, as that sequence suggests, midterm turnout has actually decreased slightly over time. This trend reversed, at least temporarily, in 2018 – that fully half of eligible voters turned out that year was considered astonishing. It was, indeed, the best midterm turnout in more than a century.[24] But it would have represented the *worst* turnout in a presidential election during that same century and for that matter during the previous century, too – since 1828, the only two presidential contests with less than 50 per cent VEP turnout have been in 1920 and 1924, the two elections after the size of the electorate was doubled by the Nineteenth Amendment's ratification of women's suffrage.[25]

This dynamic underlies one explanation for midterm loss, as a simple matter of reversion to the mean. That is: when a party wins the presidency, nearly by definition it had a good year, meaning that numerous down-ballot members of the party will have ridden into office on the president's 'coat-tails'. At that point, the party in the White House controls more congressional seats than usual, beyond its expected level of support in the country – it has picked up House members in competitive swing districts that are then ripe for the picking two years later. The party's fortunes surge, then decline. And the more 'seat exposure', the greater the risk: as James E. Campbell put it, 'the bigger they are, the harder they fall'.[26] In 2008, for instance, Democrats won nearly fifty seats in districts also won by Republican presidential candidate John McCain, only to lose three-quarters of those in 2010.

If the midterm electorate were simply a smaller replica of two years prior its downsizing wouldn't matter much. But the 'surge and decline' metaphor contemplates key differences in the make-up of the sequential turnout.[27] Presidential elections are highly salient and feature national organisations trying to drive up participation. Voters excited about their candidate show up in droves and, as noted, elect members of his party as a more or less accidental by-product. However, two years later, many of those voters will stay home. At that point, the motivation to get to the polls rests with those angry at the incumbent president (since, as prospect theory predicts, those who lose are asymmetrically passionate compared to those who win).[28] And presidential approval nearly always declines over time. Even those who voted for the president may have changed their minds, as their previous champion creates an aggregating coalition of the disgruntled, simply by making the inevitably difficult decisions the job requires. Either way, the midterm electorate is – all else equal – less favourable to the president than the one that elected them just two years before.

All else may veer from the entirely equal. Shorn of (at least some of) the money and media coverage of the presidential contest, midterms tend to attract the most dedicated voters. In the United States, that suggests an older, wealthier, more educated, and (by correlation) whiter electorate.[29] Those demographics traditionally skew Republican, potentially buffering GOP losses. (V. O. Key hypothesised as early as 1942 that 'consistently lower participation in . . . congressional elections [may] contribute to intergovernmental friction by placing in offices below the Presidential rank a generally more conservative group'.[30]) By the late 1980s, a dedicated focus on casework and district-level issues had helped enhance the power of incumbency, leading Morris Fiorina to conclude in 1989 that the 'the House of Representatives is more insulated from national currents than in any previous period of American history'.[31] As discussed below, however, that trend now seems to have reversed, with the value of incumbency tailing off. And in 2018, at least, both sides sought to nationalise the election.[32]

Referendum voting

Scholars have long sought to establish a connection between electoral outcomes and economic conditions. Indeed, according to Robert Erikson, the 'hypothesis that the state of the economy matters at election time may be as widely accepted today as any hypothesis about elections and voting behavior'.[33] Even so, shifting that hypothesis from presidential elections (where the correlation of economic 'fundamentals' to the incumbent party's share of the two-party vote is comfortingly linear) to congressional races, and then again to midterm loss, is a trickier proposition. Edward Tufte's seminal presentation of the case in the 1970s argued that midterm elections were, indeed, merely a rational assessment of the president's performance, and could be explained by variation in economic conditions and the president's overall standing. 'The midterm vote is neither a mystery nor an automatic swing of the pendulum,' he argued, but rather 'a referendum'.[34] To test his thesis, Tufte used just three independent variables: the change in national real per capita disposable income in the year preceding the election, presidential approval polls immediately before election day, and a 'standardized vote' that sought to control for overall partisanship by calculating the deviation in the current year's vote from the incumbent party's long-term vote share. Following his lead, numerous analysts gave particular emphasis to the impact of economic measures as they extended the 'referendum' model in time and utilised new measures.[35]

However, as new elections were added (the original Tufte analysis included only eight midterms, starting in 1946), scholars found a diminishing connection between aggregate economic conditions and the midterm vote. Robert Erikson concluded that income changes were both statistically and substantively insignificant to the midterm vote when controlling for the partisan vote breakdown just two years prior.[36] Others, examining individual-level survey data, found scant evidence that congressional voters' choices were triggered by their own pocketbook, potentially undermining the micro-foundations of the macro-behaviour Tufte and others had posited.[37] A later study used state-level voting and economic data as a way of pushing past this impasse.[38] It found no connection between state-level per capita income change when controlling for the lagged congressional vote share for the president's party, for incumbency, and for presidential approval. However, consistent with Tufte's theory, *national*-level change in per capita income or unemployment did matter to the state-level vote. This suggested midterm voters might not hold members of Congress responsible for local conditions but rather for the performance of the US economy as a whole, perhaps using that performance as a rough proxy for the general governing capacity of the party in power.

Balancing

Yet the same study also found support for a third strand of the midterm loss literature: the mere existence of a president of a particular party led to a lower vote for that president's party two years on. In the late 1980s, Erikson termed this the '"presidential penalty" explanation', finding that 'electorates are biased or predisposed to vote against the presidential party, regardless of the objective circumstances'.[39] But why? Erikson suggested several possibilities. One was driven by the notion of 'negative voting' noted above, and the likelihood that voters were more likely to be motivated to show up at the midterm polls if they held negative views of the president. Another was that citizens were primed at midterm to respond more to negative cues regarding the performance of the president's party than to positive ones. 'The skewed result', he said, would have the 'appearance of a "protest vote," even when the electorate as a whole has little to protest'.[40]

However, Erikson also bruited a 'balancing' theory that has since received substantial scholarly attention. Voters, this model suggests, are generally moderate, and prefer incremental policy shifts to radical change. Since in the American system large-scale reforms are only plausible under unified party government, many voters prefer divided control of the branches of government. And midterms serve as voters' opportunity to create divided government or at least to downsize the party in power and check its policy ambitions. This suggests a clear motive for moderate voters to overtly balance the partisan make-up of the federal government, grounded not in brute presidential punishment but in substantive policy concerns.

The scope of the governing party's losses might be offset somewhat by a high level of presidential approval, but also by earlier results. When casting votes in a presidential election the results are unknown, preventing voters from being able to balance their ballots at the time – by this reasoning, the more uncertain the result of a presidential election (the more 'electoral surprise'), the higher the subsequent midterm loss. Ken Scheve and Michael Tomz concluded that 'the more surprised moderate voters are about the outcome of a presidential election, the lower the probability that they will support the president's party in the following midterm contest'.[41] Some argue this requires overly generous assumptions about how much attention Americans pay to policy specifics. Still, in later work, Erikson likewise found evidence of 'anticipatory balancing' when polling predicted a presidential landslide.[42] The effect would be to tamp down coat-tails in a presidential election – a prediction that finds some support in the 2020 results, where Joe Biden's win was long forecast but the down-ballot 'blue wave' failed to materialise.

Voter behaviour – as expressed through any of these theories – is also affected by who is on the midterm ballot. Perhaps the safest assumption in politics (or political science) is that no one likes to lose an election: better not to run at all, to withdraw from the field, and await a more propitious opportunity. Thus the very roster of midterm candidates reflects strategic decisions made by individual members of Congress and their potential challengers, based on national conditions, the president's standing, the eagerness of activists and donors, the results of the American equivalents of by-elections, and, for that matter, scattered anecdote. As leading scholars of this phenomenon observe, 'Signs and portents are readily available, widely discussed, and taken seriously.'[43] As such national conditions are on the ballot after all, but by indirect means: it is not unusual for retirements from Congress to surge in years where a party expects serious headwinds, and a campaign waged over an open seat is far more competitive. For instance, twenty-eight Democratic representatives decided to retire rather than seek re-election in 1994; twenty-two of those seats went to the GOP in November.

The rich get richer in other ways, too: the party favoured by national context can recruit a larger proportion of well-financed, qualified candidates while the other offers up correspondingly more less-experienced and lesser-funded opponents. In 1994, thirty-four Democratic incumbents also lost, as Republicans were able to field a particularly strong group of challengers.

It is harder to generalise midterms' impact on presidential power and governance. Still, as Andrew Busch writes, they should be seen as an independent variable – a cause – rather than merely as a dependent variable, an effect, measured by the empirics of seats lost or vote share diminished.[44] Most broadly, adopting the 'balancing' reasoning above (though not the methodology), he argues that midterms are a crucial means for checking presidential power. That check can be either straightforwardly negative, but it can also be creative, spurring renewed political bargaining and policy accommodation.

Certainly, presidential support in Congress declines after the midterm, and more than can be explained simply by the drop-off from a productive honeymoon and first '100 Days', broadly defined. Using various measures ranging from *Congressional Quarterly* box-scores to the presidential support scores developed by scholars such as Jon Bond and Richard Fleisher, Busch calculates a consistent decline after the midterm by as many as ten percentage points. Updating that calculation for Bush and Obama shows a similar pattern. In 2009 and 2010, for instance, Obama was successful on an astonishing 91 per cent of the roll call votes on which he took a position, according to *Congressional Quarterly*. In 2011 and 2012, that figure was just over 55 per cent. His second term repeated the same trend from a lower baseline, with a 63 per cent success rate in 2013–14 falling to 42 per cent in 2015–16.[45]

Another measure of presidents' legislative success is the proportion of presidential proposals enacted into law. Over the 1949–96 period, this, too, shows a significant drop-off across midterm loss. In 1993–4, for instance, Clinton's ranking on an index of 0–3, where a '3' represents something close to the transcription of administration bills into the statute books, was 1.9. In 1995–6, it was more than a third lower, at 1.2. Nor does a dramatic shift require fully divided government. Harry Truman's success score in 1949–50 was 2.1 – but in 1951–2, only 0.8.[46] Lyndon Johnson's flood of Great Society measures in 1965–6 likewise slowed to a trickle in 1967–8, after Democrats lost forty-eight seats at the midterm. At that point, as White House aide Ken O'Donnell would sardonically comment, 'he couldn't get Mother's Day through', symbolically unable to rally Congress even to endorse motherhood and apple pie.[47]

Figure 1.3 details these and the other post-war twentieth-century presidencies on this measure. Given a limited number of annual

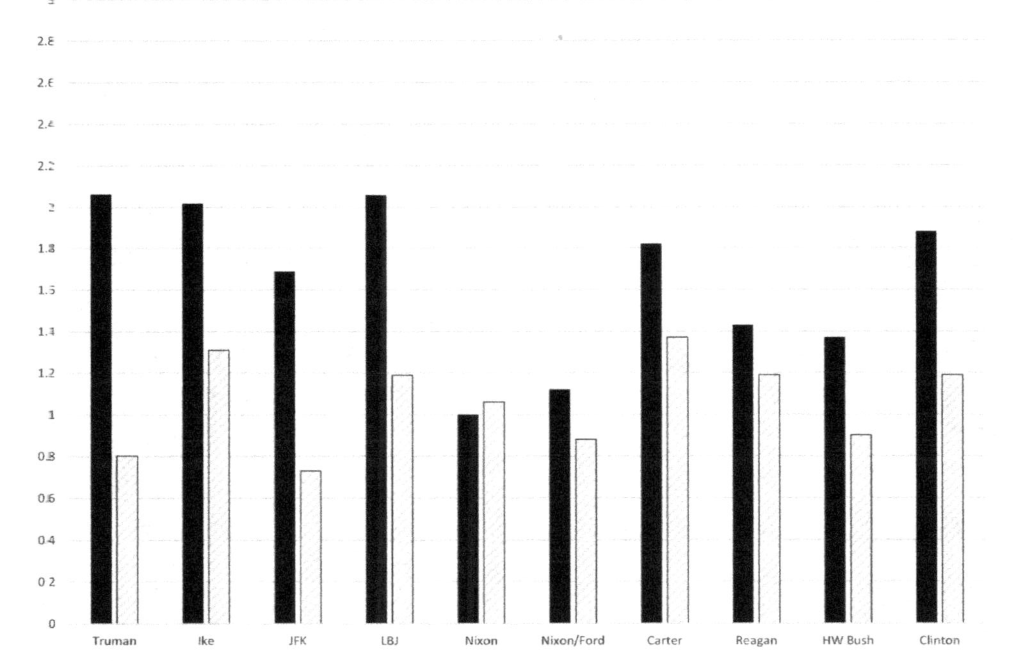

Figure 1.3 Legislative success, pre- and post-midterm, 1949–1996

Source: Calculated from Andrew Rudalevige, *Managing the President's Program: Presidential Leadership and Legislative Policy Formulation* **(Princeton, NJ: Princeton University Press, 2002), Table A.7**

observations, the absolute numbers should be taken with a grain of salt, and obviously other caveats apply, too – John F. Kennedy was killed before completing even a single year in office after the 1962 midterm, and Richard Nixon resigned his office before the 1974 election. Even so, the consistency of the trend is striking. In these data, only Nixon, in 1971–2, did better after the midterms than before, and that by a tiny amount (1.00 versus 1.06) that mostly highlights the low level of legislative success in his first two years in office.

Scholarship is mixed on whether divided government can be as productive as when it is unified – an early affirmative consensus on that point has faded over the past twenty years, with the past three presidents (Bush, Obama, Trump) having successively served as the most polarising chief executives since the Civil War.[48] Even stipulating that divided governments can forge meaningful legislation, it is clear that midterm shifts in the make-up of Congress will reshape the substance of the statutory record. Given Bill Clinton's 1992 platform, for instance, he would presumably have pushed welfare reform had Democrats retained the majority in the 104th Congress after the 1994 midterms. But would the resulting law have looked the same as the one he was forced to negotiate with Newt Gingrich's GOP in 1996? Almost certainly not. This suggests that some midterms serve a 'calibrating' purpose, as Busch puts it, serving to 'blunt and redirect change' by imposing new constraints on presidential policymaking.[49] Other elections in this category are 1938 (FDR), 1982 (Reagan), and – though outside Busch's timeline – 2010 (Obama). In all of these cases, of course, the president would go on to win re-election. But to achieve that, they governed differently than they had done previously. Clinton 'triangulated', positioning himself relative to congressional Democrats as well as against the new Republican majority. For his part, by 2011 Obama had declared that 'we can't wait for an increasingly dysfunctional Congress to do its job'. Instead, he pledged, 'Where they won't act, I will. I've told my administration to keep looking every single day for actions we can take without Congress.' A long list of executive directives designed to spur the faltering economy soon accreted on a White House website.[50]

Change can be tracked even within the parameters of continuing, rather than newly created, divided government. The 1958 midterms did not fundamentally reshape the partisan make-up of American government. But it expanded narrow Democratic congressional majorities, especially in the Senate, to bring to power 'a large and substantially unified class' of liberals in both chambers.[51] That had crucial implications for the ability of future Democratic presidents to press forward with a more activist agenda.

As that suggests, some midterms seem 'preparatory' (in Busch's typology) to a change in White House control and a new policy agenda. The 1958 midterm provided John Kennedy's demand to 'get America moving again' with a critical mass of open ears on Capitol Hill.[52] (And Lyndon Johnson, especially from 1964 to 1966, proved particularly skilled at turning ears into 'yes' votes.) Meanwhile, even before the 1960 election, Eisenhower found it harder to muster legislative support even for his foreign policy and defence initiatives, which to that point had attracted broad bipartisan backing. Even so, the Democratic victory in the subsequent presidential race rested on extraordinarily fine margins. If Nixon could come so close to extending the Eisenhower administration, one can certainly see a non-term-limited Ike himself winning in 1960. In that sense, 1958 was a hint more than a guarantee. LBJ's drubbing in 1966, similarly, did not prefigure a Republican landslide in 1968: Nixon won, this time, but with only 43 per cent of the national popular vote.[53] Even a midterm like 2006, which in retrospect seems to signpost Barack Obama's sweeping victory two years later, was not a static-free signal at the time. It is important to realise that Republican nominee John McCain was favoured in many polls into the early autumn of 2008. Only with the financial market meltdown did Obama move decisively ahead.[54]

Theory meets Trump: the 2018 midterms

As mentioned at the outset, Donald Trump did know the history of midterm loss, observing that 'it's very rare that a party who has the presidency does well'.[55] But a month before the election, he claimed to personify that rare case. Trump insisted that 'this is a different presidency and this is the greatest economy ever. So, we'll have to test that.'[56] How did the test go?

On one level, the answer is simple: badly. Republicans lost more than forty House seats, and with them the majority. Hillary Clinton had won the national popular vote in 2016 by two percentage points; House Democrats expanded that margin to nine points in 2018. Democrats had particular success in 'swing' or 'battleground' districts. Of eighty-three such districts identified by the political website *Ballotopedia*, forty-six changed party hands – and forty-five of those were in a Democratic direction.[57] In part, this was because Democrats were particularly well funded, especially in competitive races: in contests decided by ten percentage points or less, the *median* Democratic challenger spent more than $4 million – 3.5 times what they raised in the prior midterm in 2014 – besting the median Republican incumbent by $1.1 million. On the flip side, the median Democratic incumbent in such races was able to outspend the median GOP challenger by more than $1 million.[58] The immediate practical upshot brought Representative Nancy Pelosi of California back to the House Speaker's chair. Democrats would have control of all House committees, and not incidentally their subpoena power.

The Senate results were far better for Trump's Republicans, though falling short of expectations given that Democrats faced 'an almost impossible', 'lopsided', 'terrible' – indeed, historically bad – electoral map.[59] Thirty-five seats were on the ballot, including both of Mississippi's and Minnesota's, and Democrats had to defend three-quarters (twenty-six) of them, the ironic legacy of their solid showing in 2012.[60] Ten Democratic seats were in states won by Trump in 2016. Of the nine GOP incumbents, by contrast, only one (Dean Heller of Nevada) held office in a state won by Hillary Clinton. David Wasserman's calculations for the political website *Five Thirty-Eight* indicated that since '52 seats are in states where the 2016 presidential margin was at least 5 percentage points more Republican than the national outcome', it was possible for Democrats to 'have a pretty good midterm by historical standards' – winning every state that Clinton won or lost by fewer than three percentage points – and still lose five Senate seats. In the end, they lost two.

Trump's quick claims of a 'close to complete victory . . . A great victory', then, fell short.[61] If he was, indeed, 'extraordinarily happy', that did not last past Speaker-in-waiting Pelosi's first comments. Even as she stressed her desire to find 'common ground', she delighted in 'restoring again, the checks and balances conditioned by our founders'. That, she promised, rested on the 'Constitutional responsibility to have oversight . . . [I]f we see a need to go forward, we will.'[62] The new majority would, of course, go forward with the impeachment of the president just a year later.

Do the 2018 results give us any leverage on the hypotheses from the research literature described in the previous section? As noted there, the 'decline' side of surge-and-decline diminished somewhat in 2018, given that midterm turnout, at fifty per cent of eligible voters, was the highest since 1914. In 2014, by contrast, turnout had been just 36.7 per cent; in 2010, slightly over 40 per cent. Thus, even though 2016 turnout was itself relatively high, at 60.1 per cent, the gap between presidential election and midterm was relatively low: in recent times, only the drop from 1972 to 1974 was lower (see Figure 1.2, above). This was buttressed by expanded early absentee and mail-in voting – about 40 per cent of the total 2018 vote was cast that way, representing over 45 million ballots.

Still, the make-up of the 2018 electorate did differ from 2016's in ways that hurt the president. The Pew Research Center's comprehensive study of 2018 voters found that slightly more of Clinton's 2016 supporters than Trump's made it to the polls, and that slightly fewer of them defected to a candidate of the other party (though more than 90 per cent in each group were consistent with their earlier partisan choice).[63] Further, the relatively large number of voters who supported a third party in 2016 (some 6 per cent of the overall electorate) broke towards Democratic candidates by twelve percentage points in 2018. And while only one in ten 2018 voters had not voted at all in 2016, that group voted Democratic by a wide margin, 68–29 per cent.

Offsetting the traditional Republican demographic advantage in midterm voting was a counter-surge (so to speak) in enthusiasm among those who vote less frequently at the midterm, notably young and non-white voters. According to *Washington Post*/ABC News polling, in 2014, just 48 per cent of non-white registered voters said they were 'absolutely certain to vote' in the midterm – but in October 2018 that figure was 72 per cent. That was just a few percentage points behind white voters, after a more than twenty-point gap in 2014.[64] Ultimately, the size of the Black and Latino voting bloc in 2018 was down just three percentage points from its level in 2016.[65]

Young registered voters (defined in the poll as under 40) also expressed far more interest in the 2018 midterm than usual: in 2014, just 42 per cent said they would vote, but 67 per cent in 2018.[66] At the polls, age mattered greatly for vote choice, with younger voters breaking even more heavily Democratic than they had in 2016. Pew's subsequent findings, breaking age cohorts into 18–29-year-olds and 30–49-year-olds, showed that youngest group favouring Clinton by 30 percentage points in 2016, but Democratic candidates by forty-nine percentage points in 2018. The 30–49-year-old group's Democratic lean went from eleven to twenty-one points. Granted, not all of those younger voters made it to the polls – those over sixty-five years of age turned out at three times the rate of the 18–29-year-old cohort despite their similar share of the population. But while senior citizens favoured the GOP, that gap was just six points (itself down from nine in 2016).[67]

Was the vote a referendum on the issues facing the nation, notably the economy? If so, it turned out oddly. Trump, again, asserted that 'Republicans have created the best economy in the HISTORY of our Country – and the hottest jobs market on planet earth', that 'our Economy is setting records on virtually every front'. He tweeted that 'The Economy is soooo good, perhaps the best in our country's history (remember, it's the economy stupid!), that the Democrats are flailing & lying like CRAZY!'[68]

While the superlatives were misplaced, the pre-pandemic American economy was indeed performing well. In 2018, US incomes rose by 2.4 per cent, adjusting for inflation, with a jump of 4.6 per cent in the third quarter (July–September) leading to the election, while gross domestic product was up 3.4 per cent for that quarter and 2.9 per cent for the year.[69] Unemployment stood at just 3.7 per cent by October. And economic growth was stronger in blue regions than red. (The one-sixth of US counties won by Clinton in 2016 accounted for 64 per cent of the nation's GDP.)[70] A solid majority of Americans had a favourable view of the economy, with measures of consumer confidence and personal finances particularly strong.[71]

Referendum theory suggests this performance should have buffered Republican candidates, at least in part. That it did not reflects that voters' assessments of the president himself were far less positive. 'There's Never Been a President This Unpopular with an Economy This Good', read a *Bloomberg News* headline above a chart detailing the gap between economic perceptions and presidential approval.[72] Trump ran well behind where he 'should' have been given past data linking approval to the state of the economy: the last time the public had felt as optimistic about the economy as they did in autumn 2018 was 1997, when Bill Clinton boasted a 56 per cent approval rating.[73] But a week before the 2018 elections, Gallup reported that only 40 per cent of the public approved of Trump's performance. Fifty-five per cent disapproved.[74]

That figure had not varied much in Trump's twenty-one-plus months in office to that point. Trump's first Gallup poll in January 2017 showed that 44 per cent of Americans approved of his performance, hardly a traditional 'honeymoon', but even so his peak rating through the midterm; the lowest figure during that time was 36 per cent. Thus a Gallup graph of the period traces a nearly (and compared to his predecessors, a strikingly) flat line, just above and below that 40 per cent level. That stability was constant across partisan subsets of the electorate, but at radically different levels. As of the midterm, nearly nine-tenths of Republican voters saw Trump favourably – but only 7 per cent of Democrats, while independents tracked at just 38 per cent. Few had changed their minds over the course of Trump's term. It was hard to argue he had given anyone a reason to do so.

In that sense, the election was indeed a referendum, but on matters other than economic performance. In fact, notwithstanding his quoted boasts, Trump's own closing arguments for Republican midterm success did not mention the economy:

'This will be an election of Kavanaugh, the caravan, law and order and common sense,' the president summarised at an 18 October rally.[75] This litany of issues made reference to the recent confirmation of Supreme Court justice Brett Kavanaugh despite what conservatives saw as unfair demonisation over accusations of past sexual misconduct, a 'caravan' of Central American would-be immigrants to United States supposedly organised by Democratic officials, and imagined urban (read: Black) riots. But it had a tenuous relationship to the facts, and even less to voters' key concerns and which party they thought could best address them.

Indeed, less than a week before the election, Peter Baker and Linda Qiu of the *New York Times* noted that 'the president has spoken of riots that have not happened, claimed deals that have not been reached, cited jobs that have not been created and spun dark conspiracies that have no apparent basis in reality. He has pulled figures seemingly out of thin air, rewritten history and contradicted his own past comments.'[76] More than four-fifths of registered voters ranked the economy and health care as key to their vote, well above immigration or the Supreme Court.[77] And only on stewardship of the economy and the related issue of taxation did Republicans even come close to parity with Democrats as the party more trusted to manage those issues well. On immigration, Democrats got the nod by twelve percentage points (50–38 per cent); on the Supreme Court, their lead was eleven points (49–38 per cent). Trump did not accept this: when asked, for instance, whether he was 'concerned that Democrats are going to be more energized coming into the midterms now that Kavanaugh [has been confirmed]', the president replied that 'I think a lot of Democrats are going to vote Republican', on the grounds that the party-in-Congress's rush to judgement on Kavanaugh had outraged its own loyalists. Yet 76 per cent of voters overall said 'equal treatment of men and women in U.S. society' was 'especially important in their vote', and gave Democrats a twenty-six-point (55–29 per cent) lead in addressing that issue.[78] Suburban and female voters skewed strongly away from Trump's stated priorities and for that matter from the tone of his rhetoric.[79] Any benefit of the doubt given to Trump when he faced another unpopular candidate head-to-head in 2016 had dissipated two years on.

More generally, Trump's tactics were hardly calibrated to attract voters from across the aisle. Indeed, elsewhere in his 18 October speech, Trump claimed that 'radical Democrats' were 'the party of crime', desperate 'to impose socialism on our incredible nation'. A few days earlier, he had declared that 'Democrats want to open America's borders and turn our country into a friendly sanctuary for murderous thugs from other countries who will kill us all'.[80] Readers may not require formal fact-checking to appreciate that this was not, in fact, part of the Democratic platform.

In the end, the biggest issue was the president himself. That was no accident: as Senator Chris Coons (D-DE) observed, 'No matter what it is that's going on in our country or the world, he wants to be the subject of the news.'[81] Trump threw himself into the midterm campaign, crisscrossing the country and inserting himself into local races. He barnstormed through eleven rallies in eight days in late October and early November, building on what he had emphasised to Mississippi voters on 2 October: 'I'm not on the ticket, but I am on the ticket, because this is also a referendum about me and the disgusting gridlock that they'll put this country through . . . I want you to vote. Pretend I'm on the ballot.'[82] In Florida, later that month, voters said they would do just that. 'I'm here because of President Trump,' one told a reporter. 'I trust the candidates that the president supports.' Another, though, reached a rather different conclusion from a similar starting point. 'My vote is driven by Trump 1,000 percent,' she said. 'I just find him despicable.'[83]

Florida was not an outlier – but, despite Trump's confidence, the second opinion outnumbered the first. One Kaiser Family Foundation Poll tracking swing-state voters in Colorado found that, while health care was, indeed, the largest substantive issue troubling Democratic and independent voters (it was third for Republicans), a 'candidate's support for or opposition to President Trump' was twice or three times more important still.[84] In a national poll, some two-thirds of voters said Trump would be a key factor in their vote. Women, especially suburban women, were disproportionately likely to say so. And Trump's approval rating among women was even worse than detailed above, at just 27 per cent by late October. Overall, nearly two-thirds of voters who saw Trump as a major factor in their vote said they would vote Democratic.[85]

That suggests a more personal 'presidential penalty' than usually implied in the midterm loss literature. In 2014, just a quarter of voters saw Barack Obama as a major factor in their vote, and more than half 'not a factor at all' (only 31 per cent said this of Trump).[86] But that is not the whole story. The 2018 midterms also served, of course, as an exemplar of partisan balancing in the manner Erikson and others have proposed. Given that the outcome of the 2016 presidential race was predicted by very few – including, by most accounts, Trump himself – the 2018 results also support the 'electoral surprise' hypothesis. Voters who had expected a President Hillary Clinton to check a Republican Congress now saw the need, and had the chance, to buffer GOP power instead.

Other systematic factors played out, too. A flurry of pre-emptive retirements meant that forty-four Republican seats lacked incumbents to defend them, by far the highest total since 1974. And the unexpected GOP success in 2016 meant additional battleground districts to defend in 2018. Gary Jacobson's research adds an additional factor: the sudden peak of a long-developing trend, namely the correlation between evaluations of the president and the generic vote for Congress noted above. Over time those responses became increasingly aligned, suggesting that party identification was increasingly dominant in the voting calculus at all levels. From the 1940s through the 1970s, the congruence of pre-election polls tracking presidential approval and congressional preferences was only about 70 per cent, rising only to 74 per cent in the 1980s and 1990s.[87] In the twenty-first-century midterms prior to 2018, the congruence rose to 82 per cent. But for 2018 the figure was an all-time high of 93 per cent. Not surprisingly, this itself correlated very closely with other measures of polarisation, notably the immense gap in approval of Trump between Democratic and Republican voters.[88] As Nathaniel Rakich writes, 'Once upon a time, people really did vote for person over party . . . [and] a voter's preferences were only loosely moored to partisanship. But those days are over.'[89] Thus the GOP's midterm loss in 2018 was both 'an extreme referendum' on Trump, the president and person, and a sign of the intensive nationalisation of congressional elections.[90]

Midterm loss and presidential power

The impact of the 2018 midterm results on the remainder of Trump's time in office was hinted at above. Congressional productivity even during unified government in 2017–18 had been sporadic, with just 429 laws passed during the two years of the 115th Congress. (This compares to over 900 laws passed during the so-called 'Do Nothing' Congress of 1947–8.) But in the 116th Congress that ran to 3 January 2021, even that figure plummeted: to 283, including the only veto override of Trump's presidency.[91] Party seats in Congress are, after all, the gold standard for presidents' legislative success. And even had Trump been the assiduous bargainer his 'art of the deal' persona promised, the opportunity for Clintonesque triangulation was limited by the polarisation between the parties. Legislative stalemate was always the most likely outcome of the 2018 midterms, and with two exceptions – the huge spending bills prompted by the coronavirus pandemic in 2020, and the slate of federal judges confirmed with increasing rapidity by the still-Republican Senate – it prevailed. Even before the new Democratic House majority formally took office, gridlock over budget negotiations shut down significant portions of the federal government. A deal would not be reached until late January 2019.

Another predictable outcome was a surge in executive orders and regulations evading the need for new statute. While he had decried Obama's 'We can't wait' campaign at the time, Trump used similar reasoning, if more inflammatory language. 'Democrats are actively blocking the things that we want. And what we want is good for people,' the president said in August 2020. 'Therefore, I'm taking Executive action. We've had it.'[92] He also evaded the appropriations process by declaring a 'national emergency' in early 2019 to unlock spending for the border wall

Congress had refused to fund. The actual emergency posed by the COVID-19 crisis unsurprisingly prompted its own flurry of administrative directives.

While the GOP Senate busied itself with judicial nominations, the Democratic House turned to aggressive oversight. The year that began with a government shutdown ended in impeachment, via a series of committee-driven investigations, lawsuits over executive privilege and congressional prerogative, and testimony from executive branch whistle-blowers. After the Senate quickly acquitted Trump in early 2020, the president's behaviour after his failed re-election campaign led to an unprecedented second impeachment. Throughout, Trump railed against 'PRESIDENTIAL HARRASSMENT' and (on Christmas Day 2019) plaintively wondered aloud 'why should Crazy Nancy Pelosi, just because she has a slight majority in the House, be allowed to Impeach the President of the United States?'[93] The answer was inexorably bound up in midterm loss.

To be sure, the impeachment of Joe Biden is not the likely outcome of the 2022 midterms. But even before he was inaugurated, Biden and his staff were planning strategies that would avoid his own midterm 'shellacking'.[94] Given that Democrats control the Senate only by virtue of Vice President Kamala Harris's tie-breaking vote and the House by a handful of switched seats, midterm loss far short of the historical average would return Republicans to power on Capitol Hill in 2023. Indeed, given the GOP's control of state legislatures, the redistricting required by the 2020 Census could itself be enough for the party to net the five seats needed to take back the House. The likelihood of impending gridlock helped unify otherwise disparate Democrats around Biden's hugely ambitious legislative agenda in the 117th Congress.

Either way, 2022 will be a good measure of some of the competing trends discussed above, shaping whether its impact will be merely 'calibrating' or 'preparatory', in Busch's terms. Turnout hit a modern high in 2020, with nearly two-thirds of eligible voters getting to the polls (or to their mailbox); to dampen the decline after that surge, Democrats hoped to cement the educated white suburbanites Trump had alienated to their base. Republicans in numerous states, for their part, sought to make the logistics of voting – whether on the day or in advance – more difficult.[95] Trump himself, of course, would not be on the ballot, a factor that could reduce turnout on both sides of the aisle.

On paper, the Senate map favoured Democrats, at least relative to 2018; they had to defend just fourteen of the thirty-four seats at stake, and could contest open seats in key swing states after Republican incumbents retired from the field. Of the eight races *Roll Call* handicappers ranked as most competitive, four were held by each party – but six were in states Biden had won (albeit barely in several cases). Would party loyalty outweigh the traditional midterm dynamic?[96] That question was key in the House as well, as elections nationalise and the benefits of incumbency decline. Twenty years ago, incumbency added some eight points to a candidate's vote share; in 2018, at least, that dropped to under three points. All politics, it seems, are no longer local.[97]

If the correlation between presidential approval and the generic congressional vote remains sky-high, that could help Democrats in 2022 where it hurt Republicans in 2018. As of July 2021, Biden's approval (according to Gallup) had not dipped below 50 per cent, and polls of registered voters in early August placed it in the mid- to upper 50s.[98] He would bank on an aggressive coronavirus vaccination programme and a related post-pandemic economic surge – as well as, perhaps, the GOP's continuing fealty to former President Trump – to keep it there.

Would (as *538.com* put it) 'everything [be] partisan and correlated and boring' in 2022?[99] 'Sleepy Joe' certainly hoped so. Given the governing implications of midterm loss, a boring election night is something any president looks forward to.

Notes

1. DNC chair David Wilhelm quoted in Adam Clymer, 'The 1994 Elections, Congress: The Overview', *New York Times*, 10 Nov. 1994, p. A1; William J. Clinton, press conference of 9 Nov. 1994, American Presidency Project [hereafter APP], https://www.presidency.ucsb.edu/documents/the-presidents-news-conference-1235, accessed 14 Mar. 2022.

2. George W. Bush, press conference of 8 Nov. 2006, APP, https://www.presidency.ucsb.edu/documents/the-presidents-news-conference-1, accessed 14 Mar. 2022.
3. Barack Obama, press conference of 3 Nov. 2010, APP, https://www.presidency.ucsb.edu/documents/the-presidents-news-conference-1115, accessed 14 Mar. 2022. He said again, in a press conference on 22 December 2010, that in 'the midterm elections . . . we took a shellacking'. See APP, https://www.presidency.ucsb.edu/documents/the-presidents-news-conference-1114, accessed 14 Mar. 2022.
4. Olivia Nuzzi, 'My Private Oval Office Press Conference, *New York*, 10 Oct. 2018, https://nymag.com/intelligencer/2018/10/my-private-oval-office-press-conference-with-donald-trump.html, accessed 14 Mar. 2022.
5. https://www.govinfo.gov/content/pkg/DCPD-201800771/pdf/DCPD-201800771.pdf, accessed 14 Mar. 2022.
6. Bernard Grofman, Thomas L. Brunell, and William Koetzle, 'Why Gain in the Senate but Midterm Loss in the House? Evidence from a Natural Experiment', *Legislative Studies Quarterly* 23 (1998): pp. 79–89 (quotation at p. 79); see also Alan I. Abramowitz, Albert D. Cover, and Helmut Norpoth, 'The President's Party in Midterm Elections: Going from Bad to Worse', *American Journal of Political Science* 30 (1986): pp. 562–76.
7. In 1902, Teddy Roosevelt's Republicans did gain nine seats in the House, but this was a loss nonetheless: the chamber was expanded that year to track the national population growth reflected in the 1900 census, and Democrats gained twenty-five seats. We could also include 1866, since, while Andrew Johnson was nominally a Republican, he had been a Democrat prior to 1864 and campaigned heavily against congressional Republicans at the midterm only to see them gain at least nine net seats (exact calculations of loss/gain are tricky in this case since not all states had yet been readmitted to the Union).
8. In nineteen cases, the president's party lost seats; in 1982 and 1998, the president's party neither gained nor lost seats. (Some sources list a one-seat gain for Reagan's GOP in 1982. But Republicans held the same number of seats after the election as before, taking a seat formerly held by an independent while losing one net seat to Democrats.)
9. V. O. Key Jr, *Politics, Parties, and Pressure Groups*, 5th edn (New York: Crowell, 1964), p. 568.

10. Gary C. Jacobson, 'Extreme Referendum: Donald Trump and the 2018 Midterm Elections', *Political Science Quarterly* 134 (2019): pp. 9–38 (quotation at p. 9).
11. Ashley Parker and Josh Dawsey, '"I Am on the Ticket": Trump Seeks to Make the Election About Him, Even If Some Don't Want It to Be', *Washington Post*, 18 Oct. 2018, www.washingtonpost.com/politics/i-am-on-the-ticket-trump-seeks-to-make-the-election-about-him-even-if-some-dont-want-it-to-be/2018/10/17/069406f6-d0bc-11e8-a275-81c671a50422_story.html, accessed 14 Mar. 2022.
12. Bill Clinton, press conference of 18 Apr. 1995, APP, https://www.presidency.ucsb.edu/node/220794, accessed 14 Mar. 2022.
13. This astonishing idea came from Democratic Senator William Fulbright of Arkansas, future employer of a young Bill Clinton (among his other legacies). See Harry S. Truman, press conference of 11 Nov. 1946, APP, https://www.presidency.ucsb.edu/node/232244, accessed 14 Mar. 2022.
14. There is at least some research on whether governors also face a midterm loss phenomenon; they probably do. See Olle Folke and James M. Snyder, 'Gubernatorial Midterm Slumps', *American Journal of Political Science* 56 (2012): pp. 931–48; Michael Bailey and Elliott Fullmer, 'Balancing in the U.S. States, 1978–2009', *State Politics & Policy Quarterly* 11 (2011): pp. 148–66.
15. In *Presidential Power*, Richard Neustadt defined 'Washingtonians' as all those with an interest in American national power and policy dynamics, whether or not resident in the District of Columbia.
16. Pearl O. Ponsford, *Evil Results of Mid-Term Congressional Elections and a Suggested Remedy* (Los Angeles, CA: University of Southern California Press, 1937).
17. The president's Gallup job approval numbers never dipped below 60 per cent during the course of 1998 (his average annual approval prior to 1996 was well under 50 per cent). Two-thirds of respondents consistently said Clinton should not be impeached. See Andrew Rudalevige, 'The Broken Places: The Clinton Impeachment and American Politics', in Michael Nelson, Barbara A. Perry, and Russell L. Riley, eds, *42: Inside the Presidency of Bill Clinton* (Ithaca, NY: Cornell University Press, 2016), pp. 141–2.
18. Sometimes special elections are added to this total. If a vacancy occurs in the US Senate, governors often have the authority to appoint a successor who holds the seat until the next federal election.

19. Grofman et al., 'Why Gain in the Senate . . .?', p. 84.
20. This kind of '*p*-hacking' (slang for auditioning combinations of variables to improve the statistical fit of a given model, as measured probabilistically, hence *p*) is scientific malpractice in some contexts, but can be useful for purely predictive purposes. For a broader Senate forecast model (not aimed specifically at midterms), see Carl Klarner and Stan Buchanan, 'Forecasting the 2006 Elections for the United States Senate', *PS: Political Science and Politics* 39 (2006): pp. 849–55; it is perhaps worth noting, though, that they gave Democrats 'little chance of taking control of the Senate in 2006'.
21. See, e.g., Alan Abramowitz, 'Forecasting the 2022 Midterm Election with the Generic Ballot', *The Crystal Ball*, University of Virginia Center for Politics, 10 June 2021, https://centerforpolitics.org/crystalball/articles/forecasting-the-2022-midterm-election-with-the-generic-ballot/, accessed 14 Mar. 2022. Gallup's version of the 'generic ballot' question is: 'If the elections for Congress were being held today, which party's candidate would you vote for in your congressional district – the Democratic Party's candidate or the Republican Party's candidate?'
22. Andrew Rudalevige, 'Revisiting Midterm Loss', *American Politics Research* 29 (Jan. 2001): pp. 25–46 (quotation at p. 27).
23. This measure of the 'voter eligible population' (VEP) usually yields a somewhat higher turnout estimate than that for the 'voting age population' (VAP), since across American history numerous people have been old enough to vote but not eligible to do so – for instance, prisoners (and often former prisoners) and individuals not legally in the United States but who are counted in Census data. Many others were long barred from participating by Jim Crow statutes and related 'rules' backed up by local political establishments and mob violence.
24. McDonald calculates that 50.4 per cent of the VEP cast ballots in 1914. See http://www.electproject.org/national-1789-present, accessed 14 Mar. 2022.
25. In practice, only white women, at least in the South until after 1965.
26. James E. Campbell, 'Explaining Presidential Losses in Midterm Congressional Elections', *Journal of Politics* 47 (1985): pp. 1140–57 (quotation at p. 1140); see also Barbara Hinckley, 'Interpreting House Midterm Elections: Toward a Measurement of the In-Party's "Expected" Loss of Seats', *American Political*

Science Review 61 (1967): pp. 691–700; D. Roderick Kiewiet and Douglas Rivers, 'A Retrospective on Retrospective Voting', *Political Behavior* 6 (1984): pp. 369–93.

27. The classic article is Angus Campbell, 'Surge and Decline: A Study of Electoral Change', *Public Opinion Quarterly* 24 (1960): pp. 397–418; see also James E. Campbell, 'The Presidential Surge and Its Midterm Decline in Congressional Elections', *Journal of Politics* 53 (1991): pp. 477–87.
28. Prospect theory is associated with the work of economists Daniel Kahneman and Amos Tversky. But for an early discussion of the power of 'negative voting' in midterms, see Samuel Kernell, 'Presidential Popularity and Negative Voting', *American Political Science Review* 71 (1977): pp. 44–6.
29. See John Aldrich, Jamie Carson, Brad Gomez, and David Rohde, *Change and Continuity in the 2016 and 2018 Elections* (Washington, DC: Sage/CQ Press, 2019), esp. ch. 4, for a discussion of demographics and voter turnout.
30. V. O. Key, *Politics, Parties, and Pressure Groups* (New York: Thomas Y. Crowell, 1942), p. 609.
31. Morris Fiorina, *Congress: Keystone of the Washington Establishment*, 2nd edn (New Haven, CT: Yale University Press, 1989), p. 83.
32. Stuart Rothenberg, 'Breaking the Midterm Mode: Both Parties Make It about Trump', *Roll Call*, 15 Oct. 2018, https://www.rollcall.com/2018/10/15/breaking-the-midterm-mode-both-parties-make-it-about-trump/, accessed 14 Mar. 2022.
33. Robert Erikson, 'Economic Conditions and the Congressional Vote: A Review of the Macrolevel Evidence', *American Journal of Political Science* 34 (1990): pp. 373–99 (quotation at p. 373).
34. Edward Tufte, 'Determinants of Outcomes of Midterm Congressional Election', *American Political Science Review* 69 (1975), pp. 812–26 (quotation at p. 826); and see also Tufte, *Political Control of the Economy* (Princeton, NJ: Princeton University Press, 1978).
35. For a more extensive literature review, see Rudalevige, 'Midterm Loss Revisited'; Folke and Snyder, 'Gubernatorial Midterm Slumps'.
36. Robert Erikson, 'The Puzzle of Midterm Loss', *Journal of Politics* 50 (1988): pp. 1011–29 (at p. 1020).
37. See, among many others, Alan Abramowitz, 'Economic Conditions, Presidential Popularity, and Voting Behavior in Congressional

Midterm Elections', *Journal of Politics* 47 (1985): pp. 31–43; Lyn Ragsdale, 'The Fiction of Presidential Events', *American Politics Quarterly* 8 (1980): pp. 375–98.

38. Rudalevige, 'Midterm Loss Revisited', from which the following discussion is drawn.
39. Erikson, 'Puzzle of Midterm Loss', p. 1012.
40. Ibid., p. 1014.
41. Kenneth Scheve and Michael Tomz, 'Electoral Surprise and the Midterm Loss in U.S. Congressional Elections', *British Journal of Political Science* 29 (1999): pp. 507–21 (quotation at p. 507); see also Alberto Alesina and Howard Rosenthal, *Partisan Politics, Divided Government, and the Economy* (New York: Cambridge University Press, 1995).
42. Robert Erikson, 'Explaining Midterm Loss: The Tandem Effects of Withdrawn Coattails and Balancing', *Journal of Politics* 50 (2010): pp. 1011–29.
43. Gary C. Jacobson and Jamie Carson, *The Politics of Congressional Elections*, 10th edn (Lanham, MD: Rowman & Littlefield, 2019), p. 214; for a foundational statement, see Jacobson and Samuel Kernell, *Strategy and Choice in Congressional Elections* (New Haven, CT: Yale University Press, 1981).
44. Andrew Busch, *Horses in Midstream: U.S. Midterm Elections and Their Consequences, 1894–1998* (Pittsburgh, PA: University of Pittsburgh Press, 1999), p. 7.
45. Calculated by the author from various issues of *CQ Weekly*, 2009–17. Note that the overall figures may be inflated both by presidents' careful choice about what issues they take a position on and by the large number of confirmation votes on the Senate calendar. For a wider discussion, see Andrew Rudalevige, *Managing the President's Program: Presidential Leadership and Legislative Policy Formulation* (Princeton, NJ: Princeton University Press, 2002), ch. 3.
46. Rudalevige, *Managing the President's Program*, calculated from p. 184, Table A.7. Note that, in Figure 1.3, the results for Eisenhower and Reagan are averaged across their two terms (and midterms).
47. Quoted in Andrew Rudalevige, 'The Presidential Charm Offensive', *The Monkey Cage*, 8 Mar. 2013, available at https://themonkeycage.org/2013/03/the-presidential-charm-offensive/, accessed 14 Mar. 2022.
48. At least as measured by the gap in presidential approval between Democrats and Republicans for each. See David Mayhew, *Divided*

We Govern, 2nd edn (New Haven, CT: Yale University Press, 2002), for early and optimistic empirics on the productivity of divided government.

49. Bush, *Horses at Midstream*, p. 121 and ch. 5 generally.
50. Obama, 'Remarks in Las Vegas', 24 Oct. 2011, APP, https://www.presidency.ucsb.edu/node/297388
51. Busch, *Horses at Midstream*, p. 97. See, too, James Sundquist, *Politics and Policy: The Eisenhower, Kennedy, and Johnson Years* (Washington, DC: Brookings Institution, 1968).
52. V. O. Key suggests that the 1958 gains were so large they left few additional seats for Democrats to capture and thus offset midterm loss in 1962: 'Democrats did not win in 1960 the seats they would have been expected to lose in 1962' (*Politics, Parties, and Pressure Groups*, 5th edn, p. 571).
53. He beat LBJ's vice president, Hubert Humphrey, by about half a million votes nationally, a margin of 0.7 per cent. This was good enough for a 301–191 electoral college victory, though, with independent George Wallace picking up the remaining forty-six.
54. See, e.g., James E. Campbell, 'The Exceptional Election of 2008: Performance, Values, and Crisis', *Presidential Studies Quarterly* 40 (2010): pp. 225–46.
55. https://www.govinfo.gov/content/pkg/DCPD-201800771/pdf/DCPD-201800771.pdf, accessed 14 Mar. 2022.
56. Olivia Nuzzi, 'My Private Oval Office Press Conference', *New York*, 10 Oct. 2018, https://nymag.com/intelligencer/2018/10/my-private-oval-office-press-conference-with-donald-trump.html, accessed 14 Mar. 2022.
57. 'United States Congress Elections, 2018', *Ballotopedia*, https://ballotpedia.org/United_States_Congress_elections,_2018, accessed 14 Mar. 2022.
58. Noah Rudnick, 'The Year of the Green Wave', *Crystal Ball*, 31 Jan. 2019, Center for Politics, University of Virginia, https://centerforpolitics.org/crystalball/articles/the-year-of-the-green-wave/, accessed 14 Mar. 2022.
59. See, respectively, Tim Reid, 'Democrats Face "Almost Impossible Map" to Retake U.S. Senate', *Reuters*, 24 Aug. 2018, https://www.reuters.com/article/us-usa-election-democrats-explainer-idUSKCN1L920M, accessed 14 Mar. 2022.; Larry J. Sabato and Kyle Kondik, 'How'd We Do?', *Crystal Ball*, 7 Nov. 2018, Center for Politics, University of Virginia, https://centerforpolitics.org/crystalball/articles/howd-we-do/, accessed 14 Mar. 2022.; and

David Wasserman, 'The Congressional Map Has a Record-Setting Bias against Democrats', *FiveThirtyEight*, 7 Aug. 2017, https://fivethirtyeight.com/features/the-congressional-map-is-historically-biased-toward-the-gop/, accessed 14 Mar. 2022.

60. In Mississippi, Republican Cindy Hyde-Smith had been appointed to succeed Thad Cochrane, who had retired midterm due to ill health, while incumbent Roger Wicker was running for re-election after his full six-year term. Likewise, Minnesota featured Amy Klobuchar's regularly scheduled bid for re-election as well as Tina Smith's special election; Smith was appointed to the seat formerly held by Al Franken, who announced his resignation in late 2017.
61. https://www.govinfo.gov/content/pkg/DCPD-201800771/pdf/DCPD-201800771.pdf, accessed 14 Mar. 2022.
62. Transcript of Pelosi press conference, 7 Nov. 2018, available at http://www.cnn.com/TRANSCRIPTS/1811/07/wolf.02.html, accessed 14 Mar. 2022.
63. Statistics in this paragraph are drawn from Scott Keeter and Ruth Igielnik, 'Democrats Made Gains from Multiple Sources in 2018 Midterm Victories', Pew Research Center, 8 Sept. 2020, https://www.pewresearch.org/methods/2020/09/08/democrats-made-gains-from-multiple-sources-in-2018-midterm-victories/, accessed 14 Mar. 2022.
64. Scott Clement and Dan Balz, 'Voters Say They Are More Likely to Cast Ballots in This Year's Midterm Elections', *Washington Post*, 13 Oct. 2018, https://www.washingtonpost.com/politics/voters-say-they-are-more-likely-to-cast-ballots-in-this-years-midterm-elecions/2018/10/13/c8dd8198-ce63-11e8-a360-85875bac0b1f_story.html, accessed 14 Mar. 2022.
65. Keeter and Igielnik, 'Democrats Made Gains'.
66. Clement and Balz, 'Voters Say'.
67. Keeter and Igielnik, 'Democrats Made Gains'.
68. Tweets of 5 Nov. 2018, 24 Aug. 2018, and 10 Sept. 2018. See thetrumparchive.com for a searchable database of Trump tweets, which, of course, are no longer available on the Twitter site itself.
69. Data from the news release of 28 Mar. 2019, Bureau of Economic Analysis, US Department of Commerce, https://www.bea.gov/news/2019/gross-domestic-product-4th-quarter-and-annual-2018-third-estimate-corporate-profits-4th, accessed 14 Mar. 2022.
70. See Andrew Rudalevige, 'The Meaning of the Election: The President as Minority Leader', in Michael Nelson, ed., *The Elections of 2016* (Thousand Oaks, CA: CQ Press/Sage, 2017), p. 225.

71. See Alexandre Tanzi and Rob Miller, 'There's Never Been a President This Unpopular with an Economy This Good', *Bloomberg*, 12 Sept. 2018, https://www.bloomberg.com/news/articles/2018-09-12/trump-is-more-unpopular-than-any-president-with-a-strong-economy, accessed 14 Mar. 2022; for specifics of Bloomberg's Consumer Comfort Index (CCI), including the 'economic' and 'personal finances' subindices, see, e.g., https://www.langerresearch.com/wp-content/uploads/CCI_04-02-20.pdf, accessed 14 Mar. 2022.
72. Tanzi and Miller, 'There's Never Been a President This Unpopular with an Economy This Good'.
73. Jacobson, 'Extreme Referendum', p. 11.
74. The Gallup data here and discussed in the next paragraph are available at https://news.gallup.com/interactives/185273/presidential-job-approval-center.aspx, accessed 14 Mar. 2022.
75. Trump, 'Remarks at a "Make America Great Again" Rally in Missoula, Montana', 18 Oct. 2018, APP, https://www.presidency.ucsb.edu/node/332470, accessed 14 Mar. 2022.
76. See Peter Baker and Linda Qiu, 'Inside What Even an Ally Calls Trump's "Reality Distortion Field",' *New York Times*, 31 Oct. 2018, https://www.nytimes.com/2018/10/31/us/politics/fact-check-trump-distortion-campaign.html, accessed 14 Mar. 2022. 'You should probably dial down the lying', former Trump communications director Anthony Scaramucci advised the president live on CNN in October.
77. Gary Langer, 'Trump's Approval Improves, Yet Dems Still Lead for the House', *ABC News*, 14 Oct. 2018, https://abcnews.go.com/Politics/trumps-approval-improves-dems-lead-house/story?id=58469893, accessed 14 Mar. 2022. The headline is technically accurate relative to an August poll by the same news organisations, but Trump's approval had risen only to 41 per cent, with 54 per cent disapproval.
78. Langer, 'Trump's Approval Improves, Yet Dems Still Lead for the House'.
79. Domenico Montenaro, 'Poll: Trump Seen as Important Factor in Americans' Vote, as Democrats Open Up Lead', *NPR*, 26 Oct. 2018, https://www.npr.org/2018/10/26/660670687/poll-trump-seen-as-important-factor-in-americans-vote-as-democrats-open-up-lead, accessed 14 Mar. 2022.
80. Chris Kenning, 'Trump Rallies Kentucky Supporters', *Courier-Journal*, 13 Oct. 2018, https://www.courier-journal.com/story/news/

politics/2018/10/13/president-donald-trump-speaks-richmond-kentucky/1577851002/, accessed 14 Mar. 2022.

81. Ashley Parker and Philip Rucker, 'Trump Colors the Fall Campaign Landscape: "He's Been the Only Thing That Matters"', *Washington Post*, 8 Sept. 2018, https://www.washingtonpost.com/politics/trump-colors-the-fall-campaign-landscape-hes-been-the-only-thing-that-matters/2018/09/08/fd1a9a06-b2d7-11e8-a20b-5f4f84429666_story.html, accessed 14 Mar. 2022.; see also Rothenberg, 'Breaking the Midterm Mode'.
82. See the transcript of the 2 Oct. 2018, rally in Southaven, Mississippi, at https://factba.se/transcript/donald-trump-speech-maga-rally-southaven-ms-october-2-2018, last accessed. This was the second time in that speech Trump made this appeal, having earlier said that 'I'm not on the ballot, but in a certain way, I'm on the ballot.'
83. Quoted in Lisa Lerer, 'Trump Has Become a Midterms Rorschach Test', *New York Times*, 25 Oct. 2018, https://www.nytimes.com/2018/10/25/us/politics/on-politics-trump-midterm-influence.html, accessed 14 Mar. 2022.
84. Kaiser Family Foundation and Colorado Health Foundation Survey, Oct. 2018, available at https://files.kff.org/attachment/Report-Coloradans-Perspectives-on-Health-Quality-of-Life-and-Midterm-Elections, accessed 14 Mar. 2022.
85. Montenaro, 'Poll: Trump Seen as Important Factor in Americans' Vote'. Jacobson likewise found that 63 per cent of prospective voters 'said their vote would be about Trump', a new record high (56 per cent said the same of Obama in 2010). Jacobson, 'Extreme Referendum', p. 23.
86. Montenaro, 'Poll: Trump Seen as Important Factor in Americans' Vote'.
87. Jacobson, 'Extreme Referendum', p. 19.
88. Ibid., pp. 19–20.
89. Nathaniel Rakich, 'Everything Is Partisan and Correlated and Boring', *FiveThirtyEight.com*, 20 Nov. 2018, https://fivethirtyeight.com/features/everything-is-partisan-and-correlated-and-boring/, last accessed 14 Mar. 2022.
90. Jacobson, 'Extreme Referendum', p. 23; see also Rothenberg, 'Breaking the Midterm Mode'.
91. The override vote enacting the Defense Authorization Act – which Trump had vetoed because it sought to rename US military bases named after Confederate Civil War generals (by definition, traitors to the United States) – came on 1 January 2021. For annual figures,

see https://www.senate.gov/legislative/ResumesofCongressionalActivity1947present.htm, accessed 14 Mar. 2022.

92. Remarks of 8 Aug. 2020, APP, https://www.presidency.ucsb.edu/node/343275, accessed 14 Mar. 2022.
93. Tweet of 25 Dec. 2019; Trump tweeted about 'presidential harassment', usually in all-caps, nearly forty times. See, e.g., his tweets of 7 Feb. 2019, 19 Dec. 2019, and 9 July 2020, at the Trump Twitter archive cited earlier.
94. Natasha Korecki and Christopher Cadelago, 'Inside Joe Biden's Plan to Avoid a Midterm "Shellacking"', *Politico*, 12 Jan. 2021, https://www.politico.com/news/2021/01/12/joe-biden-plan-midterms-shellacking-458316, accessed 14 Mar. 2022.
95. Geoffrey Skelley, 'How the Republican Push to Restrict Voting Could Affect Our Elections', *FiveThirtyEight.com*, 17 May 2021, https://fivethirtyeight.com/features/how-the-republican-push-to-restrict-voting-could-affect-our-elections/, accessed 14 Mar. 2022.
96. Stuart Rothenberg, 'Will Straight-Ticket Voting Upset the Midterm Dynamic in Battle for Senate?', *Roll Call*, 16 June 2021, https://www.rollcall.com/2021/06/16/the-senate-in-2022-midterm-dynamic-or-straight-ticket-voting/, accessed 14 Mar. 2022.
97. Nathaniel Rakich, 'How Much Was Incumbency Worth in 2018?,' *FiveThirtyEight.com*, 6 Dec. 2018, https://fivethirtyeight.com/features/how-much-was-incumbency-worth-in-2018/, accessed 14 Mar. 2022.; for earlier research, see, among others, Andrew Gelman and Gary King, 'Estimating Incumbency Advantage without Bias,' *American Journal of Political Science* 34 (1990): pp. 1142–64; Gary King and Andrew Gelman, 'Systematic Consequences of Incumbency Advantage in U.S. House Elections', *American Journal of Political Science* 35 (1991): pp. 110–38.
98. See, e.g., the *Investor's Business Daily* poll released 2 Aug. 2021, which showed Biden's approval at 52 per cent overall and 57 per cent among registered voters: https://twitter.com/dcg1114/status/1422210274673651716, accessed 14 Mar. 2022.
99. https://fivethirtyeight.com/features/everything-is-partisan-and-correlated-and-boring/, accessed 14 Mar. 2022.

2

From Election to Re-election: The Electoral Politics of Presidency and Party, 1960–2012

Sarah Tiplady

Midterms are part of a political system characterised by frequent elections; in a political system also characterised by a focus on the presidency, these are contests when the White House is not subject to electoral competition but when there are many candidates representing – and opposing – the president's party. The relationship between president and party is one that has been the subject of scholarly neglect by contrast with other aspects of the presidency – not surprisingly, perhaps, because this is a system further characterised, at least for much of the period investigated in this book by weak parties and, increasingly, by 'candidate-centred' politics.[1] Through an investigation of midterms, this book explores the relationship between presidents and parties, analysing the meaning and the impact of these elections when a president is not on the ballot. At the heart of this chapter is the relationship between president and party; it scrutinises the extent to which successful presidential candidates over time have employed party-oriented – as opposed to candidate-centred – rhetoric on the campaign trail, in search of the White House, by comparison with incumbent presidents seeking re-election. It finds that there has been much more discussion of party during these campaigns than prevailing understandings of candidate-centred politics suggest; it also finds that there are significant differences between successful initial campaigns and re-election bids. In turn, this creates a context within which to reflect on midterms and their meanings.

The focus, then, for this exploration of the relationship between president and party involves campaign rhetoric, specifically campaign speeches, between 1960 and 2012. All campaign speeches from presidential election and re-election campaigns have been analysed on a weekly basis, focusing on the use of party within speeches; that is the use of party affiliation to reinforce predispositions of the electorate or encourage the electorate to vote for the candidate in question.

Use of party in campaign speeches

Presidential candidates can try to use their party affiliation, as a Democrat or Republican, to reinforce any predispositions the electorate may have, encouraging the electorate to vote for them.[2] Conversely, some of the electorate may use the party as a way to decide how to vote. The electorate does not always vote based on the party they generally affiliate with, but in trying to gain as many votes from a broad coalition as possible, candidates will want to use party in rhetoric to appeal to party-faithful voters. However, there may be times that candidates will want to be considered a partisan, and other circumstances during the campaign where it may be beneficial to be seen as being above party or as being bipartisan in their rhetoric.[3] This study adapts the method used by Jesse H. Rhodes's analysis of presidential campaign speeches to identify the use of classic partisan rhetoric, cross-partisan rhetoric, and above-party rhetoric, in order to understand how candidates have used discussions of party in their presidential campaigns.[4]

A number of indicators were used to identify paragraphs in campaign speeches that referred to party. Not every paragraph or every speech had evidence of the use of party, and not all presidential candidates used all three types of party rhetoric (classic partisan, cross-partisan, above party). The indicators used to identify party paragraphs were: 'democrat', 'republican', 'RNC/Republican National Committee', 'DNC/Democratic National Committee', 'party', 'bipartisan(ship)', and presidents' names of the thirty years prior to when the candidate in question was running (a period commonly considered to represent a generation).[5] As an example, with Obama this would include any reference to Carter, Reagan, George H. W. Bush, Clinton, and George W. Bush.[6] The identified party paragraphs were then coded into mutually exclusive and exhaustive variables:

- *own-party positive*, where the candidate speaks positively about their own party, personally identifies with the party or party members, or praises the party's principles or values;
- *own-party negative*, where the candidate tries to distance themself from the party, or criticises the party, its members, principles, or values;
- *opposition-party positive*, where the candidate speaks positively about the opposition party, positively or personally identifies with the opposition party or party members, or praises the opposition party's principles or values;
- *opposition-party negative*, where the candidate criticises the opposition party, its members, principles or values;
- *bipartisanship*, where the candidate praises both parties working together, gives examples of working together or discussing a desire to work together in the future;
- *both other*, where both parties are mentioned in comparison with each other;
- *above party*, where the candidate refers to placing a priority on being an American, unity, the public in general – rather than, or above, party – or where the candidate mentions being an American first, and claims not to be affected by party considerations;
- *not-party statement*, where party indicators were used but the statement was not actually about party).[7]

The above indicators were then used to identify rhetoric as classic partisan, cross-partisan, or above party in nature. These variables were defined as follows:

- *Classic partisan*: the aggregation of own-party positive, opposition-party negative, and 'both other' variables and was anticipated to be used where candidates use partisanship to their advantage in a classic sense, talking positively of their own party and negatively of the opposition party.

- *Cross-partisan*: the aggregation of own-party negative, opposition-party positive, and bipartisan variables and was considered to be used by candidates when they wanted to indicate willingness to work across the party lines, as well as to appeal to independents, opposition party supporters, and undecided voters.
- *Above party*: this variable was not aggregated and captured the times when a candidate wanted to show they would work, or have worked, above party to appeal to a broader section of the electorate.[8]

Campaigns of this period were analysed using this method to assess the use of party in campaign speeches on a weekly basis. The campaign period was identified as the point at which both parties had only one candidate running (which could be ahead of national conventions). For each week of the campaign – running from Wednesday to Tuesday so that the last Tuesday is election day – the three variables have been identified as a percentage of all paragraphs with party rhetoric for the week. For example, for the whole amount of party paragraphs that were identified for a given week, the percentage that is classic partisan, cross-partisan, or above party has been calculated. This split of classic partisan, cross-partisan, and above-party rhetoric will be discussed for the elections where there was a candidate seeking re-election, or an incumbent president (who had assumed office since the last presidential election) running to stay in the White House, in order to explore the change in the relationship between party and president on the campaign trail while a president is in office.

The era of Democratic dominance and Republican resurgence

The Great Depression and the New Deal marked the start of a period in electoral politics in which measures of party identification indicated that a majority of Americans preferred the Democratic Party. In 1960, for example, at the start of the period explored in this chapter, almost one-half of Americans identified as Democrats and fewer than three in ten identified as Republicans, with the others seeing themselves as independent of such a party attachment, according to the Gallup polling organisation. Only in the 1980s did the Republican Party start to achieve enduring success in challenging the coalition mobilised by Franklin Roosevelt as president. (Nevertheless, even in 1984, when Ronald Reagan won re-election by a landslide, Gallup reported that about four in ten Americans remained Democratic Party identifiers, and still not quite three in ten were Republican Party identifiers.[9]) Clearly, this disparity in party identification did not prevent Republican victory, and even in 1960 Kennedy's margin over his rival Richard Nixon was slender, but between 1932 and 1994 Republican success in winning congressional majorities was infrequent (both houses following the elections of 1946 and 1952; the Senate only following the elections of 1980, 1982, and 1984). But this disparity created for each party a different context in which campaigns were conducted. Daniel Galvin has shown, furthermore, that the problem of minority status encouraged Republican presidents during this era to engage in 'presidential party building' – an array of efforts to boost the capacity and effectiveness of the party as a political organisation – whereas their Democratic counterparts, not facing a similar challenge, failed to do so.[10] A study of campaign rhetoric is on the whole in harmony with this understanding of the relationship between president and party. Between the 1960s and the 1980s, presidents seeking re-election were less partisan on the campaign trail than they had been in first seeking the White House – a tendency especially visible among the era's Republicans.

The sequence of Democratic victories of 1960 and 1964 presents an unusual case because – as a result of John F. Kennedy's assassination in 1963 – Lyndon B. Johnson, on the national ticket in the former as vice-presidential candidate, was seeking first election in his own right in the latter. Figure 2.1 shows the use of classic partisan, cross-partisan, and above-party rhetoric for each week of John F. Kennedy's 1960 campaign and of Lyndon B. Johnson's 1964 campaign. Although there are likely to be some differences in the use of party given that LBJ was running instead of JFK in 1964, the use of cross-partisan and above-party rhetoric in that year is in fact very different from

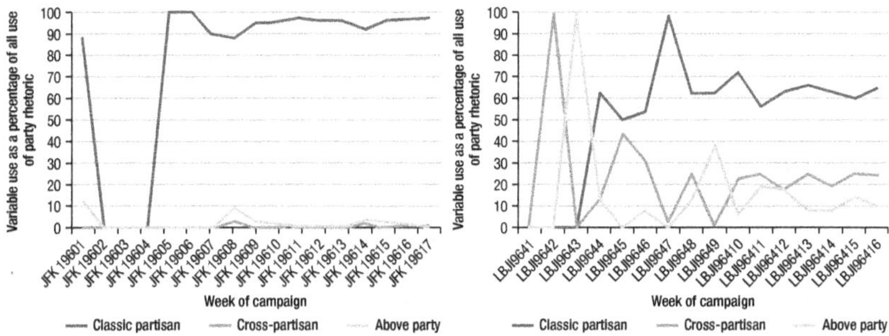

Figure 2.1 The use of classic partisan, cross-partisan, and above-party rhetoric in each week of John F. Kennedy's 1960 and Lyndon B. Johnson's 1964 campaigns

the 1960 campaign. In 1960, JFK used classic partisan rhetoric almost exclusively, with some limited use of above-party rhetoric in the second half of the campaign and rare use of cross-partisan rhetoric. By comparison, LBJ in 1964 started off using cross-partisan and above-party rhetoric, and in only one week of the whole campaign did he almost exclusively use classic partisan rhetoric; there was definite use throughout of a mix of the three partisan rhetoric variables.

Four years of Republican control of the White House under Richard Nixon saw a not dissimilar shift away from a rhetorical emphasis on partisanship in campaign politics. In 1968, as shown in Figure 2.2, Nixon's party rhetoric was heavily focused on the classic partisan variable. While there was some use of above-party rhetoric, and minimal use of cross-partisan rhetoric, the use of classic partisan rhetoric was never lower than 67 per cent in any given week of the 1968 campaign. In contrast, when Nixon in 1972 did start using party rhetoric in his campaigning, all three variables were much more evident. While the predominant variable was still classic partisan, more often than not only 50–60 per cent of party rhetoric was classic partisan rhetoric, even dropping as low as 25 per cent in one week, rather than generally being 70–80 per cent of party rhetoric in 1968.

In 1976, the institutional setting for Gerald R. Ford's presidential bid resembled Johnson's of 1964 in the sense that both were

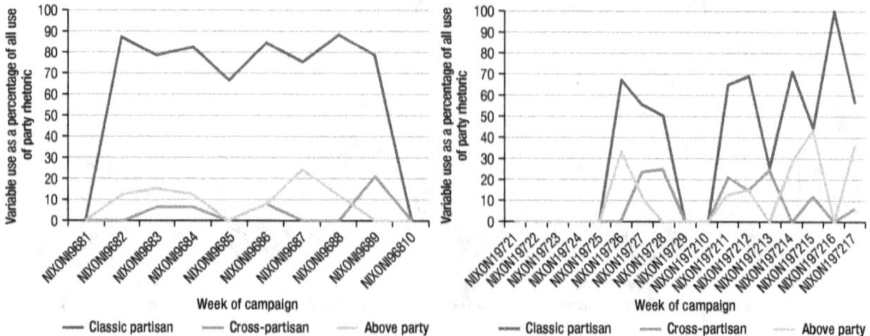

Figure 2.2 The use of classic partisan, cross-partisan, and above-party rhetoric each week in Richard Nixon's 1968 and 1972 campaigns

the incumbent but neither had been presidential candidate four years earlier. (Unlike Johnson, however, Ford had also not been on the national ticket, and he assumed the vice presidency in 1973 after scandal forced the resignation of Spiro Agnew; furthermore, the circumstances of Ford's accession to the presidency, the result of Nixon's Watergate-impelled resignation, were quite different.) But Ford's campaign rhetoric, with regard to the presidency–party relationship, was more similar to Kennedy's in 1960 and Nixon's in 1968 than to Johnson's in 1964. As Figure 2.3 shows, Ford in 1976 predominantly used classic partisan rhetoric to appeal to voters. One week exceptionally saw Ford use only cross-partisan rhetoric, but generally use of this and above-party rhetoric was minimal.

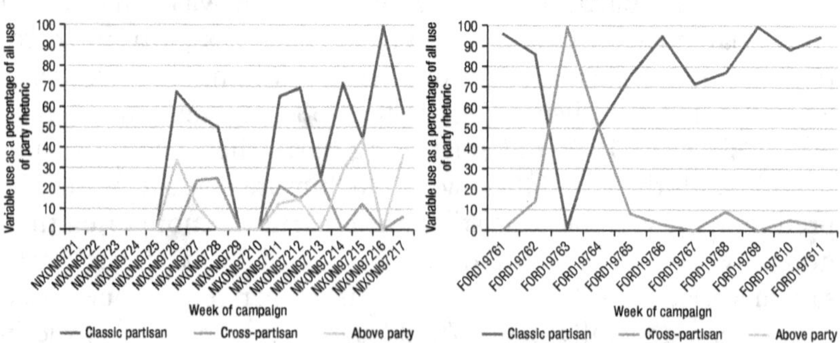

Figure 2.3 The use of classic partisan, cross-partisan, and above-party rhetoric each week in Richard Nixon's 1972 and Gerald R. Ford's 1976 campaigns

Successfully opposing Ford in 1976, Jimmy Carter's campaign also employed party-related rhetoric in a manner similar to Kennedy's in 1960 and Nixon's in 1968, as Figure 2.4 shows. The majority of his party rhetoric saw Carter use classic partisan rhetoric. Only in three of the eleven campaign weeks was there any minimal use of above-party or cross-partisan rhetoric. This did not change in his re-election campaign. In fact, while exceptionally in one week the use of classic partisan rhetoric dropped to only 50 per cent, the rest of the use of party rhetoric was focused on the classic partisan variable, and the above-party variable was not visible at all throughout the campaign. Four years later, Carter did not change how he spoke about party in seeking re-election. As in 1976, the majority of his re-election campaign saw him appealing to the Democratic Party faithful using classic partisan rhetoric. Such a focus proved unsuccessful, and Carter became one of the few presidents in American history who failed to win a bid for re-election.

When Carter stressed party in 1980, it was in opposition to a Republican candidate, Ronald Reagan, who quite similarly made use of party-oriented rhetoric. As Figure 2.5 shows, in his 1980 campaign Reagan, acting similarly to many candidates when first seeking election to the White House, employed classic partisan rhetoric with minimal use of cross-partisan and above-party rhetoric across the whole period. In his re-election campaign, there was a mix of classic partisan and cross-partisan rhetoric, as well as two weeks of the sixteen campaign weeks where cross partisan rhetoric

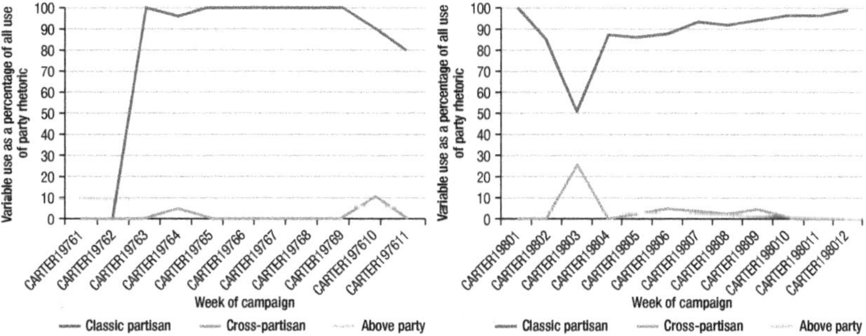

Figure 2.4 The use of classic partisan, cross-partisan and above-party rhetoric in each week of Jimmy Carter's 1976 and 1980 campaigns

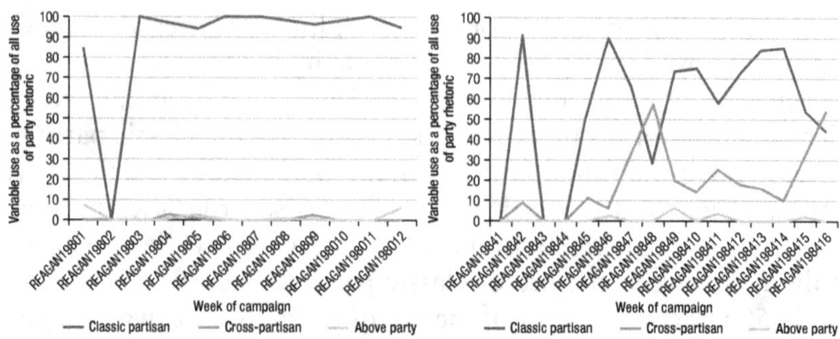

Figure 2.5 The use of classic partisan, cross-partisan, and above-party rhetoric in each week of Ronald Reagan's 1980 and 1984 campaigns

was 50 per cent of the party rhetoric; Reagan's rhetoric on the campaign trail was thus much more cross-partisan in nature.

During this period – one of dominance for the Democratic Party – there was thus a tendency for successful Republican non-incumbent candidates for the White House to be no less partisan than their Democratic counterparts. When seeking re-election, by contrast, they were likelier to engage in outreach beyond their own party. Such efforts to achieve outreach are also visible in midterm contests – as perhaps most notably Richard Nixon did in 1970, a campaign that Sarah Thelen analyses in Chapter 9. The midterm task for Democrats, by contrast, was more likely to activate their coalition, an endeavour that characterises both John F. Kennedy in 1962 (as Mark Eastwood shows in Chapter 7) and Lyndon B. Johnson in 1966 (as Mark McLay shows in Chapter 8). Always complicating a president's engagement with a midterm campaign, however, has been the historic tendency for the party in control of the White House to suffer loss – so that an effort whether to achieve outreach to supporters of the opposing party or to activate a party's existing coalition did not have especially promising odds at best.

Beyond Reagan

The Reagan years signalled the arrival of a new era in electoral politics, one of new strength for the Republican Party. And yet

Republicans did not achieve the long-harboured goal of majority status in place of their Democratic rivals. Instead, Republican growth, Democratic decline, and an entrenched tendency among Americans to see themselves as independent of party affiliation created an era of relative balance in party competition. Whereas, according to Gallup data about party identification, in 1980 45 per cent of Americans considered themselves Democrats, 23 per cent Republicans, and 29 per cent independents, by 1988 the Democratic share of electorate had fallen to 35 per cent, the Republican share had grown to 30 per cent, and at 31 per cent the proportion of independents had remained roughly the same. The years since Reagan have become characterised by inter-party competition of a more bitter kind, as both parties engaged in battle to consolidate their own coalition of support.

Over time, presidents seeking re-election were less likely to play up cross-partisan appeals and were, instead, more likely to concentrate on partisan appeals, as they did in first seeking election to the White House. Such change was not, however, immediate; George H. W. Bush in 1988 and Bill Clinton in 1992 had a focus on partisan rhetoric in a manner not dissimilar from their predecessors from 1960 to 1980. It was in seeking re-election when they started to demonstrate a difference of approach, with Bush remaining somewhat more partisan-focused in 1992 than previous incumbent Republicans, and with Clinton less partisan-focused in 1996 than Carter had been when defending the White House against Reagan.

When in 1988 he campaigned to succeed Reagan, whom he had served as vice president for eight years, George H. W. Bush, as Figure 2.6 shows, did not start using party rhetoric until nine weeks into the campaign and then on the whole used classic partisan rhetoric to appeal to voters. Some cross-partisan rhetoric was introduced as well, with an exceptional week where minimal above-party rhetoric was also used. In his unsuccessful bid for re-election in 1992, Bush employed party rhetoric throughout the whole campaign period, still predominantly using classic partisan rhetoric, but mixing this especially in the first half of the campaign with cross-partisan rhetoric. There were also more weeks where above-party rhetoric was used by Bush in his re-election

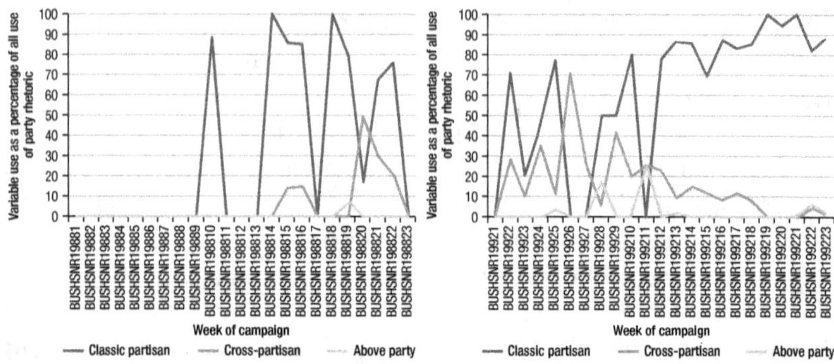

Figure 2.6 The use of classic partisan, cross-partisan, and above-party rhetoric in each week of George H. W. Bush's 1988 and 1992 campaigns

campaign. Rather than just focusing on the party faithful, Bush was trying to appeal to others.

In 1992, Bill Clinton, as Figure 2.7 shows, did not start using party rhetoric until seven weeks into the campaign. As in all the campaigns for first election to the White House studied thus far, Clinton mainly used classic partisan rhetoric. This was mixed with some above-party rhetoric, together with very minimal cross-partisan rhetoric. This was substantially different in his 1996 re-election campaign; for the first twenty-four weeks of the campaign, Clinton used classic partisan rhetoric and cross-partisan rhetoric in almost a balanced fashion; in some weeks the majority of party rhetoric was cross-partisan, and in other

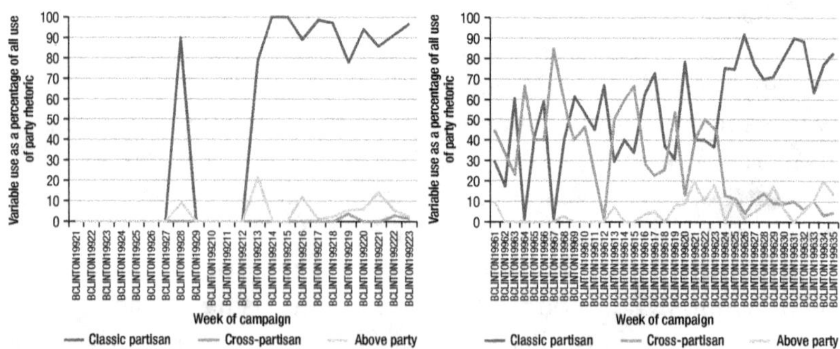

Figure 2.7 The use of classic partisan, cross-partisan, and above-party rhetoric in each week of Bill Clinton's 1992 and 1996 campaigns

weeks it was classic partisan in nature. From week 18 of the election, above-party rhetoric was fairly consistently used as well, although this was always 20 per cent or less of the party rhetoric.

An anti-politics tide characterised midterm contests of the 1990s – with contrasting implications. The 1990 midterms were held midway through the Gulf War – considered to have bipartisan support largely – with the invasion of Kuwait occurring that August. Meanwhile, the economy was turning sluggish, and Bush was losing support even though the war effort was not unpopular. On election day, incumbency seemed to be the main victor, with the Democrats picking up just a handful of seats in the House and achieving a net gain of just one in the Senate. Turnout, at only 36 per cent, matched that of 1986 in marking a post–World War II low. While observers noted an anti-Congress and anti-politics climate that explained this phenomenon, the impact at the polls was little change.[11] Four years later, things were very different, and for the first time since 1952 Republicans won control of both the House (through a net gain of fifty-two seats) and the Senate (through a net gain of eight seats). While Clinton was unpopular and there was economic anxiety (even though assessments of the nation's economic situation were generally positive), the Democratic-run Congress also suffered from unpopularity.[12] Turbulence once more characterised the midterm campaigns of 1998, but the status quo was again successful (with the Democrats defying the historic trend of midterm loss to achieve a net gain of five in the House and to maintain its overall number in the Senate). The focus for this turbulence was scandal, but while the Monica Lewinsky scandal fostered disillusionment with Clinton, the aggressive way in which Republicans pursued the investigation of the president created a backlash against their party.[13]

The relationship between president and party was then different as the twentieth century turned to the twenty-first. The rhetoric of both George W. Bush and Barack Obama was less partisan when they first sought election to the White House; their rhetoric, by contrast, became more partisan when seeking re-election as the presidential incumbent.

George W. Bush's initial presidential campaign rhetoric in 2000 was different from those previously explored, as Figure 2.8 suggests. Bush from week 9 of the campaign onwards had very mixed and fairly balanced use of both classic partisan and cross-partisan rhetoric, with minimal instances of above-party rhetoric. This actually decreased slightly in 2004, with Bush making greater use of classic partisan rhetoric, although he still used cross-partisan rhetoric to a substantial degree throughout, with exceptional use of above-party rhetoric in only two weeks of the campaign.

In Obama's campaign for the presidency in 2008, he predominantly used classic partisan rhetoric, as Figure 2.9 shows, but with a good mix of both cross-partisan and above-party rhetoric

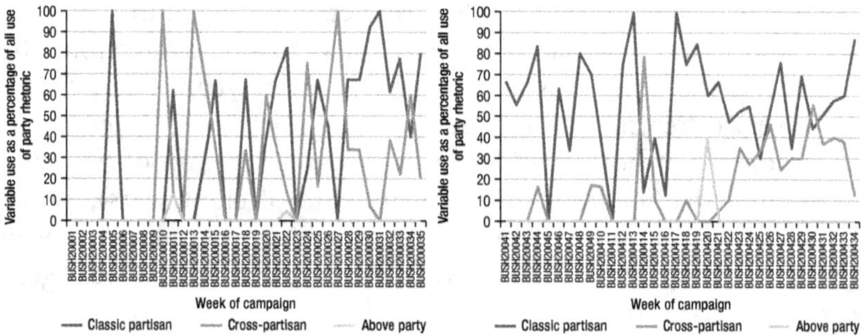

Figure 2.8 The use of classic partisan, cross-partisan, and above-party rhetoric in each week of George W. Bush's 2000 and 2004 campaigns

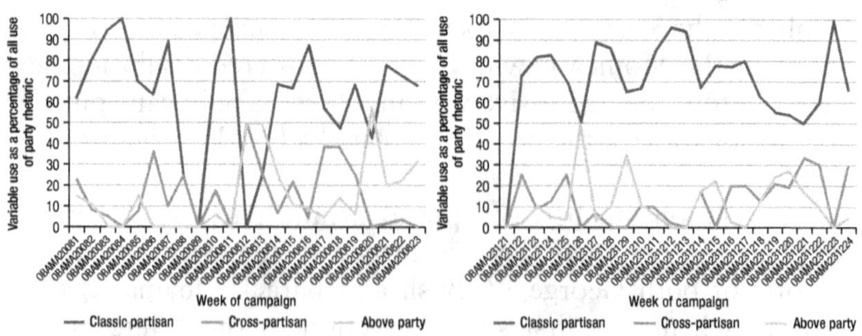

Figure 2.9 The use of classic partisan, cross-partisan, and above-party rhetoric in each week of Barack Obama's 2008 and 2012 campaigns

also employed throughout. There were weeks where the use of party rhetoric was at least 50 per cent above-party rhetoric, and while the use of classic party rhetoric never fell below 40 per cent of party rhetoric, the use of cross-partisan rhetoric also in certain weeks was almost as high as 40 per cent of party rhetoric. This, again, was different from most other initial presidential campaign races that have been explored here. Obama's re-election campaign in 2012, like George W. Bush's, actually saw Obama using more classic partisan rhetoric throughout the campaign than in 2008. While above-party rhetoric and cross-partisan rhetoric were still used consistently throughout the re-election campaign, this was generally in slightly lower proportions; it was on average around 20–30 per cent for both, with classic partisan rhetoric not falling lower than 50 per cent throughout the re-election period.

During the post-Reagan years – a period of relative balance between the parties with regard to the size of their respective base among voters, causing journalists John Micklethwait and Adrian Wooldridge in 2004 to label the United States 'the 50:50 nation' – the relationship between president and party has thus been different from how it was during the period explored in Parts Two and Three of this book.[14] Bush and Obama were less likely to employ partisan rhetoric when first seeking election but more likely to do so when seeking re-election. According to political scientists, this has been a period of revitalised but also redefined partisanship, one of centralised party leadership within the executive branch.[15]

If the period analysed in Parts Two and Three often involved, on the one hand, Democratic efforts to activate an electoral coalition that enjoyed the support of an enduring electoral majority, and on the other, Republican efforts of outreach to disaffected voters within that coalition, instability and volatility have more recently characterised inter-party competition and thus midterm campaigns. While the elections of 2000 resulted in victory for a presidential candidate without a popular vote majority for the first time since 1888, the Republican Party lost further ground in the House and retained control of the Senate only through the vice president's casting vote (a majority soon lost when Vermont's James Jeffords abandoned his Republican attachment to become an independent). But the political environment after the terrorist attacks of September 2001 created a context for Republican gains in the 2002 elections – the first time since 1934 that a president's party increased its congressional representation in first-term midterms. Four years later, by contrast, Republicans suffered significant midterm losses because of Bush's poor response to the Hurricane Katrina disaster, the unpopularity of the Iraq War, the failure of the administration's Social Security reform project, and a set of congressional scandals.[16] If the issues were different during the Obama years, the climate of turbulence amid partisan division was similar. The year 2010 saw the Affordable Care Act become law, the economy was still recovering with unemployment worse than when he took office, anti-Obama sentiment was strong, and the Tea Party movement was growing in influence after its founding a year earlier. The Republicans gained more seats than the 1994 midterms, winning sixty-three House seats, even though they just fell short of taking control of the Senate.[17] This was, Obama said, a 'shellacking'.[18]

Conclusion

Between the 1960s and the 1980s, presidents seeking re-election were less partisan on the campaign trail than they had been in first seeking the White House – a tendency especially visible among the era's Republicans. This was exemplified by Nixon's two campaigns: in 1968 heavily focused on the classic partisan variable, but in 1972 using more above-party and cross-partisan rhetoric as well. Ronald Reagan's election in 1980 made use of party-oriented rhetoric, but that in 1984 switched to more of a mix of classic partisan and above-party rhetoric, with cross-party rhetoric also used. During this period – one of dominance for the Democratic party – there was thus a tendency for successful Republican non-incumbent candidates for the White House to be no less partisan than their Democratic counterparts. When seeking re-election, by contrast, they were likelier to engage in outreach beyond their own party. Such efforts to achieve outreach are also visible in midterm contests and the midterm task for Democrats, by contrast, was more likely to activate their coalition. Always complicating a president's engagement with a midterm campaign, however, has been the historic tendency for the party in control of the White House to suffer loss – so that an effort whether to achieve outreach to supporters of the opposing party or to activate a party's existing coalition did not have especially promising odds at best.

The Reagan years signalled the arrival of a new era in electoral politics, one of new strength for the Republican Party. The years since Reagan have become characterised by inter-party competition of a more bitter kind, as both parties engaged in battle to consolidate their own coalition of support. Over time, presidents seeking re-election were less likely to play up cross-partisan appeals and were, instead, more likely to concentrate on partisan appeals, as they did in first seeking election to the White House. The relationship between president and party was then different as the twentieth century turned to the twenty-first. The rhetoric of both George W. Bush and Barack Obama was less partisan when they first sought election to the White House; their rhetoric, by contrast, became more partisan when seeking re-election as the presidential incumbent.

Notes

1. Martin P. Wattenberg, *The Rise of Candidate-Centered Politics: Presidential Elections of the 1980s* (Cambridge, MA: Harvard University Press, 1991). A rare exception to the neglect of presidential duties with regard to party is James W. Davis, *The President as Party Leader* (New York: Praeger, 1992). Sean J. Savage has written a series of historical studies of individual presidents with this focus: *Roosevelt: The Party Leader, 1932–1945* (Lexington, KY: University Press of Kentucky, 1991); *Truman and the Democratic Party* (Lexington, KY: University Press of Kentucky, 1997); *JFK, LBJ, and the Democratic Party* (Albany, NY: State University of New York Press, 2004). Also relevant is Daniel J. Galvin, *Presidential Party Building: Dwight D. Eisenhower to George W. Bush* (Princeton, NJ: Princeton University Press, 2010).
2. John S. Jackson III and William Crotty, *The Politics of Presidential Selection*, 2nd edn (New York: Longman, 2001); Daron R. Shaw, *Race to 270: The Electoral College and the Campaign Strategies*

of 2006 (Chicago, IL: University of Chicago Press, 2006); Nelson W. Polsby, Aaron Wildavsky, Steven E. Schier, and David A. Hopkins, *Presidential Elections: Strategies and Structures of American Politics*, 14th edn (Lanham, MD: Rowman & Littlefield, 2016); James W. Ceaser and Andrew W. Busch, *Red over Blue: The 2004 Elections and American Politics* (Lanham, MD: Rowman & Littlefield, 2005); John Sides, 'The Consequences of Campaign Agendas', *American Politics Research* 35 (2007): pp. 465–88.

3. Sarah Tiplady, 'US Presidential Campaign Strategy, 1960–2012: Observing and Explaining Change in Rhetoric', PhD thesis, University of Keele, 2019.
4. Jesse H. Rhodes, 'Party Polarization and Ascendance of Bipartisan Posturing as a Dominant Strategy in Presidential Rhetoric', *Presidential Studies Quarterly* 44 (2014): pp. 120–42.
5. Tiplady, 'US Presidential Campaign Strategy', p. 219.
6. Ibid.
7. For the full codebook for this analysis, see Tiplady, 'US Presidential Campaign Strategy'.
8. Ibid., pp. 225–6.
9. Pew Research Center, 'Trends in Party Identification, 1939–2014', 7 Apr. 2015, https://www.pewresearch.org/politics/interactives/party-id-trend/, accessed 15 June 2021.
10. Galvin, *Presidential Party Building*.
11. Pippa Norris, 'The 1990 Mid-term US Elections: Campaign and Results', *Political Quarterly* 62 (1991): pp. 461–75; Rhodes Cook, 'Reflections on the 1990 Election', *Public Perspective* 2, 2 (Jan./Feb. 1991): pp. 9–10.
12. Gary C. Jacobson, 'The 1994 Elections in Perspective', *Political Science Quarterly* 111 (1996), pp. 203–23; Alan I. Abramowitz, 'The End of the Democratic Era? 1994 and the Future of Congressional Election Research', *Political Research Quarterly* 48 (1995): pp. 873–89; Charles O. Jones, 'Foreword', in Philip A. Klinkner, ed., *Midterm: The Elections of 1994 in Context* (Boulder, CO: Westview, 1996), p. ix.
13. Gary C. Jacobson, 'Impeachment Politics in the 1998 Congressional Elections', *Political Science Quarterly* 114 (1999): pp. 31–51; Alan I. Abramowitz, 'It's Monica, Stupid: The Impeachment Controversy and the 1998 Midterm Election', *Legislative Studies Quarterly* 26 (2001): pp. 211–26; Benjamin Highton, 'Bill Clinton, Newt Gingrich, and the 1998 House Elections', *Public Opinion Quarterly* 66 (2002): pp. 1–17.

14. John Micklethwait and Adrian Woodridge, *The Right Nation: Conservative Power in America* (New York: Penguin, 2004).
15. Sidney M. Milkis and Jesse H. Rhodes, 'George W. Bush, the Republican Party, and the "New" American Party System', *Perspectives on Politics* 5 (2007): pp. 461–88; Richard M. Skinner, 'George W. Bush and the Partisan Presidency', *Political Science Quarterly* 123 (2008–9): pp. 605–22; Sidney M. Milkis, Jesse H. Rhodes, and Emily J. Charnock, 'What Happened to Post-Partisanship? Barack Obama and the New American Party System', *Perspectives on Politics* 10 (2012): pp. 57–76.
16. James E. Campbell, 'The 2002 Midterm Election: A Typical or an Atypical Midterm?' *PS: Political Science and Politics* 36, 2 (2003): pp. 203–7; Gary C. Jacobson, 'Terror, Terrain, and Turnout: Explaining the 2002 Midterm Elections', *Political Science Quarterly* 118 (2003): pp. 1–22; Robert Mason and Iwan Morgan, 'The Ongoing Republican Search for a New Majority since 1980', in Robert Mason and Iwan Morgan, eds, *Seeking a New Majority: The Republican Party and American Politics, 1960–1980* (Nashville, TN: Vanderbilt University Press, 2013), pp. 216–18.
17. John H. Aldrich, Bradford H. Bishop, Rebecca S. Hatch, D. Sunshine Hillygus, and David W. Rohde, 'Blame, Responsibility, and the Tea Party in the 2010 Midterm Elections', *Political Behavior* 36 (2014): pp. 471–91; Jamie L. Carson and Stephen Pettigrew, 'Strategic Politicians, Partisan Roll Calls, and the Tea Party: Evaluating the 2010 Midterm Elections', *Electoral Studies* 32 (2013): pp. 26–36.
18. Andrew Rudalevige, '"A Majority is the Best Repartee": Barack Obama and Congress, 2009–2012', *Social Science Quarterly* 93 (2012), pp. 1272–94 (at p. 1283).

3

Accountability Regimes, Partisanship and Midterm Mandates: Midterms in Contemporary America

Nadia Hilliard

Elections serve as the most fundamental form of political accountability, and midterm elections provide an opportunity for citizens to participate in a single moment of collective accountability for the US president. Yet midterm elections serve not only as a judgement on the past performance of the president and his party; they also provide an opportunity to put in place a sub-federal accountability regime that oversees the president's actions, a regime comprised of governors, state attorneys general, and mayors. It is this regime, reaching from city halls to the US Capitol building – and not simply the congressional midterm elections with which we are more familiar – that carries with it a 'midterm mandate' to redirect the president's agenda. By reinterpreting, refusing to implement, or directly challenging federal policy, these actors complement Congress's oversight function of the president.

Using the 2018 elections as a focus, this chapter surveys the growing importance of midterm elections as an opportunity to elect a cohort of actors who supply new sources of executive oversight. In surveying existing literature on governors, state attorneys general, and mayors, it argues that these are political actors of increasing salience on the national political scene as sources of accountability, and documents recent changes in midterm campaign strategy and donations that reflect this growth. Ultimately, the mandates carried and defended by this regime of subnational actors are transforming the significance of midterms on the national level.

According to conventional wisdom, midterm elections serve as a referendum on, or reassessment of, the existing administration and Congress. The 2018 midterms were no exception: Gary Jacobson labelled them an 'extreme referendum', 'the most sweeping and discordant national referendum . . . since the Great Depression'.[1] They reassessed not only the president, Donald Trump, and the Republican Party, but also Congress as an institution. Although midterms can serve as an assessment of the policy record of the preceding two years, they can also lead to horizontal accountability – that is, accountability between branches and levels of government. Midterms shape not only the partisan composition of Congress, but also subnational political institutions, and this, too, can provide a significant challenge to presidential authority. Winners in these elections complement the oversight activity in Congress. The 2018 midterms were also a commentary on the oversight role that the Republican-controlled 115th Congress played – or failed to play – in keeping the executive branch in check.

In theory, midterm elections serve as a 'referendum' on the administration's first two years: voters pass judgement, usually critical, on the president. Yet the reality is more complex and more interesting. Midterms do indeed express the electorate's assessment of the president's policy record, but they also indirectly respond to the performance of Congress. On the one hand, issue accountability, the degree to which members of Congress base their roll call voting on their constituents' preferences (and the degree to which it is congruent with campaign promises), figures minimally in congressional elections.[2] Kathleen Bawn and her co-authors have called this an '"electoral blind spot," within which voters are unable to reliably ascertain policy positions or evaluate party performance', thereby causing a primary mechanism of vertical, electoral accountability to break down.[3] On the other hand, contemporary midterm elections can create a form of accountability indirectly, by performing the symbolic function of passing public judgement as well as the practical function of instating a set of actors who will, in theory, oversee and counterbalance the actions of the administration. The 'shellacking' that the Democrats received in the 2010 midterms stood as a powerful rhetorical rebuke of the Obama administration as well as a reordering of the composition of Congress, governorships, and state attorneys general towards Republican dominance. In short, even if voters do not respond in an informed way to their national representative's policy record, they can nonetheless cast votes for subnational actors who perform, in part, the role of executive overseer.

This chapter provides an overview of the way that subnational elections affect presidential accountability and power. First, I outline the political context that has produced these alternative sources of accountability. Three interrelated phenomena have enabled the growth of this subnational accountability regime: the shift to 'coercive federalism' since the 1970s; the partisan polarisation that has intensified since the 1990s; and the broad growth of executive power since the New Deal. Taken together, they lessen vertical accountability in Congress (such as issue accountability in congressional elections) and horizontal accountability exercised by Congress towards the executive (congressional investigations). I then consider a concomitant and growing source of electoral accountability at the subnational level: the army of governors, state attorneys general, and mayors who support or contest federal policy. Finally, I reflect on the implications of this shift for democracy in the contemporary United States. Throughout the chapter, I focus primarily on the Trump presidency and the 2018 midterm elections, but also consider the degree to which their features illustrate broader trends in American electoral politics, modes of accountability, and federal relations. In the context of a steadily more 'coercive' federalism, as well as the ever-growing administrative state, subnational and bureaucratic forms of accountability have assumed heightened salience as components of an accountability regime that ultimately tames the presidential mandate.

While Paul Nolette has argued for the importance of contemporary federalism and polarisation in enabling the growth of state attorney general activism,[4] I argue that a third factor – the growth of executive power – also contributes to this phenomenon and that the same factors have enabled other subnational actors to play a complementary oversight role.

Federalism

The centrality of single-party control of the White House and Congress has traditionally underpinned scholarly writing on midterm elections. But, in a federal system, the success of a President depends also on the capacity and willingness of state and local actors to implement (or resist) federal directives. The twentieth-century trend towards a stronger and more centralised federal government observed by scholars such as Martha Derthick has persisted,[5] despite attempts by Presidents Richard Nixon and Ronald Reagan to institute a 'New Federalism'.[6] Moreover, the 'fragmented' shape of contemporary American federalism[7] has generated intensified conflict between states and the federal government,[8] with polarisation between states becoming more prominent. Thirty-seven states were governed under unified government after the 2012 elections – an unusually high number, historically.[9] The effect of these federal dynamics, according to Nolette and Colin Provost, is that 'polarisation across all levels of government [has] increased'.[10] So, too, has the partisanship of subnational actors, such as attorneys general.

Polarisation

Partisan polarisation diminishes the efficacy and legitimacy of congressional oversight committees. Although Douglas Kriner and Liam Schwartz have demonstrated that divided government engenders intensified congressional oversight activity in recent decades,[11] the success and efficacy of such investigations are dependent on their bipartisan composition; bipartisan investigations create greater impact than partisan.[12] Congress's investigative powers surpass those of the courts, having expanded across the twentieth century to include not only the right to subpoena witnesses for a specific case (as a court would), but also 'to anticipate all possible cases which may arise thereunder'.[13] Despite these strengths, investigations without cross-party support can be discredited as 'partisan witch-hunts' that lead to few, if any, consequences.[14] As Paul Light has concluded, if the 'question . . . is whether today's bitter partisanship is degrading the good investigation with ever-increasing limits on freedom to investigate', then '[t]he answer is not clear yet, but the signs are not good'.[15] Out of sixteen federal investigations between 1945 and 2012, Light scored only two as having a 'great deal of impact'.[16] However, diminished oversight capacity on the congressional level opens a space for alternative sources of accountability – namely, subnational actors – to emerge.

Executive power

Finally, the well-documented growth of executive power since World War II[17] has provided the president with a wealth of tools that circumvent congressional scrutiny. Executive orders provoke particular ire among the president's foes, regardless of party affiliation. In recent decades, presidents from both parties have enhanced the executive's capacity to circumvent Congress: think, for instance, of Obama's extensive executive rulemaking, such as the Deferred Action for Childhood Arrivals policy, or of George W. Bush's expansion of national security powers. These longer-term developments are at least in part a function of polarisation and have set an institutional stage that minimises the capacity of Congress to exercise effective oversight.

These three developments have created an 'accountability gap' in the oversight of the executive. Although proponents of a strong or unitary executive, such as Eric Posner and Adrian Vermeule,[18] celebrate the latitude afforded to the president by these diminished restraints, the executive has not strengthened without unintended consequences: such a concentration of power has contributed to heightened political polarisation. This weakened accountability on the federal level has also enabled subnational forms of accountability to flourish, in part replacing Congress's traditional oversight function. Before outlining the developing subnational forms of accountability, I first detail the failure of existing congressional oversight of the Trump administration.

In the first two years of Trump's presidency, oversight of the administration on the federal level was concentrated in two areas: congressional investigations and the special investigation (the 'Mueller investigation'). From one perspective, Congress stayed very busy with its investigations of the executive branch. By May 2019, the Trump administration had faced over fifty probes from the House alone.[19] The House committees of the 116th Congress held a total of 405 hearings and sent 1,318 letters to executive branch agencies to conduct oversight of administration policies.[20] Even the Senate, which remained in Republican hands for the entirety of Trump's presidency, undertook two major investigations of Trump's possible collusion with Russia during the 2016 elections. The 'blue wave' that gave the House to the Democrats following the 2018 midterms added vigour to the House investigations and enabled Trump to become the first president to be impeached twice.

Despite the apparent intensity of congressional oversight during Trump's presidency, few consequences resulted from these probes. The congressional investigations were highly politicised, and even when investigations found fault with the administration, Congress refrained from acting on the findings. The most significant, the Senate Intelligence Committee investigation led by Richard Burr (R-NC), explored the question of Russia's alleged interference in the 2016 elections. Prior to the 2018 elections, the Burr committee issued preliminary reports citing ample evidence that the Trump campaign colluded with Russian officials for electoral gain. But Burr clashed publicly about the committee's findings with the top Democrat on the panel, Mark Warner, and in the final report of nearly 1,000 pages, no statements regarding 'collusion' are to be found.[21] Rather than undermine the work of the three-year investigation with public disagreement, the committee refrained from drawing direct conclusions about collusion in the report itself, and simply presented the fruits of its labour. An earlier, parallel investigation by the House Intelligence Committee dissolved into a series of partisan attacks by spring of 2018, with each party in the committee producing separate reports targeted at the opposing party.[22] A third investigation, by the Senate Judiciary Committee, looked at the June 2016 meeting between Trump campaign officials and a Russian lawyer, but Republican members of the committee refrained from drawing conclusions from more than 2,500 pages of documents released by the committee.[23] And though Trump was impeached twice, in neither case was he convicted and removed by the Senate. In each of these cases, the process of accountability was terminated before any consequences resulted.

As well as the congressional probes, the Special Counsel, or 'Mueller investigation', dominated headlines before and after the 2018 midterms. Importantly, the Mueller investigation operated under a different legal framework from the Special Counsel law that governed other high-profile investigations, such as the Iran-Contra investigation and the Clinton–Lewinsky affair. That framework, which required investigators to submit their findings to Congress if they uncovered impeachable offenses, expired in 1999.[24] In contrast, Mueller was only permitted to notify his superiors in the Department of Justice (DOJ) of his findings, and only at the discretion of the DOJ would the details of the report be available to the public. A redacted version of the report was released in April 2019, and though the report provided details of possible collusion and attempts at obstruction of justice, Mueller and his team ultimately left the question of accountability – that is, consequences – in the hands of Congress.[25]

The intensity of investigation, and subsequent failures of Congress and of the Special Counsel to provide consequential accountability for Donald Trump and his administration, are distinctive to the Trump presidency, but also manifest broader trends in the capacity of these traditional sources of oversight to fulfil their function. Accordingly, the traditional understanding of midterm elections as a source of accountability loses potency. This begs the question: what role do midterm elections play in a highly polarised, 'dysfunctional' Congress?[26] In particular, in the context of a Congress in which the oversight function was not always, or effectively, exercised? The 'blue wave' of the 2018 elections certainly intensified the pace of investigations coming from the House, including but not limited to the impeachment investigations. The elections resulted in a Democratic net gain of forty-one seats in the House of Representatives and a Republican net gain of two seats in the Senate, leading to respective partisan control over those two chambers.

In contrast to the extensive but ultimately weak oversight outlined above, the 'blue wave' also ushered in a robust subnational set of officials who, from 2019 onwards, provided a robust and ultimately consequential form of accountability. These actors spearheaded state-level challenges to specific federal policies. Though subnational election cycles do not always coincide with congressional midterm years, they often feature and benefit from the voter turnout of the national elections. In 2018, thirty-six governorships and thirty attorney general seats were at stake. Both positions have been instrumental in challenging federal policy coming from both the president and from Congress. Mayors, too, have protested federal directives and forced federal policy to undergo scrutiny.

Subnational accountability regime: a midterm mandate for accountability

Although scholars and voters overlook midterm elections in equal measure, these elections take on renewed significance if one looks beyond congressional elections to the myriad state and local elections that occur in each election cycle. As surveyed above, the results of mid-cycle elections affect not only the interests represented in a particular Congress, but also, in theory, the strength and efficacy of its oversight function. This latter function is affected primarily in two ways: the partisan composition of Congress (and its willingness to hold the president to account), and in the subnational 'accountability regime' that issues challenges from outside of Washington, DC. The role of subnational elected officials in challenging Trump administration policy was extensive and targeted policy areas ranging from environmental regulation to immigration policy to tax law. Although the local and regional resistance to federal policy under Trump was strong, this mode of holding the federal government to account has grown irrespective of partisanship since the 1990s. Below, I survey the role that governors, state attorneys general, and mayors played in countering federal policy under Trump, and consider the broader political meaning of their behaviour.

Governors

Of the thirty-six governorships up for election in 2018, seven flipped from blue to red, leading to a rough split between the parties in governors' mansions (twenty-three Democrat and twenty-seven Republican). This wave of opposition-party governor elections is typical of recent midterms: in 2018, Democrats gained seven governorships; in 2010, Republicans gained six governorships; in 2006, Democrats gained six governorships; and in 1994, Republicans gained ten governorships. Governors combat federal policy in two main ways: bringing lawsuits against the president or his or her administration and refusing to implement federal directives. Here, these mechanisms are explored with reference to specific governors' actions toward the Trump and Obama administrations.

Democratic governors during the Trump administration sued and boycotted a wide range of social and fiscal policies. For instance, the governors of New York, New Jersey, Connecticut, and Maryland sued the administration over a change in federal tax law known as the SALT (State and Local Tax deduction) cap,[27] and though initially unsuccessful, this effort led to a series of appeals and ultimately helped to motivate a bipartisan caucus within the House of Representatives to repeal the cap.[28] Governors have not only used lawsuits to assert their opposition to Trump administration policy. The governors of New York, Hawaii, Oregon, Washington, and Illinois all refused to participate in the proposed gag rule of the federal Title X family planning programme, which bars clinicians at facilities that receive Title X funding from referring pregnant women to abortion providers.[29] Less than a year following Trump's election, Governor Jerry Brown of California signed into law 'sanctuary state' legislation in defiance of the administration's immigration policies. In September 2018, he signed the first piece of state-level legislation against Trump's executive order to allow drilling off the coast of California. After Brown refused to implement a series of federal directives ranging from immigration enforcement to marijuana policy, the Trump administration itself initiated a legal battle with California by suing the state over three 'sanctuary' immigration laws in 2018.[30] Ultimately, the legal battle made its way to the state Supreme Court, where it was upheld in 2020.[31] But this political strategy was not limited to Democrats; Texas, like California under Trump, had earlier flaunted its defiance of numerous Obama-era federal policies, with Attorney

General-cum-Governor Greg Abbott of Texas continuing to wage his war against Obama even after leaving the attorney general's seat. He continued to sue the federal government and made Texas one of twelve states refused to adopt Medicaid expansion following the passage of the Affordable Care Act.[32] At the behest of Senate majority leader Mitch McConnell, five Republican governors (of Texas, Louisiana, Wisconsin, Indiana, and Oklahoma) refused to implement the Obama administration's climate change regulations in 2015.[33]

State attorneys general[34]

State attorneys general serve as the chief legal advisor and law enforcement official in each state, but because they set law enforcement priorities and allocate resources accordingly, they function as de facto policymakers as well.[35] In recent decades, however, and especially since the Clinton years, attorneys general have discovered a new function: litigator against the federal government. Accordingly, state attorneys general steadily challenged Trump administration policies. These state-level elections are not limited to midterm years, but their campaigns are increasingly directed towards national politics rather than solely state-level concerns.

According to one observer, 2018 was a 'high octane year for state-attorneys-general elections'.[36] Of the thirty attorney general seats at stake in the 2018 elections, nine were battleground races, putting three Democrats and six Republican seats in play. The Democrats ultimately gained four seats in Nevada, Colorado, Wisconsin, and Michigan, all of which quickly joined multistate lawsuits contesting Trump administration policies.[37] But the importance of state attorneys general as political actors on the federal stage is not new. The rise of the 'activist attorney general' began during the Clinton administration when forty-six attorneys general sued the nation's four largest tobacco companies, a situation that resulted in the states' ability to recover the costs associated with smoking-related illnesses. Although much attorney general activism has been partisan in nature – with Democratic attorneys general suing the Bush administration for a failure to uphold the Clean Air Act, and Republican attorneys general suing over specific provisions of the Affordable Care Act – the activism itself has been a two-party affair. It is important to note, too, that these challenges did not originally appear purely along partisan lines; the Clinton-era tobacco suit, for instance, brought together parties from both sides. But the attorneys general themselves have hardened into partisan camps with expanding institutional bases. The Republican Attorneys General Association, or RAGA, was established in 1999, at first as a wing of the Republican State Leadership Committee (RSLC) and, from 2014, as an independent body.[38] Its Democratic counterpart, DAGA, was formed in 2002.

What is new about lawsuits by attorneys general, in the Trump and post-Trump era, is the pace. To illustrate: under Obama, attorneys general initiated seventy-eight multistate lawsuits. Nearly a third came from Greg Abbott, Texas attorney general from 2002 until 2015, and governor of Texas from 2015, who attempted to sue the Obama administration forty-four times over the course of Obama's two terms.[39] The number intensified from Obama's first term to his second term, as the pace of lawsuits quickened in response to the pace of executive orders issued from the White House.[40] The Trump administration saw nearly as many challenges in his first month in office. California attorney general Xavier Becerra brought over twenty lawsuits against the Trump administration in 2017 alone. Eighteen other attorneys general attempted to sue the administration for violating the constitutional rights of children and families in the months ahead of the 2018 midterm elections. This acceleration reflects not only partisan animosity, but also the Supreme Court's 2007 ruling on a Bush-era challenge, *Massachusetts v. E.P.A.* (549 U.S. 497, 519–21), which strengthened states' 'special solicitude' to sue the federal government as quasi-sovereign entities and opened the floodgates for lawsuits by attorneys general.[41]

Although most of the lawsuits against Obama and Trump were filed by multiple states, some individual attorneys general have made it a mission to attack the sitting president with a steady stream of lawsuits. As noted above, Attorney General Greg Abbott of Texas targeted Obama, and Xavier Becerra, whose tenure as California attorney general coincided with

Trump's presidency, followed in kind against Trump with a total of 122 lawsuits against Trump.[42] Maura Healy of Massachusetts similarly developed a reputation for being part of 'the Democratic resistance' against Trump, taking part in nearly seventy lawsuits against him.[43] In a 2018 campaign advertisement entitled 'Preoccupied', for his first run for Colorado attorney general, Phil Weiser claims that it was Donald Trump's election that inspired him to run for the position, and that 'ever since, I've been writing down all the ways I could protect Colorado from Donald Trump'.[44] This reorientation of focus towards federal activity represents a profound shift in the political role played by state attorneys general.

The Trump administration was the target of a total of 138 multistate lawsuits from state attorneys general. To put this in recent historical perspective, trends from Nolette's database demonstrate the speed of the increase in multistate lawsuits against sitting presidents: thirty against Reagan; twenty against George H. W. Bush; forty-two against Clinton; seventy-six against George W. Bush; and seventy-eight against Obama. Although the lawsuits in each administration are heavily, and increasingly, partisan, they are not uniformly so; six against the Trump administration came from Republican states. And, unlike the congressional investigations, state attorney general legal activity has had success in reining in executive activity. As of November 2020, 79 per cent of the suits filed against Trump were settled in favour of the attorney general.[45] The scope and target of the lawsuits varies widely, from contesting the so-called Muslim travel ban and family separations at the US–Mexican border to regulating automobile emissions and upholding various clauses of the Affordable Care Act.[46] The attorneys general of Maryland and Washington, DC, led a lawsuit alleging that Trump violated the Foreign Emoluments clause of the constitution.

The political significance of the attorneys general is evident not only in the frequency of their challenges, but also in their expanded repertoire of policy tools, including amicus briefs and joint letters to federal officials. Nolette and Provost demonstrate that state attorneys general are more active and target an increasingly wide range of policy areas.[47] And though the work of attorneys general is mainly partisan, Nolette and Provost call attention to certain areas of bipartisan activity, including investigations into corporate fraud and criminal justice. A bipartisan group of attorneys general have, for instance, led the way in investigating the opioid crisis.[48]

The rise of the politicised, activist attorneys general, and their expanded toolkit, respond in part to the inability of Congress to hold the federal executive to account, and to the legislature's gradual delegation of policy making authority to the president. The rapidly growing power of state attorneys general has also sparked rule changes that deepen their partisan character. In a 2017 vote taken by the Republican Attorneys General Association (RAGA), a long-standing agreement between Democrat and Republican attorneys general not to target the opposing party's incumbent officeholders in elections was overturned.[49] Not only did the end of this 'incumbency rule' eliminate any vestiges of bipartisanship in the attorney general community, but it also led to an unprecedented level of attorney general campaign spending in 2018, including out-of-state donations that have prompted ethics investigations.[50] The phenomenon of the attorneys general is also transforming the landscape of electoral campaigning. As the policy networks of attorneys general have expanded, donors have increasingly channelled funds to races for attorney general, leading to what the executive director of the Democratic Attorneys General Association (DAGA) calls an 'arms race' in attracting larger donations.[51] Between 2003 and 2013, the Chamber of Commerce gave 100 times more to RAGA (now the Republican State Leadership Committee) than it did to the Democratic counterpart, DAGA, founded in 2002.[52] Similarly, trial lawyers have given considerably more to DAGA, though with slightly less imbalance.

As with governor activism, 'resistance' is not a one-way street. Twelve Republican attorneys general supported the revised travel restrictions proposed by Trump in 2017 by submitting a federal appeals court brief.[53] Former federal attorney general Jeff Sessions initiated his own counter-lawsuits, including one against California to force it to arrest and hand over illegal immigrants, and a second, also against California, over its net-neutrality laws. Ultimately, California won the immigration battle, and, following a separate, 2019 counter-lawsuit brought before the DC Circuit Court of Appeals, confirmed its authority to uphold its net-neutrality laws.[54]

Mayors

Resistance to federal policy does not end with the states. The largest US cities are overwhelmingly Democratic, and these mayors repeatedly challenged the Trump administration's directives. Republican mayors also took aim at federal policy alongside their Democratic counterparts: a bipartisan group of sixteen mayors organised in June 2018 to oppose the administration's family separations policy.[55] Prior to the 2018 midterms, Democrats held the mayoral office in sixty-one of the largest 100 cities, and twenty-five of those 100 held races in 2018.[56] Of those in play, twelve were held by Democrats; ten by Republicans; and three by independents. Although the 2018 elections handed one Democratic mayorship (in Lexington, Kentucky) to Republican Linda Gorton, Democratic mayors collectively defied the Trump administration threat to 'sanctuary cities' in April 2019 by declaring that they would welcome illegal immigrants.[57] Following the deployment of federal law enforcement agents to control the widespread riots in summer 2020, multiple mayors of major cities contested the Trump administration's 'law and order' strategy.[58]

Although these examples draw from opposition to Donald Trump and his agenda, the collective actions on the part of major US municipalities should not be overlooked as specific to a particular presidential administration. Richard Schragger argues that, despite important challenges from states, cities have experienced an 'economic and popular resurgence' in the twenty-first century and have been 'pressing the existing limits of their regulatory authority in areas like labor and employment, antidiscrimination law, immigration, and environmental protection'.[59] Rahm Emanuel, one-time chief of staff to President Obama, left his privileged position in Washington in 2010 to serve as mayor of his hometown, Chicago. His move from Washington to Chicago – the reverse of the state-to-national trajectory traditionally followed by aspiring politicians – hints at the growing centrality of subnational arena for contemporary governance. In his post-presidential political life, one of Barack Obama's primary strategies has been to work with US mayors.[60] And in his post-mayoral memoir, *The Nation City: Why Mayors Are Now Running the World*,[61] Emanuel primarily celebrates the technicalities of municipal policy innovation as being the fruits of universities and networks between mayors. But his focus on the local did not prevent him issuing a well-publicised renunciation of the president by declaring Chicago a 'Trump-free zone'.[62] The Chicago mayor also delivered a letter signed by multiple mayors asking the president to reconsider his stance on immigration.[63]

Although cities found their independence from the federal government reduced during the COVID-19 pandemic, Emanuel's argument that American cities now bear the epithet of 'laboratories of democracy' suggests a deeper shift towards local authority. Mayoral elections on midterm ballots have gained in significance for both governing capacity and as a source of indirect federal oversight.

Conclusion

Midterm elections offer voters an opportunity to modify a presidential mandate not only by recasting the partisan composition of Congress but also by voting for a host of subnational political actors capable of holding the president to account. Perhaps to even greater effect than the so-called 'blue wave' in Congress, the cohort of subnational actors ushered in after the 2018 elections decisively altered the political landscape in which subsequent oversight took place. At stake in contemporary midterms is not only the partisan make-up of Congress, but also the intergovernmental sources of accountability and the balance of power between levels of government. In the twenty-first century, state-level activism enables fruitful opposition to executive policies that have been stymied by congressional gridlock. The significance of the trends outlined above stretches far beyond opposition to a particularly contested president.

We are seeing a shift in the location of both federal-level policy battles and the source of federal oversight and accountability *away* from Congress. Increasingly, we see partisan battles fought in the courts as legal battles by subnational actors rather than as political battles between the executive and legislative branches. As Paul Nolette has observed, these struggles are increasingly fought not only between levels of government but also between attorneys general themselves, thus repositioning partisan, national-level political battles as conflicts between individual states.[64] Moreover, partisanship is differentially distributed across federal levels: in today's political climate, cities are often heavily Democratic, whereas the Senate institutionalises a deep conservative bias. Yet, partisan control over the different branches and levels of federalism varies widely across time. Although federal battles have to some degree always been partisan battles, the current situation complicates traditional narratives of that partisan divide. Progressive voices have begun to consider the idea of 'states' rights' as an instrument to protect their own interests.[65]

Although midterms continue to provide an opportunity for a national 'referendum' on the president, the shift in the centre of gravity of midterm elections, from a square focus on national, congressional candidates to a range of subnational actors, is also a commentary on Congress as an institution. Midterms provide a public that is disillusioned with Congress the opportunity to legitimise alternative centres of political authority with their votes. Politically, we have seen Congress progressively delegate authority to the executive over the course of many decades.[66] This has no doubt contributed to the rise of activist attorneys general, governors, and mayors as de facto policymakers on the national level. David Mayhew's classic intuition[67] that the American political system has the capacity to self-correct finds support in these developments – where the executive has usurped authority from Congress, and Congress has fallen into dysfunction, subfederal democratic processes demonstrate signs of resurgence and health.[68] Although political theorist David Runciman cautions about the practical limits of subnational democracy,[69] midterm elections might well continue to gain in import for their role in ushering in subnational governance and accountability regimes.

Notes

1. Gary C. Jacobson, 'Extreme Referendum: Donald Trump and the 2018 Midterm Elections', *Political Science Quarterly* 134 (2019): pp. 9–38.
2. Benjamin Highton, 'Issue Accountability in U.S. House Elections', *Political Behavior* 41 (2019): pp. 349–67.
3. Kathleen Bawn, Martin Cohen, David Karol, Seth Masket, Hans Noel, and John Zaller, 'A Theory of Political Parties: Groups, Policy Demands and Nominations in American Politics', *Perspectives on Politics* 10 (2012): pp. 571–97 (quotation at p. 571).
4. Paul Nolette, 'State Litigation during the Obama Administration: Diverging Agendas in an Era of Polarized Politics', *Publius* 44 (2014): pp. 451–74.
5. Martha Derthick, 'Crossing Thresholds: Federalism in the 1960s', *Journal of Policy History* 8 (1996): pp. 64–80.
6. Ann O'M. Bowman and George A. Krause, 'Power Shift: Measuring Policy Centralization in U.S. Intergovernmental Relations, 1947–1998', *American Politics Research* 31 (2003): pp. 301–25.
7. J. Mitchell Pickerill and Cynthia J. Bowling, 'Polarized Parties, Politics, and Policies: Fragmented Federalism in 2013–2014', *Publius* 44 (2014): pp. 369–98.
8. Nolette, 'State Litigation', p. 453.
9. Ibid., p. 453. See also Dan Balz, 'Red, Blue States Move in Opposite Directions in a New Era of Single Party Control', *Washington Post*, 29 Dec. 2013, A1, https://www.washingtonpost.com/politics/red-blue-states-move-in-opposite-directions-in-a-new-era-of-single-party-control/2013/12/28/9583d922-673a-11e3-ae56-22de072140a2_story.html, accessed 6 Aug. 2021.
10. Paul Nolette and Colin Provost, 'Change and Continuity in the Role of State Attorneys General in the Obama and Trump Administrations', *Publius* 48 (2018), pp. 469–94 (quotation at p. 471).
11. Douglas Kriner and Liam Schwartz, 'Divided Government and Congressional Investigations', *Legislative Studies Quarterly* 33 (2008): pp. 295–321.
12. Paul C. Light, 'Investigations Done Right and Wrong: Government by Investigation, 1945– 2012', Governance Studies at Brookings, Dec. 2013, p. 8. https://www.brookings.edu/wp-content/uploads/2016/06/LIghtPaperDec2013.pdf, accessed 31 July 2021.

13. *Townsend v. United States*, 95 F.2d 352, 361 (D.C. Cir. 1938), quoted in Carl Levin and Elise J. Bean, 'Defining Congressional Oversight and Measuring Its Effectiveness', *Wayne Law Review* 64 (2018): p. 5.
14. Kimberly Breedon and Christopher Bryant, 'Executive Privilege in a Hyper-Partisan Era', *Wayne Law Review* 64 (2018): pp. 65–95 (quotation at p. 92).
15. Light, 'Investigations Done Right and Wrong', p. 11.
16. Ibid., p. 14.
17. See, among others, Garry Wills, *Bomb Power: The Modern Presidency and the National Security State* (London: Penguin, 2010); Desmond King and Robert Lieberman, 'The Ironies of State Building: A Comparative Perspective on the American State', *World Politics* 63 (2009): pp. 547–88; Eric Posner and Adrian Vermeule, *Executive Unbound: After the Madisonian State* (Oxford: Oxford University Press, 2011).
18. Posner and Vermeule, *Executive Unbound.*
19. Alex Moe, 'House Investigations of Trump and His Administration: The Full List', *NBC News*, 27 May 2019, https://www.nbcnews.com/politics/donald-trump/house-investigations-trump-his-administration-full-list-n1010131, accessed 2 Aug. 2021.
20. Molly E. Reynolds and Jackson Gode, 'Tracking House Oversight in the Trump Era', Brookings Institution, Jan. 2021, https://www.brookings.edu/interactives/tracking-house-oversight-in-the-trump-era/, accessed 1 Aug. 2021.
21. Jeremy Herb and Marshall Cohen, 'How a Senate Panel Went beyond Mueller in Documenting Trump Campaign Contacts with Russia', *CNN*, 23 Aug. 2020, https://edition.cnn.com/2020/08/23/politics/senate-intelligence-committee-report-russia-trump/index.html, accessed 1 Aug. 2021.
22. Mike Memoli, 'House Intelligence Committee Releases Full Report on Russia Investigation', *NBC News*, 27 Apr. 2018, https://www.nbcnews.com/politics/congress/house-intelligence-committee-releases-full-report-russia-investigation-n869656, accessed 2 Aug. 2021.
23. Philip Ewing, 'Senate Committee Releases 2,500 Pages about 2016 Trump Tower Meeting', *NPR*, 16 May 2018. https://www.npr.org/2018/05/16/611477917/senate-committee-releases-2-500-pages-about-2016-trump-tower-meeting, accessed 5 Aug. 2021.
24. Darren Samuelsohn, 'Mueller Report PSA: Prepare for Disappointment', *Politico*, 19 Oct. 2018, https://www.politico.com/

story/2018/10/19/mueller-investigation-findings-914754, accessed 5 Aug. 2021.

25. Lev Sugarman, 'Full Text of the Mueller Report's Executive Summaries', *Lawfare* blog, 18 April 2019, https://www.lawfareblog.com/full-text-mueller-reports-executive-summaries, accessed 3 Aug. 2021.
26. Sarah Binder, 'The Dysfunctional Congress', *Annual Review of Political Science* 18 (2015): pp. 85–101.
27. Andrew Cuomo, 'Governor Cuomo Announces New York, New Jersey, and Connecticut Launch Coalition to Sue the Federal Government Over Federal Tax Bill', press release of Governor Andrew M. Cuomo, 26 Jan. 2018, https://www.governor.ny.gov/news/governor-cuomo-announces-new-york-new-jersey-and-connecticut-launch-coalition-sue-federal, accessed 5 Aug. 2021.
28. Laura Davison, 'SALT-Cap Repeal Gains Momentum with House Bipartisan Caucus', *Bloomberg*, 15 Apr. 2021, https://www.bloomberg.com/news/articles/2021-04-15/push-to-end-salt-cap-grows-with-new-bipartisan-house-caucus, accessed 5 Aug. 2021.
29. Karen Pierog, 'Illinois to Defy Trump Administration's Abortion Referral "Gag Rule"', *Reuters*, 18 July 2019. https://www.reuters.com/article/us-usa-abortion/illinois-to-defy-trump-administrations-abortion-referral-gag-rule-idUSKCN1UD32V, accessed 6 Aug. 2021.
30. Associated Press, 'California Gov. Brown Denounces Jeff Sessions over Federal Immigration Lawsuit', *KPBS*, 7 Mar. 2018. https://www.kpbs.org/news/2018/mar/07/gov-brown-denounces-jeff-sessions-over-california-/, accessed 5 Aug.2021.
31. Bob Egelko, 'Calif. Supreme Court: All Cities Have to Follow State Sanctuary Law', *San Francisco Chronicle*, 3 Apr. 2020, https://www.police1.com/federal-law-enforcement/articles/calif-supreme-court-all-cities-have-to-follow-state-sanctuary-law-uRSBZ6V7hEIxWhiF/, accessed 6 Aug. 2021.
32. Sarah Miller, Norman Johnson, and Laura R. Wherry, 'Medicaid and Mortality: New Evidence from Linked Survey and Administrative Data', NBER Working Paper No. 26081 July 2019, Revised Jan. 2021, JEL No. I1, I13.
33. Coral Davenport, 'Republican Governors Signal Their Intent to Thwart Obama's Climate Rules', *New York Times*, 2 July 2015, https://www.nytimes.com/2015/07/03/us/republican-governors-signal-their-intent-to-thwart-obamas-climate-rules.html, accessed 5 Aug. 2021.

34. Paul Nolette has produced the most robust scholarship on developments in state AG activity, including a State Litigation and AG Activity Database. See https://attorneysgeneral.org/multistate-lawsuits-vs-the-federal-government/list-of-lawsuits-1980-present/.
35. 'Attorney General (State Executive Office)', *Ballotpedia*, United States, 2021. Web Archive. https://ballotpedia.org/Attorney_General_(state_executive_office), accessed 5 Aug. 2021.
36. Emma Platoff, 'America's Weaponized Attorneys General'. *The Atlantic*, 28 Oct. 2018, https://www.theatlantic.com/politics/archive/2018/10/both-republicans-and-democrats-have-weaponized-their-ags/574093/, accessed 9 Aug. 2021.
37. 'Attorney General elections, 2018', *Ballotpedia*. United States, 2021. Web Archive. Accessed 5 Aug. 2021, https://ballotpedia.org/Attorney_General_elections,_2018.
38. 'Republican Attorneys General Association', *Ballotpedia*. United States, 2021. Web Archive, https://ballotpedia.org/Republican_Attorneys_General_Association, accessed 5 Aug. 2021.
39. Dan Frosch and Jacob Gershman, 'Abbott's Strategy in Texas: 44 Lawsuits, One Opponent: Obama Administration; Former Attorney General, Now Governor, Has Led a Red-State Revolt against the White House', *Wall Street Journal* (Online), 24 June 2016, https://www-proquest-com.libproxy.ucl.ac.uk/newspapers/abbotts-strategy-texas-44-lawsuits-one-opponent/docview/1799228255/se-2?accountid=14511, accessed 29 July 2021.
40. Troutman Pepper, 'State Watchdogs: As Biden Takes Office, Republican Attorneys General Likely to Challenge Administration on Many Fronts', *JD Supra*, 5 Mar. 2021, https://www.jdsupra.com/legalnews/state-watchdogs-as-biden-takes-office-7149235/, accessed 6 Aug. 2021.
41. David S. Green, '*Massachusetts v. EPA* Without Massachusetts: Private Party Standing in Climate Change Litigation', *Environs* 36 (2012): pp. 35–63, https://law.ucdavis.edu/centers/environmental/files/Doremus%20Writing%20Winners/2012Green.pdf, accessed 4 Aug. 2021.
42. Nicole Nixon, 'California Attorney General Files Nine Lawsuits In One Day As Trump Leaves Office', *CapRadio*, 19 Jan. 2021, https://www.capradio.org/articles/2021/01/19/california-attorney-general-files-nine-lawsuits-in-one-day-as-trump-leaves-office/, accessed 5 Aug. 2021.
43. Brooks, Anthony. 'Healey v. Trump: The Mass. AG Continues to Challenge the President – A Lot, *WBUR News*, 17 May 2018,

https://www.wbur.org/news/2018/05/17/healey-trump-legal-challenges, accessed 4 Aug. 2021.

44. Phil for Colorado, 'Preoccupied – Phil Weiser for Colorado Attorney General', YouTube video, 0:37, 22 May 2018, https://www.youtube.com/watch?v=7PsdTnqEucM, accessed 9 Aug. 2021.
45. Eric Ortiz, 'State Attorneys General Have Sued Trump's Administration 138 times – Nearly Double Those of Obama and Bush', *NBC News*, 16 Nov. 2020, https://www.nbcnews.com/politics/politics-news/state-attorneys-general-have-sued-trump-s-administration-138-times-n1247733, accessed 5 Aug. 2021.
46. Ibid.
47. Nolette and Provost, 'Change and Continuity'.
48. Brian Mann, 'State Attorneys General Reach a $26 Billion National Opioid Settlement', *All Things Considered*, NPR, 21 July 2021. https://www.npr.org/2021/07/21/1018881195/state-attorneys-general-26-billion-opioid-settlement, accessed 5 Aug. 2021.
49. Dan Levine, 'Exclusive: As Democratic Attorneys General Target Trump, Republican AGs Target Them', *Reuters*, 28 Mar. 2017. https://www.reuters.com/article/us-usa-politics-republican-ags-exclusive-idUSKBN16Z1A5, accessed 5 Aug. 2021.
50. Jared Bennett, 'Why State Attorneys General Races Are the Next Frontier for Out-of-State Influence', Center for Public Integrity, 3 Nov. 2018. https://publicintegrity.org/politics/state-politics/why-state-attorneys-general-races-are-the-next-frontier-for-out-of-state-influence/, accessed 5 Aug. 2021.
51. Alan Neuhauser, 'State Attorneys General Lead the Charge against President Donald Trump', *US News & World Report*, 27 Oct. 2017. https://www.usnews.com/news/best-states/articles/2017-10-27/state-attorneys-general-lead-the-charge-against-president-donald-trump, accessed 5 Aug. 2021.
52. Ben Wieder, 'Big Money Comes to State Attorney-General Races', *Atlantic Monthly*, 8 May 2014. https://www.theatlantic.com/politics/archive/2014/05/us-chamber-targets-dems-in-state-attorney-general-races/361874/, accessed 5 Aug. 2021.
53. Dan Levine, 'Exclusive: As Democratic Attorneys General Target Trump, Republican AGs Target Them', *Reuters*, 28 Mar. 2017. https://www.reuters.com/article/us-usa-politics-republican-ags-exclusive-idUSKBN16Z1A5, accessed 9 Aug. 2021.
54. Rob Bonta, 'Attorney General Becerra Continues Defense of State Net Neutrality Law in Federal Court', State of California Department of Justice, Attorney General, Press Release, 22 Feb. 2021. https://

oag.ca.gov/news/press-releases/attorney-general-becerra-continues-defense-state-net-neutrality-law-federal, accessed 9 Aug. 2021.

55. Abigail Simon, 'How President Trump Is Spurring Mayors to Speak Up on National Issues', *Time*, 29 June 2018. https://time.com/5325646/donald-trump-mayors/, accessed 9 Aug. 2021.
56. 'United States Municipal Elections', *Ballotpedia.* United States, 2021. Web Archive. https://ballotpedia.org/United_States_municipal_elections,_2018, accessed 9 Aug. 2021.
57. 'U.S. Mayors Decry Trump Sanctuary City Threat, "Prepared to Welcome" migrants', Reuters, 12 Apr. 2019. https://www.reuters.com/article/us-usa-immigration-sanctuary-mayors-idUSKCN1RO2E3, accessed 9 Aug. 2021.
58. Shane Savitsky, 'Cities Resist Trump's Summer of Security', *Axios*, 22 July 2020. https://www.axios.com/cities-resist-trumps-summer-of-security-7206c7d6-d96b-4404-a66f-e7c38d952aff.html, accessed 9 August 2021; Alana Wise, 'Mayors Demand Congress Block Trump from Deploying Federal Agents to Cities', *NPR*, 27 July 2020, https://www.npr.org/sections/live-updates-protests-for-racial-justice/2020/07/27/895904023/mayors-demand-congress-block-trump-from-deploying-federal-agents-to-cities, accessed 9 Aug. 2021.
59. Richard C. Schragger, 'The Attack on American Cities', *Texas Law Review* 96 (2018): pp. 1163–233.
60. Christiana Prignano, 'Former President Obama Urges Mayors to "Speak the Truth" as they Battle Coronavirus', *Boston Globe*, 10 Apr. 2020, https://www.bostonglobe.com/2020/04/10/nation/former-president-obama-urges-mayors-speak-truth-they-battle-coronavirus/, accessed 9 August 2021; Joseph Ax, 'Obama Calls on all U.S. Mayors to Pursue Policing Reforms in Wake of Protests', *Reuters*, 3 June 2020, https://www.reuters.com/article/us-minneapolis-police-obama-idUSKBN23A3FG, accessed 9 Aug. 2021.
61. Rahm Emanuel, *The Nation City: Why Mayors Are Now Running the World* (New York: Knopf, 2020).
62. Susan B. Glasser, 'Trump and Rahm Emanuel Both Love a Fight, Especially against Each Other', *New Yorker*, 14 Feb. 2018, https://www.newyorker.com/news/news-desk/why-declaring-chicago-a-trump-free-zone-isnt-enough, accessed 6 Aug. 2021.
63. Bill Ruthhart, 'How Emanuel Worked to Maximize His Meeting with Trump', *Chicago Tribune*, 7 Dec. 2016, https://www.chica

gotribune.com/politics/ct-mayor-rahm-emanuel-donald-trump-meeting-20161207-story.html, accessed 9 Aug. 2021.

64. Paul Nolette, 'State Litigation during the Obama Administration: Diverging Agendas in an Era of Polarized Politics', *Publius: The Journal of Federalism* 44 (2014): pp. 451–74.
65. Jonathan Taplin, 'Rebirth of a Nation', *Harper's*, Nov. 2018, pp. 27–35.
66. Thomas E. Mann and Norman J. Ornstein, *It's Even Worse Than It Looks: How the American Constitutional System Collided with the New Politics of Extremism*, expanded edn (New York: Basic, 2016), p. 166.
67. David R. Mayhew, *Divided We Govern: Party Control, Lawmaking, and Investigations, 1946–1990* (New Haven, CT: Yale University Press, 1991).
68. I thank Gareth Davies for raising this point.
69. David Runciman, 'Ask Mike – City Government', *London Review of Books* 42, 12 (18 June 2020), pp. 27–8.

Part Two

Testing the New Deal Coalition

4

Swing Time: The New Deal Midterms of 1934 and 1938

Iwan Morgan

Franklin D. Roosevelt's landslide victories in the presidential elections of 1932 and 1936 are conventionally regarded by scholars as the primary indicators of the political realignment that occurred in the turbulent era of the Great Depression. A case can be made, however, that the midterm elections of 1934 and 1938 merit equal attention in any assessment of the scale of partisan change in the New Deal years – both in terms of its magnitude and limitations. In 1934, the Democrats added to their already huge majorities in both houses of Congress, thereby bucking the historic trend that the president's party loses seats in at least one chamber in the midterm elections of his or her first term – for the only time between 1902 and 2002. On its front page, the *New York Times* adjudged the result 'the most overwhelming victory in the history of American politics' not only for the Democratic Party but also for Franklin D. Roosevelt and the New Deal. In 1938, by contrast, the Democrats' loss of seventy-two seats in the House of Representatives was their second highest after the 105 lost in 1894. In picking up eight Senate seats, the Republicans also made their largest midterm gains hitherto in the upper chamber, going two better than their previous best in 1898. As a further indicator of GOP success, none of its incumbent congressional candidates failed to win re-election, an achievement unmatched until the 1994 midterms. According to the *New Republic,* the outcome made the future of liberalism, seemingly so assured a few years earlier, 'full of danger and uncertainty'.[1]

Although the national Democratic Party experienced triumph in 1934 and tribulation in 1938, the two midterm elections provided significant confirmation of the political realignment of the New Deal era that underwrote its majority status and predominantly liberal identity. The key difference between them was that the 1934 elections boosted New Deal liberalism and the 1938 elections constituted a setback for it. In the latter, FDR's failure to purge conservative Democrats in the congressional primaries and the Republican revival in the congressional elections encouraged the development of an informal bipartisan conservative coalition in Congress. As well as stymying the prospects for further New Deal reform in the Depression decade, this alliance became a significant obstacle to the enactment of new liberal programmes for the next quarter century. Nevertheless, the 1938 elections had positive significance for liberalism in one important regard. Roosevelt's attempted purge may not have eliminated its principal conservative targets but his direct and indirect interventions in Democratic primaries had the effect of defining the national party as liberal in both its mainstream ideology and programmatic agenda.

The pre–New Deal Democratic Party

The Democratic Party that Roosevelt inherited lacked a coherent political identity, had a narrow voter base, and was internally divided. Since the Civil War it had elected just two presidents, Grover Cleveland (1881–5 and 1893–7) and Woodrow Wilson (1913–21), and enjoyed two-chamber control of Congress for only ten years in aggregate.[2] The white, rural, small-town Protestant South, the party's largest and most reliable source of electoral support, had little in common with the rising but still-secondary constituency of northern, urban, Catholic, and Jewish ethnic Americans. Their falling out over the culture wars of the 1920s pertaining to Prohibition, immigration, and nativism threatened to tear the party apart. The Democrats reached their lowest ebb in 1924 when they required 103 ballots to nominate a compromise presidential candidate at their national convention and carried only 28.8 per cent of the popular vote, their lowest ever share, in the presidential election.[3]

Withdrawing from politics after contracting polio in 1921, Roosevelt returned to the front line in time to witness first-hand the 1924 debacles. Thereafter, he sent some 3,000 Democrats a circular letter laying out 'certain fundamental truths' necessary for their party's revival. As well as calling for organisational and financial improvements, he urged that it should become 'the party of progress and liberal thought' in opposition to Republican pro-business conservatism. In his assessment, the Democrats could only regain national power by moving away from disruptive cultural issues to find unity in support of progressive socio-economic reform that benefited the broad mass of ordinary voters.[4] His hope to convene a national conference to agree the way forward foundered on the rocks of Democratic divisions. Nevertheless, he continued over the next eight years to hone ideas about party development that he would put into practice when president.

The Great Depression created the political environment for economic issues to take precedence over cultural questions in the Democratic agenda. Challenging conventional historical opinion that FDR improvised the New Deal when in office, Eric Rauchway persuasively argues that the positions he took in the 1932 campaign and maintained throughout the long interregnum between his election and inauguration followed the liberal principles he had laid down in his 1924 letter to co-partisans.[5] In Roosevelt's calculation, the success of his presidency depended on achieving two corollary goals: the transformation of the Democratic Party from the minority to the majority party and its reconstruction as a liberal party that would sustain the New Deal programme of federal socio-economic activism during his tenure and build on its legacy thereafter. Nevertheless, he believed that their dual attainment required him to pursue a supra-partisan strategy to bring progressive-minded Republicans and independent voters into the Democratic tent. In the 1932 election, accordingly, he eschewed direct attacks on the Grand Old Party (GOP) itself and invited the support of 'those nominal Republicans who find that their conscience cannot be squared with the groping and failure of their party leaders'. Ernest Lindley, a journalist close to FDR, later observed that his 'consistent ambition for many years . . . was to form a new liberal party by attaching the Republican Progressives and miscellaneous liberals to the Democratic Party, thus effecting a new political alignment which had meaning'.[6]

The outcome of the 1932 presidential election owed more to popular disillusionment with Herbert Hoover's failure to restore the depressed economy than to positive enthusiasm for FDR. Nevertheless, the scale of the Democratic victory vindicated Roosevelt's hopes of building a new party. He won a greater share of the popular vote (57.4 per cent) and of the Electoral College vote (88.8 per cent) than any previous Democratic presidential candidate. He ran well in all parts of the country except New England and the rural Northeast. Building on the foundations laid by Alfred E. Smith in his unsuccessful presidential campaign of 1928, he made a particularly strong showing in urban areas. Roosevelt swept America's twelve largest cities with an aggregate majority that exceeded 1.5 million votes – dwarfing Smith's plurality of 20,000.[7] He drew his core urban support from organised labour, ethnics, lower-income voters, the unemployed, and women (he was the first Democrat to carry a majority of women voters since the national advent of female suffrage). At the same time, FDR's coat-tails helped the Democrats gain their highest-ever majorities over the Republicans in the House of Representatives (313 seats to 117) and Senate (sixty seats to thirty-five).

The 1934 midterms: consolidating the New Deal voter coalition

It was inconceivable to many pundits that the Democrats could sustain that level of congressional strength in the 1934 midterm vote given the disadvantages they carried into the election. Roosevelt's personal prestige remained tremendously high but he was not on the ticket and every president's party tended to lose seats in off-year contests. Two years of New Deal experimentation had made the federal government an important presence in the lives of many Americans, but there were signs of grassroots discontent that it had done more for bankers and big business than for ordinary citizens. Most significantly, even though the economy was in recovery (GDP growth of 10.8 per cent in 1934 compared with a decline of 1.2 per cent in 1933), this had not translated into substantial expansion of jobs. In late 1934, the unemployment rate was still staggeringly high at 21.7 per cent of the labour force, not much improved on the 23.6 per cent level when Hoover crashed to defeat in 1932.

Despite all this, the Democrats passed their first national electoral test of the Roosevelt presidency with flying colours. They made a net gain of nine seats in the House to secure an enlarged majority over the Republicans of 322 to 103 and a remarkable gain of nine in the thirty-six Senate seats (including special elections) being contested for a majority of 69–25. While midterm elections often turn on state and district issues, the 1934 contests were effectively nationalised by both parties into a referendum on Rooseveltian reform. Whatever its shortcomings, the New Deal, among other things, had established the federal government as the main provider of unemployment relief, had stabilised the banking system to halt the panics that threatened financial meltdown in early 1933, had reversed the collapse of agricultural prices, had guaranteed farm and home mortgage insurance to halt foreclosures, and had belatedly commenced to defend organised labour's collective bargaining rights. The House and Senate elections were largely fought on whether such unprecedented federal activism in economic affairs constituted a necessary and effective response to the Great Depression or whether it entailed excessive regimentation that threatened full recovery and liberty.

As Robert Mason points out, the Republican National Committee (RNC) initially advocated 'a balance between accommodation and attack' in GOP election strategy. In June 1934, it issued a statement that supported engagement with economic problems 'in a broad, liberal and progressive spirit, unhampered by dead formulas or too obstinately clinging to the past' but warned that an overly powerful federal government posed a threat to democracy, constitutionalism, and free enterprise.[8] Since it was difficult to develop a message that straddled these contrary assertions with a constructive alternative, most GOP candidates preferred to give vent to their anti-statist convictions in the belief that the New Deal's failure to achieve recovery would hurt the Democrats. Much to Democratic delight, the still very unpopular Herbert Hoover joined in the assault with gusto. One month before the election, he published *The Challenge to Liberty*, whose warnings of the New Deal's totalitarian consequences received mixed reviews. *The Christian Century* typically acknowledged it as a significant critique but questioned the former president's capacity to accept change.[9] Intended as a manifesto for the GOP campaign, it was a damp squib in that regard, but an undeterred Hoover continued to speak out against the New Deal's collectivist threat through to election day.

FDR stayed true to his supra-partisan strategy of 1932 in the belief that this would work to his party's advantage. Despite his admiration for Thomas Jefferson, he resolutely stayed out of Democratic celebrations of the party's founder in 1934. 'Our strongest plea to the country', he told one confidant, '. . . is that the recovery and reconstruction program is being accomplished by men and women of all parties.' Expecting the Republicans to take a highly partisan approach, he added, 'In that kind of foolishness lies our strength.'[10] Accordingly, FDR did not participate actively in the campaign but he was ever-present in it in other ways.

In a Fireside Chat in late June, Roosevelt set the Democratic midterm theme: '[T]he simplest way for each of you to judge recovery lies in the plain facts of your own individual situation. Are you better off than you were last year? Are your debts less burdensome? Is your bank account more secure? Are your working conditions better? Is your faith in your own individual future more firmly grounded?' In the pre-election months, the Democratic National Committee (DNC) produced a barrage of literature lauding the president and his programmes in support of an affirmative answer to all these questions. Virtually every Democrat running for congressional or state office outside the one-party South ran on their support for the Roosevelt record. Sensing the national mood, House Speaker Henry Rainey of Illinois, shortly before his sudden death in August, had counselled Democrats in marginal districts that their best hope of victory was 'to preach the Roosevelt philosophy and stand behind the President'.[11]

Seeking to understand their sweeping defeat, many Republicans subscribed to a 'bought vote' theory that the New Deal had corrupted beneficiaries of its programmes into voting Democratic. This grossly misrepresented popular support for Roosevelt and the New Deal and overlooked the GOP's failure to offer an alternative that did not entail a return to the past.[12] It also ignored Democratic progress in consolidating the urban electoral coalition initially mobilised by Al Smith in 1928 and enlarged by FDR in 1932. Outside the South, the party's victory in the midterms was built on the votes of labour union families, unorganised workers, the unemployed, ethnics, women, and African Americans.

In national terms, the Democrats actually lost House seats to the Republicans in predominantly rural districts in some western and midwestern states, including five in Michigan. However, seats they picked up in predominantly urban areas in Connecticut, Illinois, Massachusetts, Missouri, and, most notably, Pennsylvania gave them a net gain. The pattern of gain in urban-industrial northern states was even more evident in the Senate – the Democrats captured seats in Connecticut, Rhode Island, New Jersey, Pennsylvania, Ohio, and Indiana. Their other three pick-ups were in the border states of Maryland, Missouri, and West Virginia. In Missouri, future president Harry S. Truman inflicted a landslide defeat on the GOP incumbent, Roscoe Patterson. The Republican had taken 52 per cent of the vote to win election in 1928, but Truman boosted the Democratic share from 48 per cent to 60 per cent, with the assistance of massive voter registration drives by Democratic organizations in Kansas City and St Louis.

Nowhere was the transformation of the Democrats' urban power more evident than in Pennsylvania, a state that Hoover had carried by 150,000 in 1932 – thanks to Roosevelt winning just 45 per cent of the vote in Philadelphia, the only big city where he had not gained a majority. In 1934, however, the Keystone State elected its first Democratic governor since 1890 (George Earle, who launched a 'Little New Deal' in state government) and its first Democratic senator since 1874 (Joseph Guffey, who became a '100% New Dealer' in office). The Democrats also won twelve additional House seats to boost the size of their

Pennsylvania delegation to twenty-five and shrink the Republican complement to nine. Guffey had joined with Pittsburgh mayor David Lawrence to renew the Pennsylvania Democratic Party as a predominantly urban one. The foundations of their success were the popularity of FDR, their receipt of New Deal patronage, and extensive voter registration drives that resulted in the Democratic share of Pennsylvania's registered voters doubling from 21 per cent in 1932 to 42 per cent in 1936.[13]

The 1934 midterms are also significant for being the elections in which African Americans finally turned Abraham Lincoln's portrait to the wall. While some in the African American elite, such as Robert Vann, publisher of the *Pittsburgh Courier*, the nation's largest-circulation Black-owned newspaper, had urged support for FDR in 1932, rank-and-file voters deserted the Republicans in significant numbers only in Detroit and Manhattan. The Democrats remained in their eyes the lily-white party of the Jim Crow South. In 1934, however, Democratic congressional candidates and local party organisations made a concerted attempt to woo Black voters. Local machines in, among other places, Chicago, Detroit, Kansas City, New York, Pittsburgh, and St Louis dispensed patronage to African American leaders, and federal relief projects put increasing numbers of Black Americans on their rolls. Most notably, in the Illinois 1st congressional district that included Chicago's South Side Black ghetto, the Kelly–Nash machine ran African American Arthur Mitchell, who had switched parties only two years earlier, against Republican Congressman Oscar de Priest, the solitary Black member of the House of Representatives. Campaigning on a 'Forward with Roosevelt' slogan to highlight his opponent's opposition to federal relief, Mitchell rolled out a victory by 53 to 47 per cent of the vote to become the first ever Black Democrat in Congress.[14]

As had long been the case, Republican registration continued to exceed Democratic registration in 1934, but the margin had narrowed. The voter registration drives conducted by many urban Democratic organisations give weight to the scholarly contention that mobilisation of new or uncommitted voters rather than partisan conversion of existing ones underlay the creation of the Democratic majority in this era. The most significant exponent of this viewpoint, Kristi Andersen, calculates that some three-quarters of the total Democratic gains in the New Deal era came from the support of hitherto uninvolved voters, notably second-generation immigrant ethnics, women, and African Americans. In her calculations, the elections of 1934 had pivotal significance in this development. Though some 12.5 per cent down from the 1932 presidential election, the voting-eligible turnout of 44.5 per cent in 1934 was significantly higher than that of 36.7 per cent in the previous off-year elections of 1930.[15]

The Democratic midterm success produced a mandate for the New Deal to expand in a new direction. It facilitated the enactment early in the next Congress of the so-called 'Big Bill', the Emergency Relief Appropriation Act of 1935, whose authorisation of \$4.8 billion dwarfed previous spending on work-relief and public works. This signalled the New Deal's turn from efforts to promote a top-down approach to recovery through helping business, banks, and farm owners in 1933 to a more direct emphasis on aiding the Democratic base of organised labour, the unemployed, and those in the lower half of the income distribution. Despite resistance and delaying tactics from conservative Democrats, Congress approved a blitz of liberal measures in what historians have characterised as the 'second hundred days' in mid-1935. These included the Social Security Act, the National Labor Relations Act, the Public Utility Holding Company Act, and a wealth tax.

The 1938 midterms: the Republican comeback

The coat-tail effects of Roosevelt's landslide re-election in 1936 produced even larger Democratic majorities of 334–88 over the Republicans in the House and 75–17 in the Senate. This level of strength was unsustainable for much longer, but the scale of Democratic decline from the highs of 1934 and 1936 was far greater than party leaders anticipated. Overly confident that the Republican Party was still unpopular in the country at large, Roosevelt told DNC chairman James Farley that he expected only minimal losses of one Senate seat and up to sixteen House seats in 1938. Instead, his party suffered what Farley called 'the great turnover': the GOP gained eighty-one seats in the House, seventy-two of them captured from Democrats and the rest from smaller parties, eight in the Senate (where the Democrats were defending thirty-two seats), and twelve governorships.[16] In a post-election news conference, FDR was less than truthful in claiming that he had expected to lose sixty-five House seats and eight in the Senate, but denied that the outcome would make it more difficult to enact a liberal programme.[17] If he truly believed this, he was deluding himself. The huge Democratic losses may not have threatened the party's large majorities in both chambers, but they significantly altered its composition to the benefit of the party's conservative wing.

The losses arguably represented more than a normal swing of the pendulum against the majority party after six years in power. There were numerous factors at work to produce such a large-scale shift towards the GOP, many of them pertinent to candidates and issues at district and state levels. There were some common threads in the national electoral patchwork, however. Most significant was the onset of what Republicans called the 'Roosevelt Recession'. The first annual increase in unemployment since FDR took office, this halted the promising recovery seemingly in train at the time of the 1936 elections. Joblessness rose to 19 per cent in 1938, compared to 14.7 per cent in 1937, a level it would not fall below again until 1941. The Committee for Industrial Organization (CIO) sit-down strikes of 1937 in the automobile and steel industries, which FDR had not condoned but failed to stop, were unpopular with many voters. Meanwhile, farmers outside the South complained of declining commodity prices and of Works Progress Administration (WPA) work-relief projects depriving them of cheap labour.[18]

Broadly, the Democrats held on to their New Deal voter base, but voting-eligible turnout of 46.6 per cent was well down on the 61 per cent rate in the 1936 presidential election. Middle-class voters, for whom labour union militancy was particularly concerning, turned out in large numbers to back the Republicans. In 1936, GOP presidential candidate Alf Landon had narrowly won the outer suburbs of many cities where FDR had trounced him. The suburban shift towards the Republicans intensified two years later. The small-town vote that had gone to Landon in 1936 also continued to trend much more heavily towards the GOP than in the 1934 midterms.

In terms of electoral geography, the Democrats fared badly in some states that had been bedrock supporters in the previous New Deal elections. These included Connecticut, New Jersey, and Pennsylvania, but in general the party's vote in bigger northern cities held up better than in smaller ones. In Pennsylvania, for example, the Republicans made an aggregate gain of twelve House seats, but only half of these numbered among those the Democrats had captured in 1934. The region where the Democrats fared worst, however, was the Upper Midwest. They lost thirteen House seats and one Senate seat in Ohio, six House seats in Indiana, three House seats and a Senate seat in Wisconsin, and three House seats in Michigan, where Governor Frank Murphy also lost his bid for re-election. Meanwhile, the Republicans profited at the expense of left-leaning smaller parties, picking up five House seats from the Progressives in Wisconsin and three from the Farmer–Labor Party in Minnesota. The region had been hard hit by the recession, had been on the front line of the sit-down strikes – Frank Murphy's sympathy for the United Automobile Workers' use of this tactic in their battle for employer recognition of their union was the main factor in his defeat – and its farmers were resentful of a decline in corn, hog, and dairy prices.[19]

Also instrumental in the Republicans' success was learning from their previous mistakes: GOP candidates who unseated Democratic incumbents generally abstained from direct attacks on the New Deal's social welfare provision, focusing their fire instead on its inefficiencies and throttling of private enterprise's capacity to boost recovery. A case study of their success in Indiana offers some illumination of this strategy. In a state that was once a bedrock of old-guard conservatism, Republicans cosied up to the Townsend Clubs, approving their calls for more generous pensions than provided under the New Deal's social security legislation. The endorsement of these senior-citizen organisations was thought to have tipped the balance to the GOP in the congressional districts that included Terre Haute and South Bend.

In Fort Wayne and other cities, moreover, local Republicans attacked the inadequacy of WPA resources to provide relief for the rising number of unemployed. These tactics helped to capture six congressional seats and reduce the winning margin of Senator Frederick Van Nuys, who had trounced Senate Majority Leader James Watson by 209,000 votes in 1932, to a bare 5,000, which was eked out with the help of ballot-rigging in Gary. It was small wonder that some Democratic county chairmen complained of being out–New Dealed by the opposition.[20]

Such local manoeuvring was hardly a foundation for a national strategy. Despite their successes in 1938, Republicans were far from being agreed about whether their best hope for the next presidential election lay in accommodating or attacking the New Deal. Hitherto the fault lines in this intra-party debate had lain between western progressives and eastern conservatives. Now they lay between two different groups – eastern moderates willing to accept the main elements of the New Deal and western and midwestern conservatives sceptical of activist government in principle.

The intra-party divide was encapsulated by the two Republicans who attained national prominence as a result of the 1938 midterms. New York County district attorney Thomas E. Dewey, who had made his name as a racket-buster, came within 65,000 votes, 1 per cent of the total ballots, of unseating popular incumbent Herbert Lehman in the Empire State's gubernatorial election. Focusing his campaign on state issues, he broadly accepted the New Deal's social goals while criticising its economic record and centralising tendencies. In private, he identified conservatives' influence within the GOP as the greatest obstacle to its electoral success in the next presidential election. By contrast, Robert Taft, son of President William Taft, interpreted his defeat of Ohio's incumbent senator, Robert J. Bulkley, whom FDR had endorsed in his primary race, as a repudiation of the later New Deal's leftward turn. While approving its humanitarian assistance for senior citizens and the unemployed, he attacked its excessive regulation of economic enterprise, encouragement of labour militancy, and appropriation of arbitrary powers to carry out its programme.[21]

Whither the Democratic Party? The 1938 midterms and beyond

For the time being, the congressional wing of the Republican Party was dominated by conservatives intent on halting the New Deal's expansion of statism. They found willing allies in conservative Democrats, predominantly southerners and those with a rural base elsewhere in the nation. Party strength in the 76th Congress suggested overwhelming Democratic strength over the Republicans by 260 to 169 seats in the House and sixty-nine to twenty-three in the Senate. However, many of the defeated Democratic incumbents in the 1938 midterms had been reliable supporters of the New Deal. Their departure increased the relative strength of conservatives within Democratic ranks, particularly those from the South. In the three previous New Deal Congresses, southerners had represented a large minority of Democrats in each chamber, instead of their habitual majority, but in the 76th Congress of 1939–40 they constituted 54 per cent of the party total in the House and were on their way to renewing their majority in the Senate (attained in the next Congress). It soon became evident that at least thirty Democrats were hostile to the New Deal and another fifty were unreliable supporters of it in the House, and anywhere between twenty and thirty Democrats were inclined to join with the GOP against the president's programmes in the Senate.[22]

Conservative Democrats, particularly those from the South, had grown increasingly concerned at FDR's efforts to liberalise the Democratic Party and its programmatic agenda at the expense of their traditional dominance of it. Initially, they had assumed, as historian Susan Dunn observes, 'that they were merely leasing out their party on a short-term basis to Roosevelt and his progressive agenda' until the temporary emergency of the Great Depression subsided.[23] Their growing realisation of Roosevelt's transformational intent for party and nation caused a change of heart. While FDR was too popular to attack openly in his first term, the failure of his efforts to pack the Supreme Court with liberal justices in 1937 emboldened conservative Democrats to oppose him. As Senator Josiah Bailey of North Carolina, informed the like-minded Senator Harry Byrd of Virginia, 'What we have to do is to preserve, if we can, the Democratic Party against his efforts to make it the Roosevelt party.'[24] This was the context for Roosevelt's effort to assert greater control over the congressional party through intervening in the 1938 Democratic primaries to secure the nomination of candidates supportive of the New Deal.

Roosevelt's unsuccessful efforts to purge conservatives in the Democratic primaries dominated the early historiography of his role in the midterms. According to James MacGregor Burns, FDR could have used the massive patronage resources at his disposal to strengthen liberal forces in state parties when the New Deal's prestige and his own were at their peak in his first term, but left it too late to act. In contrast, James Patterson argues that the very nature and organisation of state parties, which favoured conservative rural interests, made them resistant to the liberalising influence of presidential intervention. Nevertheless, later scholars such as Sean Savage contend that Roosevelt's role in the 1938 midterms entailed far more than the attempted purge and should be seen in broader perspective.[25]

In early 1938, Roosevelt used the presidential podium to insist that the Democratic Party had to be an indisputably liberal party. In particular, his address to the Jackson Day dinner, a key event in the Democratic calendar, emphasised that it had to be a national party concerned with the welfare of the majority, which required it to 'slough off any remains of sectionalism and class consciousness'.[26] This rhetorical barrage was intended to soften up his intra-party opponents for the front-line advance of pro–New Deal candidates in the primaries. The offensive got off to a good start. On 4 January, Lister Hill, a liberal-leaning congressman running with Roosevelt's endorsement, won the special Democratic primary to fill Alabama's Senate seat (vacated by Hugo Black on his elevation to the Supreme Court) by a margin of 61 to 34 per cent over the race-baiting anti–New Deal former senator, Thomas Heflin. This encouraged FDR, acting through his son and White House secretary, James Roosevelt, to endorse Senator Claude Pepper, a liberal stalwart, in his quest for renomination in the Florida senatorial primary against Congressman Neil Wilcox, a New Deal foe, and David Sholtz, a former governor and moderate conservative. 'The issue', Pepper wrote in his diary, 'is the New Deal or not – liberalism versus reaction.' With financial and patronage assistance from the administration, which also mobilised federal appointees in his support, he ran out the clear winner with 58 per cent of the vote on 3 May. The outcome, Roosevelt wrote to a British friend, 'seemed to prove that the voters' hearts (and heads!) seem still to be in the right place'.[27]

Pepper's success in Florida encouraged what the press called an 'elimination committee', supposedly consisting of James Roosevelt, presidential aide Thomas Corcoran, and WPA director Harry Hopkins, to seek the ouster of an incumbent for the first time. Their target was Guy Gillette of Iowa, a moderate conservative whose sin was to oppose FDR's judicial reorganisation plan, but their efforts to oust him were disorganised, limited, and crucially lacked presidential endorsement for their favoured candidate, Representative Otha Wearin. With the state Democratic organisation in his corner, Gillette secured an easy victory with a vote greater than the aggregate for his three primary opponents. Senator Burton Wheeler of Montana, who had led the battle against FDR's court bill, called the outcome 'a repudiation of the backseat drivers in Washington' in their attempt to pack the Senate.[28]

At this point, Roosevelt himself decided to take charge of the campaign to promote liberal candidates in the Democratic primaries. By now, he was widely perceived in Congress and the press as its moving force, so other setbacks would inevitably be interpreted as signalling his declining hold over the national party, regardless of whether he was directing operations or not. Announcing his intentions in the Fireside Chat on 24 June, he urged primary voters to consider whether the candidate they supported adhered to the liberal or conservative 'school of thought'. Distinguishing between his role as president and party leader, he asserted his responsibility in the latter capacity to carry out 'the definitely liberal declarations of principle set forth in the 1936 Democratic platform'. It therefore followed, he said, that 'I have every right to speak in those few instances where there may be a clear issue between candidates for the Democratic nomination involving these principles, or involving a clear misuse of my own name.'[29]

On this basis, Roosevelt proceeded in the months that followed to endorse liberal-leaning Democrats facing conservative primary opponents. On his train trip west to board a navy cruiser at San Diego for a sea trip, he stopped off to speak in support of Senator Alben Barkley of Kentucky, Senator Hattie Caraway of Arkansas, Senator Elmer Thomas of Oklahoma, and Representative Lyndon B. Johnson of Texas, all of whom won their primary races. Presidential endorsements for Congressman Maury Maverick of Texas and Senator William Gibbs McAdoo of California proved less effective – the former, a New Deal champion, was ousted by a conservative primary challenger and the latter went down to the more liberal Sheridan Downey.[30]

Only in five contests did FDR's involvement entail more than rhetorical endorsement. In Kentucky, Alben Barkley was the beneficiary not only of being anointed in person as Roosevelt's preferred candidate but also of increased WPA spending for his state, the contributions canvassed from the local officials of every federal agency, and the votes of relief workers directed by the WPA to support him. He eventually took 56 per cent of the primary vote to defeat Governor Albert Chandler, who had a powerful state government machine at his disposal and had support from conservative Democrats. More was involved in the contest than just the re-election of a pro–New Deal senator. Roosevelt had used his influence to secure Barkley's election as Senate Majority Leader, by a bare one-vote margin, over Pat Harrison of Mississippi in 1937. If this administration loyalist had fallen in the primary, the Senate leadership would have passed to one of the most conservative southern Democrats.[31]

In three other cases, Roosevelt made overt interventions to oust conservative senators in favour of their liberal primary challengers. His targets were Walter George of Georgia, Ellison 'Cotton Ed' Smith of South Carolina, and Millard Tydings of Maryland, but each was too entrenched in terms of their state party organisation and voter support to be dislodged. Only in Maryland did Roosevelt campaign vigorously but he could not transfer his popularity to his hand-picked candidate, David Lewis, an obscure congressman. Tydings benefited from greater statewide name recognition, aroused popular animus against outside interference and outspent his challenger by nearly a two-to-one ratio. In Georgia and South Carolina, efforts to mobilise WPA voter support had little effect because relief workers were predominantly poor whites and African Americans, who did not have suffrage eligibility. George and Smith were also effective in arousing popular outrage against presidential interference in their states as the modern equivalent of the Reconstruction carpetbaggers. For good measure, George called it a 'second march through Georgia' to remind voters of a Civil War episode that lived in infamy in the state's memory.[32]

Roosevelt, meanwhile, tasted success in his campaign to purge Congressman John O'Connor of New York, who had stymied New Deal legislation as Rules Committee chair. The president's endorsement of his challenger, James Fay, carried more weight in O'Connor's district on New York's East Side, where low-income voters predominated. Moreover, in contrast to the attempted Senate purges, which largely entailed unsystematic and disorganised half-measures, his aides worked full-time on the campaign. When Fay won the general election against O'Connor, who ultimately ran as a Republican, the *New Republic* exulted, 'This single victory is enough to justify the whole [purge] effort.'[33] This arguably underestimated what Roosevelt had achieved in the midterm primaries. His principal interventions had secured two major successes in preserving a loyal Senate leader and removing the most strategically obstructive House committee chair. His lesser interventions were also broadly successful in helping liberal incumbents gain primary election success. Nevertheless, his failure to unseat three conservative senators have received far greater weight in New Deal scholarship than his successes.

Without doubt, the failed purges demonstrated that Roosevelt could not remake the national Democratic Party into an entirely liberal one because its conservative wing was too strong, particularly in its habitual southern base. Even had he succeeded in ousting George, Smith, and Tydings, their removal would not have sufficed to effect party transformation. That project required much greater time, energy, and resources than the president could have given. Nevertheless, Roosevelt's interventions in the 1938 midterms ensured that conservatives would never regain leadership over the national party. He had succeeded through his words and actions in establishing the liberal purpose of the national party mainstream, consolidating the influence of New Deal supporters within it, and relegating conservatives to play the role of obstructive minority. The purge also forced conservative Democrats to become more overt in their opposition to the New Deal by making it more difficult for them to identify with Roosevelt and his programme when running for re-election and sabotaging his agenda when back in Congress.

Even though FDR eschewed further use of the purge tactics employed in 1938, he regarded them as just one round in his ongoing struggle to ensure the future of liberalism in the Democratic Party. A month after the election, he picked up an honorary degree from the University of North Carolina, the intellectual centre of southern liberalism. In his acceptance address, he declared that liberal forces, far from being 'on their way to the cemetery' as reported in press commentary on the 1938 midterms, 'would come to life again with more strength than they had before'. He went on to proclaim the importance of a liberal America for democracy at home and abroad:

> We are not only the largest and most powerful democracy in the whole world, but many other democracies look to us for leadership in order that world democracy may survive. I am speaking not of the external policies of the United States Government. . . . What I would emphasize is the maintenance of successful democracy at home. Necessarily democratic methods within a nation's life entail change . . . the kind of change to meet new social and economic needs through recognized processes of government.[34]

Some eighteen months later, FDR would accept his party's nomination for an unprecedented third term in office, compel its acceptance of an out-and-out New Dealer, Secretary of Agriculture Henry Wallace, as his running mate, and ensure that his lieutenants dominated the formulation of its domestic platform. This marked his successful 'purge' of conservative influence in the presidential wing of the party as a means of preserving the vision he had outlined in his North Carolina address. In a paradoxical demonstration of FDR's enduring popularity in the South and the declining significance of the region in the New Deal voter coalition, he won every southern state in the 1940 election but would still have been elected without carrying a single one – as had been the case in 1932 and 1936.

Conclusions: the meaning of the New Deal midterms

Despite their different outcomes, the 1934 and 1938 midterm elections were important in the development of liberalism in the United States. The former manifested the consolidation of a New Deal urban-voter coalition and the latter confirmed its continuation to underwrite liberal ascendancy in the presidential wing of the party. Roosevelt had long hoped that the New Deal's modernisation of the South would bring it into the liberal mainstream of the Democratic Party, but the 1938 midterms indicated that the regional power of conservatism in its congressional bailiwick was too strong. He now acknowledged, 'It takes a long, long time to bring the past up to the present.'[35]

In 1934, FDR had maintained his supra-partisan stance in the hope of attracting support from liberal-inclined Republicans and independents. In 1938, he operated more as a partisan because of his concerns to stifle conservative influence within his own party, but took some satisfaction that the poor showing of independent progressive parties in the Upper Midwest spelled the end of their Third Party threat. 'They must and will come to us *if* we remain definitely the liberal party,' he told one correspondent.[36] Ultimately, he hoped for a realignment that would offer voters a choice between a liberal Democratic Party and a conservative Republican Party. The 1938 midterm elections signified that this would not happen anytime soon because conservatives held too much power in the congressional wing of the Democratic Party and the GOP had still not resolved the question of whether it wanted to be a conservative party.

Notes

1. 'Tide Sweeps Nation', *New York Times*, 7 Nov. 1934; 'What the Election Means', *New Republic*, 23 Nov. 1938, p. 59.

2. The Democrats controlled both the House of Representatives and the Senate in 1879–81, 1893–5, and 1913–19. In addition, they controlled the House alone in 1875–9, 1883–9, 1891–3, 1911–13, and 1931–3.
3. For the Democrats in the 1920s, see: David Burner, *The Politics of Provincialism: The Democratic Party in Transition, 1918–1932* (New York: Knopf, 1968); and Douglas B. Craig, *After Wilson: The Struggle for the Democratic Party, 1920–1934* (Chapel Hill, NC: University of North Carolina Press, 1994).
4. The most thorough treatment of this is Joseph Laycock, 'A Party in Peril: Franklin Roosevelt, the Democratic Party, and the Circular Letter of 1924', PhD dissertation, Bowling Green State University, 2016 (esp. ch. 4).
5. Eric Rauchway, *Winter War: Hoover, Roosevelt, and the First Clash over the New Deal* (New York: Basic Books, 2018).
6. Franklin D. Roosevelt, 'Address Accepting the Presidential Nomination at the Democratic National Convention in Chicago', 2 July 1932, online by Gerhard Peters and John T. Woolley, The American Presidency Project [henceforth APP], https://www.presidency.ucsb.edu/node/275484; Ernest Lindley, *The Roosevelt Revolution: First Phase* (New York: Viking, 1933), p. 10.
7. All but four – Los Angeles (5th), St Louis (7th), Baltimore (8th), and San Francisco (11th) – were in the North. See https://www.census.gov/population/www/documentation/twps0027/tab01.txt.
8. RNC, 'Statement of Party Policy', 6 June 1934, in Robert Mason, *The Republican Party and American Politics from Hoover to Reagan* (New York: Cambridge University Press, 2012), p. 47.
9. Herbert Hoover, *The Challenge to Liberty* (New York: Charles Scribner's, 1934); 'Mr Hoover and the New Deal', *Christian Century*, 3 Oct. 1934, pp. 1230–2. See, too, Alan Nevins, 'The Battle of 1936 Begins', *Saturday Review of Literature*, 6 Oct. 1934, pp. 155–72.
10. Roosevelt to Colonel Edward M. House, 10 March 1934, in Elliott Roosevelt, ed., *FDR: His Personal Letters, 1928–1945* [hereafter *FDR: HPL*] I (New York: Duell, Sloan and Pearce, 1950), p. 394.
11. Roosevelt, 'Fireside Chat', 28 June 1934, APP, https://www.presidency.ucsb.edu/node/208443; Donald Ritchie, *Electing FDR: The New Deal Campaign of 1932* (Lawrence, KS: University Press of Kansas, 2007), pp. 184–5.
12. E. Francis Brown, 'The Moral of the Elections', *Current History* 41 (Dec.1934): pp. 279–83; Mason, *Republican Party*, pp. 49–50.

13. Joseph Alsop and Robert Kitner, 'The Guffey, Biography of a Boss, New Style' and 'The Guffey – The Capture of Pennsylvania', *Saturday Evening Post*, 26 Mar. and 16 Apr. 1938; Bruce Stave, *The New Deal and the Last Hurrah: Pittsburgh Machine Politics* (Pittsburgh, PA: Pittsburgh University Press, 1970).
14. Arthur Krock, 'Did the Negro Revolt?' *Opportunity* 11 (Jan. 1933): p. 19; 'They Stand Out from the Crowd', *Literary Digest*, 8 Dec. 1934, pp. 90–1; Harvard Sitkoff, *A New Deal for Blacks: The Emergence of Civil Rights as a National Issue: The Depression Decade* (New York: Oxford University Press, 1978), pp. 88–90.
15. Kristi Andersen, *The Creation of a Democratic Majority, 1928–1936* (Chicago, IL: University of Chicago Press, 1979), esp. pp. 33–8. For turnout data, see Michael McDonald's calculations for eligible voters in 'National General Election VEP Turnout Rates, 1789 to the Present', *United States Election Project*, http://www.electproject.org/national-1789-present, accessed 14 Mar. 2022.
16. One of the GOP Senate gains resulted from a special election in Oregon, where a Democrat had been appointed temporarily to fill a seat held by a Republican.
17. James Farley, *Jim Farley's Story* (New York: McGraw-Hill, 1948), p. 148; transcript, press conference no. 499, 11 Nov. 1938, Franklin D. Roosevelt Library, Hyde Park, NY [hereafter FDRL], http://www.fdrlibrary.marist.edu/_resources/images/pc/pc0072.pdf, accessed 14 Mar. 2022.
18. See the reports to Farley from state party chairmen and other officials in Official File [OF] 300 and Democratic National Committee papers, both in FDRL.
19. RNC, 'Republican Gains in the 1938 Elections', Dec. 1938, reel 1, *Papers of the National Republican Party,* II: *Reports and Memoranda of the Research Division of the Headquarters of the Republican National Committee, 1938–1980* (Bethesda, MD: University Publications of America, 1986); Milton Plesur, 'The Republican Congressional Comeback of 1938', *Journal of Politics* 24 (1962): pp. 525–62.
20. Indiana Democratic State Committee, 'Result of the Indiana Elections, 1938', undated, and Joseph Suelzer to James Farley, 22 Dec.1938, OF 300, box 42, FDRL.
21. Richard Norton Smith, *Thomas E. Dewey and His Times* (New York: Simon & Schuster, 1982), pp. 265–74; Mason, *Republican Party*, pp. 76–7.

22. Ira Katznelson, *Fear Itself: The New Deal and the Origins of Our Time* (New York: Norton, 2013), pp. 151–2; James Patterson, *Congressional Conservatism and the New Deal: The Growth of the Conservative Coalition in Congress, 1933–1939* (Lexington, KY: University Press of Kentucky, 1967), pp. 289–90.
23. Susan Dunn, *Roosevelt's Purge: How FDR Fought to Change the Democratic Party* (Cambridge, MA: Belknap Press, 2010), pp. 81–92 (quotation at p. 82).
24. Bailey to Byrd, 25 Sept. 1937, in Patterson, *Congressional Conservatism*, p. 191.
25. James MacGregor Burns, *Roosevelt: The Lion and the Fox* (New York: Harcourt, Brace, 1956), pp. 376–80; Patterson, *Congressional Conservatism*, pp. 261–87; Sean Savage, *Roosevelt the Party Leader, 1932–1945* (Lexington, KY: University Press of Kentucky, 1991), pp. 129–58.
26. Roosevelt, 'Address at the Jackson Day Dinner, Washington, DC', 8 Jan. 1938, APP, https://www.presidency.ucsb.edu/node/209617, accessed 14 Mar. 2022. See, too, Dunn, *Roosevelt's Purge*, pp. 94–102.
27. Claude Pepper, *Pepper: Eyewitness to a Century* (New York: Harcourt Brace Jovanovich, 1987), pp. 52–73 (quotation at p. 66); Roosevelt to Arthur Murray, 13 May 1938, *FDR:HPL*, II, p. 781; Savage, *Roosevelt the Party Leader*, pp. 133–4.
28. Dunn, *Roosevelt's Purge*, pp. 114–19 (quotation at p. 117).
29. Roosevelt, 'Fireside Chat', 24 June 1938, APP, https://www.presidency.ucsb.edu/node/208978, accessed 14 Mar. 2022.
30. Dunn, *Roosevelt's Purge*, pp. 120–46.
31. Felix Belair, 'Not Interfering', *New York Times*, 9 July 1938, p. 1; Savage, *Roosevelt the Party Leader*, pp. 138–43.
32. Patterson, *Congressional Conservatism*, pp. 279–85; Dunn, *Roosevelt's Purge*, pp. 152–201.
33. 'After the "Purge" at Home', *New Republic*, 19 Oct. 1938, p. 292.
34. Roosevelt, 'Address at University of North Carolina, Chapel Hill, North Carolina', 5 Dec. 1938, APP, https://www.presidency.ucsb.edu/node/209376, accessed 14 Mar. 2022.
35. Quoted in Bruce Schulman, *From Cotton Belt to Sunbelt: Federal Policy, Economic Development, and the Transformation of the South, 1938–1980* (New York: Oxford University Press, 1991), p. 53.
36. Roosevelt to Josephus Daniels, 14 Nov. 1938, *FDR:HPL*, II, p. 827.

5

The Domestic Politics of War: Franklin D. Roosevelt and the 1942 Midterm Elections

Andrew Johnstone

At a 30 October 1942 press conference, President Franklin Roosevelt issued a brief statement on the following week's midterm elections. Expressing his hope that all Americans would go out and vote on 3 November, he stated that 'we are engaged in an all-out war to keep democracy alive. Democracy survives through the courage, fortitude and wisdom of many generations of fighting Americans. And that includes using not only bullets but also ballots.'[1] Despite the ongoing nature of World War II, midterm elections continued as usual. Elections had taken place during previous American wars, and it was important that they took place during this war, a war being fought in the name of democracy against the forces of fascist dictatorships.

Yet, despite the unusual wartime nature of the 1942 midterms, these elections have been largely overlooked. Historian Sean Savage notes that not enough has been written on the 1942 elections. In one of the few books to examine the significance of midterm elections, government scholar Andrew Busch deems 1942 a 'normal midterm' largely because the party of the president saw losses in Congress, though that party did not go on to lose the White House in the next presidential election. Studies of the war and of the Roosevelt years tend to come to similar conclusions. Robert Dallek describes the outcome as 'typical of a midterm election'. James MacGregor Burns, paying more attention to the elections than most, still describes it as 'a typical off-year congressional election, hardly influenced by the great issues of war and peace'.[2]

However, World War II significantly affected the 1942 midterms. In fact, the war defined the elections. The outcome of the elections may be seen as 'normal' – congressional losses for the party of the presidency – but the context and the conduct certainly cannot be seen as that of a normal midterm. An examination of that context highlights the importance of contingency in 1942. The idea of a 'normal midterm' suggests that Democratic losses were inevitable in 1942, but this was not the case. The specific nature of the war and the home front clearly affected the election results. Polls suggest that, had the elections come a few months earlier, the results could have been very different. Similarly, had the elections come just a few weeks – or even days – later, then the results could have been far better for the Democrats.

At first glance, the 1942 results may look unsurprising. A Republican resurgence reduced the Democratic majorities in both the House and Senate. Democrats lost seven Senators to leave them with fifty-seven; the Republicans gained eight to bring them up to thirty-eight. In the House, the Democratic majority was slashed from ninety-one to thirteen, leaving them with 222 seats compared to the 209 held by Republicans. Those losses were mostly among northern liberal Democrats rather than southern conservative ones, which broadly ensured the incoming 78th Congress became more conservative than its predecessor. Yet the contingent nature of the midterms results is evident in polls taken throughout 1942. Polls created to track trends ahead of the elections suggested that had the midterms been held earlier in the year, they would have seen a much more successful outcome for the Democrats. Gallup polls showed that the Democrats would have made significant gains of approximately thirty-eight seats in the House had the elections been held in early May. Those numbers shrank over the summer to an increase of ten seats by mid-June, and while the projected gain was just eight by mid-August, it was still a gain. By the end of September, polls predicted that Republican gains of twenty-one seats were likely in November, and the final increase was even greater. Even allowing for the relatively primitive nature of polling at this time, the downward trend through the summer was clear.[3]

A number of reasons account for this decline in support for the Democrats, all of which are directly connected to the war. These include dissatisfaction with the war both at home and abroad, Franklin Roosevelt's limited political interaction with the campaign, and low voter turnout. While other long-term and local factors existed, the war was the most significant influence on the elections. As 1942 progressed, Americans became increasingly unhappy with the impact of government on the home front. At the same time, they had no significant advances to celebrate on the battlefield. Popular satisfaction in both of these areas might have led to greater support for the party in control of the executive branch. Yet for a number of reasons, Roosevelt chose to play a very limited role in the campaign, which certainly did not help the Democratic performance. The lack of a clear motivation to vote Democratic, combined with wartime restrictions, also led to low turnout at the polls.

While the election results were a Democratic disappointment, the aftermath had a mixed effect on Roosevelt's mandate. The midterms did not adversely affect Roosevelt's foreign policy mandate. In addition to the public's existing faith in the president as commander in chief, the following two years saw the development of an increasingly bipartisan consensus on an internationalist foreign policy. The elections affected Roosevelt more significantly in the realm of domestic politics. As a result of divisions within his own party, Roosevelt subsequently faced an increasingly conservative congressional coalition that moved to roll back the New Deal. Public dissatisfaction with the war in a brief window of late 1942 therefore had a lasting impact on domestic politics.

The war at home

It was clear in the aftermath of the midterms that the results were largely due to popular dissatisfaction with the war at home. As is so often the case in American politics, domestic issues and the economy were paramount, but the war's particular effect on the home front economy was crucial. In George Gallup's pre-election analysis, the downward trend in Democratic support through 1942 reflected 'a feeling of dissatisfaction among many voters with the manner in which the war effort is being administered'. A later Gallup survey from December 1942 listed the public's main complaints with the government's handling of the war: excessive bureaucracy, a sense that rationing should have started earlier, a belief that the draft and manpower requirements had taken too many working men away from farms rather than using unemployed men, and frustration with a general lack of preparedness. Overall, surveys suggested the Roosevelt administration's policies were perceived to be hindering rather than helping the ordinary American's economic advancement, and not doing enough to drive the war effort.[4]

Editorials in the press reinforced this critical view of the administration. Many newspapers reported the results as a major blow for Roosevelt and his government. An Office of War Information Intelligence Report noted that most editorial writers saw the election results as 'a rebuke to the Administration'. It noted that the *Detroit News* described the results as 'a protest against stumbling and fumbling'. The conservative Scripps-Howard papers were quoted as saying that the American people were protesting against the 'inefficient, ankle-deep conduct of the war'. More specifically, the way the government dealt with the wartime economy was a consistent bone of contention.[5]

In addition to Gallup polls and press reports, a more selective and qualitative survey of Democratic candidates confirmed that these wartime factors directly affected the election results. In the aftermath of the elections, the Democratic National Committee (DNC) asked its candidates why they believed the results had gone so badly. The responses covered much the same ground as the Gallup survey. DNC secretary Edwin Pauley identified eighteen different reasons, of which four appeared in more than a third of the 192 individual responses: resentment of the conduct of the war, the resentment of farmers, the resentment of bureaucracy, and the resentment of the Office of Price Administration (OPA), and particularly its head, Leon Henderson. More than half of the congressmen surveyed blamed the OPA in some part for the midterm results.[6]

Described as the 'most universal and serious complaint of all', the OPA was the government agency responsible for fixing prices and introducing rationing. However, the criticisms were less about the principle of rationing and were more personally directed at veteran New Dealer Henderson, the OPA, and its methods. Pauley wrote that the all-powerful Henderson 'stood like a tower' among the complaints, 'like Satan in *Paradise Lost*'. One Congressman blamed the Democratic setbacks on Henderson's 'unreasonable, arbitrary and dictatorial conduct'. Democrats criticised Henderson for being both too partisan and insufficiently partisan, too bureaucratic, and too eager to implement rationing and fix prices. These issues upset Americans who suffered as a result of specific policies such as price fixing, but also those more ideologically opposed to government restrictions. As one congressman put it, 'he wants us to get into a hair shirt not because all the wool and cotton shirts are gone but because it will be good for us to be uncomfortable as hell in a hair shirt. How much farther does he have to go to be a complete convert to the authoritarianism of Mr. Hitler?'[7]

Farmers were especially frustrated by the government's economic management, with some degree of justification. Having been badly affected through the 1930s by the Great Depression, many farmers felt that the government was neglecting their interests once more in favour of urban manufacturing jobs. They directed their ire at Congress as well as numerous parts of the executive branch's war bureaucracy, from the OPA to Roosevelt himself. Wanting more money for their produce, farmers were particularly unsettled by Roosevelt's September Fireside Chat that urged a ceiling on previously exempt farm prices. At the same time, farmers watched as urban wages slowly rose, which incentivised manpower to move from rural to urban areas. Of course, this frustration ignored the government's efforts to stabilise wages, as well as its willingness to subsidise agricultural goods.[8]

However, farmers were not the only sector of society that felt aggrieved by government policy. Just as farmers resented urban labour, Sean Savage suggests that organised labour felt Roosevelt's administration was 'too deferential to big business', which may have contributed to the low turnout from urban voters expected to support Democrats.[9] The uneven impact of the war economy in 1942 left many Americans feeling that the war effort was hitting them harder than other sectors of society, and in a managed economy they blamed Roosevelt's policies and Democratic lawmakers for the injustice. While the war ultimately transformed the American economy and brought it out of the Great Depression, that transformation was still in process in 1942. The midterm backlash against Roosevelt's wartime economic policies was in large part because the economy had not yet been saved by the war.

In addition to pitting Americans against each other economically, the dislocation and disruption of the war highlighted social issues. Racial issues caused significant problems for the Democratic Party, especially in the solidly Democratic South where Jim Crow laws ensured segregation remained in place. Arkansas Congressman William F. Norrell blamed 'agitation for social equality against the races' for the midterm results. Georgia representative Stephen Pace specifically blamed First Lady Eleanor Roosevelt – known for her civil rights activism – for trying to arouse African Americans and 'compel their admittance into places where they are not wanted'. Comments from local southern party officials the following year reinforced this negative view of the party's approach to racial issues and of Eleanor Roosevelt in particular. Although the government introduced very few wartime policies on the specific issue of race relations, initiatives such as Executive Order 8802 (which prohibited discrimination in the employment of workers in defence industries) created suspicion among the party's southern white base about the government's racial policies that had lasting significance for the party. In contrast, the party's liberal supporters of equal rights felt the party was not doing enough for African Americans. New York's Joseph Gavagan, who had fought hard for anti-lynching legislation, argued that one of the reasons for the national defeats was 'a complete lack of confidence' on the part of African Americans that they were 'receiving a fair deal from the administration'.[10]

Democrats also recognised that the overly bureaucratic nature of wartime government was responsible for the election setbacks. The public resented not only the arrogance of power displayed by officials such as Henderson but also the excessive paperwork required by agencies like the OPA. In a broader sense, some survey responses suggested a sense of growing frustration with the increased power of the executive branch, which came under even greater criticism than it had in the New Deal years.[11] Indeed, a longer-term view of the 1942 midterms might suggest that the Republican gains were a result of growing dissatisfaction with almost a decade of New Deal policies. A poll from December suggested that the public thought Republican gains were primarily due to dissatisfaction with the Roosevelt administration's dominance of politics and with a vague 'New Dealism'. Yet while New Deal policies clearly came under attack, the explosion of wartime bureaucracy dwarfed that of the New Deal and brought with it specific economic issues and complaints that went beyond critiques of 'big government'.[12]

Democratic candidates advanced numerous other home front–related reasons to explain why the party had suffered losses beyond the OPA, dissatisfied farmers, and excessive bureaucracy. Examples included unhappiness with the teenage draft, a hostile anti-Democratic press, and continued midwestern opposition to the war (notably from Americans of German heritage). While some anti–New Deal complaints could clearly be traced back to the pre-war years, almost all of the concerns related to the immediate transformations of society and the economy brought about by the war. Some concerns were quite specific to politicians – such as complaints that Democrats felt overly constrained by the 1939 Hatch Act's restrictions on political campaigning by federal employees – but most were also concerns of the general public.[13] Yet popular dissatisfaction with the war did not just relate to domestic matters, as polls also revealed a lack of satisfaction with the military conduct of the war.

The war abroad

Indeed, the limited progress with the war hurt the Democrats in the midterms. Both public polls and analysis from politicians suggest that a lack of war progress played a key part in voter dissatisfaction, though it was a less significant factor than domestic issues (perhaps unsurprisingly given the more local nature of midterm elections). Public confidence in Roosevelt was high, primarily as a result of his war leadership. A *Fortune* survey conducted by Elmo Roper in 1943 revealed that 70.4 per cent of Americans believed Roosevelt was doing a good job as a war leader, while only 56.2 per cent thought he was doing a good job dealing with problems at home. Yet despite high satisfaction with their commander-in-chief, limited success on the battlefield led to 'impatience of the American people, because we had not made the progress in the prosecution of the war prior to the election that they felt should have been made'.[14]

Neither theatre of war offered significant signs of American progress. Progress against Japan in the Pacific was slow. The Battle of Midway in June had largely halted Japanese advances, but the military had not yet launched a successful counteroffensive. The war in Europe offered even fewer reasons for optimism. By October 1942, the Axis powers controlled much of Europe, having pushed deep into the Soviet Union, yet after almost eleven months at war American soldiers were still not involved in combat. The limited success in both areas was reason for Democratic voters to stay at home. The significance of Europe here is more speculative but also more significant for the potential morale boost it offered. Progress in the European theatre would have provided a reason to galvanise voters, a fact made all the more clear when, just five days after the elections, the North African landings took place (Operation Torch) and American troops finally began the fight against Germany and Italy in earnest.

Roosevelt would have loved Operation Torch to be a week earlier, but he admirably refused to play politics with a military decision. When asked by the press on 10 November why the date of the North African landing was put after the election, the president stated that the date was decided without consideration for the election. Roosevelt did not mention that General Dwight Eisenhower had selected the date back in September. Instead, he joked that Economic Stabilization Director James Byrnes had asked why the president could not have moved the election back a week; after all, he had moved Thanksgiving forward a week that year. The exchange highlighted the president's unwillingness to intervene and his acknowledgement that, while the decision was clearly unfortunate for domestic political reasons, it was one for the military rather than the Democratic National Committee.[15]

In the immediate aftermath of Operation Torch, the damaging political implications of the delay were all too clear to Democratic candidates who strongly believed that the timing of Torch had a negative effect on the election. Congressman Pete Jarman of Alabama blamed the election results on the fact that 'no victory had occurred in the war', even if none had been likely up to that point. 'Had the election occurred the week after the invasion of North Africa,' Jarman added, 'we would have twenty-five Democratic Congressmen with us hereafter who will not be here.' Florida's Joe Hendricks was even more forceful, arguing that, if the North Africa campaign had begun a week before the election, 'the Republicans would not have gained more than ten seats in the House'. Instead, 'people were just beginning to feel the sacrifices and had not yet had anything to show results'. The *New Republic* suggested that 'the returns might not have been completely reversed, but it is hard to believe that the President's supporters would not have shown more strength'.[16]

The *New Republic* also criticised those who accused the president of playing politics with the war, countering that it was in fact those critics who were playing politics with the war by raising the issue in the first place. The magazine noted that Roosevelt could have moved the operation ahead, but he did not. Instead, 'he allowed military considerations to dictate the schedule, without thought of the elections. And he allowed no hint of the coming offensive to be noised about in the campaign.' Michigan Representative John Dingell agreed that, if the North Africa campaign had started before the election, then the government would have been criticised for timing them accordingly but the Democrats would have 'enjoyed another landslide as I see it'. By taking the correct military decision, Roosevelt and the Democrats lacked a significant military engagement in the European theatre that had the potential to raise morale. As House chief assistant whip Thomas Ford put it, 'we were too noble to start a second front before election [*sic*]. So we got kicked in the pants.'[17]

In addition to frustration that the fighting against Germany had not yet begun, the other main complaint about the war strategy as of 3 November 1942 was with the war against Japan. Polls suggested frustration in the Pacific where the war was not progressing as quickly as expected. The survey of congressional candidates revealed 'the well established [*sic*] conviction that America could "lick Japan with one hand tied" but wasn't doing it'. Just as the North Africa campaign came too late for the election, so too did the naval victory at Guadalcanal in the Solomon Islands the following week. The drawn-out nature of the island-hopping Pacific campaign did not lend itself to dramatic quick victories. As Roosevelt himself explicitly acknowledged in his September Fireside Chat, even the Battle for Midway felt more like the defeat of a Japanese offensive than a rollback of Japanese advances, no matter how significant that battle turned out to be in the long run.[18] As of election day, the end of the war in both theatres looked a very long way away.

Roosevelt's non-campaign

The president's September Fireside Chat came at a time when many congressional politicians were actively campaigning, but Roosevelt did not join them. Indeed, the president's limited and relatively apolitical campaign also contributed to the Democratic disappointment in 1942. A need to prioritise wartime unity over partisanship partly inspired Roosevelt's decision to play a limited role in the campaign. But Roosevelt also drew historical lessons from two previous sets of midterms: those of 1918 and 1938. By refusing to make the midterms a national issue, Roosevelt avoided the partisanship of the previous world war, when Woodrow Wilson called for a Democratic Congress in 1918. That decision had damaging implications for Wilson's peace-making efforts over the following two years, as a resentful Republican-controlled Congress ultimately rejected membership in the League of Nations. Roosevelt also learned from his own personal experience and the damaging effects of his intervention in the 1938 midterms. Then, as Iwan Morgan explores in the previous chapter, his mostly unsuccessful attempts to create a more liberal party by working against the re-election of conservative Democrats led to reduced majorities as well as accusations of dictatorship that resonated with voters in the era of Hitler and Stalin. But, in 1942, Roosevelt's unwillingness to capitalise on his own popularity affected the success of his party.[19]

As early as February 1942, Roosevelt made it clear he had learned from Wilson's mistake in the aftermath of an address from DNC Chairman Edward J. Flynn. In a highly partisan statement, Flynn claimed that 'no misfortune except a major military defeat could befall this country to the extent involved in the election of a Congress hostile to the President.' Defusing any potential backlash, the president responded that 'when a country is at war we want Congressmen, regardless of party – get that – to back up the Government of the United States, and who have a record of backing up the Government of the United States in an emergency, regardless of party.' As the year progressed, some of the anti-Roosevelt press suggested that the president would take advantage of the war to cancel the elections. Of course, he did no such thing and largely went out of his way to avoid politicising the elections.[20]

Yet the hands-off approach failed. Commentators subsequently criticised Roosevelt for taking an apolitical strategy. As historian James MacGregor Burns observes, one commentator 'noted acidly that Wilson had called for a Democratic Congress in 1918 and lost seats in the House and Senate: Roosevelt had not called for anything and lost twice as many'. The *New Republic* blamed the party and its leader. The progressive journal criticised the Democratic National Committee for its view that 'politics was improper in wartime'. Yet it criticised the president even more than the DNC, with Roosevelt blamed for inaction and learning the wrong lesson from 1918. The journal urged Roosevelt to 'realise that political management is as important as the management of the war, and as much a part of our war effort'. It also blamed White House assistant David K. Niles for bungling various political assignments, notably in Roosevelt's home state of New York.[21]

New York was one of only two states where Roosevelt openly intervened by endorsing candidates, though his efforts were unsuccessful in both New York and Nebraska. In New York, Roosevelt made some effort to dislodge his home representative and noted political adversary, Republican Hamilton Fish III. The president worked with local leaders to find a candidate who might appeal to anti-Fish Republicans, settling on Judge Ferdinand A. Hoyt. Yet despite his pre–Pearl Harbor non-interventionism, Fish's continued popularity saw him re-elected for the eleventh time.[22] Roosevelt put more effort into the New York gubernatorial race, where he initially supported Senator James Mead in the Democratic primary over former Attorney General John Bennett, who had the support of former DNC Chairman James Farley. In the absence of a third compromise candidate, Roosevelt eventually, if reluctantly, supported Bennett. In a 23 October telegram subsequently released to the press, Roosevelt called Bennett 'the best qualified of all the candidates for the Governorship'. However, with the field narrowed down to Bennett, Republican Thomas E. Dewey, the American Labor candidate Dean Alfange, and fringe communist and socialist candidates, this was relatively faint praise. Dewey won with ease.[23]

In Nebraska, Roosevelt came out in support of veteran progressive Senator George Norris. Norris, a former Republican, was a supporter of the New Deal and had served since 1936 as an Independent. In October, Roosevelt publicly offered his support to Norris, describing him as 'one of the major prophets of America' whose candidacy 'transcends State and party lines'. Claiming to have followed a rule of non-participation in state elections (and deliberately ignoring his own actions in 1938), Roosevelt described his endorsement of Norris as a 'magnificently justified exception'. The effort was unsuccessful, as Norris lost to Republican Kenneth Wherry. Roosevelt had to be selective about intervening, especially after 1938, but his few interventions must have been especially frustrating for those who unsuccessfully sought the president's support. It was hypocritical of the White House to tell party activists such as those who sought to replace Congressman Arthur Mitchell in Illinois that 'the president does not take part in local primaries or elections'.[24]

A broader national campaign from the president that focused on the positive aspects of the war effort might have had an effect.

Yet when Roosevelt had an opportunity to appear presidential on the eve of the election, he downplayed it. In the latter half of September, FDR took a two-week nationwide inspection trip of military establishments. The 8,754-mile lap of the country took in numerous manufacturing facilities, from Detroit to Seattle, and from San Diego to New Orleans. It was an ideal opportunity to publicise the war effort, but Roosevelt rejected it. Three news agency reporters who joined him were not allowed to file reports until their return to Washington. When asked near the end of the trip about the potential to politicise it, Roosevelt highlighted that he had not seen 'any candidate for office, any state chairman or national committeemen. I've seen governors, some candidates for re-election and some not, just about as many Republicans as Democrats.' When told that would disappoint people, he agreed. 'It will not only disappoint but shock them.' A poll conducted for the White House a week later suggested the public overwhelmingly agreed that Roosevelt was correct to keep the tour secret. Nevertheless, it was a missed opportunity to appear presidential and boost morale at a time when the war effort appeared to be drifting.[25]

Fortunately for Roosevelt, the Republican Party lacked a strong national figurehead in the autumn of 1942. Former presidential candidate Wendell Willkie, to the extent anyone still saw him as a party leader or even a genuine Republican, was also on a tour. He spent the campaign period on a forty-nine-day trip across the globe that resulted in his 1943 bestseller *One World*. Roosevelt approved Willkie's trip as a diplomatic and fact-finding opportunity, though it had the added advantage of removing him from the political arena at home. Both parties therefore lacked strong individual leadership. While unsurprising for midterm elections, this was a particular disadvantage to the Democrats who were unable to build upon Roosevelt's broad personal popularity. The lack of leadership also left Democratic candidates reliant on local issues. Missouri representative C. Jasper Bell complained that no national issues had been raised 'as a blanket under which all local campaigns could be made'. The Republicans, in contrast, could rely on popular frustration with the state of the war at home and abroad.[26]

It is, of course, impossible to know what might have happened had Roosevelt campaigned harder for the Democratic Party in 1942. In his 6 November press conference, Roosevelt replied 'I don't know' when asked whether the results would have been the same had he taken part in the campaign. It is possible that a backlash might have occurred as in 1918. It is also possible that by simply being seen to act in a presidential manner as a national leader – as in the autumn of 1940, when he made few overt campaign speeches but largely focused his rhetoric on Hitler rather than Wendell Willkie – that Roosevelt could have brought out the Democratic vote more effectively. Yet his campaigning was limited and he refused to capitalise on the inspection tour. In his brief message just four days before the election, Roosevelt did not urge the public to vote for particular candidates, or even to vote Democratic – he simply urged the public to get out and vote. Unfortunately for him, as historian George McJimsey writes, 'Roosevelt's nonpartisanship was an invitation to political apathy', as many Democrats did not listen and did not vote.[27]

Turnout

In the absence of leadership from Roosevelt, relief on the home front, or success on the battlefield, the 1942 election saw an apathetic electorate and a low turnout. Just 33.9 per cent of Americans voted, around twenty-eight million out of an eligible eighty million. That was eight million fewer voters than the 1938 midterms, and twenty-two million fewer voters than the 1940 election.[28] The low turnout in 1942 helps explain the midterm losses, and the White House took it seriously when examining where the campaign went wrong. Crucially, the turnout had a far more damaging effect on the Democratic Party. Polling from early 1943 suggested that Democrats had been less likely to turn out in November 1942 than Republicans. Of those polled who considered themselves Democrats, only 46 per cent voted Democrat, while 47 per cent did not vote. In contrast, of those who saw themselves as Republicans, 62 per cent voted Republican while only 34 per cent did not vote. Of the Willkie voters from 1940, 67 per cent voted Republican in 1942 with just

25 per cent not voting. In contrast, of the Roosevelt voters from 1940, just 48 per cent voted Democrat, while 36 per cent did not vote and 11 per cent voted Republican. Independents were also more likely to vote Republican.[29]

The larger the drop in turnout, the greater the Republican gain. Based on this fact, polling specialist Hadley Cantril concluded that the vote closely followed party lines, and that the Democratic defeats were 'simply because more traditional Republicans went to the polls'. In contrast, he concluded that the war, the domestic war effort, and the president and his polices had 'little or no influence' on the vote. Another polling expert, George Gallup, predicted a low turnout as early as July, arguing that the Democrats would lose more votes as a result of their younger demographics. Barriers to voting, all of which related to dislocation brought about by war, certainly affected the Democratic turnout. Some recently migrated Americans did not fit residency requirements to vote in their new states. Many young men were now fighting overseas, and not all were able to use absentee ballots. Others were unwilling or unable to escape work commitments. Yet barriers alone cannot explain the low turnout.[30]

The question that remains is why the Democratic turnout suffered so much more than that of Republican voters. While the *New Republic* argued that 'one central fact explains most of the election defeats – the great liberal rank and file of the population of the cities just didn't vote', it acknowledged that the blame for failing to inspire the voting public lay primarily with Roosevelt and the Democratic Party. C. Jasper Bell blamed voter lethargy on the 'general dissatisfaction' with the progress of the war and the handling of the war programme. Dissatisfaction with Democratic government acted as a disincentive to vote for its continuation. The government did not help itself by failing to act upon the predicted low turnout. DNC member David L. Lawrence wrote to the White House in September urging Roosevelt to deliver a Fireside Chat that encouraged people to vote regardless of affiliation, though all that eventually materialised was Roosevelt's brief statement immediately before the election. Lawrence also pressed the president to contact labour leaders Philip Murray and William Green in order to mobilise and deliver the labour vote. Roosevelt urged employers and government officials to allow time for workers to go and vote, but his appeal failed.[31]

Voter apathy was also the result of broader frustration with the war. Those frustrations peaked at a very specific point in time where the domestic sacrifices of war were not yet seen to make a difference to its prosecution. As a result, the turnout was a critical comment on the Democratic Party more than a political turn to the right. Historian Brian Waddell argues that the election was 'more an expression of apathy and of barriers to voting by displaced workers than the result of an electoral shift to the Republican party'.[32] Yet given the increasingly conservative face of the new Congress, and the rapidly evolving nature of the wartime economy and the war itself, the overall outcome was a clear challenge to the president.

Mandate

The immediate impact of the elections on Roosevelt's mandate was unclear. A small minority of Democratic voices argued that the midterms were not a significant setback. After all, they were not a defeat, with Democrats retaining majorities in both chambers of Congress. A letter to Roosevelt from Chicago attorney David Jackson highlighted the odd sense of Republican happiness and Democratic disappointment in the face of the actual results: 'I always supposed that the landslide meant a victory for the side supposed to be the beneficiary of the landslide. No one, for instance, would claim that the Detroit Lions enjoyed an overwhelming victory yesterday over the Washington Redskins when the score was 15 to 3 for the Redskins.' Of course, this optimistic assessment ignored the trend over time and the reduced majorities. Still, given the results, it was not entirely clear how the incoming Congress would move forward. Immediately after the elections, the Office of War Information noted caution among the conservative press regarding domestic issues. The *Providence Journal* said, 'as long as the war lasts, the minority members would be well advised to fight Roosevelt less and Hitler more'. Roosevelt's public response to the election results was itself cautious. In a press conference on 6 November, when asked whether his attitude to Congress had changed given the increasingly close majority, he replied, 'Why should it? I assume that the Congress of the United States is in favour of winning this war, just as the President is.'[33]

Roosevelt was correct about the war, but the implications of the midterms for domestic politics were significant. The 78th Congress ultimately worked against Roosevelt on many domestic issues. Not only did the election results ensure an atmosphere hostile to further reform, the new Congress felt emboldened to start rolling back the existing New Deal. In 1943, Congress passed the Smith–Connally Act (which limited the power of organised labour) over Roosevelt's veto, abolished the National Resources Planning Board, and dramatically pared down the Farm Security Administration and Rural Electrification Administration following budget cuts. In 1944, Congress overrode Roosevelt's veto of the Revenue Act. Popular New Deal agencies such as the National Youth Administration, the Civilian Conservation Corps, and the Works Progress Administration expired, though the increase in wartime employment made them largely redundant. Crucially, the southern conservative bloc of Democrats gained in relative importance. Southern Democrats, who had no desire for further reform, held 120 out of 222 seats in the House, and twenty-nine out of fifty-seven in the Senate. Given how often the conservatives of both parties came together, historian William O'Neill describes the 78th Congress as 'in all but name, a Republican Congress'. In terms of the bigger structural picture, any attempt at further Democratic Party realignment on ideological grounds (such as in 1938) was put on indefinite hold as a result of the war.[34]

The president did not completely give up on the reformist rhetoric, even though he had not introduced any significant reforms since 1938. His 1943 State of the Union address made it clear he had no intention of giving up on securing freedom from want for the American people. He argued the young people of the nation wanted 'assurance against the evils of all major economic hazards – assurance that will extend from the cradle to the grave. And this great government must provide this assurance.' Roosevelt's 1944 State of the Union went even further.

That address, which called for a Second Bill of Rights to ensure security and prosperity for all, was arguably the most radical speech of Roosevelt's political career. However, it became increasingly difficult for Roosevelt to achieve much in the area of reform. Roosevelt conceded in December 1943 that 'Dr. New Deal' had been replaced by 'Dr. Win-the-War'. A notable exception was the GI Bill of 1944. Still, it is clear that the midterm losses, alongside prioritising the war, affected Roosevelt's reforming vision and reduced his ability to be Dr New Deal.[35]

The midterms did not have the same negative impact on Roosevelt's foreign policy mandate. Of course, foreign policy was not really an election issue in 1942, as few questioned Roosevelt's war strategy as commander in chief. After the elections, Congress increasingly aligned with Roosevelt on the future of the nation's foreign policy. Those two years saw the creation of an increasingly bipartisan consensus on an internationalist foreign policy. Yet the coming together of both parties behind a bipartisan, global-facing, internationalist foreign policy was not inevitable. True, the internationalist/non-interventionist divide prior to the Pearl Harbor attack did not strictly follow party lines. But in late 1941, the America First Committee was investigating the possibility of running independent non-interventionist candidates in the 1942 midterms. Less than a year before the midterms, the genuine likelihood of a new third party running on foreign policy issues existed (or, more likely, the prospect of the America First Committee supporting non-interventionist candidates from either party).[36] Even after the United States entered the war and the public united behind the war effort, the nation's future foreign policy was unclear. By 1944, everything had changed.

The crucial issue was how the United States would engage with the world after the war. Post-war planning had already begun in the State Department, but in 1943 both parties showed their support for an internationalist post-war policy in Congress despite the fact that most pre-war non-interventionists had retained their seats in the midterms. In March, four senators created the bipartisan B2H2 resolution (named for its sponsors, Republicans Joseph Ball and Harold Burton and Democrats Carl

Hatch and Lister Hill). The resolution called for an international organisation to keep the peace, including the United States, to be created while the war was still ongoing. It passed by a vote of 85–5. A similar resolution in the House initiated by Democratic representative J. William Fulbright passed by 360–29, supported by 98 per cent of Democrats and 87 per cent of Republicans.[37] In many ways, these were even more forceful statements about the post-war world than those emerging from a cautious White House and State Department. The bipartisan support for an international organisation, which could by no means have been imagined in 1941, made it much easier for Roosevelt to move forward with post-war planning in 1943 and 1944.

Conclusion

In a generous post-election assessment, Democratic Pennsylvania Congressman J. Buell Snyder argued that, given the wartime context, the results represented Democratic success rather than setback. 'Fifty years from now, historians will write that it was Roosevelt's greatest victory in 1942.' Despite the challenges on the home front, the American people showed 'absolute confidence in the Administration's policy' and re-elected a majority in both houses of Congress.[38] This assessment has not aged well. The Democrats did not win a great victory. Instead, they clung to reduced majorities in the face of enormous wartime challenges that had not been resolved in the eleven months following the attack on Pearl Harbor. Those challenges of war and economic mobilisation defined the 1942 midterm elections.

Given those challenges, the 1942 midterms were anything but normal, even ignoring the trivial fact that they were the only midterm to ever occur during a president's third term. The war had too great an effect on American society to discount. The government's handling of the wartime economy was the most significant factor affecting the Democratic Party in the midterms. The heavy-handed if necessarily centralised control of the economy left many Americans looking for change by November 1942. Additionally, the Democrats failed to make a strong case to win voters. The lack of success on the battlefield left the party without a good news story, and Roosevelt chose not to make a national argument for voting Democratic. Given the economic frustration and the lack of a positive reason to vote Democratic, many regular party voters stayed at home.

Yet this outcome was not inevitable. The elections captured public opinion at a specific wartime moment in early November. Had the elections come a few months earlier, or a few days later, it could have gone very differently. While the midterms might not have had a dramatic effect on Roosevelt's foreign policy plans, the effect on domestic politics was more significant. Congress took advantage of the public's wartime frustration to put an end to further reform. While it is unlikely that a better outcome for the Democrats would have led to a substantial new era of reform, the results led to the opposite, and accelerated the rollback of the New Deal.

Notes

I am extremely grateful to Heather Dichter, Andy Johns, and Kelly Shannon for their constructive criticism on an early draft of this chapter. Thanks also to all those who attended the original conference in Edinburgh for their feedback and suggestions.

1. Franklin D. Roosevelt, *Complete Presidential Press Conferences of Franklin D. Roosevelt*, vol. 20, 1942 (New York: Da Capo Press, 1972), pp. 185–6.
2. Sean J. Savage, 'The 1936–1944 Campaigns', in William D. Pederson, ed., *A Companion to Franklin D. Roosevelt* (Malden, MA: Wiley-Blackwell, 2011), p. 106; Andrew E. Busch, *Horses in Midstream: U.S. Midterm Elections and their Consequences* (Pittsburgh, PA: University of Pittsburgh Press, 1999), p. 157; Robert Dallek, *Franklin D. Roosevelt: A Political Life* (London: Allen Lane, 2017), p. 486; James MacGregor Burns, *Roosevelt: The Soldier of Freedom* (New York: Harcourt Brace Jovanovich, 1970), p. 281.
3. Geoffrey Perrett, *Days of Sadness, Years of Triumph: The American People, 1939–1945* (Madison, WI: University of Wisconsin Press, 1973), pp. 247–8: *Washington Post*, 13 May 1942, p. 11; *New York Times*, 21 June 1942, p. 33; *New York Times*, 16 Aug. 1942, p. 40; *New York Times*, 30 Sept. 1942, p. 27.

4. *New Republic*, 21 Sept. 1942, p. 347; Gallup Survey, 15 Dec. 1942, folder 'Public Opinion Polls 1942–44', PSF 157, Franklin Roosevelt Papers [hereafter FDR Papers], Franklin D. Roosevelt Library, Hyde Park, New York [hereafter FDRL].
5. OWI Intelligence Report 49, 13 Nov. 1942, pp. 3–4, PSF 156, folder 'Office of War Information – Survey of Intelligence – Nov. 1942', FDR Papers, FDRL.
6. Pauley to Roosevelt, 12 Dec. 1942, folder 'Mayock Survey after Election 1942', box 566, Democratic Party National Committee Papers [hereafter DNC Papers], FDRL.
7. Quotations in Pauley to Roosevelt, 12 Dec. 1942, folder 'Mayock Survey after Election 1942', box 566, DNC Papers, FDRL.
8. Pauley to Roosevelt, 12 December 1942, folder 'Mayock Survey after Election 1942', box 566, DNC Papers, FDRL; Samuel I. Rosenman, ed., *The Public Papers and Addresses of Franklin D. Roosevelt, 1942* (New York: Harper & Brothers, 1950), pp. 368–77; David Kennedy, *Freedom from Fear: The American People in Depression and War, 1929–1945* (Oxford: Oxford University Press, 1999), pp. 640–1.
9. Pauley to Roosevelt, 12 Dec. 1942, folder 'Mayock Survey after Election 1942', box 566, DNC Papers, FDRL; Savage 'The 1936–1944 Campaigns', p. 106.
10. Norrell to Pauley, 18 Nov. 1942, folder 'Postmortems Correspondence 1', box 568, DNC Papers, FDRL; Pace to Pauley, 11 Nov. 1942, folder 'Postmortems Correspondence 4', box 568, DNC Papers, FDRL; Undated Comments, folder 'Miscellaneous Comments on Political Situation in 1943', box 569, DNC Papers; Gavagan to Pauley, 19 Nov. 1942, folder 'Postmortems Correspondence 1', box 568, DNC Papers, FDRL. For a collection of essays on the relationship between the war and race, see: Kevin M. Kruse and Stephen Tuck, eds, *Fog of War: The Second World War and the Civil Rights Movement* (Oxford: Oxford University Press, 2012).
11. Pauley to Roosevelt, 12 Dec. 1942, folder 'Mayock Survey after Election 1942', box 566, DNC Papers, FDRL.
12. Hadley Cantril, *Public Opinion, 1935–1946* (Princeton, NJ: Princeton University Press, 1951), p. 937.
13. Pauley to Roosevelt, 12 Dec. 1942, folder 'Mayock Survey after Election 1942', box 566, DNC Papers, FDRL.
14. The Fortune Survey, 3 May 1943, p. 12, folder 'Public Opinion Polls, 1942–44', PSF 157, FDR Papers, FDRL; Oren Harris to Pauley,

14 Nov. 1942, folder 'Postmortems Correspondence 1', Box 568, DNC Papers, FDRL.

15. Rosenman, *Public Papers and Addresses of Franklin D. Roosevelt, 1942*, p. 465; Robert Sherwood, *Roosevelt and Hopkins: An Intimate History* (New York: Harper & Brothers, 1948), p. 630.
16. Jarman to Pauley, 5 Jan.1943, folder 'Postmortems Correspondence 1', box 568, DNC Papers, FDRL; Hendricks to Pauley, 24 Nov. 1942, folder 'Postmortems Correspondence 1', box 568, DNC Papers, FDRL; *New Republic*, 16 Nov. 1942, p. 625.
17. *New Republic*, 16 Nov. 1942, p. 625. Seen in folder 'Postmortems Correspondence 1', box 568, DNC Papers, FDRL; Dingell to Pauley, 2 Dec. 1942, folder 'Postmortems Correspondence 3', box 568, DNC Papers, FDRL; Ford to Pauley, 17 Nov. 1942, folder 'Postmortems Correspondence 2', box 568, DNC Papers, FDRL.
18. Gallup Survey, 15 Dec. 1942, folder Public Opinion Polls 1942–44, PSF 157, FDR Papers, FDRL; Pauley to Roosevelt, 12 Dec. 1942, folder 'Mayock Survey after Election 1942', Box 566, DNC Papers, FDRL; Joe Starnes to Pauley, 25 Nov. 1942, folder 'Postmortems Correspondence 1', box 568, DNC Papers, FDRL; Rosenman, *Public Papers and Addresses of Franklin D. Roosevelt, 1942*, p. 375.
19. On the 1938 midterms, see: Susan Dunn, *Roosevelt's Purge: How FDR Fought to Change the Democratic Party* (Cambridge, MA: The Belknap Press of Harvard University Press, 2012).
20. *New York Times*, 7 Feb. 1942, p. 1; Rosenman, *Public Papers and Addresses of Franklin D. Roosevelt, 1942*, p. 80.
21. Unknown, quoted in Burns, *Roosevelt: The Soldier of Freedom*, p. 281; *New Republic*, 16 Nov. 1942, pp. 627–8. Seen in folder 'Postmortems Correspondence 1', box 568, DNC Papers, FDRL.
22. Grace Tully to James Kiernan, 12 Aug. 1942, folder 'New York State Politics', PSF 144, FDR Papers, FDRL.
23. Roosevelt memorandum, 14 Aug. 1942, folder 'New York S 1933–1945', OF 300, FDR Papers, FDRL; Roosevelt to Lehman, 18 Aug. 1942, folder 'New York L 1933–1945', OF 300, FDR Papers, FDRL; Roosevelt to Bennett, 23 Oct. 1942, PPF 351, FDR Papers, FDRL.
24. Press release, 20 Oct. 1942, PPF 880, FDR Papers, FDRL; Marvin McIntyre to Rev. A. Wayman Ward, 6 Feb. 1942, folder 'Illinois', OF 300, FDR Papers, FDRL.
25. Our Nation at War: Log of the President's Inspection Trip, folder 'Inspection Trip 17 Sept.–1 Oct. 1942', OF 200, FDR Papers,

FDRL; Douglas Cornell memo, 29 Sept. 1942, Folder Inspection Tour 17 Sept.–1 Oct. 1942, OF 200-2-0, FDR Papers, FDRL; Special Flash Ballot, 12 Oct. 1942, folder 'Straw Votes, 1941–42', OF 857, FDR Papers, FDRL.

26. See Samuel Zipp, *The Idealist: Wendell Willkie's Wartime Quest to Build One World* (Cambridge, MA: The Belknap Press of Harvard University Press, 2020); Bell to Pauley, 14 Nov. 1942, folder 'Postmortems Correspondence 4', box 568, DNC Papers, FDRL.
27. Roosevelt, *Complete Presidential Press Conferences of Franklin D Roosevelt*, vol. 20, 1942, p. 201; Roosevelt, *Complete Presidential Press Conferences of Franklin D Roosevelt*, Volume 20, 1942, pp. 185–6; McJimsey, *The Presidency of Franklin Delano Roosevelt*, p. 244; Perrett, *Days of Sadness, Years of Triumph*, p. 253.
28. Perrett, *Days of Sadness, Years of Triumph*, p. 253, Richard Polenberg, *War and Society: The United States, 1941–1945* (Philadelphia, PA: J. B. Lippincott, 1972), p. 189. The percentage turnout has not been lower since, though the dismal turnout of 36.4 per cent in 2014 came close.
29. Hadley Cantril polls, 4 Jan. 1943, folder 'Public Opinion Polls 1942–44', PSF 157, FDR Papers, FDRL.
30. 'What the November 1942 Election Boils Down To', 14 Dec. 1942, PPF8229, FDR Papers, FDRL; Memorandum for Stephen Early [author unknown], 5 Nov. 1942, folder 'Oct.–Dec.1942', OF 4675, FDR Papers, FDRL; *Washington Post*, 10 July 1942, p. 9; *New York Times*, 30 Sept. 1942, p. 27.
31. *New Republic*, 16 Nov. 1942, p. 627. Seen in folder 'Postmortems Correspondence 1', box 568, DNC Papers, FDRL; Bell to Pauley, 14 Nov. 1942, folder 'Postmortems Correspondence 4', box 568, DNC Papers, FDRL; Lawrence to McIntyre, 17 Sept. 1942, folder 'Elections 1937–1944', PPF 869, FDR Papers, FDRL; Polenberg, *War and Society*, p. 189.
32. Quoted in David M. Jordan, *FDR, Dewey and the Election of 1944* (Bloomington, IN: Indiana University Press, 2014), p. 15.
33. Jackson to Roosevelt, 30 Nov. 1942, folder 1942, OF 1113, FDR Papers, FDRL; OWI Intelligence Report 49, 13 Nov. 1942, pp. 3–4, PSF 156, folder 'Office of War Information – Survey of Intelligence – Nov. 1942', FDR Papers, FDRL; Rosenman, *Public Papers and Addresses of Franklin D. Roosevelt, 1942*, p. 448.
34. Kennedy, *Freedom from Fear*, pp. 625, 783; John Morton Blum, *V was for Victory: Politics and American Culture during World War*

II (New York: Harcourt Brace Jovanovich, 1976), pp. 233–44; Polenberg, *War and Society*, pp. 192–3; William L. O'Neill, *A Democracy at War: America's Fight at Home and Abroad in World War II* (New York: Free Press, 1993), p. 101.

35. Samuel I. Rosenman, ed., *The Public Papers and Addresses of Franklin D. Roosevelt, 1943* (New York: Harper, 1950), p. 31; Samuel I. Rosenman, ed., *The Public Papers and Addresses of Franklin D. Roosevelt, 1944–45* (New York: Harper, 1950), pp. 32–42; Rosenman, *Public Papers and Addresses of Franklin D. Roosevelt, 1943*, pp. 570–1. For the idea that the New Deal was effectively over by 1938, see Alan Brinkley, *The End of Reform: New Deal Liberalism in Recession and War* (New York: Alfred A. Knopf, 1995).
36. Wayne S. Cole, *America First: The Battle Against Intervention, 1940–1941* (Madison, WI: University of Wisconsin Press, 1953), pp. 180–8.
37. Roland Young, *Congressional Politics in the Second World War* (New York: Da Capo Press, 1972), pp. 191–3.
38. Snyder to Pauley, 26 Nov. 1942, folder 'Postmortems Correspondence 2', box 568, DNC Papers, FDRL.

6

Midterm Elections, the Republican Party, and the Challenge to New Deal Liberalism, 1946–1958

Robert Mason

Republicans sought to deploy the midterm campaigns from 1946 to 1958 as a means of achieving a larger revitalisation of their party's fortunes. The political context that they encountered was one of disadvantage, rooted in the economic crisis that took hold under Herbert Hoover and then in the agenda of government activism that Franklin D. Roosevelt pursued to tackle that crisis. As Iwan Morgan shows in Chapter 4, New Deal liberalism relegated Republicans to minority status in the two-party system, to habitual defeat at the polls, and to a focus on opposition in response to Democratic initiatives – an electoral descent symbolised by the historically unusual decline suffered by their party in the midterms of 1934. Taking place in the shadow of two presidential defeats for their party (those of Thomas E. Dewey in both 1944 and 1948) and then two victories (those of Dwight D. Eisenhower in 1952 and 1956), these midterm contests featured efforts by Republicans collectively to mobilise a mandate against New Deal liberalism. Hostility to organised labour was often a key thread of this odyssey. Republicans, seeing unions as powerful in building support at the polls for their Democratic rivals, pursued projects of organisational renewal that were designed to achieve a similar level of capacity in practical politics. A challenge to the labour reforms of the New Deal was, furthermore, an important target of their policy agenda.

Midterm election results twice during this period were suggestive of a watershed in public opinion and in public policy. In 1946, Republicans gained control on Capitol Hill for the first time since the arrival of the Great Depression, adding – to their existing totals – fifty-five seats in the House of Representatives (with a 53.5 per cent share of votes cast) and twelve seats in the Senate.[1] Such a level of change in the parties' fortunes characterises few midterm contests in American electoral history. But twelve years later, the elections of 1958 also involved upheaval, this time to the Republicans' detriment. Already in secure control of both Houses, Democrats made net gains of forty-nine House seats (with a 55.5 per cent share of votes cast) and twelve Senate seats, gains that advanced their party to large majorities on Capitol Hill.[2] Economic problems that created disaffection with the incumbent administration were important in both years, but in neither case did the impact on the pursuit of the president's agenda match the significance of the change in public opinion suggested by election returns. And yet even if the Republicans' electoral downturn of 1958 did not wound fatally the last two White House years of Eisenhower (the first president prevented by the Twenty-second Amendment, a product of the post-1946 Republican Congress, from seeking a third term), the longer-term implications of this liberal surge on Capitol Hill would be consequential for public policy. Whereas the Republican trend of 1946 proved to be transient, the midterms of 1958 not only confirmed the electoral strength of the congressional Democrats, but also empowered them to pursue their agenda over time. Despite Republicans' efforts during the post–World War II years to mobilise public opinion against New Deal liberalism, then, they were unsuccessful in pursuing a larger attack on their rivals' dominance in American politics. These efforts were nevertheless consequential, because their cumulative impact encouraged the Democrats to step away from a liberalising trajectory and to assert instead a commitment to moderation.

1946: 'had enough?'

The Republicans' defeats in the elections of 1944 – continuing the record of electoral failure that stretched back to the arrival of the Great Depression but marking a rebuff to the optimism that their midterm gains of 1942, discussed by

Andrew Johnstone in the previous chapter, had created – led to an agenda of organisational revitalisation at the Republican National Committee (RNC), designed to boost the party's operational capacity between campaigns.[3] It was not new for Republicans to perceive an organisational disparity between their party and the Democrats' as important in helping to explain their electoral woes, but now there was a new target for their concerns.[4] Founded in the aftermath of the 1942 midterms because union leaders saw low turnout among working-class Americans as feeding a decline in liberalism on Capitol Hill (which then facilitated the passage of the 1943 Smith–Connally Act, to prevent strikes affecting wartime production and to outlaw union contributions in federal elections), the Congress for Industrial Organization's Political Action Committee (CIO-PAC) played a role in the campaigns of 1944 that struck many as crucial.[5]

But if Republicans were able to find agreement in support of organisational change, agreement on policy was out of reach. As they started to look ahead to the midterm campaigns of 1946, the focus for this disagreement was a statement of 'aims and purposes', drafted by congressional Republicans as an interim platform for the party. Meeting in late 1945, RNC members endorsed the draft while calling for the creation of a more 'virile' and 'representative' declaration of party principles.[6] Already the statement emphasised that the inter-party difference on domestic matters was significant – between the Republicans' focus on 'American freedom' and an alternative of 'radicalism, regimentation, all-powerful bureaucracy, class exploitation, deficit spending and machine politics', offered by their Democratic rivals.[7] Even so, while moderate Republicans voiced criticism of the statement, the more significant source of disagreement was a conservative desire for a more strenuous attack on that target of radicalism and on labour.[8]

Although Republicans were not fully in agreement about how best to attack their opponents, the developments of 1946 fomented widespread discontent targeted at the incumbents. An economic shock accompanied the transition from war to peace. Supplies of housing and food were inadequate, and prices rose sharply. By year's end, the cost of living was estimated to be one-third higher than it had been at the close of World War II.[9] Most sensitive of all were meat shortages; controversies surrounding Harry Truman's imposition of price controls (lifted during campaign season) deepened his unpopularity. By late September, only one in three Americans, according to Gallup polling, voiced approval of Truman's performance as president, the office he had held for a little less than eighteen months.[10] If it was not unusual for many voters to experience dissatisfaction with the administration at the midterm moment, this dissatisfaction nevertheless reached unusual proportions in 1946. Robert Hannegan, chair of the Democratic National Committee, asked Truman to stay away from the campaign as much as possible. A radio commercial seeking to defuse high prices as a problematic issue for the party symbolised the way in which the transition from Roosevelt to Truman struck many Democrats as disadvantageous, by showcasing a recording of Franklin Roosevelt, the architect of New Deal liberalism who had died the previous spring, making the charge that Republicans were in favour of 'meat for the millionaires but not for the millions'.[11]

Post-war economic woes created labour discontent. Car workers and coal miners went on strike, and only intervention by Truman – with a threat to draft strikers into the armed forces – halted disruption of the nation's railways. Well in excess of a million working days were lost to strikes in 1946, a record.[12] Increasing numbers of Americans saw Republicans as better able than Democrats to handle labour problems.[13] Although it was a fertile moment for the Republicans' anti-labour message, there nevertheless remained qualifications to its electoral power. According to a Gallup poll of September, the most important issue for voters – as the Cold War broke out so soon after the end of World War II – was foreign policy, followed by the cost of living and then the issues of labour discontent. Those who identified with the Democratic Party, George Gallup added, focused on the cost of living, whereas those who identified with the Republican Party were more concerned about the strikes and other labour problems.[14] If anti-labour sentiment was becoming more salient, then, this was more concentrated among existing supporters of the Republicans and its potential to win the votes of others was more limited.

To harness anti-incumbent sentiment at a time of such upheaval, Republicans employed a slogan that asked voters, 'Had Enough?' According to historian James Boylan, the campaigns of Republicans often took a more specific emphasis than the generalised outreach to frustration with post-war dislocation that the slogan suggested – one that involved anti-communism. Against the context of worsened relations between the United States and the Soviet Union, Republicans not only charged Democrats with an inadequate response to a communist threat but also claimed that connections existed between their rivals' liberalism and communism. In September, Truman dismissed Commerce secretary Henry A. Wallace, his predecessor in the vice presidency, when Wallace questioned the administration's foreign policy as too harsh towards the Soviet Union; despite the dismissal, Republican national chair B. Carroll Reece called Wallace 'merely the evangel of a new party line'. The attack was part of a larger stress on anti-communism. Reece spoke of his party's opponents as the 'Democrat–P.A.C.–Communist ticket', who imperilled the nation's foreign policy as well as failing to solve labour problems at home. Not only Wallace's dismissal but other developments of campaign season as well facilitated such a message. Later in September, J. Edgar Hoover, the director of the Federal Bureau of Investigation, told the American Legion of 'diabolical plots to wreck the American way of life', the result, Hoover said, of communist infiltration in government, among organised labour and elsewhere. Republicans employed the statement in support of their anti-labour campaign against the Democrats, as they did when, in October, a Moscow radio broadcast praised the CIO-PAC. 'The Democratic Party', said Archibald H. Giroux, chair of the party's state committee in Massachusetts, 'has become infiltrated with Communist left-wing individuals whose primary hope is to throw this country into a socialized state.'[15]

The overwhelming nature of their party's victories in 1946 – which featured most CIO-PAC–endorsed candidates among the victims, as well as largely southernising the now diminished contingent of House Democrats (because representatives of the white South now constituted a larger proportion of the party's officeholders on Capitol Hill) – encouraged many Republicans to misinterpret the mandate offered by voters. This was, they suspected, a step towards the rejection of New Deal liberalism. 'For the first time in 14 years the United States no longer is in a state of emergency,' said Senator Robert A. Taft of Ohio, among the victors. 'The results of the election show that the American people definitely are opposed to giving an arbitrary central government the power and money to regulate their daily lives.'[16] But these were victories defined by an anti-incumbent tide rather than, more proactively and positively, a turn to the Republican Party, and they were victories strongly facilitated by low turnout among habitual supporters of the Democratic Party.[17] Despite the rhetoric of Republicans such as Taft, the Republican agenda of the 80th Congress successfully targeted policies likely to be more electorally appealing, rather than staging a larger attack on New Deal liberalism. As well as passing the Twenty-second Amendment, limiting presidents to two terms, and legislation to control pesticides and water pollution, the 80th Congress passed – at a third effort – a tax cut over vetoes by Truman, together with the Taft–Hartley Act, which restricted labour rights as protected by the New Deal's Wagner Act. Moreover, despite the campaign-time attacks on Truman's foreign policy, bipartisanship surrounded the development of containment measures to wage the Cold War.[18] Meanwhile, the crescendo of anti-communist attacks encouraged liberals to join the Red Scare. Not only did Truman consolidate the Democrats' anti-communism through the creation in March 1947 of the federal loyalty-security programme, but also the CIO embarked on an effort to purge Communist influence.[19] The newly found political power of the Republican Party, then, created a check on New Deal liberalism rather than a larger assertion of anti-statist principle – even if the Taft–Hartley challenge to labour rights had significant implications for the employee–employer relationship.

Still more cautious in challenging liberalism was Thomas E. Dewey in his contest for the presidency against Truman in 1948. Convinced that the minimisation of partisan controversy was likely to maximise what he believed was an electoral tide away from the Democrats, Dewey said relatively little about the 80th Congress's record when campaigning against Truman. In profound contrast, Truman's campaign was grounded in a conviction that the electoral coalition in support of New Deal liberalism remained powerful. To dramatise the difference between the parties, he attacked the Republican-controlled Congress. Sometimes rebuking audiences for the low turnout at the polls that had characterised the 1946 midterms, he told voters that, as well as cutting taxes for the wealthy, Congress had 'passed a lot of special legislation that helps special classes'.[20]

But while Dewey stepped away from the anti-communist attacks on Democrats that had been part of his own previous campaign for the White House, against Franklin Roosevelt in 1944, and then achieved such prominence in 1946, by no means all Republicans made such a change.[21] Such Republicans thus tried to press home what had seemed to be a winning issue in the 1946 midterms. Seeking re-election in Illinois, Senator Charles W. Brooks was among those who focused on anti-communism, claiming that the 'New Deal–communist–Democratic coalition' was obstructing Republican efforts to tackle subversion.[22] But Brooks proved to be one of eight Republican Senate incumbents defeated on election day, which saw the Grand Old Party (GOP) lose its majorities on Capitol Hill as well as Dewey's loss to Truman. In elections for the House of Representations, the party – with a vote share of 45.4 per cent – lost all the gains made in 1946.[23] Over the years that followed, only in the 2014 midterms, during Barack Obama's second term, would Republicans again reach the total of House seats achieved in that year of abortive breakthrough (exceeding it by one).

1950: 'liberty against socialism'

When, in early 1949, Republicans gathered in Omaha, Nebraska, for a meeting of their party's national committee, anger was the dominant response to the Dewey campaign, widely thought to have squandered an opportunity for party advance created by the 1946 midterms and the 80th Congress. For Dewey himself, the Republicans' problem remained that of an organisational disparity with their Democratic opponents. 'There is only one good party organization in the country today and that is Organized Labor,' he told Alf Landon, the party's presidential nominee of 1936.[24] But it was common among many Republicans to interpret contemporary politics, rooted in the debates about New Deal liberalism now focused on Truman's Fair Deal agenda of further domestic reform, as pitting a defence of anti-statism against a drift towards socialism. This was a defence, they believed, that Dewey had sidestepped but that urgently needed engagement for reasons not only of principle but also of electoral advantage. At the RNC meeting, Cecil Murray Harden of Indiana, newly elected to the House, told his fellow Republicans, '. . . I am supremely confident that once the Republican Party marshals its forces together and advances a concrete program for a revision of this trend toward socialism the American people will rally behind us in overwhelming numbers.'[25]

The Omaha meeting took place not only in the shadow of defeat but also in the aftermath of Truman's post-election State of the Union address, which boldly sought to pursue further the concerns of New Deal liberalism. His Fair Deal featured aid to education, action on civil rights (through the creation of a Fair Employment Practices Commission), a universal healthcare initiative, and new protections for organised labour (including the repeal of the Taft–Hartley Act). Even if Republicans no longer controlled Congress, they retained an ideological majority – via the 'conservative coalition' with southern Democrats – on some issues, however. As well as on race, opposition among southern Democrats to New Deal liberalism focused on labour rights.[26] Although the path to liberal action on protecting civil rights and on challenging union restrictions was especially difficult, the larger quest for a Fair Deal encountered many other frustrations. The 81st Congress passed legislation on housing, social security, and employment conditions, but much of the Fair Deal remained far from implementation.[27]

Still, in February 1950 the RNC joined with Capitol Hill Republicans in adopting a statement of principles that attacked 'the Administration's program for a planned economy modeled on the Socialist Governments of Europe', and in advancing the theme of liberty against socialism for the midterm campaigns of that year. A few days later, a speech in Wheeling, West Virginia, by a Republican senator seeking re-election, Joseph R. McCarthy of Wisconsin, highlighted one of the issues that the statement featured – a call to remove 'all Communists, fellow travelers and Communist sympathizers from our Federal payroll'.[28] McCarthy's claim that domestic subversion was imperilling the US cause in the Cold War achieved fresh salience as a result of North Korea's invasion of South Korea in June. The dispatch of American forces in support of the South's army did little to halt the North's advance, but the military intervention of the United Nations (UN) then turned back the invasion. When, at the start of October, UN troops moved beyond the 38th Parallel, which divided the two countries, China entered the conflict – subsequently with support from the Soviet Union. Less than a week before the midterm elections took place, the first military confrontation between the United States and China took place. Although the statement that launched the liberty against socialism assault on the Democrats had treated foreign policy briefly and vaguely, by election day questions of the United States' fluctuating fortunes in Korea were politically significant. For Richard Nixon in California, who achieved elevation from the House to the Senate, 'the major issue in my race was the issue of the Administration's foreign policy in the Far East'.[29]

For the Republicans' campaign effort, criticisms of the Democrats on the war were in some synergy with a larger effort against New Deal liberalism. More broadly, Nixon responded to his opponent Helen Gahagan Douglas's defence of the Fair Deal by branding her as 'soft on communism'; his campaign manager Murray Chotiner later commented that it was not possible to 'out-promise a New Dealer'.[30] Many other Republicans shared his tactic of comparing their opponent's voting record with that of Vito Marcantonio, an American Labor Party politician who represented a New York City district in the House. In some Democratic primaries (as in Florida, where George Smathers toppled Senator Claude Pepper's renomination bid through attacks on him as 'Red Pepper') as well as in contests between Republicans and Democrats, anti-communism was often central to campaign debate. Much newer to prominence as an anti-communist than Nixon, McCarthy nevertheless gained a reputation for deploying his newfound celebrity and notoriety to bring down leading Democrats, including Senator Millard Tydings of Maryland – chair of the subcommittee that called McCarthy's charges 'a fraud and a hoax' – and Senator Scott Lucas of Illinois. Because the electoral tide was anyway against Tydings and Lucas, and others attacked by McCarthy, these interventions were probably not responsible for their defeats. And yet the campaign not only demonstrated the power of anti-communism against the Democrats, but also convinced many contemporaries of McCarthy's persuasiveness as a campaigner.[31]

Although midterm elections have historically lacked the centralised focus afforded by the battle between two national tickets that takes place in contests for the presidency, in 1950 the Republicans' liberty against socialism theme indicated an effort to characterise the inter-party battle in a nationalised manner. The arrival of the Korean War then sharpened the salience of foreign policy. Diversity nevertheless remained visible, exemplified by the House of Representatives contests in two neighbouring Minneapolis districts. In one, Alfred D. Lindley, even though he was a moderately inclined Republican, employed the widespread tactic of comparisons with Vito Marcantonio – who 'consistently follows the Kremlin line', Lindley said – against incumbent Roy Wier, even though Wier was a centrist Democrat. For his part, Wier emphasised that his opponent was an anti-labour candidate. In the other, the interest of Walter Judd, the incumbent and a Republican, in Asian affairs facilitated, by contrast, a focus on the Korean War; even if his opponent Marcella Killen also spoke of his anti-welfare views, she similarly concentrated on foreign policy. On election day, both incumbents were triumphant, but against the context of fully dissimilar campaign debates.[32]

At first sight, the showcase for the liberty against socialism challenge to the Democratic Party took place in Ohio, because there Taft – the architect of restrictions on worker rights – was seeking re-election to the Senate, with labour leaders nationally identifying him as their chief target. That August, for example, John L. Lewis, the United Mine Workers leader, called Taft 'a relentless, albeit witless tool of the oppressors of labor'. And yet the campaign proved to be an imperfect showcase for this challenge, in part because of the anti-Taft effort's shortcomings. Analysts identified as problematic both the aggressiveness of attacks such as Lewis's, which alienated some voters, and the ineffectiveness on the campaign trail of Joseph T. Ferguson, Taft's opponent. But Taft stepped away from a more substantial defence of his conservatism in favour of a focus on the administration as soft towards communism – pointing to the war in Korea as evidence of its failings – and on organised labour as influenced by communism. The CIO-PAC, he said, 'was conceived in Communism, had Communist midwives assisting at its birth and was carefully nurtured in its formative period by Communist teachers.'[33] To explain his victory over Ferguson, which he achieved by a large margin, Taft echoed Nixon in identifying 'a vote of lack of confidence in the Administration's foreign policy primarily'.[34]

If the context of the Korean War, troubling for Americans as well as fast-moving, blurred the Republicans' liberty against socialism focus, there nevertheless remained an anti-administration tide that favoured the party's candidates, though in more limited measure than they had sought. In the Senate, the Democrats suffered a net loss of five seats, eroding their majority; the post-election balance was forty-nine to forty-seven. Their House majority experienced erosion, too, with Republicans making a net gain of twenty-eight seats. The 235–199 post-election balance understated the Republicans' electoral performance, in fact; their party gained 48.85 per cent of votes cast in House elections whereas the Democrats' share was 48.94 per cent.[35] (Among the House incumbents who suffered defeat was Vito Marcantonio, who lost to Democrat James Donovan; Donovan had focused his fire on Marcantonio's opposition to American intervention in Korea.) If a near-deadlock in some respects characterised the inter-party battleground of 1950, so too did difference. While Republicans worried that organised labour was a potent foe against them, they were the beneficiaries of increasing involvement by business in politics. This included the medical profession, mobilised against Truman's proposal for a national programme of health insurance.[36] If business opposition to the Democrats was advantageous, especially with regard to campaign funds, with weighty consequence for the party in the longer term, then in shorter-term perspective issues emerged in 1950 that would take the party to victory two years later. Not only did the war in Korea and anti-communism remain salient, and advantageous for the party, but also Republicans in 1950 had started to level accusations of corruption against their Democratic rivals (emerging especially from the findings of a Senate committee on organised crime), a theme that would become more significant in campaign debate two years later. The pursuit of a liberty against socialism message in 1950 evolved to what would become the Republican slogan of 1952: K_1C_2 (Korea, Communism, Corruption).[37]

Those who lost in the midterms included enthusiastic advocates of the Fair Deal, but it was not just the Democrats' midterm decline that impeded the pursuit of Truman's agenda for liberal advance. More generally, the war in Korea marginalised domestic reform as a priority for the administration.[38] The advances that the Fair Deal sought – not just in healthcare but also, for example, in agriculture via the Brannan Plan of farm subsidies – were therefore in eclipse.[39] If the prospects of further reform were thin, then so too, however, were the prospects of a successful challenge to the existing achievements of New Deal liberalism.[40] The anti-incumbent sentiment that Republicans harnessed did not represent the mobilisation in support of a rallying cry of liberty, as they had intended.

1954: Citizens for Eisenhower

Republican engagement with midterm campaigning took a new emphasis with Dwight Eisenhower at the White House, the party's first president in two decades. When Eisenhower won in 1952, Republicans regained control of Capitol Hill but they did so by relatively narrow margins. Although the anti-incumbent trend that typifies midterms was now against the party's candidates, possession of the White House equipped the Republicans with centralised leadership, a potential advantage in developing a campaign. Still more advantageously, Eisenhower was a politician with unusually high levels of popularity, with an appeal that far outstripped that of his party. Although his background was not in party politics, and despite an above-party image that he burnished for political advantage, Eisenhower as president pursued a serious project to revitalise the GOP's fortunes. Its policy dimension – labelled 'modern Republicanism' by Eisenhower at the time of his re-election in 1956 – moderated the party's opposition to New Deal liberalism. Ostensibly, this moderation encompassed a less hostile view of organised labour, with Eisenhower identifying a need for unions to play a central role in what historian Robert Griffith calls a 'corporate commonwealth' – a vision stressing the value of a cooperative relationship for government with business and other groups in society. And yet this vision, by seeing class conflict as a leading obstacle to the recovery of domestic tranquillity after the turbulent years of the 1930s and 1940s, did not fully challenge the party's anti-labour agenda, and in practice the role for union representatives was junior and marginal.[41]

This project for the party aimed furthermore to boost its organisational capacity, most significantly through Citizens for Eisenhower, which had successfully mobilised support for Eisenhower's candidacy in 1952. Despite its roots as a candidate-centred organisation focused on a campaign for the White House (and in promoting Eisenhower as a candidate within the Republican Party before advocating his cause in the general election against his Democratic rival Adlai Stevenson), Citizens was resuscitated for the 1954 midterms, targeted at aiding Republican candidates in marginal districts to achieve outreach to traditionally Democratic and independent voters. The Citizens congressional committee stressed that its goal was to promote support for Eisenhower on Capitol Hill, adopting a policy of non-assistance for Republican incumbents with a record of opposition to the president.[42] Even if such a conceptualisation of the role for Citizens stressed that it supplemented, not supplanted, the work of the regular party, Republicans who belonged to what was known as the 'Old Guard' and who did not share the stress on political moderation that characterised Eisenhower often viewed these 'amateur' newcomers with hostility.[43]

Privately in disagreement with the midterm strategy of outreach to those normally loyal to the Democrats and those independent of party loyalty was Richard Nixon, who as Eisenhower's vice president played a leading role on the campaign trail. Nixon saw success in such elections – when turnout was habitually lower than in elections when presidential candidates were also on ballot papers – instead as dependent on the mobilisation of a party's 'hard core'. While Nixon echoed the Citizens theme that called for the election of a Congress supportive of Eisenhower, he often did so via strident attacks on the Democrats, commenting, for example, that 'two more years of the Truman policies would have taken us straight down the road that leads to Socialism'.[44] Nixon also joined other Republicans in repeating the charge that not only had the Democrats' management of foreign policy been inadequate, but they also had failed to protect the country against domestic subversion. Joe McCarthy's descent into disgrace – with the Senate convening in special session less than a week after the midterm elections to begin a discussion of his censure – sapped the Red Scare's electoral salience nationally, however.[45]

In sharp contrast to Truman in 1946, Eisenhower campaigned actively in order to rekindle his mandate, and in particular to prevent the strengthening within the party of what behind the scenes he called its 'extreme right wing.'[46] But he did so in a manner that played down the K_1C_2 issues, which had been much discussed in 1952 on the road to Republican victory. In this way, Eisenhower's effort to rekindle his mandate involved its modification, oriented towards his moderation-focused vision for the party. Exemplifying the 'middle-of-the-road' message that Eisenhower stressed in 1954 – sympathetic to social welfare protections yet sceptical of government's growth – was a speech that initiated his campaign tour of the West. 'Never will we desert any section or people who need help that only the Federal government can give,' he said in Missoula, Montana. 'Never will we step across the line which means unwarranted intrusion into your lives.'[47] Later, visiting Denver, Eisenhower also warned against the consequences of the Democrats' recapture of Congress – amounting to 'a cold war of partisan politics', he said, because the political context of divided government was one in which 'the public good goes begging while politics is played for politics' sake'.[48]

Such a warning emphasised Eisenhower's commitment to his party at a time when many Democrats were waging campaigns that played up their affinity with the popular incumbent of the White House, especially on foreign policy.[49] The narrowness of the party division in both houses did indeed make Democratic votes crucial to presidential success in key votes on Capitol Hill during the first two years of the Eisenhower administration.[50] 'It was often difficult to discern', wrote political scientist M. R. Merrill, who tracked the campaign in the western states, 'who was more anxious to give the President the support for which he pleaded, Democrats or Republicans'.[51]

On election day, Republicans suffered a net loss of two seats in the Senate and of eighteen in the House, ceding their majorities to the Democrats – not to recapture them until 1980 and 1994, respectively. And yet for Eisenhower this outcome was, according to Merrill, 'a personal victory of the proportions of that of 1952', because Democrats had failed to attack the president much and had even sometimes competed with Republican opponents to stress agreement with his agenda.[52] Some Republicans, however, of more conservative orientation, attached blame to Eisenhower for inadequate pursuit of party principle and for inadequate promotion of the party in explaining the retreat in their fortunes on Capitol Hill.[53]

The reappearance of divided government, now with Democrats controlling Congress and a Republican in the White House, would encourage Eisenhower to claim that inter-party conflict imperilled the pursuit of his agenda, though he also stressed an above-politics posture in seeking cooperation with congressional Democrats. Cooperation, indeed, as well as conflict characterised divided government under Eisenhower. To be sure, in 1955 administration proposals on federal aid to education, federal subsidies for private health insurance, and highway construction all encountered deadlock and thus inaction, often because Democrats preferred a more generous formula of government activism (though for the more conservative in the Republican Party these proposals were too liberal). Nevertheless, more broadly Eisenhower achieved some success in gaining support among congressional Democrats; the results included the Federal-Aid Highway Act of 1956.[54]

While the Republicans' loss of Congress in the 1954 midterms spurred inter-party cooperation, disappointment with his party also encouraged Eisenhower to boost efforts to transform the GOP. There were new initiatives designed to address continuing concerns about organisational capacity, but ideology – the quest for a more moderate response to New Deal liberalism – as well as organisation informed a project to persuade Citizens activists to join the party. The results of these initiatives were, at best, limited, however. Although Eisenhower would claim success in leading the party towards modern Republicanism, in fact conservatism – sceptical of this more moderate vision – was starting to achieve intellectual and organisational revitalisation in the mid-1950s.[55]

1958: 'right to work'

Even if an economic downturn in 1957–8 – often known as the 'Eisenhower recession' – led to a decline in the president's popularity during his second term, Citizens was revived again as a vehicle for fundraising and campaign organisation in preparation for Eisenhower's second midterms.[56] Its revival actually demonstrated the failure of an aspiration to achieve integration between Citizens and the party (involving the hope that Citizens activists would join party ranks), but anyway no longer did Citizens possess the energy it had first harnessed in order to take Eisenhower to the White House in 1952. Instead anti-labour sentiment achieved renewed vitality that found an expression within a drive for 'right-to-work' legislation.[57] The CIO's merger with the American Federation of Labor (AFL) in 1955 was deepening concern among Republicans about the political power of organised labour as an opponent, while a racketeering scandal led to the creation in early 1957 of a Senate select committee to investigate labour malpractice, led by John L. McClellan, a Democrat of Arkansas. Over its three-year existence, the McClellan committee generated a series of revelations hostile to labour – a development friendly to the goals of a 'business in politics' movement that saw the structures of labour–management relations as remaining excessively protective of union rights, despite the measures of the Taft–Hartley Act that amended the reforms of the New Deal era; the movement was informed by frustrations with Eisenhower's modern Republicanism, as inadequately conservative, as well as by concern about unions' political influence. Founded in 1955, the National Right to Work Committee focused the energies of anti-labour sentiment on the union shop, seeking to portray its cause not as inimical to the interests of employees but rather as protective of their individual rights, against labour bosses.[58]

Ballots in six states featured a right-to-work initiative, and many Democrats seized the issue to mobilise support. On election day, when all initiatives except that in Kansas were defeated, Republican representation in the House sank to 153 seats (against the Democrats' 282 seats), and in the Senate the party suffered a net loss of twelve, resulting in a party division of sixty-one seats to thirty-five seats. National chair Meade Alcorn advised Eisenhower that 'the Republican party lost scores of candidates for national, state and local offices . . . largely on the right-to-work issue'. For Alcorn, more profoundly the issue shattered the modern Republican odyssey to moderate the party's image. 'The "big business versus organized labor" image', wrote Alcorn, 'was dramatically revived in the minds of a great majority of the nation's wage earners.'[59] And yet if Alcorn cited the defeat of Senator John Bricker in Ohio as emblematic of the party's slump, and if high-profile association with the right-to-work issue confounded William Knowland's effort in California to move from the US Senate to the governorship, not every anti-labour Republican was a loser in 1958. In Arizona, Senator Barry Goldwater, who had run in 1952 as an Eisenhower Republican, increased his majorities across much of the state on the basis not only of an anti-labour message, rationalised as protective of ordinary Americans, but also of a record in Washington challenging the political influence of unions.[60]

Even though the pro-Democratic surge was sizeable, Eisenhower was able to maintain his existing focus on an anti-spending agenda during his last two years in the White House. Furthermore, despite the setback to the anti-labour cause experienced by right-to-work advocates, the 86th Congress strengthened Taft–Hartley regulations of organised labour via the Landrum–Griffin Act of 1959, a response to further congressional investigation of union malpractice.[61] And yet the longer-term consequences for public policy were profound, in more firmly establishing the Democratic Party as more activist, and the Republican Party as less activist, on civil rights. Republicans who lost in 1958 were often liberals on civil rights, usually replaced by Democrats also liberal on civil rights, thus shifting the overall approach to race of both parties on Capitol Hill.[62]

Alcorn's regret that the right-to-work issue had restored the Republicans' business-oriented image was misplaced because Dwight Eisenhower – despite having sought to claim his re-election victory as a mandate for modern Republicanism – had achieved, at best, only partial success in refashioning the party anyway. To be sure, the Eisenhower administration's acceptance of New Deal reforms had led to a significant diminution in the party's reputation as hostile to welfare protections, but the Eisenhower years had been 'not equally successful . . . in dispelling the popular belief that the Republicans were the party of the great and the Democrats the party of the small', according to a group of contemporary social scientists.[63] Nevertheless, Goldwater's anti-labour victory in Arizona helped to consolidate his emergence as the leading figure among conservative Republicans. His candidacy for the presidency in 1964 would marginalise the legacy of Eisenhower's modern Republicanism.

Midterms: political science and political history

The outcomes of the 1958 elections were consequential in ways that reveal the complex, multifaceted significance of midterms. They confirmed the hollowness of Eisenhower's pursuit of modern Republicanism, which he had questionably identified as his mandate of 1956, but the defeats did less to undermine the pursuit of his second-term agenda. It would be a few years before the Democratic Party's liberalisation in Congress, especially on civil rights, a product particularly of the 1958

Senate contests, had significant consequences for public policy. Moreover, if on the Republican side the elections elevated Barry Goldwater and thus revitalised an anti-labour agenda, another victor was Nelson Rockefeller, as governor of New York, whose vision for the party was very different. The 1958 elections positioned both to pursue, over the coming years, a battle over the party's future.

In political science, the 1958 elections informed a theory seeking to explain midterm slumps in support for the president's party – that of 'surge and decline', a theory discussed by Andrew Rudalevige in Chapter 1. For Angus Campbell, a key feature of the 1958 elections was the decline in turnout at the polls that took place then – of about 25 per cent – by comparison with the elections of two years before, when Eisenhower secured re-election. They were 'low-stimulus' elections, according to Campbell, when issues did not seem so important and when candidates did not elicit so much enthusiasm; as a result, people with less interest in politics were less likely to vote. Moreover, crucially for the Republicans' decline in 1958, whereas Eisenhower had won support among many normally loyal to the Democratic Party, his absence from the ballots in 1958 allowed them to return to their preferred party.[64]

This initial formulation of the 'surge-and-decline' thesis, published in 1960, thus does not dwell on economic downturn as a reason for Republican losses or on the 'right-to-work' campaigns' impact, though it stresses Dwight Eisenhower's political appeal in explaining the 1956 'surge' in favour of the party. But the interest of contemporary political scientists in turnout closely echoes the strategic odyssey of contemporary Republicans, concerned about the apparent success of unions in mobilising voters at the polls in support of the Democratic Party. But, more profoundly, Campbell's analysis is suggestive of the difficulties that faced Republicans in challenging New Deal liberalism. In the absence of a 'high-stimulus' electoral context, existing party loyalties were the key determinants of outcomes; Campbell was among a team of political scientists whose work on parties and voters encouraged them to conclude that in this era the Democratic Party's electoral strength, allied to a popular association between

Republicans and the Great Depression as well as their agenda of New Deal liberalism, was largely impervious to successful challenge.[65] During the decade and a half after the death of Franklin Roosevelt, who had done much to reshape American politics, Republicans attempted to harness the surge-and-decline character of midterm elections in support of their endeavour to boost their party's fortunes. But if these efforts sometimes achieved gains that challenged a political trajectory among Democrats towards bolder reform, it proved not so straightforward to mobilise a mandate against New Deal liberalism.

Notes

1. William Graf, *Statistics of the Congressional Election of November 5, 1946* (Washington, DC: United States Government Printing Office, 1947), http://clerk.house.gov/member_info/electionInfo/1946election.pdf, accessed 5 Aug. 2020.
2. Benjamin J. Guthrie, *Statistics of the Congressional Election of November 4, 1958* (Washington, DC: United States Government Printing Office, 1959), http://clerk.house.gov/member_info/electionInfo/1958election.pdf, accessed 5 Aug. 2020.
3. Republican National Committee, news release, 'The Republican Party Is Now Supported by the Majority of the Voters', 19 July 1943, folder 'Republican Politics 1944', box 162, Robert A. Taft Papers, Manuscript Division, Library of Congress, Washington, DC; Jack Steele, 'Republicans Put Party on All-Year Basis', *New York Herald Tribune*, 23 Jan. 1945, p. 1, p. 11.
4. Robert Mason, *The Republican Party and American Politics from Hoover to Reagan* (New York: Cambridge University Press, 2012), pp. 70–5.
5. Nelson Lichtenstein, *Labor's War at Home: The CIO in World War II* (New York: Cambridge University Press, 1982), p. 172; 'Bloc Votes Tipped the Balance in Closest Election Since 1916', *Newsweek*, 20 Nov. 1944, p. 28.
6. Jack Steele, 'Republicans Act for "Virile" Party Policy', *New York Herald Tribune*, 9 Dec.1945, p. 1, p. 34.
7. 'Republicans' Statement', *New York Herald Tribune*, 6 Dec. 1945, p. 27.
8. Jack Steele, 'Republicans Cool to Plan of Congress Aids', *New York Herald Tribune*, 7 Dec. 1945, p. 20; Luke P. Carroll, '12 Mid-West

Republican Chiefs Issue "Declaration of Principles"', *New York Herald Tribune*, 3 Feb. 1946, p. 1, p. 28.

9. Eric F. Goldman, *The Crucial Decade – and After: America, 1945–1960* (New York: Random House, 1960), p. 25.
10. George Gallup, 'Democrat Strength Ebbs to Lowest Point in 16 Years', *Washington Post*, 16 Oct. 1946, p. 5.
11. Joseph and Stewart Alsop, 'Keeping Truman in Background is New Democratic Strategy', *New York Herald Tribune*, 25 Oct. 1946, p. 25.
12. Goldman, *Crucial Decade*, pp. 21–5.
13. George Gallup, 'GOP Wins Voters' Favor as Labor Handler', *Washington Post*, 23 June 1946, p. B5.
14. George Gallup, 'The Real '46 Issues', *Washington Post*, 29 Sept. 1946, p. B5.
15. James Boylan, *The New Deal Coalition and the Election of 1948* (New York: Garland, 1981), pp. 135–8 (quotation at p. 137); Emma Bugbee, 'Reece Declares Foreign Policy Is Major Issue', *New York Herald Tribune*, 27 Sept. 1946, p. 7; 'Chief of F.B.I. Warns of Plots by Reds in U.S.', *New York Herald Tribune*, 1 Oct. 1946, p. 17; 'Moscow Radio Praise for PAC Hit by Massachusetts G.O.P.', *Christian Science Monitor*, 21 Oct. 1946, p. 2.
16. 'Republicans See Election as Mandate from Public', *Christian Science Monitor*, 6 Nov. 1946, p. 15.
17. For contemporary criticism of mandate claims among Republicans, see Louis Bean, 'The Republican "Mandate" and '48', *New York Times* magazine, 19 Jan. 1947, p. 16, p. 52.
18. Anthony Badger, 'Republican Rule in the 80th Congress', in Dean McSweeney and John E. Owens, eds, *The Republican Takeover of Congress* (Basingstoke: Macmillan, 1998), pp. 165–84; Mason, *Republican Party*, pp. 114–16; David R. Mayhew, *Parties and Policies: How the American Government Works* (New Haven, CT: Yale University Press, 2008), pp. 194–6.
19. Jennifer Delton, *Rethinking the 1950s: How Anticommunism and the Cold War Made America Liberal* (New York: Cambridge University Press, 2013), pp. 13–31.
20. Sean J. Savage, *Truman and the Democratic Party* (Lexington, KY: University Press of Kentucky, 1997), pp. 112–43 (quotation at p. 132).
21. Richard M. Fried, '"Operation Polecat": Thomas E. Dewey, the 1948 Election, and the Origins of McCarthyism', *Journal of Policy History* 22 (2010): pp. 1–22.

22. Robert E. Hartley, *Battleground 1948: Truman, Stevenson, Douglas, and the Most Surprising Election in Illinois History* (Carbondale, IL: Southern Illinois University Press, 2013), p. 151.
23. William Graf, *Statistics of the Presidential and Congressional Election of November 2, 1948* (Washington, DC: United States Government Printing Office, 1949), http://clerk.house.gov/member_info/electionInfo/1948election.pdf, accessed 20 Aug. 2020.
24. Letter, Thomas E. Dewey to Alf M. Landon, 19 Jan. 1949, folder 3, box 24, series 10, Thomas E. Dewey Papers, River Campus Libraries, University of Rochester, Rochester, NY.
25. Transcript, Republican National Committee meeting, 26 Jan. 1949, folder 'Transcript of Luncheon Session of Republican National Committee', box 6, Hugh Scott Papers, University of Virginia Library, Charlottesville, VA.
26. Ira Katznelson, Kim Geiger, and Daniel Kryder, 'Limiting Liberalism: The Southern Veto in Congress, 1933–1950', *Political Science Quarterly* 108 (1993): pp. 283–306.
27. Barbara Sinclair, *Congressional Realignment, 1925–1978* (Austin, TX: University of Texas Press, 1982), pp. 52–3.
28. W. H. Lawrence, 'G.O.P. Poses Issue for '50 as Liberty Versus Socialism', *New York Times*, 7 Feb. 1950, p. 1.
29. Ronald J. Caridi, *The Korean War and American Politics: The Republican Party as a Case Study* (Philadelphia, PA: University of Pennsylvania Press, 1968), pp. 97–8.
30. Irwin F. Gellman, *The Contender: Richard Nixon – The Congress Years, 1946–1952* (New York: Free Press, 1999), pp. 306–43 (quotation at p. 342).
31. Richard M. Fried, 'Electoral Politics and McCarthyism: The 1950 Campaign', in Robert Griffith and Athan Theoharis, eds, *The Specter: Original Essays on the Cold War and the Origins of McCarthyism* (New York: New Viewpoints, 1974), pp. 190–222; Adam J. Berinsky and Gabriel S. Lenz, 'Red Scare? Revisiting Joe McCarthy's Influence on 1950s Elections', *Public Opinion Quarterly* 78 (2014): pp. 369–91.
32. Philip H. Ennis, 'The Contextual Dimension in Voting', in William N. McPhee and William A. Glaser, eds, *Public Opinion and Congressional Elections* (New York: Free Press of Glencoe, 1962), pp. 197–200; 'Mauseth Backed Wier–Lindley', *Minneapolis Star*, 17 Oct. 1950, p. 21; Wallace Mitchell, 'Congress Races Hold Top State Interest', *Minneapolis Sunday Tribune*, 5 Nov. 1950, p. 1.

33. James T. Patterson, *Mr. Republican: A Biography of Robert A. Taft* (Boston, MA: Houghton Mifflin), pp. 441–73 (quotations at p. 458, p. 465).
34. Caridi, *Korean War and American Politics*, p. 97.
35. William Graf, *Statistics of the Congressional Election of November 7, 1950* (Washington, DC: United States Government Printing Office, 1951), http://clerk.house.gov/member_info/electionInfo/1950election.pdf, accessed 9 Sept. 2020.
36. Joseph G. LaPalombara, 'Pressure, Propaganda, and Political Action in the Elections of 1950', *Journal of Politics* 14 (1952): pp. 300–25. On the longer-term business campaign against New Deal liberalism, see: Kim Phillips-Fein, *Invisible Hands: The Making of the Conservative Movement from the New Deal to Reagan* (New York: Norton, 2009).
37. William A. Glaser, 'Hindsight and Significance', in William N. McPhee and William A. Glaser, eds, *Public Opinion and Congressional Elections* (New York: Free Press of Glencoe, 1962), pp. 277–8.
38. Jason Scott Smith, 'The Fair Deal', in Daniel S. Margolies, *A Companion to Harry S. Truman* (Malden, MA: Wiley-Blackwell, 2012), p. 219.
39. Glaser, 'Hindsight and Significance', pp. 279–80.
40. Jonathan Bell, *The Liberal State on Trial: The Cold War and American Politics in the Truman Years* (New York: Columbia University Press, 2004), pp. 238–9.
41. Robert Griffith, 'Dwight D. Eisenhower and the Corporate Commonwealth', *American Historical Review* 87 (1982): pp. 87–122; Robert Mason, '"Down the Middle of the Road": Dwight D. Eisenhower, the Republican Party, and the Politics of Consensus and Conflict, 1949–1961', in Robert Mason and Iwan Morgan, eds, *The Liberal Consensus Reconsidered: American Politics and Society in the Postwar Era* (Gainesville, FL: University Press of Florida, 2017), pp. 186–206.
42. 'Citizens for Eisenhower to Work in Congress Race', *New York Herald Tribune*, 19 Dec. 1953, p. 3; Warren Uuna, '"Congress for Eisenhower" Is New Aim', *Washington Post*, 3 Jan. 1954, p. B6.
43. Michael Bowen, *The Roots of Modern Conservatism: Dewey, Taft, and Battle for the Soul of the Republican Party* (Chapel Hill, NC: University of North Carolina Press, 2011), pp. 185–8.

44. Irwin F. Gellman, *The President and the Apprentice: Eisenhower and Nixon, 1952–1961* (New Haven, CT: Yale University Press, 2015), pp. 232–58 (quotations at p. 242, p. 246).
45. Richard M. Fried, 'Voting against the Hammer and Sickle: Communism as an Issue in American Politics', in William H. Chafe, ed., *The Achievement of American Liberalism: The New Deal and Its Legacies* (New York: Columbia University Press, 2003), pp. 112–13.
46. Daniel J. Galvin, *Presidential Party Building: Dwight D. Eisenhower to George W. Bush* (Princeton, NJ: Princeton University Press, 2010), p. 51.
47. Robert J. Donovan, 'Eisenhower Promises Help When It's Needed', *New York Herald Tribune*, 23 Sept. 1954, p. 1.
48. 'Eisenhower Pleads for GOP Victory', *Hartford Courant*, 9 Oct. 1954, p. 1.
49. 'Eisenhower Talk Hit as "Partisan"', *New York Times*, 10 Oct. 1954, p. 71.
50. 'Democrats' Aid Gives Eisenhower Most of 1954 Congress Victories', *Atlanta Journal and Atlanta Constitution*, 30 May 1954, p. F1.
51. M. R. Merrill, 'The 1954 Elections in the Eleven Western States: Introduction', *Western Political Quarterly* 7 (1954): p. 589.
52. Merrill, 'The 1954 Elections', p. 593.
53. Chester J. Pach Jr and Elmo Richardson, *The Presidency of Dwight D. Eisenhower*, rev. edn (Lawrence, KS: University Press of Kansas, 1991), p. 73.
54. Ibid., pp. 106–7, pp. 123–5.
55. Galvin, *Presidential Party Building*, pp. 46–53; Robert Mason, 'Citizens for Eisenhower and the Republican Party, 1951–1965', *Historical Journal* 56 (2013): pp. 524–7, pp. 533–4.
56. George Gallup, 'Eisenhower Popularity Slumps in Past Month', *Washington Post*, 26 Nov. 1958, p. A21.
57. Mason, 'Citizens for Eisenhower', pp. 532–3.
58. Kim Phillips-Fein, '"As Great an Issue as Slavery or Abolition": Economic Populism, the Conservative Movement, and the Right-to-Work Campaigns of 1958', *Journal of Policy History* 23 (2011): pp. 491–512.
59. Memo, Meade Alcorn to the president, 15 Dec. 1958, folder 'Alcorn, H. Meade (3)', box 1, Administration Series, Dwight D. Eisenhower Papers as President (Ann Whitman File), Dwight D. Eisenhower Presidential Library, Abilene, KS.

60. Elizabeth Tandy Shermer, 'Origins of the Conservative Ascendancy: Barry Goldwater's Early Senate Career and the De-legitimization of Organized Labor', *Journal of American History* 95 (2008): pp. 678–709.
61. Mayhew, *Parties and Policies*, p. 185; Iwan W. Morgan, *Eisenhower versus 'the Spenders': The Eisenhower Administration, the Democrats and the Budget, 1953–60* (London: Pinter, 1990).
62. Edward G. Carmines and James A. Stimson, *Issue Evolution: Race and the Transformation of American Politics* (Princeton, NJ: Princeton University Press, 1989), p. 63.
63. Angus Campbell, Philip Converse, Warren E. Miller, and Donald E. Stokes, *The American Voter* (New York: Wiley, 1960), p. 47.
64. Angus Campbell, 'Surge and Decline: A Study of Electoral Change', *Public Opinion Quarterly* 24 (1960): pp. 397–418.
65. Campbell et al., *American Voter*.

7

'Peace need not be poison at the polls': John F. Kennedy and the Challenge of the Right in the 1962 Midterms

Mark Eastwood

Shortly before the 1962 midterm elections, President John F. Kennedy's special advisor, Arthur Schlesinger Jr, met with the Soviet ambassador to the United States, Anatoly Dobrynin. During the meeting, Dobrynin expressed particular interest in what he perceived as the growing 'strength' of conservativism in the US Congress. Not only were several prominent Republican candidates standing on conservative platforms, typified by former Vice President Richard Nixon's campaign for the California governorship, but the ultra-right-wing John Birch Society (JBS) had candidates running on the Republican ticket. Given that deep social conservativism mixed with rigid anti-communism, it is not surprising that the Soviets may have been concerned by a perceived 'rightward' turn in American politics.

Schlesinger, however, reassured Dobrynin that this was all part of the natural 'ebb and flow' of American politics and that the Soviets should not worry unduly about this apparent rise of the Right: 'observers must take care not to spend all their time watching the sideshows while the parade marches by outside.'[1] In the immediate wake of the midterms, Schlesinger's dismissal seemed well founded. *New York Times* reporter Homer Bigart described the results as 'disheartening' for conservatives, noting that the public face of American ultra-conservatism, Republican Senator Barry Goldwater of Arizona, was unavailable for comment the day after the midterms because he was unexpectedly travelling.[2] Goldwater, Bigart suggested, had slunk away with his tail between his legs. The sideshow was over.

The ready dismissal of the efforts of the Right in the 1962 midterms obfuscates a significant story about the fracturing of the Democratic Solid South, the growth of the New Right, and the beginning of electoral problems for the Democrats which would see Richard Nixon – his political career seemingly finished by defeat in the California gubernatorial election of 1962 – sweep to power in the 1968 presidential election. Viewed through the prism of winners and losers, the 1962 midterms were a trend-bucking success for Democrats. This chapter, however, argues that a closer examination of voting patterns reveals a more complex picture, with Republicans making small but significant inroads in the supposedly Solid South. President Kennedy sensed these electoral weaknesses and, the chapter explains, sought to offset them by broadening his appeal to African Americans and so-called 'peace voters'. While 1962 may have signalled a strengthening of Kennedy's presidential mandate – after the narrow victory of 1960 – it also held notes of caution ahead of the 1964 presidential election. This chapter establishes that the 1962 midterms mark an important but often overlooked milestone on the road to Republican capture of the Democratic Solid South and the rise of the New Right.

1962: a victory for the Democrats?

On first viewing, the 1962 midterm elections represent a success for the incumbent Kennedy administration. As other chapters in this volume point out, one of the very few 'iron laws' of American politics is that the president's party loses seats in midterm elections.[3] Prior to 1962, the incumbent's party had lost seats in every midterm since 1894, with the sole exception of 1934. The average number of seats lost in the House (during the period 1894–1994) was thirty-six.[4] In the Senate, where staggered terms work in the president's favour, off-year election results were slightly more positive. However, the president's party lost seats in eighteen of the twenty-six midterm elections from 1894 through 1994, with an average net loss of three seats.[5]

Prior to the 1962 elections, Kennedy's Democrats held an eighty-seven-seat majority in the House (262 Democrats to 175

Republicans) and a twenty-eight-seat majority in the Senate (64–36); the alliance of southern Democrats with Republicans meant that Kennedy's working margins were smaller, however. With such finely balanced majorities, there was both peril and opportunity in 1962. Publicly acknowledging in July that 'history is so much against us', Kennedy nevertheless added, 'If we can hold our own and win five seats or ten seats, it could change the whole opinion in the House and in the Senate . . .'[6] Republican leaders talked optimistically about winning the additional forty-four House seats they needed to take a majority; privately, they were projecting gains of ten to twenty seats. The Democrats' own projections offered a similarly negative forecast, pushing Kennedy into active participation in the campaign.[7] In doing so, the president ignored the advice of Arthur Schlesinger Jr that history suggested that active intervention in the midterms by a sitting president was a 'mistake'.[8]

Kennedy's campaigning was certainly a risk. His election in 1960 had itself been unusual, insomuch as it was the first election in the twentieth century in which a party regained control of the White House without increasing its representation in Congress. Kennedy had offered no coat-tails that down-ballot Democrats could ride to Capitol Hill. Indeed, the inverse was true, with Democratic House candidates running five percentage points ahead of Kennedy in 1960.[9] The patchy record of Kennedy's early years, particularly on foreign policy, also meant that he threatened to inject negative reactions to his prosecution of the Cold War into local election issues. With growing instability in Vietnam, failure at the Bay of Pigs and humiliation at the Vienna Summit with Khrushchev, Andrew Johns notes that the administration had become 'increasingly sensitive' about the impact of Kennedy's foreign policy on the elections.[10] Meanwhile, Kennedy's failure to act decisively on his civil rights promises of 1960 had led to increasing disquiet among some African Americans, a key constituency for national Democrats.[11]

Yet, events of early autumn of 1962 offered some optimism for Democrats. First, Kennedy actively intervened to ensure the enrolment of James Meredith, a Black US military veteran, at the previously all-white University of Mississippi in late

September, before using federal troops to quell resulting civil unrest and ensure Meredith successfully undertook his studies. Pollster Lou Harris informed Kennedy that his decisive handling of the crisis had won over voters in key northern industrial states by as much as a three-to-one margin. This, coupled with Kennedy's firm stance over Berlin, had increased the political capital of the president and allowed for cautious optimism ahead of the elections. By early October, Harris told Kennedy that he was 'more in control of this election than ever before'.[12] Then came the discovery of Soviet missiles in Cuba.

Much has been written about Kennedy's handling of the Cuban Missile Crisis, including its impact on domestic politics. In perhaps the most exhaustive analysis of its effects on the 1962 midterms, Thomas Patterson and William Brophy make clear that the crisis was not manufactured to help Democrats win the elections, nor was it a decisive factor in their outcome. Rather, it had an 'indiscriminate' effect: it 'helped some Democrats and hurt some Democrats; it buoyed some Republicans and weakened some Republicans', while 'in many instances Cuba was not even a conspicuous campaign issue'.[13] Polling data revealed no major shift after Cuba: the optimism with which Harris viewed the election for Kennedy in October remained in place by November. On the eve of the election, the *New York Times* predicted Democratic gains in the Senate, with only minor losses in the House.[14]

The results appeared even more promising. In the Senate, Democrats gained four seats and, while they did not fully buck the historical trend in the House, they recorded a net loss of just four representatives, with the Republicans gaining only one.[15] In the gubernatorial races, where the 'most significant' Republican gains had been forecast, the two parties each took seven governorships from the other party, leaving the overall partisan balance unchanged.[16] Most noteworthy of these was the defeat of Kennedy's 1960 opponent, Richard Nixon, in California. Nixon's defeat, Arthur Schlesinger Jr later admitted, gave the White House a 'special fillip of entertainment'.[17]

Nixon's loss was indicative of a widespread 'bad night' for the conservatives over whom Dobrynin had expressed growing concern. In particular, the ultra-conservative John Birch Society saw its four standard-bearer candidates defeated, including two incumbent congressmen, John H. Rousselot and Edgar W. Hiestand. In all four races, the *New York Times* concluded, their opponents managed to make 'Birchism' the single issue in each campaign, with candidates expending their energies explaining to voters why they belonged to a 'monolithic secret society' whose leader had called President Dwight D. Eisenhower an agent of communism.[18] For conservatives who accepted support from the John Birch Society but took a broader conservative stance, there was a little more success. In Kentucky's Third District congressional race, Gene Snyder, an ultra-conservative Republican, ousted the liberal Democrat, Frank W. Burke. Snyder had accepted the support of the Birch Society while courting that of more moderate conservative groups, such as Americans for Constitutional Action. There were also victories for conservatives in Colorado, Wyoming, and Utah, while the newly formed Conservative Party – a more moderate manifestation of the new conservative trend – at least did well enough in New York to guarantee the party's candidates would be on the ballot again in 1964.[19]

Virtually all of the successful conservative candidates were labelled as 'Goldwater-types', after the strongly conservative Arizona senator. Indeed, there was already a concerted campaign under way, particularly in the South, to place Goldwater on the Republican presidential ticket for 1964. However, the 1962 elections appeared to endorse a more moderate Republicanism. In looking ahead to 1964, the *New Republic* concluded that moderates were 'in the driver's seat', with New York's re-elected Republican governor Nelson Rockefeller the most likely Republican nominee, followed by newly elected moderate governors William Scranton of Pennsylvania and George Romney of Michigan.[20] In a similar 1964 preview, Barry Goldwater received a mere passing mention from liberal journalist Tom Wicker of the *New York Times*, who optimistically concluded that, with a moderate likely to win out, the 'prophet of the right-wing' was a 'star in decline'.[21]

By contrast, the *New York Times* hailed the election as a 'remarkable success' for Kennedy, which gave the young president 'greater prestige – and political strength'.[22] Schlesinger declared that the president's 'personal mandate was triumphantly refreshed'.[23] Kennedy, his aide Theodore Sorensen later wrote, knew the results 'were better than we hoped', yet he also held a shade of caution, noting that, 'we were about where we were the last two years'.[24] Despite that initial optimism, Kennedy was right to be cautious. The Senate gains and House losses had been small, meaning that the composition of Congress was changed to only a limited extent. The *Kansas City Star* argued that it had actually been a 'status quo' election where little would change in terms of congressional voting, leaving it 'a shade more conservative in the House, and a shade more liberal in the Senate.'[25] The results of the 1962 midterms appear remarkable insomuch as they were unremarkable. While Kennedy did partially buck the trend of incumbent midterm defeats, the make-up of Congress remained near-identical and he would continue to face a challenging congressional picture. For Republicans, the results were certainly not a national success, but they were far from 'clobbered' as some within the GOP initially diagnosed.[26]

What then can we learn from the 1962 midterms? The answer can be found in voting patterns, rather than outright results. As this chapter next demonstrates, voting in 1962 showed clear and emergent faults in the traditional Democratic base in the Solid South. This challenge to Democratic dominance in the South – and Republican efforts to exploit it – would stimulate Kennedy's efforts to broaden his electoral appeal to African Americans and 'peace voters', before his untimely death in 1963.

1962: fracturing of the Solid South?

One of the most significant voter trends in 1962 was the growth of the Republican vote in the South, which had long been a Democratic stronghold.[27] After World War II, Republicans had made concerted efforts to crack Democratic control. This process began with the 1948 election, when the idea of a two-party South became imaginable for the first time. The breakaway from the Democrats' presidential ticket by the States' Rights Democratic Party, or 'Dixiecrats', in 1948 was crucial in weakening the national party's position in the region. Several prominent members later defected to the Republican Party – most notably, in 1964, Senator Strom Thurmond of South Carolina, who had been the Dixiecrats' presidential nominee.[28] The presidency of Dwight D. Eisenhower in the 1950s played an important role in further expanding Republican influence. This process would culminate with the presidential election of 1968, which, Kari Frederickson has shown, made inevitable the 'region's political transition from a Democratic to a Republican stronghold'.[29] The elections of 1962 are overlooked in this story. Beyond the winners and losers column, they reveal much about Republican successes and the strategies begun under Eisenhower, notably Operation Dixie, and was essential in providing what the *New York Times* termed a significant 'toehold' in the South upon which to build towards 1968.[30]

It had been in the decade prior to Kennedy's election that the Republicans had started to make small gains in the South. In particular, the election of Republican Dwight D. Eisenhower in 1952 was, in the words of Earl Black and Merle Black, a 'path-breaking candidacy', which focused the appeal of Republican fiscal conservativism on the growing white middle class of the peripheral southern states.[31] In the election, Eisenhower carried Florida, Virginia, Tennessee, Texas and Oklahoma. Four years later, in the 1956 election, Eisenhower carried the same southern states, dropping Oklahoma but adding the Deep South state of Louisiana. Keen to capitalise on this success, Eisenhower and the GOP launched Operation Dixie, which focused on scaling up Republican apparatus throughout the South and conveying to the people of the region the importance of a two-party system. Republicans, as Joseph E. Lowndes notes, portrayed themselves as the moderate party, in stark contrast to the racial extremism of white southern Democrats. However, this focus on moderate-to-conservative voters and Eisenhower's growing support for civil rights after 1956 – particularly during the Little Rock school integration crisis – slowed Republican progress in the white South. [32]

In spite of this slowdown, Kennedy struggled in some areas of the white South in 1960. Texas and Louisiana re-entered the

Democratic fold but Kennedy lost the electoral college votes of Mississippi and half of Alabama's.[33] Two interrelated factors were at play in Kennedy's declining white southern vote. First was the issue of civil rights. Concerned about his vulnerability with African Americans, and much to the dismay of white southerners, Kennedy and the Democrats endorsed a strong civil rights plank at the Democratic National Convention. Second, the Republicans were well placed to capitalise on this white southern unease because of the apparatus Eisenhower had put in place. Particularly significant was Operation Dixie, which now pivoted from presenting Republicans as the moderate party on the race issue to attacking the Democrats' civil rights plank as 'a direct slap in the face' to southern Democrats.[34] Conservative Republicans were growing increasingly attractive in the South. Most popular after Nixon was Barry Goldwater who, Operation Dixie reported, could speak in three separate cities each day and still not fulfil the sheer number of speaking requests he was receiving across the South.[35] Cracks were beginning to appear in the Solid South. Nixon won 46 per cent of the vote in the region and carried three peripheral states – Florida, Tennessee, and Virginia. Significantly, Republicans also made headway for the first time further down the ticket. In five gubernatorial races, Lowndes writes, the Republican candidates increased their vote by '105 percent above the 1956 level or by over one million votes'.[36] Such was the success in the South in 1960 that the GOP expanded their activities for 1962 and beyond.

Even before the 1962 midterms, Kennedy was dealt a blow in the South. His Vice President, Lyndon B. Johnson, had made the unusual decision in 1960 to run both on the presidential ticket and for re-election as a senator for Texas. After becoming vice president in 1961, a special election was held to fill his vacant Senate seat. Against a divided Democratic Party, the conservative Republican John Tower – whom Johnson had defeated in 1960 – won 50.6 per cent of the vote to the Democrats' 49.4 per cent and became the first Republican senator for the South in the twentieth century. While Democrats dismissed the outcome as a fluke, Kenneth Bridges argues that Tower's victory was a 'harbinger' of the party's growth: the GOP could finally be considered a viable alternative in the South.[37] This was a trend that would continue in the 1962 midterms.

Going into 1962, both parties had an eye on the South. Republicans hoped to build on the inroads of the previous decade and to ride the shockwave created by Tower's election to create a genuine two-party state in the region. Democrats, meanwhile, sought to consolidate their position, using the popularity of Vice President Johnson to offset growing southern disquiet. However, the party was also conscious of a 'white backlash' to civil rights in the South and began to pursue a coalition of 'new liberals' from the growing urban and suburban areas above the Mason–Dixon line which, James Reston reported, was designed to help 'overcome' potential Republican growth in the South.[38]

After the election, both parties claimed to have been the more successful in the region. The GOP, Democrats argued, had failed to make the significant gains that Republicans had hoped for. Republican candidates were unable to dislodge any southern senators, winning seats in only Colorado and Wyoming. In the House, they picked up a total of just five southern seats. Four new Republican congressmen came from Kentucky, Tennessee, Texas, and North Carolina, while Republicans won one of the four new seats Florida had gained resulting from the state's population growth.[39] In the gubernatorial races, Henry Bellmon became Oklahoma's first ever Republican governor. In Texas, however, the success of John Tower could not be translated into winning the governor's mansion, with Lyndon Johnson's protégé, John B. Connally, defeating Republican Jack Cox. The Republicans, claimed Texas Democratic chairman, Eugene Locke, had 'failed' in their project to make Texas, and indeed the South, a two-party state.[40]

How then were the Republicans able to claim success? The answer lies in the number and strength of votes the GOP polled. In the previous off-year election, Republicans received just 606,000 votes across the South. In 1962, they won more than two million votes.[41] They may not have claimed many new seats in the region, but Republicans ran the Democrats far closer than before. In Senate races, James D. Martin lost to the veteran

Democrat Lister Hill by just nine-tenths of 1 per cent, while in South Carolina Republican W. D. Workman Jr took 42.8 per cent of the vote, a 25 per cent swing from Democrats to Republicans. Incredibly tight races could also be found in the House, with Democratic incumbent, Clifford Davis, defeating his Republican challenger by 1 per cent. Even in the Texas gubernatorial race, Jack Cox still polled over 45 per cent against the Johnson-backed Connally. The Democrats may have prevailed in the South in 1962, but, as Joseph E. Lowndes concludes, Republicans 'did extraordinarily well around the South by southern standards'. Success trickled down from the top of the ticket, with 'major gains' made in local elections in Georgia, Alabama, Texas, Tennessee, and North Carolina.[42] Even in states where Democrats easily defeated Republicans, the *New York Times* noted, many Republicans still polled 'sizeable' numbers for the first time.[43] Admitting defeat in Texas, Jack Cox 'promised' Democrats that the battle for the South was just beginning, with a true two-party state as the prize.[44] The elections of 1962 may not have been the end of the Democratic Solid South, but this was the moment when southern Republicanism was felt in a 'major way' for the first time, according to Andrew Busch, a force that would 'blossom' by 1966.[45] In the more immediate term, President Kennedy faced a re-election campaign in 1964. The final section of this chapter considers the impact of the midterms on Kennedy's early strategising for 1964, as the administration sought to offset a weakening position in the South.

1964: the challenge ahead

The votes of African Americans had been crucial in Kennedy's victory in 1960. Had only whites voted, Nixon would have carried 52 per cent of the popular vote and would have won Illinois, Michigan, Texas, South Carolina, and, possibly, Louisiana. Kennedy needed to lose only two of those five states to have lost the election.[46] Despite this, and the progressive civil rights plank the Democrats had adopted in the campaign, Kennedy had been slow to act on the issue once in office. The president felt he simply did not have the congressional majorities to push through an ambitious civil rights programme. As Mark Stern has written, not only was it exceedingly difficult to pass any legislation, given that white southerners controlled the majority of congressional committees, but Kennedy feared that Congress would then retaliate by 'wreaking havoc' on the rest of his legislative programme.[47] The result was a cautious approach to questions of civil rights.[48]

By 1962, however, this approach was giving Kennedy a problem. African Americans – along with some white voters – were becoming increasingly dissatisfied by his timidity on civil rights. During the 1960 campaign, Kennedy had promised to eliminate housing discrimination 'by a stroke of the presidential pen'. Two years later, and after no significant improvements, civil rights campaigners began sending thousands of pens to the White House and greeting him in public with signs reading 'Pick Up the Pen, Mr. President'.[49] Kennedy's cautiousness ahead of the midterms led some African American voters to inform the *New York Times* that they were considering 'staying home' that November. Kennedy's intervention in the University of Mississippi crisis promised to 'hold African Americans in line' for the Democrats, but it also reflected the importance of an active civil rights policy for the president in holding on to the votes which carried him to a slim majority in 1960.[50] Conversely, where he had – often reluctantly – intervened in civil rights, Kennedy earned the ire of white southerners. Historians have, for example, drawn a clear link between the white southern 'backlash' to Kennedy's involvement at the University of Mississippi and Republican gains in the South in the 1962 midterms.[51] During his first two years in office, Kennedy had attempted to make enough progress on civil rights to appeal to African Americans, without alienating the white South. By late 1962, this balancing act appeared increasingly unachievable.

The significance of the African American vote in 1960 meant that Kennedy needed to maintain and expand their electoral support ahead of 1964. However, the midterms had revealed that any close association with civil rights threatened Kennedy's support in an already fracturing white South. The Republicans sensed this growing vulnerability. Republican strategists, Kenneth Bridges explains, saw race as the 'wedge' that could lead Republicans back to the White House. After 1962, many southern Republicans intensified their oppositional stance to civil rights, aiming to 'make the party more palatable to politically homeless conservatives and an attractive alternative to the remainder'.[52] This, however, meant a further embrace of the conservativism that had not fared too well nationally in 1962. Now, though, a rightward move for the party was, William Rusher argued in *National Review*, the only feasible way to beat Kennedy in 1964. This meant, Rusher concluded, an embrace of Barry Goldwater, the conservative candidate who had been immensely popular across the South in 1962 and who might 'carry enough Southern and Border States to offset the inevitable Kennedy conquests in the big industrial states of the North and still stand a serious chance of winning the election'.[53] If 1962 had highlighted to Republicans, especially those in the South, that conservativism and opposing civil rights might offer the best path back to the White House, it also stressed to national Democrats the importance of the Black vote in mitigating against a loss of white southern support.

The year 1963 marked a turning point in Kennedy's approach to civil rights. Alongside renewed efforts at a legislative breakthrough, the events in Birmingham, Alabama, that April – where the city's police force reacted with extreme violence towards organised non-violent civil rights protestors, including many children – brought civil rights to the fore, both nationally and internationally, and sharpened Kennedy's focus. As non-violent protests spread across the South that summer, Kennedy's speeches gave 'presidential sanction', as Schlesinger later put it, to the movement.[54] Gone was the previously timid approach. In June 1963, Kennedy sent his Civil Rights bill up to the Hill. As the chair of the Westchester County (New York) Democratic Committee predicted, if civil rights legislation were 'on the books and off television by January [1964], we will do better than '60'.[55] However, given the congressional composition after 1962, Kennedy knew that securing any legislative breakthrough before 1964 would be difficult.

Kennedy's new stance on civil rights legislation drew the ire of Democratic representatives in the states of the former

Confederacy. In the weeks before he sent the bill to Congress, Kennedy was already feeling the 'sting of retribution' as eighteen Southern congressmen reversed their previous votes in support of the administration's Area Redevelopment bill, contributing to a narrow 209–208 defeat.[56] By the autumn of 1963, according to one poll, the civil rights issue had already turned 4.5 million white voters against the administration. This 'white backlash' was not just confined to the South. Northern Democrats also reported growing unrest among their white constituents about the pace of progress on civil rights. African Americans, according to one respondent, were being 'crammed down our throats' by the administration. Some Democrats, Arthur Schlesinger Jr concluded, 'thought that civil rights might very well lose the election for Kennedy in 1964'.[57] At the same time as Kennedy's white southern support was waning, the Republicans were firming up their own strategy ahead of the election. Responding to criticisms that their campaign had become a race-based one, Republican strategist F. Clifton White later wrote that, although Republicans had never suggested writing off African American and minority voters, they had to nevertheless 'face political realities'. Republicans were highly unlikely to win the presidency on the basis of support in northern states alone, and, as such, the 'only hope' the party had 'was to win the Southern states'.[58] The tacit acknowledgement was that opposing civil rights and the white southern vote were the way to achieve that.

Prior to 1962, Kennedy had balked at the political damage an activist civil rights agenda might bring, especially in the South. Now, however, in the face of increasing southern unrest and despite significant Republican growth in the 1962 midterms, he persevered with his support for civil rights. In part, this was due to the growing strength and momentum of the civil rights movement, as well as an apparent newfound 'legitimate interest', in the words of Derek Catsam, in pursuing civil rights legislation.[59] At the same time, the difficulties he would face in 1964 were never far from his mind. While a more positive stance on civil rights would cement his support among African Americans, Kennedy, Robert Dallek writes, worried privately whether enough African Americans would turn out to vote in 1964 to 'make a significant difference' in offsetting the losses in the white vote his civil rights position would bring.[60]

How then did Kennedy plan to broaden his electoral appeal? First, it must be noted that Kennedy did not entirely give up on the white South. In particular, Dallek has noted that Kennedy subscribed to Lou Harris's view of a 'New South', in which segregation and conservativism did not dominate. Instead, Harris argued, there was a new class of educated, industrial white southerners whose vote might help to mitigate broader losses in the region. While he may have been optimistic about his appeal to the 'New South' voter, Kennedy also recognised that his support among other marginal groups, especially women, was 'soft'.[61] There was, however, one significant issue by which Kennedy might firm up some of this support: peace.

As the Cold War arms race intensified in the 1950s, there developed a small but increasingly vocal peace movement in the United States, including Women Strike for Peace (WSP) and the Committee for a Sane Nuclear Policy (SANE). These groups began life with an initial goal of ending nuclear testing as the first step on the road to abolishing nuclear weapons and ending the Cold War.[62] In the 1962 midterms, the organisations supported a number of 'peace candidates' in their bid for office. Although much less extreme than the John Birch Society, peace candidates remained on the margins of mainstream political debate in the early 1960s. And, much like the John Birch Society, their 1962 candidates were dismissed as offering a poor electoral showing and, according to the *New Republic*, 'sinking without a trace'.[63]

The mood among the activists, however, was much more optimistic. The majority of their candidates had lost in 1962, but three successful peace candidates were elected to the House of Representatives, including two in California where the incumbent JBS representatives had been ousted from office. As a single-issue platform, peace candidates, like JBS candidates, remained on the margins. However, what 1962 had shown was that peace, like conservativism, could win over voters as a broader electoral issue. In New York alone, WSP reported that they had mobilised 50,000 voters for peace, regardless of their party affiliation.[64] In a post-election conference in California, the mood among the peace organisations was one of 'optimism bordering on jubilation'. The lesson of 1962, activist Paul Albert celebrated, was that peace 'need not be poison at the polls'. In the wake of the midterms, the movement doubled down on their electoral efforts, recognising that 'to get peace as soon as possible ... the only answer is politics. Serious, realistic, effective political action.'[65]

As peace groups intensified their initiatives for 1964, President Kennedy was embarking on his own efforts to defuse Cold War tensions. This began with the American University speech in the summer of 1963 and culminated in the signing of the Limited Test Ban Treaty with the United Kingdom and Soviet Union, which ended above-ground nuclear testing. Domestic political considerations and the growing influence of the peace movement were a significant factor in Kennedy's renewed pursuit of a treaty after the 1962 midterms.[66] Conservatives and Cold War hawks vigorously opposed the treaty and the apparent relaxation of tensions with the Soviet Union. However, among moderates and peace groups the treaty was immensely popular. In the aftermath of the treaty's signing, Kennedy undertook a pre-1964 election tour of the American West. To some surprise within the administration, Theodore Sorensen recalled, the treaty was extremely popular, even in the 'the heart of right-wing territory'.[67] Just as Kennedy had increased his commitment to civil rights after the 1962 midterms, so, too, had he intensified his support for peace issues and a relaxation of Cold War tensions. In doing so, he continued to alienate those ultra-conservatives whom Barry Goldwater and the Republicans were courting, but, more importantly, it won Kennedy support among moderates and even some less hard-line conservatives. It was these votes that could help him offset the losses in the South which the GOP and Kennedy's civil rights stance threatened to inflict. The 1962 midterms had indicated that Kennedy could rely less and less on the idea of a Democratic Solid South. But he could also exploit other areas of the electorate as a tool to redress declining support in the white South. The 'peace discourse' which, Arthur Schlesinger Jr admitted, had given the Left a 'moment of genuine hope' after 1962 could, Kennedy strategised, become a significant political lever ahead of 1964.[68]

One crucial element of Kennedy's courting of the peace vote was the centrality of women within the movement. In the aftermath of the 1962 midterms, Kennedy was increasingly wary of his 'soft' electoral position with women.[69] Aligning with the priorities of the peace movement offered one way for Kennedy to restore his appeal. WSP was at the forefront of women's engagement with the peace issue. Founded in 1961, in response to the growing crisis over nuclear testing, WSP's first significant action was to bring out 50,000 women in sixty cities for a general peace demonstration in November of 1961. They framed their protest through the lens of gender, charging Kennedy and his administration with failing to protect the nation from the dangers of nuclear weapons and asserting that it was their motherly duty to protect their families. This framing helped broaden their appeal to include more moderate-conservative women by centring on the traditional family structure. Following their first 'strike', WSP celebrated that fact that, for the first time since the move for women's suffrage, 'the New York newspapers have given a women's movement front page coverage'.[70]

Increasingly, WSP came to focus its efforts on lobbying and political activism. In May 1963, for instance, 1800 WSP members, representing thirty-seven states, descended on Washington to lobby their representatives in Congress to support a nuclear test ban treaty. For a president concerned about the softness of his position with female voters, securing the support of an organisation like WSP could make a crucial difference at the polls. As WSP co-founder Dagmar Wilson wrote, if agreement could be struck between the president and WSP, the organisation would 'go all out for him' in 1964, such that 'he might win by a landslide . . . instead of the narrow margin he gained in 1960'.[71] While his increasing support for peace and relaxation of the Cold War appealed to moderate and even conservative voters, Kennedy made sure to go out of his way to reinforce the centrality of women to the movement's success. Like WSP, he did so in a manner centred on traditional notions of the family in order to make his message palatable to moderate and conservative voters.[72] Giving an exclusive interview to seven women's periodicals, Kennedy talked openly about the importance of women's engagement in issues of war and peace.[73] Responding to Kennedy's interview, Dagmar Wilson celebrated the fact that WSP had been at the fore of creating what was now being termed the 'Mothers' Vote'.[74] This represented not just a success for the movement but also the realisation of Kennedy's own attempts to broaden his support ahead of the 1964 election. A letter from Coretta Scott King – prominent civil rights leader – to WSP which argued that 'peace among nations and peace in Birmingham, Alabama, cannot be separated' reflected an explicit linkage of two core issues that Kennedy hoped would offset his weakened position in the South: civil rights and the (female) peace vote.[75] Quite how this would have played out in 1964 remains unknown, with Kennedy's assassination fundamentally changing the landscape of the election.

Initially, the 1962 midterm elections appear remarkable insomuch as they were one of the two occasions between 1894 and 1998 when the rule of incumbent midterm losses was bucked. Yet, if we look beyond the outcome of the races to the voting trends, we see that 1962 was a crucial election in signposting the breakdown of the Democratic Solid South. Although the impact of this process on the presidential ticket would be felt vehemently in 1968 with the election of Richard Nixon – supposedly the main victim of the 1962 midterms – even the death of President Kennedy could not fully offset these issues in the 1964 election. Lyndon Johnson carried all of the country against Barry Goldwater, with the exception of Arizona and the Deep South. The civil rights problem for the Democrats in the South, which became increasingly evident in and after the 1962 midterms, remained a problem for Johnson. Despite winning the presidency, Johnson – his own political career forged in the South – lost the overall southern popular vote (49 per cent to 48.9 per cent) and 'overwhelmingly' lost the Deep South Black Belt region, altering 100 years of political alignment.[76]

The warning signs were there in 1962, and Kennedy did seek to address losses in the South by focusing on civil rights and broadening his appeal to moderates and women through a more vocal pursuit of 'peace' issues. Johnson would continue these efforts, passing crucial civil rights legislation and continuing to align with the peace movement, going as far as to personally thank

SANE for 'all the help you've been to me' in his 1964 election.[77] However, in the South, the die was cast. While the 1962 midterm elections appeared to reaffirm President Kennedy's mandate, they also exacerbated the growing fault lines which would see the Democrats ousted from the Oval Office in 1968, with the transfer of the Solid South from Democrat to Republican.

Notes

1. 'Memorandum from the President's Special Assistant (Schlesinger) to Secretary of State Rusk', 20 Aug. 1962, *Foreign Relations of the United States, 1961–1963*, vol. V: *Soviet Union*, ed. Charles S. Sampson and John Michael Joyce (Washington, DC: Government Printing Office, 1998), Document 223.
2. Homer Bigart, 'Election Returns are a Blow to the Right Wing', *New York Times*, 8 Nov. 1962.
3. Alan I. Abramowitz, Albert D. Cover, and Helmut Norpoth, 'The President's Party in Midterm Elections: Going from Bad to Worse', *American Journal of Political Science* 30 (1986): p. 563.
4. Andrew E. Busch, *Horses in Midstream: US Midterm Elections and Their Consequences* (Pittsburgh, PA: University of Pittsburgh Press, 1999), p. 14.
5. Busch, *Horses in Midstream*, p. 16.
6. Arthur M. Schlesinger Jr, *A Thousand Days: John F. Kennedy in the White House*, 1983 edn (New York: Greenwich House, 1983), pp. 756–7; 'Transcript of the President's News Conference on Foreign and Domestic Affairs', *New York Times*, 24 July 1962.
7. Thomas G. Paterson and William J. Brophy, 'October Missiles and November Elections: The Cuban Missile Crisis and American Politics, 1962', *Journal of American History* 73 (1986): pp. 90–1.
8. Schlesinger, *Thousand Days*, p. 757.
9. Paterson and Brophy, 'October Missiles', p. 91.
10. Andrew L. Johns, *Vietnam's Second Front: Domestic Politics, theRepublican Party and the War* (Lexington, KY: University Press of Kentucky, 2010), p. 27.
11. Derek C. Catsam, 'Civil Rights', in Mark J. Selverstone, ed, *A Companion to John F. Kennedy* (Malden, MA: Wiley Blackwell, 2014), pp. 540–57.
12. Paterson and Brophy, 'October Missiles', p. 92.
13. Ibid., p. 92.

14. Tom Wicker, 'Democratic Gain in Senate Likely; Party Could Add 1 to 3 Seats in 39 Election Races', *New York Times*, 1 Nov. 1962.
15. Benjamin J. Guthrie, *Statistics of the Congressional Election of November 6, 1962* (Washington, DC: Government Printing Office, 1963), p. 46.
16. Tom Wicker, 'GOP Gain Likely in Governorships', *New York Times*, 4 Nov. 1962.
17. Schlesinger, *Thousand Days*, 833.
18. Homer Bigart, 'New York Conservatives Claim a Moral Victory in Showing on First State-Wide Test', *New York Times*, 7 Nov. 1962.
19. Ibid.
20. 'Whose Victory Was It?' *New Republic*, 17 Nov. 1962, p. 5.
21. Tom Wicker, 'Election Returns Bring into Focus the Personalities for '64', *New York Times*, 11 Nov. 1962.
22. Tom Wicker, 'President Elated', *New York Times*, 8 Nov. 1962.
23. Schlesinger, *Thousand Days*, p. 833.
24. Theodore Sorensen, *Kennedy*, Harper Perennial Modern Classics edn (New York: Harper Perennial, 2009), p. 354.
25. 'Opinion of the Week: At Home and Abroad', *New York Times*, 11 Nov. 1962.
26. Cabell Phillips, 'Kennedy and Democratic Aides Heartened by Victory at Polls', *New York Times*, 8 Nov. 1962.
27. While recognising the political, cultural, and economic nuances of the idea of the 'US South', for the purposes of this essay 'the South' refers to the southern states identified by the US census (South Carolina, Mississippi, Florida, Alabama, Georgia, Louisiana, Texas, Virginia, Arkansas, North Carolina, Tennessee, Missouri, Kentucky, Oklahoma, and West Virginia) excluding Delaware and Maryland, which became more politically aligned with northern states in the 1960s. An important area of distinction is between the Deep South (Georgia, Alabama, South Carolina, Mississippi, and Louisiana) and the remaining states, which I term the 'peripheral' southern states for ease of distinction. 'The South' here also refers exclusively to white southerners, in large part because of the suppression of the Black and minority vote in those states. See: US Census Bureau, 'Census Regions and Divisions of the United States', www2.census.gov/geo/pdfs/maps-data/maps/reference/us_regdiv.pdf, accessed 21 July 2020.
28. Kari Frederickson, *The Dixiecrat Revolt and the End of the Solid South, 1932–1968* (Chapel Hill, NC: University of North Carolina Press, 2001).

29. Ibid., p. 4.
30. Tom Wicker, 'Seen In Results of Congress Election', *New York Times*, 8 Nov. 1962.
31. Earl Black and Merle Black, *The Rise of Southern Republicans* (Cambridge, MA: Harvard University Press, 2002), p. 24.
32. Joseph E. Lowndes, *From the New Deal to the New Right: Race and the Southern Origins of Modern Conservatism* (New Haven, CT: Yale University Press, 2008), pp. 45–6.
33. Frederickson, *Dixiecrat Revolt*, p. 235.
34. Lowndes, *New Right*, p. 58.
35. Ibid., p. 59.
36. Ibid., p. 59.
37. Kenneth Bridges, *Twilight of the Texas Democrats: The 1978 Governor's Race* (College Station, TX: Texas A&M University Press, 2008), p. 11.
38. James Reston, '50 Million Vote', *New York Times*, 7 Nov. 1962.
39. Wicker, 'Seen in Results'.
40. 'Republicans Fail to Make Texas a 2-Party State', *New York Times*, 11 Nov. 1962.
41. Lowndes, *New Right*, p. 64.
42. Ibid., p. 64.
43. Claude Sitton, 'GOP's Strength on Rise in South', *New York Times*, 7 Nov. 1962.
44. 'Republicans Fail to Make Texas a 2-Party State', *New York Times*, 11 Nov. 1962.
45. Busch, *Horses in Midstream*, p. 147.
46. Schlesinger, *Thousand Days*, p. 930.
47. Mark Stern, 'Calculating Visions: Civil Rights Legislation in the Kennedy and Johnson Years', *Journal of Policy History* 5 (1993): p. 233.
48. Nick Bryant, *The Bystander: John F. Kennedy and the Struggle for Black Equality* (New York: Basic Books, 2006).
49. Catsam, 'Civil Rights', p. 541.
50. 'Negro Democrats Find Ticket Dull', *New York Times*, 3 Nov. 1962.
51. Bridges, *Texas Democrats*, p. 11; Lowndes, *New Right*, p. 64. Indeed, this 'backlash' was not just limited to the South. Lisa McGirr has made clear that in the West, too, Democrats drawn into conservative circles in the 1960s had an important impact on the rise of the New Right: Lisa McGirr, *Suburban Warriors:*

The Origins of the New American Right (Princeton, NJ: Princeton University Press, 2001).

52. Bridges, *Texas Democrats*, p. 12.
53. Quoted in Lowndes, *New Right*, p. 66.
54. Schlesinger, *Thousand Days*, p. 964.
55. Robert Dallek, *John F. Kennedy: An Unfinished Life* (New York: Penguin, 2003), p. 687.
56. Stern, 'Calculating Visions', p. 235.
57. Schlesinger, *Thousand Days*, pp. 967–8.
58. Quoted in Lowndes, *New Right*, p. 67.
59. Catsam, 'Civil Rights', p. 545.
60. Dallek, *Unfinished Life*, p. 688.
61. Ibid., pp. 688–9. The idea of a racially moderate, economically focused New South has persisted since the end of Reconstruction but has continuously failed to materialise in a meaningful way. See: Howard N. Rabinowitz, *The First New South, 1865–1920* (Arlington Heights, IL: Harlan Davidson, 1992), pp. 1–4.
62. The most complete history of these movements remains Lawrence S. Wittner, *The Struggle against the Bomb*, 3 vols (Stanford, CA: Stanford University Press, 1993–2003).
63. 'Whose Victory Was It?', p. 4.
64. 'Press Release', 2 Nov. 1962, folder 'Literature: 1961–63', box 1, series C1, Women Strike for Peace [hereafter WSP], Swarthmore College Peace Collection, Swarthmore, PA [hereafter SCPC].
65. Paul Albert, 'Political Action Workshop', 16 Nov. 1962, folder 'Regional Conference: The Search for Survival, 1962', box 8, series A, SANE Inc., Records [hereafter SANE], SCPC.
66. Mark Eastwood, 'Anti-Nuclear Activism and Electoral Politics in the 1963 Test Ban Treaty', *Diplomatic History* 44 (2020): pp. 133–56; Paul Rubinson, '"Crucified on a Cross of Atoms": Scientists, Politics, and the Test Ban Treaty', *Diplomatic History* 35 (2011): pp. 283–319.
67. Sorensen, *Kennedy*, p. 744.
68. Schlesinger, *Thousand Days,* p. 749; Lawrence Freedman, *Kennedy's Wars: Berlin, Cuba, Laos and Vietnam* (New York: Oxford University Press, 2000), p. 275.
69. Dalek, *Unfinished Life*, p. 688.
70. Memo, n.d. 1961, folder 'Literature, 1961', box 1, series A2, WSP, SCPC.
71. Dagmar Wilson to Norman Cousins, 27 May 1963, folder 'Letters to Officials', box 1, series A3, WSP, SCPC.

72. Kennedy's focus on traditional family structures was also clear in his civil defence campaigns. See: Thomas Bishop, *Every Home a Fortress: Cold War Fatherhood and the Fallout Shelters* (Amherst, MA: University of Massachusetts Press, 2020).
73. Ray Robinson, 'President Kennedy Talks about You, Your Children, and Peace', *Good Housekeeping*, Nov. 1963, p. 73.
74. Dagmar Wilson, 'WSP 2nd Anniversary' (1 Nov. 1963), folder 'Test Ban', box 2, series acc. 94A-051, WSP, SCPC.
75. Dorothy Bernstein, 'Test Ban Lobby Report – May 7', 1963, folder 'Literature January – December 1963', box 1, series A2, WSP, SCPC.
76. Stern, 'Calculating Visions', p. 240.
77. 'SANE Conference Sets New Policies', *SANE World* 4, Jan. 1965.

Part Three

The Republican Resurgence

8

War on Poverty Stalled, Nixon Recalled: Republican Revival and the 1966 Midterm Elections

Mark McLay

The 1966 midterm elections foreshadowed the next two decades of American politics. The contest sounded the starting gun for an era of Republican ascendance in which the Grand Old Party (GOP) proved adept at seizing executive control but was never quite able to break the Democratic Party's iron grip on Congress. On a regional level, the elections also proved predictive, with the Republican Party making significant inroads into the Mountain West, the Democrats cementing their control of the East, and the Midwest emerging as the true battleground of American politics. Despite GOP hopes, Republican gains in the South were modest – a sign of the region's stubborn loyalty to local southern Democrats that would stymie the GOP's congressional ambitions for a couple of generations. Elsewhere, the dominant politicians of the following two decades – Richard Nixon and Ronald Reagan – played a starring role in the contest. In terms of voter attitudes, the 1966 elections signalled a growing unease with America's war in Vietnam and a mounting disillusionment with the antipoverty elements of President Lyndon B. Johnson's 'Great Society'. Regarding the latter, however, the lack of Republican opposition to popular elements of the Great Society – such as Medicare, the Elementary and Secondary Education Act (ESEA), and the two landmark civil rights laws – confirmed that such legislation was now deeply woven into the fabric of American government and society.

In winning 48.7 per cent of the House popular vote – the best Republican result in a decade – the GOP ensured that the previous elections were a blip rather than a trend in American politics. In 1964, Johnson had routed conservative Republican candidate, Barry Goldwater. In the wreckage of that lopsided presidential contest – in which LBJ won the highest popular vote percentage in modern presidential history – Republicans sank to their lowest numbers in the House of Representatives since Franklin D. Roosevelt's 1936 landslide. Given the scale of the repudiation, commentators speculated on whether the GOP remained a viable competitor for the dominant Democratic Party.[1] Such conjecture soon proved wide of the mark. In 1966, the Republicans gained forty-seven seats in the House, three in the Senate, all while netting eight governor's mansions. At local level, the gains went further, with Republicans netting control of a further eight legislatures and 503 state legislative seats. Johnson's landslide, rather than precipitating another prolonged spell of Democratic control of Washington, proved the beginning of a more tightly contested partisan era.

Scholarship on the 1966 midterm elections is in significant agreement that the results indicated disenchantment with the Great Society and liberalism writ large. Andrew Busch, who posits that 1966 was a 'pre-aligning midterm' – which Busch defines as a midterm that stood on the vanguard of change in American politics – argues that Republican gains 'ended the Great Society period and foretold the period of Republican ascendancy'.[2] Similarly, Gareth Davies notes that the 'results indicated that Americans were "tired of being improved"', and Matthew Dallek places 1966 as the year in which American conservatism shook off its extremist image and thus became electorally viable.[3] While scholars are right to suggest that elements of the Great Society were checked, they have ignored the fact that many of the big ticket items in Johnson's programme continued to expand. Rather, the 1966 midterm elections proved crucial in halting social welfare programmes that were perceived as solely helping poor people in the cities, who were disproportionately Black – most notably, the War on Poverty. Many Republicans elected in 1966 would go on to support further expansion of Great Society initiatives that were not aimed at racial minorities. Godfrey Hodgson is therefore overzealous in claiming that 'the meaning of 1966 [. . .]

was that the Republican Party was now turning away from the "me-too" policies it had followed since the New Deal'.[4]

The 1966 results impacted two presidencies. Most obviously, they impacted Johnson's domestic mandate (as will be discussed below, Johnson's Vietnam War mandate was barely altered). After the freewheeling legislative years of the 89th Congress, in which LBJ and liberal Democrats had passed an array of laws under the guise of the Great Society, the 90th Congress saw a reassertion of the 'conservative coalition', an alliance of conservative Republicans and southern Democrats. Nonetheless, while Johnson was stymied from advancing the bold proposals of his early presidency, there was no significant rolling back of those laws already on the books – and some programmes continued to expand. Even the War on Poverty, the most politically vulnerable initiative, survived a concerted conservative backlash. Beyond Johnson, the 1966 elections proved crucial in shaping the mandate that Richard Nixon would win in 1968. The 1966 Republican comeback, of which Nixon was a prominent campaigning figure, relied upon two key qualities: party unity and pragmatism. Regarding the latter, Republicans spent 1966 campaigning not against the popular achievements of Johnson's Great Society, such as Medicare, for the elderly, or aid to education, but instead focused their ire pragmatically on the antipoverty efforts that were increasingly tied up with 'white backlash' racial politics. Nixon would prove himself adept at learning victory's lessons.

The campaign

The 1966 campaign was shaped by significant national issues that played a key role in swaying a significant portion of the electorate back towards the Republican banner. By 1966, worrying trends, which would culminate in a traumatic year in 1968 for the country, were becoming evident. The most glaring evidence of this bubbling unease was the president's sharply declining popularity. Having rode high since assuming the presidency, Johnson's approval ratings in 1966 sunk below 50 per cent on various issues, including his handling of the Vietnam War, the economy, Civil Rights, and the War on Poverty. Republicans, who had struggled to articulate a convincing critique of Johnson in 1964 – not helped by their own significant divisions – were more successful in their 1966 cross-examination. As one Republican adviser put it, 'there's only one issue in 1966, [. . .] the confidence of the people in the character of LBJ'.[5] Through a disciplined campaign, in which the GOP projected a unified image to the electorate, the Republicans took aim at Johnson and his increasingly divided Democratic Party on a host of issues that ultimately led to a GOP revival.

While the Vietnam War provided the mood music for the 1966 elections, it lacked the volume to dominate the campaign. Yes, there was growing anxiety among the electorate that the United States' all-conquering military had not quickly vanquished a supposedly weak enemy. The televised congressional hearings on Vietnam that began in 1966, organised by war sceptic Senator J. William Fulbright (D-AK), also served to highlight that the war was beginning to pose challenges to Democratic Party unity. Nonetheless, the anti-war movement was in its infancy, and the events that would truly shake the public's confidence in the war effort – Johnson's surtax in 1967 and the Tet Offensive in 1968 – remained in the future. Vietnam, crucially, was also not a starkly partisan issue. As the Fulbright hearings demonstrated, Democratic disquiet was on the rise, as many party leaders wrestled with their desire to support their president and growing discomfort with the rising body count in Vietnam. Equally, while most Republicans believed in a more hawkish approach to the war, there were many outspoken GOP candidates who sought a quick peace. As a compromise, the Republican campaign settled on attacking the commander in chief's credibility – in line with a growing media narrative that portrayed Johnson as dishonest – rather than an outright assault on his war leadership. 'There's no longer a Credibility Gap,' charged House minority leader Gerald Ford (R-MI), 'it's become a Credibility Canyon.'[6] Overall, the war in South-east Asia may not have taken centre stage in the campaign, but it was a backdrop that worked against the incumbent president and his party.

Domestic issues assumed vital importance in the 1966 elections. The key domestic issues in 1966 can be summed up succinctly:

inflation and race relations. Similar to Vietnam, these issues worked in tandem to create a toxic environment for LBJ and his party. While FDR had been able to boast of the New Deal's accomplishments in his trend-bucking 1934 midterms, rising inflation and fraught racial tensions meant that Johnson could not emulate his political hero. Having lost the ability to claim the nation was at peace, the president was also forced to defend himself from accusations that his policies had undermined economic prosperity and social harmony.

In early 1966, leading Republicans decided to focus their campaign on blaming Johnson's Great Society spending for triggering sharp inflation in the United States. Indeed, perhaps the most important role the Vietnam War played in the 1966 campaign was not in discussions of war and peace, but in fostering the 'guns or butter' debate, whereby Republicans claimed the nation could ill-afford both the Great Society and the Vietnam War.[7] In a radio appearance of February 1966, Ford damned inflation as 'legalized robbery'.[8] Meanwhile, Senator George Murphy (R-CA) mocked LBJ's tin-eared plea for housewives to buy less at the grocery store as a way of limiting inflation:

> I know the housewives are confused this week when the President said take out your lead pencils and just trim down the shopping list. If the Administration really wants to curb inflation and hold down the cost of living wouldn't it make more sense for the Great Society to go on a fiscal diet and just cut out all the unnecessary government sweets?[9]

Republicans were so convinced that the inflation angle was their path to success that the Republican Congressional Committee printed and distributed one million replica 'Lyndon' dollar bills. This 'Great Society funny money', the Republicans advised, could be redeemed 'for full value on Election Day'.[10] The president, however, was not laughing when the Consumer Price Index recorded a 5 per cent rise, pushing him to suspend tax credits and cut $3 billion from the federal government's budget.[11]

Observing ongoing inflation, the nation's leading columnists quickly predicted significant Republican gains.[12] Arthur Krock, writing in the *New York Times*, stated in March that Republicans stood ready to gain from the prices of meat and eggs jumping by 19 per cent and 27 per cent, respectively.[13] By September, 85 per cent of Americans told pollsters that they felt negatively about the cost of living. Inflation, a somewhat dour economic issue that rarely attracted glossy headlines, almost certainly benefited Republican fortunes as voters began to feel the pinch in their pocketbooks.

Race relations, at the centre of national life throughout the 1960s, endured no such problem in dominating the frontpages. In 1964, with the Civil Rights Act recently passed, these headlines had been broadly positive. By 1966, however, the nation was in the midst of a white backlash to racial progress. At the same time, many Black Americans were restless with the slow pace of change, leading to a fracturing of the civil rights movement between those who continued to pursue non-violence and those who felt that such an approach was too naïve to ever achieve real change. Both 1965 and 1966 had witnessed various uprisings and violent clashes in the nation's cities. Most notably, the explosive and prolonged Watts Riots (as they were known), which took place in August 1965, served to intensify the white backlash to any further legislation that was viewed as benefiting racial minorities.

A side-effect of this shift was that many white Democratic voters either crossed over to support Republican candidates or dropped out of the electorate altogether. Political scientist Philip Converse observes that an unusually large portion of voters – most of whom were former Democrats – abandoned their party identification in 1966. Converse convincingly posits that such a change could only have been triggered by a dramatic event, such as Watts, and the subsequent large number of racial uprisings that took place in 1966.[14] In late October, *Congressional Quarterly* noted that 'White resentment over rapid Negro rights advancements, commonly known as the "white backlash," has taken on major proportions in the 1966 elections'.[15] Former Republican president, Dwight Eisenhower, declared that voters were rightfully angry over 'deliberate riots engendered for no purpose except to hurt the rest of us'. Ike encouraged the GOP to position itself in direct opposition to crime and rioting.[16] Many

Republican candidates across the country heeded their former leader's words and began to exploit the issue that would soon become known as 'law and order'.[17] As election day neared, pollsters found that the racial question was emerging as the top domestic issue for voters.[18] As will be discussed below, this had significant ramifications for Lyndon Johnson's mandate in the final two years of his presidency.

It is fair to conclude that election day arrived in a favourable political environment for Republicans, who stood to benefit from the unresolved Vietnam War, rising inflation, and deteriorating race relations. For LBJ, beyond a vague notion of continued prosperity, the consolidation of Black voters behind the Democratic Party, and the stubbornness of the southern electorate, little else gave the president cause for optimism. As such, the 'shellacking' – the term a future Democratic president would popularise in the wake of a chastening midterm result – that Johnson received was entirely predictable. What remained unclear, however, was the effect that the midterm elections would have on his presidency, and particularly, his Great Society.

Hitting the weak spot

Lyndon Johnson's presidency was shaped by his Great Society agenda at home – particularly the racial elements of this vision – and the Vietnam War abroad. Regarding the latter, the 1966 elections would have little impact on his mandate to continue the war in Southeast Asia. As already discussed, Democrats and Republicans largely fudged the complex Vietnam issue during the campaign. The same, however, could not be said of Johnson's domestic agenda. In seeking to realise his Great Society vision, Johnson had shepherded a range of programmes through Congress, including two civil rights acts, and a massive expansion in the federal government's spending on health care (Medicare and Medicaid) and education. Immigration was reformed, the arts received substantial funding, while Washington expanded its efforts to curb pollution and increase consumer rights. And yet, an observer of the Republican campaign in 1966 would have heard almost nothing about these initiatives.

In 1966, it was another Great Society initiative – the War on Poverty – that served as the Republican bogeyman. Republicans, the vast majority of whom opposed the War on Poverty when it was conceived as the Economic Opportunity Act (EOA) of 1964, advanced a successful two-pronged attack on the antipoverty effort throughout the year. In Congress, leading Republicans relentlessly attacked the War on Poverty as incompetent and corrupt, while also offering a Republican alternative – the 'Opportunity Crusade' – to Johnson's antipoverty programmes. Meanwhile, on the campaign trail, the War on Poverty became the 'poster child' policy for Republican claims that Johnson's administration had worsened racial violence and crime, driven inflation, and created a welfare state that was encouraging dependency rather than self-reliance. Most of all, many Republicans argued, the American system of private enterprise was the greatest antipoverty vehicle that humanity had yet invented, and it should be left alone to continue to do its work. The 1966 elections thus served to weave much of Johnson's Great Society into the American political tapestry, but by the end of proceedings, the War on Poverty was hanging by a thread.

By the beginning of 1966, the War on Poverty – led by the newly-created Office of Economic Opportunity (OEO) – had been running for over a year. Republicans were distinctly unimpressed by the results. Senate Minority Leader Everett Dirksen (R-IL) spoke for most of his colleagues when he told the press in January, that with regards to the War on Poverty, 'The field results are coming back now [. . .] They don't look good in print.'[19] Arguing that the nation needed to choose between guns and butter, the avuncular minority leader posited that Republicans wanted to see the antipoverty programmes cut back to allow American troops to flourish in Vietnam. Meanwhile, two rising Republican stars – Reps. Al Quie (R-MN) and Charles Goodell (R-NY) – went to the House floor, on an almost daily basis in March, to cite what they condemned as the War on Poverty's failures, and which they believed demonstrated that the antipoverty effort was both incompetent and corrupt. Summing up one particularly controversial OEO initiative, Goodell chronicled: 'Falsified and padded payrolls, forged identity cards and checks, political favoritism, sloppy administration, controversy and bitterness'.[20] With the EOA requiring congressional renewal in 1966, Republican leadership steeled themselves for a rare battle in the 89th Congress. Up to this point, Johnson's liberal landslide in 1964 had robbed the Republicans of the power they enjoyed through the unofficial but crucial conservative coalition with southern Democrats. The battle over the War on Poverty's renewal in 1966, however, signalled the perils that lay ahead for Johnson if Republicans made significant gains in the midterm elections.

Congressional Republicans spent the renewal fight denouncing Johnson's War on Poverty, seeking amendments and spending cuts to the legislation, and offering their own constructive alternative – the 'Opportunity Crusade'.[21] These efforts were not in vain. Republicans – together with some sceptical southern Democrats – successfully voted to reduce the antipoverty budget to $1.75 billion (Johnson had requested $2.5 billion). Meanwhile, the GOP successfully pushed amendments to the antipoverty bill that forbade assistance to anyone involved in starting a riot and which barred OEO employees from engaging in political activity. Quie also successfully proposed the biggest change to the antipoverty effort's operation, with an amendment that enhanced representation of the poor in the effort to fight poverty. Unsurprisingly, Republicans were unsuccessful in passing the Opportunity Crusade – a thorough proposal that sought to enhance the role of private enterprise in the fight against poverty. While southern Democrats were willing to support small changes to the War on Poverty, the majority were unwilling to overhaul their president's signature initiative.[22]

By the end of the prolonged battle – Johnson only signed the EOA renewal bill on Election Day – the Republicans were successful on three fronts: the public had reduced confidence in the War on Poverty, the party had restricted spending on the antipoverty programmes, and, by offering a thorough alternative, they had conveyed the impression that the GOP were reasonable opponents rather than reactionaries. This latter point stood in stark contrast to the extremism with which Barry Goldwater's campaign had tarred the party in 1964. All in all, congressional efforts in 1966 suggested that Johnson's antipoverty mandate was at risk should Republicans make significant gains in the midterm elections.

Republican efforts in Congress were mirrored on the campaign trail. Yet, while congressional leaders had denounced the antipoverty effort as corrupt and incompetent, many Republican candidates charged the War on Poverty with stirring up racial violence and encouraging welfare dependency among low-income Americans. At the forefront of this campaign was the former actor turned California gubernatorial candidate, Ronald Reagan. In 1964, Reagan had made attacking the War on Poverty central to his message in a highly popular speech on behalf of Goldwater, and in 1966 he doubled down on this approach.[23] Reagan was emphatic in his view that the War on Poverty was both unnecessary and motivated by Johnson's political considerations rather than a desire to enrich America's poor. 'For 200 years we successfully fought a War on Poverty with our system of capitalism and free enterprise,' Reagan argued.[24] In late 1965, he told the *Sacramento Bee* that the War on Poverty was 'a $1.8 billion campaign fund for the Administration'.[25] His antipoverty critique, however, went beyond such standard Republican criticisms.

In addition to his condemnation of student protestors in California, Reagan's high-profile campaign weaved together the issues of poverty, race, welfare, and the proper size of the federal government. In many ways, it provided the blueprint for how conservative Republicans would talk about such issues during their rise in the following two decades. When asked for his opinion on the underlying reasons behind the Watts uprising, Reagan spoke of 'recent immigrants from the Deep South' who had arrived in California believing 'the streets were paved with gold and [. . .] there were also promises made in connection with some of the poverty programs'.[26] Reagan also mocked the media for being unaware that there was brewing voter resentment over the growth in the welfare rolls throughout the 1960s.[27] In a thunderous speech to Republicans at a packed Patton Center in New York, Reagan decried the incumbent administration, claiming he was afraid of his own government. In listing the changes he would make, the first example he cited was the 'poverty program'.[28]

Crucially, Reagan – just like congressional Republicans with the Opportunity Crusade – offered an alternative to Johnsonian liberalism. Reagan promised that, if he was installed in Sacramento, his administration would launch a 'Creative Society' – the crux of which advocated replacing Washington-led government initiatives with local, private enterprise-fuelled alternatives. In outlining his vision, Reagan took aim at LBJ's legislative tide: 'A great society must be a free society, and to be truly great and really free, it must be a creative society calling on the genius and power of its people. Legislation alone can't solve our problems, nor will they disappear under a shower of tax dollars'. As for the antipoverty effort, Reagan looked to the private sector: 'A creative society mobilizing the business and industrial community to pinpoint who is unemployed, where and why, and then how to make a place for them in our productive free economy can fight a war on poverty 1000 times more effectively than government.'[29] Interestingly, while Reagan's Creative Society vision had a clear alternative to the War on Poverty, it said precious little about other Great Society initiatives, like Medicare and aid to education. Instead, the Creative Society aimed directly at the Great Society's weak spot – the War on Poverty.

Reagan may have been the leading anti–War on Poverty voice among Republican candidates, but he was far from the only one. Even progressive Republicans, who sympathised with the War on Poverty's aims, expressed dismay at the antipoverty effort and called for a Republican rethink. For example, Edward Brooke (R-MA), who ended the election year as the first Black American elected to the Senate since Reconstruction, made the War on Poverty's failures key to his campaign. Despite deeming the War on Poverty an 'excellent idea', Brooke believed that the OEO had 'failed spectacularly' at designing programmes that would provide the poor with sustainable employment, and thus a permanent route out of poverty.[30] Brooke, noting that Johnson was adept at starting programmes rather than seeing them through to completion, contested that it was Republicans who could turn Democratic dreams into reality.[31] While Brooke and Reagan were coming at the same issue from different political philosophies, and espoused differing concerns, they both hammered home the same message to voters: the War on Poverty was not working, and only Republicans could fix it. When election day arrived and Republican gains mounted, it was unsurprising that the media quickly speculated that the War on Poverty – which had to be renewed again in 1967 – faced a precarious future.[32]

The Great Society goes on, the War on Poverty stalls

While Johnson initially put on a brave face in the wake of results that dramatically reduced his majorities in Congress, his actions spoke of a president aware that his mandate had been altered by the campaign and the results. On election day, as he signed the Economic Opportunity Act's renewal amid predictions of Democratic losses, he had unconvincingly claimed that there was now a settled American consensus for tackling poverty.[33] Following the results, in a private conversation with Vice President Hubert Humphrey, Johnson spoke confidently that he could gain support for his liberal programmes from the moderate and progressive Republicans who had emerged victorious. In analysing Democratic losses, Johnson blamed his own side's 'ultra-liberalism'.[34] Indeed, the 1966 election highlights the uneasy relationship LBJ had with his own party – a party he often struggled to lead effectively.[35] His advisers, however, differed in their diagnosis, warning the president that '[t]he Great Society has become associated in the public mind with eliminating ghettos and generally pouring vast sums into the renovation of the poor and the Negro. The average American is tired of it.'[36]

From November 1966, through until he officially withdrew himself from the upcoming presidential election in March 1968, Johnson shrewdly moved to mute Republican arguments that had been aired during the campaign. In the election's aftermath, he fired off a memo to his cabinet instructing them to engage in 'creative federalism' – a riposte to GOP arguments that Johnson's programmes (particularly the War on Poverty) were leading to an overcentralised government in Washington.[37] Similarly, Johnson avowed that he, too, was a deep believer in the power of American private enterprise to solve social problems. In January 1967, his State of the Union address specifically called on 'the genius of private industry' to help rebuild the nation's cities; soon after, James Reston noted in the *New York Times* that Johnson was increasingly 'reaching out to private institutions [. . .] for help in dealing with social and economic problems'.[38] And, in preparation for an election he would never fight, Johnson began a concerted effort to attack Republican negativism – deeming the GOP the 'wooden soldiers of the status quo'.[39]

Johnson's legislative moves in his final two years in office also demonstrate the midterm effect. In one sense, much of his Great Society agenda continued. Medicare and aid to education were ratified and expanded upon by Congress – the latter with 80 per cent of Republicans voting in favour.[40] The administration also passed legislation that provided further funding for the arts (Public Broadcasting), consumer protections (Truth-In-Lending), pollution control (Air Quality Act), and even greater rights for racial minorities (Indian Bill of Rights, Fair Housing). Such achievements show that the 1966 midterm election did not completely obliterate the liberal reform agenda of the 1960s.

The War on Poverty, however, proved the exception to this rule. Indeed, it was somewhat of a political miracle that the Economic Opportunity Act survived the final two years of the Johnson presidency. Even more surprising was that it took the combination of an intense summer of racial uprisings and violence, combined with sympathetic moderate and progressive Republicans, to save the antipoverty effort. By the summer of 1967, it appeared that Republicans and southern Democrats would revive the old conservative coalition – once again a force after the midterm results – to scrap the War on Poverty when it came up for renewal. During the summer, huge racial uprisings in Detroit and Newark, and the resulting white backlash that followed from conservatives in Congress, initially appeared to hammer in the final nail in the War on Poverty's coffin. Ultimately, liberal Democrats and a handful of moderate and progressive Republicans – urged on by the White House – rallied to provide just enough votes to secure the antipoverty effort for a further two years.[41] As such, while the 'long, hot summer' of racial uprisings initially threatened the War on Poverty, violence in the cities ended up saving the poverty programmes by pushing moderate and progressive Republicans to stand in the way of their conservative colleagues.

Still, this desperate effort to save the War on Poverty was illustrative of how tenuous Johnson's antipoverty mandate remained. In 1968, when the Kerner Commission – which had been appointed to investigate the reasons for racial uprisings – recommended that the president launch a much greater War on Poverty to tackle the problems of the cities, the president tucked the report in a drawer and showed little appetite for a legislative fight he knew he would almost certainly lose.[42] The midterm campaign had thus played a significant role in both strengthening much of Johnson's Great Society, while simultaneously weakening the antipoverty nucleus of that agenda.

The big winner

Perhaps the 1966 midterm campaign's greatest victor was a politician who never stood for election: Richard Nixon. The former vice president visited thirty-five states and eighty-six congressional districts throughout the campaign. These were strategically chosen to maximise Nixon's presence in districts the GOP was likely to win, thus ensuring that Nixon – his political career in tatters after losing both the 1960 presidential election and the 1962 California gubernatorial contest – was well placed to seek the Republican nomination again in 1968.[43] Serving as the Republican Party's 'chief strategist' and most relentless optimist, Nixon was vindicated by the extent of GOP gains – most of which took place in districts he had visited.[44] Importantly, the 1966 Republican campaign served as a precursor for Nixon's own presidential campaign in 1968. The latter, just like the former, would be built on three pillars: Republican unity, fudging Vietnam, and attacking the War on Poverty while ignoring the rest of the Great Society.

An important reason for Republican success in 1966 was the party's quick and successful healing of the fracture that had split the party in 1964. As Charles Goodell noted in late 1966, 'there has been an overwhelming sentiment among Republicans to pull together'.[45] Two years earlier, many Republican moderates and progressives had refused to endorse Goldwater. This was a decision born partly from ideological differences, particularly Goldwater's 'nay' vote on the Civil Rights Act of 1964, but mostly as a result of the Goldwater campaign delighting in antagonising moderates and progressives.[46] In the wake of the 1964 landslide defeat, the party quickly moved to reunite. It installed Ray Bliss, a pragmatist, at the head of the Republican National Committee (RNC), and formed the Republican Coordinating Committee (RCC) to provide a coherent policy apparatus that would listen to all party voices, so that, rather than focusing on their differences, Republicans were able to unite in opposing the Johnson administration.

Nixon – who had made a career out of identifying the middle ground in the Republican Party and promptly placing himself in this spot – was at the forefront of this drive for unity. Second to reviving his own career, Nixon's primary goal was to turn the Republican Party from a permanent minority party into one capable of achieving majority status in Congress. 'I try to pound this into the heads of Republicans,' Nixon told journalist Jules Witcover, 'We have to win.'[47]

For Nixon, Republican inroads into the Democratic Party's southern bastion were crucial to Republican chances. As such, while many moderates and progressives remained squeamish about embracing southern conservatives – some of whom espoused nakedly racist rhetoric – Nixon spent substantial time in Dixie stumping for GOP candidates. For instance, during a visit to Jackson, Mississippi, Nixon raised money for avowed segregationists.[48] While in the region, Nixon penned a newspaper column advising that the Republican Party avoid trying to 'squeeze the last ounces of political juice from the rotting fruit of racial injustice'.[49] Still, when questioned about his visit, Nixon weakly put forward that 'the national Republican Party [. . .] should state its own support for civil rights forthrightly and try to convince the state parties to agree. It cannot dictate to them.'[50] Overall, Nixon's tour ingratiated him to key Republican politicos – and many voters – in the South and provided him with a strong base from which to launch his candidacy. As Busch notes, the 1966 elections 'laid the groundwork for Nixon's 1968 sunbelt strategy'.[51] In 1968, Nixon's ability to win votes in all regions of the country proved crucial in the general election.

On Vietnam, Nixon danced between espousing support for a wartime President and a condemnation of Johnson's policies in South-East Asia. The shrewd and slippery politician who would vaguely promise 'peace with honor' in 1968 was already in evidence in 1966. Rising tensions between the current president and the former vice president came to a head as the election neared its climax. When, in late October, Johnson travelled to the Philippines in an attempt to secure peace in Vietnam, Nixon questioned whether this timely trip was a 'quest for peace or a quest for votes'. 'There have been many firsts in the Johnson Administration,' Nixon suggested, 'but this is the first time a president may have figured the best way to help his party is to leave the country.' Nixon's running commentary on Johnson's Vietnam actions provoked a furious response from LBJ, who, during a cantankerous press conference, damned Nixon as merely a 'chronic campaigner' who was ill-informed.[52] By singling out Nixon, Johnson played an important role in re-establishing the former vice president, whose stock had fallen following his loss in 1962, as a serious player in American politics.

With regards to domestic issues, the echoes of 1966 can be seen clearly in Nixon's successful pursuit of the White House two years later. In 1966, Nixon followed the Republican blueprint of frequently attacking the War on Poverty, while largely ignoring the rest of Johnson's Great Society programmes. In January, Nixon deemed the antipoverty effort politically motivated and corrupt, chastising it in a speech: 'when the poverty program was initiated it was to be a program of the poor, by the poor and for the poor. It has become a program of the politicians, by the politicians and for the politicians.'[53] In June, he claimed that Johnson's inflationary spending would in reality 'wage war on the poor' as their spending power would be reduced.[54] Finally, Nixon chastised Johnson's War on Poverty for overpromising poor minorities and thus inflaming the 'urban slums' from which racial violence had emerged.[55] And, in a hint at the 'law and order' rhetoric that Nixon would famously employ in 1968, he condemned liberals – such as Vice President Humphrey – who expressed their understanding for why poor racial minorities might be prone to rioting. 'Leaders who encourage disobedience', Nixon observed, 'are responsible for the poor, the ignorant, and the impressionable who follow their advice.'[56]

Overall, Nixon was successfully in placing himself firmly in the Republican mainstream, and perhaps even – in light of the GOP's significant gains on election day – the American mainstream.

Conclusion

The 1966 midterm elections had an immediate impact on American politics. As soon as the new Congress was sworn in, it was clear that President Johnson was no longer the dominant figure – capable of cajoling legislation from Congress at his whim – that he had been during the two years prior. Nonetheless, LBJ's domestic agenda largely pressed on, and legislation continued to be passed at a fairly frequent rate by historical standards – the Great Society was far from dead. Regarding the War on Poverty, however, Johnson's signature programme barely clung to life as a newly assertive conservative coalition reasserted itself in Congress. For those paying attention, therefore, it would come as no surprise when the 1966 campaign's most notable campaigner – in accepting the Republican nomination for president in 1968 – told the millions of Americans watching at home that the 'clearest choice among the great issues of this campaign' was that a Republican administration would choose a different path to the War on Poverty. Of the rest of the Great Society, Nixon was silent.

Notes

1. Theodore H. White, *The Making of the President, 1968* (New York: Atheneum Publishers, 1969), p. 31.
2. Andrew E. Busch, *Horses in Midstream: U.S. Midterm Elections and Their Consequences, 1894–1998* (Pittsburgh, PA: University of Pittsburgh Press, 1999), pp 100–1.
3. Gareth Davies, *From Opportunity to Entitlement: The Transformation and Decline of Great Society Liberalism*

(Lawrence, KS: University Press of Kansas, 1996), p. 145; Matthew Dallek, *The Right Moment: Ronald Reagan's First Victory and the Decisive Turning Point in American Politics* (New York: Simon & Schuster, 2000), p. xi.

4. 'Me too' was a term used by conservative Republicans to denigrate moderate Republicans who supported some or all of the socio-economic policies of the post–New Deal liberal agenda. Godfrey Hodgson, *The World Turned Right Side Up: A History of the Conservative Ascendancy in America* (Boston, MA: Houghton Mifflin, 1996), p. 120.
5. Robert T. Hartmann to Richard M. Nixon, 26 Jan. 1966, box 62, Robert T. Hartmann Papers, Gerald R. Ford Library, Ann Arbor, MI.
6. Gerald R. Ford, Speech to Republican Associates of San Diego County, 15 Apr. 1966, box 59, Robert T. Hartmann Papers, Gerald R. Ford Library.
7. 'House Money Bill Vote to Run GOP Gauntlet', *Associated Press*, 1966; Everett M. Dirksen on ABC's *Issues and Answers*, 9 Jan. 1966, Dirksen Congressional Center, Pekin, IL.
8. Gerald R. Ford, RNC Radio Feed, 28 Feb. 1966, box 411, Papers of Frederick Panzer, Lyndon B. Johnson Library.
9. George Murphy, RNC Radio Feed, 8 Apr. 1966, box 411, Papers of Frederick Panzer, Lyndon B. Johnson Library, Austin, TX.
10. 'Inflation Pitch: GOP Prints "Lyndon Money"', *Washington Star*, 25 Sept. 1966.
11. Davies, *From Opportunity*, p. 133.
12. David S. Broder, 'G.O.P. Chiefs Urge a Cut in Spending', *New York Times*, 29 Mar. 1966; Tom Wicker, 'The Inflation Debate', *New York Times*, 30 Mar. 1966.
13. Arthur Krock, 'In the Nation: The Democrats' G.O.P. Salvage Corps', *New York Times,* 31 Mar. 1966.
14. Philip E. Converse, *The Dynamics of Party Support* (Los Angeles: SAGE, 1976), pp. 72–110; Richard L. Strout, 'U.S. Impact of GOP Victories', *Christian Science Monitor*, 13 Nov. 1966.
15. 'CQ Fact Sheet – On Racial Issues on 1966 Elections', *Congressional Quarterly*, 28 Oct. 1966.
16. Dwight D. Eisenhower quoted in 'CQ Fact Sheet – On Racial Issues on 1966 Elections', *Congressional Quarterly*, 28 Oct. 1966.
17. Gerald R. Ford remarks at GOP dinner, Fort Wayne, IN, 28 Oct. 1966, box 59, Robert T. Hartmann Papers, Gerald R. Ford Library.

18. 'CQ Fact Sheet – On Racial Issues on 1966 Elections', *Congressional Quarterly*, 28 Oct. 1966.
19. Everett M. Dirksen on ABC's *Issues and Answers*, 9 Jan. 1966, Dirksen Center.
20. Charles Goodell, Poverty Memo, *Congressional Record*, 17 Mar. 1966.
21. Mark McLay, 'A High-Wire Crusade: Republicans and the War on Poverty, 1966', *Journal of Policy History* 31, 3 (2019): pp. 382–405.
22. 'Antipoverty Funds Reduced and Earmarked', *CQ Almanac 1966*, 22nd edn (Washington, DC: Congressional Quarterly, 1967), pp. 250–65.
23. Ronald W. Reagan, 'A Time for Choosing', 27 Oct. 1964, Ronald Reagan Library, Simi Valley, CA.
24. Ronald W. Reagan quoted in *Seattle Post-Intelligencer*, 19 June 1966, folder 68, box 8, series j.3, RG4, Nelson A. Rockefeller Papers, Rockefeller Archive Center, Sleepy Hollow, NY.
25. Ronald W. Reagan quoted in *Sacramento Bee*, 24 Oct. 1965, folder 68, box 8, series j.3, RG4, Nelson A. Rockefeller Papers, Rockefeller Archive Center.
26. Ronald W. Reagan, Press Conference, 4 Jan. 1966, box c30, 1966 Campaign, Reagan Library.
27. Ronald W. Reagan, Remarks in Hayward, CA, 27 Sept. 1966, box c30, 1966 Campaign, Reagan Library.
28. Ronald W. Reagan, 'The Myth of the Great Society', Patton Center, New York, 1966, Ronald Reagan Library Audiovisual Composite Collection.
29. Ronald W. Reagan, 'A Plan for Action', 4 Jan. 1966, box c30, 1966 Campaign, Reagan Library.
30. Edward W. Brooke on ABC's *Issues and Answers*, 4 Sept. 1966, box 562, Edward W. Brooke Papers, Library of Congress, Washington, DC; Edward W. Brooke, 'Fighting for a Future: The Poor in America', 13 Sept. 1966, box 568, Brooke Papers.
31. Edward W. Brooke, 'New Face in the Senate: Edward Brooke of Massachusetts', *CBS News Special*, box 562, Brooke Papers.
32. Edmond Lebreton, 'Reinforced Hill Republicans Pick Targets From President's Programs', *Washington Post*, 22 Nov. 1966; Lyn Shepard, 'U.S. legislative logjam seen', *Christian Science Monitor*, 12 Nov. 1966.

33. Lyndon B. Johnson, 'Statement by the President Upon Signing Bill to Provide for Continued Progress in the Nation's War on Poverty', 8 Nov. 1966, The American Presidency Project.
34. Lyndon B. Johnson and Hubert H. Humphrey phone conversation, Nov. 1966, Miller Center, University of Virginia, http://millercenter.org/presidentialrecordings/lbj-wh6611.02-11023, accessed 27 Aug. 2021.
35. Sean J. Savage, *JFK, LBJ, and the Democratic Party* (New York: State University of New York Press, 2012).
36. Henry Wilson to LBJ, 10 Dec. 1966, reel 19, *Political Activities of the Johnson White House, 1963–1969* [microform], ed. Paul L. Kesaris (Frederick, MD: University Publications of America, 1987).
37. LBJ, 'Memorandum on the Need for "Creative Federalism" through Cooperation with State and Local Officials', 11 Nov. 1966, The American Presidency Project.
38. James Reston, 'Washington: "The Eleventh Commandment"', *New York Times*, 2 Apr. 1967.
39. LBJ, Remarks to Delegates to the National Convention, AFL-CIO, 12 Dec. 1967, The American Presidency Project.
40. Gareth Davies, *See Government Grow: Education Politics from Johnson to Reagan* (Lawrence, KS: University Press of Kansas, 2007), p. 73.
41. Mark McLay, 'The Republican Party and the Long, Hot Summer of 1967 in the United States', *Historical Journal* 61 (2018): pp. 1089–111.
42. Kerner Commission, *Report of the National Advisory Commission on Civil Disorders* (Washington, DC: US Government Printing Office, 1968).
43. Jules Witcover, *The Resurrection of Richard Nixon* (New York: G. P. Putnam's Sons, 1970), p. 124.
44. Busch, *Horses*, p. 105.
45. Charles Goodell, Interview with Robert Peabody, 3 Aug. 1966, Robert L. Peabody Research Interview Notes, 1964–7, box 2, Gerald R. Ford Library.
46. See Robert David Johnson, *All the Way with LBJ: The 1964 Presidential Election* (New York: Cambridge University Press, 2009).
47. Witcover, *Resurrection*, p. 176.
48. 'Nixon Says National GOP Should Not Dictate Anti-Segregation Stand to State GOPs', *New York Times*, 7 May 1966.
49. Witcover, *Resurrection*, p. 131.

50. 'Nixon Says National GOP', *New York Times*, 7 May 1966.
51. Busch, *Horses*, p. 104.
52. Alex Marshburn, 'The Manila Communiqué: Nixon's Comeback', 20 May 2015, Nixon Foundation.
53. Richard M. Nixon, 29 Jan. 1966, box 24, Graham Molitor Papers, Rockefeller Archive Center.
54. Nixon quoted in *Washington Post,* 5 June 1966.
55. Richard Nixon quoted in Alexander Bloom and Wini Breines, eds, *'Takin' it to the Streets': A Sixties Reader* (New York: Oxford University Press, 1995), p. 295.
56. Ibid.

9

'The power of their votes': Richard Nixon, the Silent Majority, and the 1970 Midterm Elections

Sarah Thelen

'Remember, the four-letter word that is most powerful of all the four letters in the world is vote – v-o-t-e,' thundered President Richard Nixon. It was a blustery October day in the final weeks of the 1970 congressional campaign, and he had just arrived in Grand Forks, North Dakota, hoping to mobilise those gathered on the airport runway to support Republican candidates. With Air Force One behind him and flags and bunting whipping in the wind, the president argued that the Silent Majority – to which many there presumably felt they belonged – was best served by electing candidates who would support the president in Washington, DC. As the crowd listened and the wind buffeted their signs, Nixon stressed that he was not in Grand Forks for partisan reasons, but rather that he was there 'in behalf [*sic*] of the United States of America'. Reiterating a common refrain, the president reminded his listeners: 'It's time for the great silent majority of this country to stand up and be counted.' And, confident that this crowd, at least, agreed, a smiling and relaxed Nixon waded into the cheering crowd shaking hands with his supporters.[1]

Similar scenes took place in Columbus, Ohio; Ocean Grove, New Jersey; Kansas City, Missouri; Albuquerque, New Mexico; and many other cities and towns across the United States in the weeks before US voters went to the polls on 2 November 1970. Having faced a Democratic Congress for his first two years in office, Nixon hoped to regain Republican control – or at least to weaken Democratic power – in the 1970 midterm elections. To this end, Nixon and his aides worked to rally the so-called 'Silent Majority' behind the president's favoured candidates. Initially an attempt to rally supporters against the anti–Vietnam War movement, the Silent Majority idea made public participation in political events both socially and politically acceptable for many citizens who associated demonstrations and protests with the anti-war and civil rights movements. Their visible support, in turn, enabled Nixon to claim to speak for the majority of Americans against a noisy minority protesting in the streets. Looking back on the successful mobilisation of the Silent Majority in November 1969, the 'Hard Hat' protests in May 1970 – when thousands of pro-war, pro-president construction workers disrupted anti-war vigils in New York City – and the large turnout at a flag-drenched Fourth of July event on the National Mall, Nixon and his team saw the Silent Majority as some of the president's most reliable supporters.

This support, in turn, doubtless contributed to Nixon's own decision to involve himself so directly in the campaign. This decision was contrary to the established political wisdom as 'everyone' – even, indeed, the president – 'knew' that the president's party would lose seats in the midterms.[2] But Nixon, convinced that 'there's a realignment going on', was determined to do everything within his power to secure a popular mandate for his policies[3] – which, since the president himself was not on the ballot, meant that Nixon and his surrogates could not explicitly tout his strengths and policies without appearing opportunistic, or worse, enabling opponents to cast themselves as victims of a White House attack.[4] Instead, the White House campaign emphasised the need for voters to elect senators and representatives who would work with the president and support his initiatives, which, in turn, would serve as a mandate for Nixon's foreign and domestic policies. White House reliance on the Silent Majority to deliver this mandate made the 1970 campaign the first true test of its political – rather than rhetorical – strength. But no one in Nixon's White House, not even the president himself, saw the campaign in that light at the time. Instead, they simply assumed that the Silent Majority would vote Republican and therefore planned a campaign which placed this group front and centre. But, in the end, the Silent Majority did not deliver a Republican victory in 1970 and instead of forming the foundation for a political realignment over the next two years, the campaign marked the end of the idea as an organising force in the administration.

The Silent Majority

In the summer of 1970, though, Nixon and his aides were confident that the Silent Majority was a winning theme for the upcoming election. That Nixon could so confidently count on the support of this Silent Majority was due to his staff's careful cultivation of this group in the previous year. Although not a new idea, Nixon's Silent Majority was called into being at the close of an otherwise unremarkable speech on 3 November 1969. Timed to slow the growing momentum of the anti-war movement, the speech was the centrepiece of White House efforts to regain the initiative in the domestic debate over the Vietnam War. Specifically, it was a response to the very visible participation of over two million people from all walks of life in the 15 October 1969 Moratorium protests in cities and states across the country.[5]

The diversity of participants in the October protests complicated White House efforts to paint those who opposed the war as a radical, dangerous minority. Nixon and his aides feared that, if anti-war sentiments became mainstream, they would encourage still more protests which would, in turn, encourage continued North Vietnamese intransigence and prolong the war.[6] In an effort to reframe the domestic narrative in his favour, Nixon addressed the nation on 3 November 1969. Rather than offering new information or policies, the speech described the situation in Vietnam when the president took office and explained the steps he had taken to end the war since his inauguration. Nixon argued that he was making progress, and would continue to do so, but that he needed domestic support – for 'North Vietnam cannot defeat or humiliate the United States. Only Americans can do that.'[7] In many ways an unremarkable speech, it is unlikely that it would be remembered at all except that, in a sharp break with tradition, Nixon closed not with the usual presidential appeal for national support, but directly – and explicitly – asked 'the great silent majority' for their support.[8]

And the Silent Majority answered almost immediately. Inundated with telephone calls, telegrams, letters, and petitions from people identifying themselves as part of this new group, White House officials identified over two hundred thousand 'known supporters' in just fifteen days.[9] Many of these newly vocal members of the Silent Majority had never been politically active before, but Nixon's speech – and this new identity – gave them a space in which to push back against the recent changes in US society. Most importantly, the Silent Majority identity provided them with a way to oppose the anti-war movement, and so they enthusiastically joined National Unity Week events – celebrating Veterans Day on 11 November and, more importantly, countering the 15 November anti-war protests. These immediate responses contributed to the creation of local organisations which, in the words of White House aide Alexander Butterfield, spread 'like wild fire' following the speech.[10]

Agnew's Social Issue Appeals

With such enthusiastic support from the Silent Majority, White House officials from the president down were confident that this group presaged a political realignment which would put the Republicans in power after years of Democratic dominance. This, in turn, led Nixon and his aides to make the Silent Majority their primary focus in the 1970 campaign. Having decided to take a more active role in the midterm campaign than was usual for a sitting president, Nixon took full control. Based on speechwriter Pat Buchanan's analysis of *The Real Majority* – a best-selling analysis of how Democrats should appeal to what the authors, Richard M. Scammon and Ben Wattenberg, described as 'the Social Issue' so as to counter Republican gains – the president placed the Social Issue firmly in the centre of the administration's plans for the 1970 campaign.[11] In his view, not only was it clearly good politics to appeal to this group, but doing so played to his strengths, specifically his popularity among the Silent Majority.

Although Nixon had given the group life and shape in his 3 November 1969 speech, many of its members most closely identified with the vice president. This made Vice President Spiro T. Agnew the obvious choice to serve as what one aide later called the 'cutting edge' of the administration's campaign.[12] His involvement was a clear sign of the president's interest in the campaign, but few observers were fully aware of how very involved the president was even as early as Agnew's first official campaign speech on 10 September in Springfield, Illinois. The day before, Nixon met with the White House speechwriters assigned to accompany the vice president – William Safire and Patrick Buchanan – along with congressional liaison Bryce Harlow, White House chief of staff H. R. Haldeman, and other staffers to discuss the vice president's campaign. Agnew himself was notably absent, but Nixon proceeded to give his aides what Safire later described as effectively a master class in political campaigning. Indeed, after the meeting, he and his colleagues, Safire later recounted, 'staggered out . . . looking as if we had been two-hour display of political pyrotechnics'.[13]

Determined to get out ahead of the Democrats on the Social Issue, Nixon told the Agnew team to paint their opponents as radicals, to 'put 'em all in a bag', but, at the same time, Agnew was not to attack his opponents directly. Doing so, Nixon feared, would make the target 'a martyr'.[14] Instead, the president suggested a backhanded compliment: 'I don't question his sincerity – he deeply believes this radical philosophy.'[15] The key, as Nixon saw it, was to force Democratic candidates to defend themselves by explicitly rejecting leftist policies, thereby alienating potential supporters while also making it 'comfortable, fashionable' for more centrist and conservative Democrats to vote against their party.[16]

And so Agnew, Safire, Buchanan, and their unabridged dictionary took to the campaign trail in September 1970. Their activities were noisy, exciting, and – for certain political watchers – fun. Getting Agnew on the hustings early was a purposeful attempt to put the Democrats on the defensive, and so, in his first speech, Agnew attacked the 'pusillanimous pussyfooters' in Congress who were so slow to send useful legislation to the president.[17]

The next day, in San Diego, California, the vice president attacked Democrats as not only the 'hysterical hypochondriacs of history' but also the 'nattering nabobs of negativism'.[18] And while the Silent Majority roared approval, the media, Democrats, and – indeed – even many Republicans, cried foul. Writing some years later, Safire remembered that Agnew's 'attack, delivered with a merry bravado, was not received in good humor', ultimately resulting in the vice president becoming a 'lightning rod for a delayed counterattack'.[19]

But even as they crisscrossed the country appearing at events for Senate and gubernatorial candidates, signs of the vice president's liabilities were clear, for anyone willing to see them – most notably, the consistent reluctance – and outright refusal – of Republican candidates to schedule joint appearances with the vice president. As Agnew became increasingly defined by his bombastic rhetoric and attacks on the radical liberals, or 'radiclibs', in Congress, many candidates, as Robert Mason notes, 'concluded that Agnew's reputation was negative enough to be hostile to their prospects'.[20] But even as they saw the vice president as 'too divisive, too polarising', few candidates turned down the chance to have Agnew appear at a closed-door fundraising event – and the vice president would go on to raise almost three million dollars in the course of his campaigning.[21]

These doubts about Agnew's political utility reflected broader national attitudes. Not only did an early October White House poll find that the current approach to the campaign was likely to lead to a net loss of thirty House seats and to defeat in most of the Senate races, but polls covered in the national media reported similarly dismal prospects.[22] At the same time, Agnew was still quite popular among the Silent Majority rank and file, which further complicated Republican campaigning. For example, in late October, even as his popularity soared among Republicans, pollster George Gallup described him as 'the most unpopular man holding high office in the last decade' among non-southern Democrats.[23] While this regional popularity reflected Nixon's own views of the political potential of division and polarisation and was gratifying in light of the administration's goal of expanding Republican strength in the South, it complicated their hopes to run a national campaign centred on Agnew's Social Issue, Silent Majority message.

Nixon on the campaign trail

Even so, the White House did not significantly change course other than to 'switch the spotlight from the "hot" Agnew . . . to the "cool" Nixon'.[24] Nixon claimed in his 1978 memoir that he had not intended to campaign personally, but Safire recalled in 1975 that the plan had always been for Nixon, as the campaign advanced, to 'replac[e] the Vice President as the center attraction'.[25] On the stump, the president reiterated Agnew's Social Issue appeal to the Silent Majority, but with a more 'presidential' packaging. This, the White House hoped, would appeal to moderates who agreed with the core message but were put off by Agnew's reputation and style. Essentially, the plan was for the president's campaigning to parallel Agnew's, 'but on the high road'.[26]

Nixon's standard stump speech was central to this effort. In it, Nixon argued that he had done his best to keep his 1968 campaign promises – on the Vietnam War, on the domestic economy, crime, and government reform – but had been stymied by 'obstructionists and extremists' in Congress.[27] Nixon's repeated emphasis on the idea – and importance – of a 'majority of one' in the Senate simultaneously emphasised the importance of the decision facing voters and offered an implicit justification for Nixon's active involvement.[28] Nixon consistently framed his participation in national terms and argued that '[t]he issues before America these days are too important to think in terms simply of a party label. We have to think in terms of what is best for America.'[29] Nixon cast himself as an apolitical patriot who just happened to support the Republican candidates at each campaign stop. The president was always careful not to attack the Democratic candidates personally – usually describing both candidates as 'good men' – but was always at pains to point out that only one could be relied upon to support the president's agenda and, by extension, the national interest.[30]

A far cry from Agnew's excoriation of the 'pusillanimous pussyfooters' earlier in the campaign, such patriotic appeals would,

Nixon and his aides hoped, convince more voters to pull the lever for the Republicans. Nixon closed his speeches with a reminder that the protesters were a minority of the population – both in general and even among the young – and that it just seemed otherwise because the media lavished so much attention on them. It was at this stage that Nixon returned to a more full-throated appeal to the Silent Majority: invoking protests and disruptions at that particular event or, if it had been quiet, at a recent appearance and reminding his listeners that the best way to respond to this noisy minority was with the power of their votes. Specifically, he urged them, 'Don't answer in kind. . . . The way you answer is by the most powerful action, more powerful than any four-letter epithet that you can imagine . . . by your votes.'[31]

In their efforts to convince the Silent Majority that they did, indeed, outnumber the protesters and government critics, Nixon and his aides benefited from the seemingly sudden appearance, in the summer of 1970, of the Black Silent Majority Committee on the political scene. Organised by Clay Claiborne, a former Republican Party official, the group first appeared in July and held its formal launch event in Washington, DC, in October.[32] While Claiborne claimed that he had organised the group to demonstrate that the 'Black community has a "silent majority" just as concerned about law and order as white citizens', the primary organising impetus came from the White House.[33] Administration officials were familiar with such a covert role as much of the success of earlier Silent Majority promotion – from the initial response to Nixon's November 1969 speech to the creation of 'Americans for Winning the Peace' groups in opposition to the McGovern–Hatfield Amendment that summer – was rooted in similar 'astroturf', or false grassroots, organising.[34] Distracted by the rest of the 1970 campaign, aides were not as involved in the Black Silent Majority Committee as in previous efforts, but they kept a close eye on the group and welcomed its active support.

Claiborne's statements on behalf of the group echoed the president's anti-communist, patriotic, and law-and-order rhetoric rather than engaging with substantive questions of racial equality or civil rights. As such, the group was a useful foil for the administration as aides sought to keep the campaign – and the broader domestic political conversation – centred on the president's strengths. Tellingly, Claiborne's language most closely paralleled the vice president's in his castigating a 'tiny insidious cluster of militants who . . . do not represent the overwhelming majority of people' and urging the 'millions of black citizens who believe in the American way of life to wake up. We've got to stop being shouted down by a handful of shabby agitators.'[35] While Claiborne's confession in November 1970 that his appeal had at that point been more successful with white than Black Americans highlights the limits of such divisive rhetoric, the Nixon administration was less concerned with the realities of the group than with the fact that it existed at all.[36] Even when much of the coverage of the group highlighted Claiborne's Republican Party ties and questioned its grassroots legitimacy, it was still a useful counterpoint to charges of political narrowness for Nixon and other Silent Majority proponents. More importantly, although never a major player, the group would continue to grow over the next two years making it both more powerful – and by its deeper roots – more credible in the 1972 campaign.

While White House officials were pleased with the Black Silent Majority Committee and Claiborne was certainly determined to stay relevant, this group was never an administration priority. Administration officials saw the utility of expanding the scope of the Silent Majority beyond its core membership of white, middle- and working-class citizens, but were consistently more interested in developing ties to this core group. Indeed, much of Nixon's stump speech was designed specifically to appeal to them. On the campaign trail, the president addressed their unease about Vietnam and stressed that he was ending the war; stoked their fears of inflation and crime; and reassured them that they were, indeed, a majority – no matter what media coverage might suggest. Beyond formal campaign appearances, the Nixon White House sought to deepen ties with this group by cultivating the so-called 'white ethnics' as well as the more conservative elements of the labour movement. Stops such as Nixon's Columbus Day visit to an Italian community centre in Stamford, Connecticut, were the logical extension of White House invitations for labour leaders before the campaign season.[37] Additional meetings whenever Nixon's schedule allowed and publicising previous meetings ensured continual coverage of White House efforts to court groups such as the Sons of Italy and the Polish American Congress.[38] Furthermore, Nixon's rhetoric consistently emphasised an idealised patriotism and almost-mythic view of American ideals shared by many of his listeners.

Beyond the practical utility of their votes in the midterm election, Nixon and his aides were eager to cultivate ties to these groups, many of whom were as fiercely proud of their immigrant ancestors as they were of their American citizenship, because they saw an opportunity to recruit a core Democratic constituency for the GOP. The Hard Hat protests that spring – both the violent near-riots and the peaceful marches – encouraged White House aides to put more effort into recruiting members of what had seemed to be a solidly Democratic constituency. Nixon and his staff hoped to pull enough of the most conservative unionists away from the Democrats to tip the election in their favour. Gleefully reporting back to Chief of Staff H. R. Haldeman, Colson described the potential for a mass defection of the New York labour vote from the Democrats on the back of foreign policy concerns even though the Democratic candidate, Richard Ottinger, was 'a pro-labor liberal'.[39] Indeed, Colson went further, anticipating the eventual approach Nixon would use to build his landslide constituency in 1972 and described many in the labour movement as 'anti-student dissent, pro the American flag and worried about the encroachment . . . of other minorities like the blacks'.[40] And, so, with a few nods to local ethnic and demographic groups, Nixon easily cast a seemingly solidly Democratic constituency as the core of his Silent Majority.

Similarly, Nixon and his aides – particularly speechwriter and arch-conservative Pat Buchanan – worked to cultivate ties to the conservative movement, even at the expense of Republican candidates. A growing force in US politics, a group of conservative leaders had worked hard in the 1950s and 1960s to distance themselves and their movement from the paranoid anti-communism of the John Birch Society.[41] Represented instead by the more intellectual and mainstream conservatism exemplified by William

F. Buckley's *National Review*, its members were an important part of the Republican Party, but were becoming worryingly independent by 1970. While the potential of a third-party challenge from the Right was always a concern, Nixon welcomed the Conservative Party's involvement in the New York Senate race. Indeed, a Conservative Party victory in that race would be particularly gratifying as it would not only prove the electoral potential of Hard Hat support and conservative positions but also have the added bonus of punishing one of Nixon's Senate critics.[42] New York Senator Charles Goodell had been appointed to Robert F. Kennedy's Senate seat in 1968 and, although a Republican, had proven to be a thorn in Nixon's side almost from the start. Very critical of the Vietnam War and much more liberal than many Republicans, Goodell might have managed to retain Nixon's support – or, at least, avoided his active opposition – if he had seemed likely to win. As Nixon noted in September, 'if I thought Goodell had a chance of winning, we would be for him. Since he doesn't, we drop him over the side.'[43] Furthermore, by effectively punishing Goodell for challenging his administration's policies, Nixon intended White House involvement in the New York campaign to serve as a 'a signal for others to stick with us in the future'.[44]

To ensure his critic's defeat, Nixon authorised active – if subtle and deniable – White House support for the Conservative Party's James L. Buckley. A third-party candidate, Buckley benefited from his close ties to the conservative movement – his brother was conservative doyen William F. Buckley, founder of *National Review* and an advisor of sorts to Young Americans for Freedom, the conservative counterpart to the Left's Students for a Democratic Society. But in a winner-take-all political system as in the United States, even strong third-party candidates with unpopular opponents were rarely expected to win their races. Nixon sought to tip the balance, but without creating additional political problems for himself. A canny politician first and foremost, Nixon knew that any active support for a third-party candidate – regardless of how closely that candidate's views hewed to his own – at the expense of his own party would be a boon to the Democrats. So, instead, Nixon, as had Agnew before him, carefully avoided endorsing Goodell in New York and emphasised the need for New York voters to elect a senator who would support the president. And just in case the message was unclear, when the president stopped in Westchester, New York, on his first formal day of campaigning in October, he was promptly swarmed by a group of young Buckley supporters the moment he disembarked. The Secret Service did not push them away, and the president happily talked with the group for a few minutes. The press was watching, and the images of the president shaking hands and smiling while surrounded by Buckley campaign signs was a clear sign of the president's support.[45]

And even when not implicitly endorsing third-party challengers, Nixon's campaigning was designed to appeal to the more conservative elements of the electorate. This group, Nixon gambled, was on his side regardless of party affiliation, and he hoped to secure a mandate by appealing to both their individual worries and their national pride. Highlighting his role as president, echoing his listeners' patriotism, economic worries, anti-communism, and national pride, Nixon sought to incorporate conservative and Silent Majority ideas into effectively every aspect of his campaigning. In this, his domestic critics proved invaluable. Throughout the campaign, and his presidency more generally, Nixon used disruptive and radical protesters as foils to highlight his own moderation and patriotism. Weaving references to hecklers and protesters – whether at the event in question, a previous one, or in general media coverage – throughout his standard stump speech Nixon explicitly appealed to the patriotism and 'Americanism' of his audience and supporters. Thus, even as he claimed to deplore their actions, he and his aides welcomed the interruptions and attacks from his critics – with 'get a fuck Nixon sign up' an early campaign task.[46]

A noisy end to the campaign

Thus, Haldeman and other staffers were not surprised when, less than a week before election day, after protesters failed to interrupt his speech in San Jose, California, the president loitered longer than necessary outside the venue waiting for his motorcade to arrive.[47] Once a crowd had gathered – as the president knew it would – he flashed his trademark 'V' sign as he got into his car. The reaction was immediate and he narrowly missed the cascade of rocks and other projectiles that rained down in response, breaking the windows of the bus carrying aides and journalists.[48] Nixon later explained his decision to provoke the crowd, writing: 'I could not resist showing them how little respect I had for their juvenile and mindless ranting.'[49] Haldeman noticed his mood at the time, recording in his diary that 'All through the day he delighted in giving the "V" to the peaceniks.' The violent response in San Jose was the perfect opportunity for the combative campaigner to push back against his critics, and he expected his staff to 'crank it up' to ensure it became a 'really major story'. Still energised by the encounter – and undaunted at having set his bedroom chimney on fire – the president discussed the day's events and plans for managing the story over the next few days with Haldeman. Eventually convinced to sleep in the smoke-free guest house, the president discussed the day over beer with Haldeman until the early morning.[50]

Although still determined to make sure the media gave the events in San Jose the attention he felt they deserved, the president opted to give his usual speech in Anaheim, California, the next day. Safire later explained Nixon's decision not to deliver the 'tough, but calm' speech requested immediately after the events in San Jose with the theory that Nixon was so '[c]oncerned about overreacting, he did not react at all'.[51] Back on the high road, the president released a measured statement and was at pains in Anaheim to stress that the violent protesters represented neither the people of San Jose nor the nation. But as stories began to downplay the danger and violence of the events in San Jose, the president changed course again and delivered a hard-hitting speech in Phoenix, Arizona, two days later. Addressing the crowd gathered in the hot airplane hangar – with periodic pauses for their applause and roars of approval – the president's voice boomed and echoed as he excoriated the violent protesters and those who enabled and defended them. His audience, he argued, were the true Americans, as they had rejected the permissiveness that allowed this sort of violence to take place and spread.

And, therefore, they had an obligation to support candidates who would support the president in his efforts to isolate and marginalise such violent and divisive elements of society.[52]

Elevated by the enthusiasm of his audience and the satisfaction of fighting back against his critics, the president decided that the speech would be his election-eve broadcast. He and his closest aides were convinced that full-throated advocacy for patriotism and traditional values would convince the Silent Majority that Nixon's candidates would protect an amorphous 'American way of life' threatened by the radical permissiveness of the Democrats. Safire and other aides therefore rushed to find and edit a recording of the speech in time to air roughly twenty-four hours after Nixon finished speaking in Phoenix. They managed it, but in the end, their efforts were for naught as the resulting footage – despite hours of editing work – was of such poor quality that a number of Republicans complained to their local television stations, charging them with intentionally sabotaging the broadcast.[53] The grainy picture and echoey audio combined with the bombastic and angry speech itself negated much of Nixon's work to frame himself as a patriotic, non-partisan national symbol. Echoing some of the worst excesses of Agnew's less successful campaigning, the speech broadcast further undermined Nixon's quest for a mandate by creating an opportunity for the Democrats to present themselves as the moderate, responsible choice. The calm and measured nature of the address, delivered by Senator Edmund Muskie of Maine, that the Democratic Party televised on election eve, was a striking contrast to the president's anger, and while many in the Silent Majority shared Nixon's fury, seeing it in their living rooms was a different matter.

Spinning the results and looking to 1972

When the votes were tallied it was immediately clear that the administration's Silent Majority appeals had failed to counterbalance party loyalty and 'pocketbook issues'.[54] Despite administration efforts – including presidential campaign visits to twenty-one states on top of Agnew's months of campaigning – Republicans lost eleven congressional seats and the same number of statehouses.

Nixon, his staff, and other Republicans sought to minimise the appearance of defeat by pointing to gains in the Senate, but could not change the results which left the Democrats firmly in control of both houses of Congress. Indeed, the Democrats expanded their House majority by twelve seats including the defeat of nine Republican incumbents running for re-election. While Nixon and his staff comforted themselves with the knowledge that their opponents had lost three seats in the Senate, it did little to change the reality of a Democratic Congress. Worse yet – particularly as a bellwether of the broader political mood – were the state races in which the Democrats won twenty-one gubernatorial races, defeating eleven Republican incumbents. In the wake of these disappointing results, Nixon and his aides spent the next few days '[d]riving hard to get interpretation our way, as major victory in the Senate', but were fighting an uphill battle.[55] Not only had the president failed to secure his mandate, but media coverage portrayed the results as a loss for the president and not just the candidates.

Reviewing the results years later, Nixon described the 1970 returns as an 'excellent showing' since the president's party traditionally lost seats in a midterm election. He pushed a similar line in November 1970, but few were convinced by the White House argument that 'compared to the usual off-year losses . . . we did well'.[56] Publicly, Nixon sought to put a positive spin on the results – even going so far as to frame them as encouraging since 'the move is to the right, whatever the party labels'.[57] But it was a stretch, and privately, he was far more pessimistic. Safire later recalled a discussion with the president during which Nixon, in between unenthusiastic bites of cottage cheese and peaches, blamed the candidates even as he recognised that 'it's no alibi for us, and you don't kick anybody when they're down'.[58] But even as Nixon worked to spin the election results – pointing to the ideological shift, to the gains in the Senate, and so on – he was planning for 1972.

Conclusion: from a Silent Majority to a New Majority

Frustrated and disappointed, the president 'brooded' about the results for days, eventually calling a high-level political meeting at his house in Florida. Gathered in Key Biscayne, Nixon, Haldeman, and other senior White House staffers discussed the 1970 campaign, analysing all aspects with an eye toward Nixon's 1972 re-election campaign. They debated administration personnel changes as well as key issues for the next two years including the economy, government reform, the future relationship with Congress ('we don't work with Congress, we go against them'), intentions to postpone a USSR summit until it 'serves our purpose', decisions to privilege defence spending and 'squeeze the Great Society programs', the 'need for new roles for VP, positive and constructive', and intentions to 'take *very* conservative civil rights line'.[59] Concluding that they needed to 'de-escalate the rhetoric without de-escalating the substance' of the administration's Silent Majority appeals, Nixon and his team also recognised that the 1970 results demonstrated the liabilities of depending on that group.

Having failed to deliver a mandate for Nixon in 1970, the Silent Majority lost its hold over White House public opinion programmes. The idea never quite disappeared, but the Silent Majority was soon just one among many groups and identities courted by the Nixon White House. By 1972, all of these 'miscellaneous cats and dogs', as Colson described them, would be grouped into a 'New Majority' expected to sweep Nixon to re-election.[60] But even as the president and surrogates celebrated this 'new majority', they primarily targeted the individual cats and dogs – the ethnic, religious, veteran, racial, regional, and other demographic groups – they saw as vital to the president's anticipated 1972 victory. In the end, there were myriad '______ for Nixon' groups including 'Democrats for Nixon', 'Intellectuals for Nixon', 'Concerned Vietnam Veterans for Nixon', and over thirty ethnicity-based groups running the gamut from Armenians to Ukrainians.[61] Central to this early attempt at identity politics were the groups cultivated in the 1970 campaign – the core Silent Majority of conservatives, workers, and 'white ethnics' who, perhaps, did not quite vote the way the administration hoped, but who, Colson and others were convinced, could be brought fully into the Nixon fold with the proper policies and approaches.

That the Nixon White House was able to reach so many blue-collar workers through patriotic and identity-driven appeals is a testament to the strength of those ideas. They overcame significant union frustrations with administration policies – wage-and-price controls, the suspension of the Davis–Bacon Act mandating union wages for anyone regardless of union membership working on a federal construction project, the push to desegregate building sites and unions – to the point where, five decades later, the 'white working class' is now as closely associated with the Republican Party as it once was with the Democrats. But these results were far from certain in the wake of the 1970 defeats for Republican candidates. It took a dramatic shift in White House policies and a creative interpretation of the 1970 results to cement the alliance between the Republicans and the working class. And, perhaps, that relationship is one of the lasting legacies of Nixon's unusual decision to intervene in the midterm elections. He might have failed to convince the Silent Majority to vote Republican that year, but he laid the foundations for his 1972 landslide when many of these same groups decided, after all, to vote Nixon.

Notes

1. Richard Nixon, 'Remarks on Arrival at Grand Forks, North Dakota', 19 Oct. 1970, American Presidency Project [hereafter APP], https://www.presidency.ucsb.edu/documents/remarks-arrival-grand-forks-north-dakota, last accessed 14 Mar. 2022.
2. H. R. Haldeman, *The Haldeman Diaries: Inside the Nixon White House* (New York: G. P. Putnam's, 1994), p. 205; William Safire, *Before the Fall: An Inside View of the Pre-Watergate White House* (1975; New Brunswick, NJ: Transaction, 2005), p. 322. For an example of the potential dangers of midterm campaigns, see Iwan Morgan's chapter in this volume.
3. Safire, *Before the Fall*, p. 316.
4. Ibid., p. 320.
5. Tom Wells, *The War Within: America's Battle over Vietnam* (Berkeley, CA: University of California Press, 1994), p. 371.
6. Sarah Thelen, 'The Importance of Being Popular: Richard Nixon, Henry Kissinger, and Domestic Support for the Vietnam War', in David Fitzgerald, David Ryan, and John M. Thompson, eds,

Not Even Past: How the United States Ends Wars (New York: Berghahn, 2020), pp. 21–44.

7. Richard Nixon, 'Address to the Nation on the War in Vietnam', 3 Nov. 1969, APP, http://www.presidency.ucsb.edu/ws/?pid=2303, last accessed 14 Mar. 2022.
8. Ibid.
9. Memo, Alex Butterfield to H. R. Haldeman, 18 Nov. 1969, folder 'Memos/Alex Butterfield (November 1969)', box 54, White House Special Files: Staff Member and Office Files [hereafter WHSF: SMOF] – H. R. Haldeman, Nixon Presidential Library and Museum, College Park, MD [hereafter NPLM] (Collections of Richard Nixon's presidential materials that were consulted at the National Archives in College Park, Maryland, are now housed at the Richard Nixon Presidential Library and Museum, Yorba Linda, California); Richard M. Scammon and Ben J. Wattenberg, *The Real Majority* (New York: Coward-McCann, 1970).
10. Memo, Alex Butterfield to Richard Nixon, 24 Nov. 1969, folder 'Alex Butterfield (Nov 1969)', box 1, WHSF: SMOF – Alexander P. Butterfield, NPLM.
11. Richard M. Nixon, *RN: The Memoirs of Richard Nixon* (London: Sidgwick & Jackson, 1978), p. 491.
12. Safire, *Before the Fall*, p. 317.
13. Ibid., p. 322.
14. Ibid., p. 320.
15. Ibid., p. 319.
16. Ibid., p. 320.
17. John R. Coyne Jr, *The Impudent Snobs: Agnew vs. the Intellectual Establishment* (New Rochelle, NY: Arlington House, 1972), p. 361.
18. Safire, *Before the Fall*, p. 323.
19. Ibid., p. 323.
20. Robert Mason, 'Spiro Agnew: A Political Biography', forthcoming, ch. 6.
21. Ibid.
22. Nixon, *RN*, 492.
23. Mason, 'Spiro Agnew: A Political Biography', ch. 6; 'Gallup Rating High', *New York Times*, 25 Oct. 1970, p. 78.
24. Safire, *Before the Fall*, pp. 325–6.
25. Ibid., pp. 325–6.
26. Memo, Charles Colson to H. R. Haldeman, 12 Oct. 1970, p. 2, folder 'Haldeman Staff Memos–Cole–Dent October 1970', box 65, WHSF: SMOF – Haldeman, NPLM.

27. Ibid., p. 2.
28. This construction was a common refrain in Nixon's campaign speeches. See, e.g., Richard Nixon, 'Remarks at East Tennessee State University', 20 Oct. 1970, APP, https://www.presidency.ucsb.edu/documents/remarks-east-tennessee-state-university, last accessed 14 Mar. 2022; Richard Nixon, 'Remarks at Tallahassee, Florida', 28 Oct. 1970, APP, https://www.presidency.ucsb.edu/documents/remarks-tallahassee-florida, last accessed 14 Mar. 2022; Richard Nixon, 'Remarks at Rockford, Illinois', 29 Oct. 1970, APP, https://www.presidency.ucsb.edu/documents/remarks-rockford-illinois-0, last accessed 14 Mar. 2022; Richard Nixon, 'Remarks in San Jose, California', 29 Oct. 1970, APP, https://www.presidency.ucsb.edu/documents/remarks-san-jose-california-0, last accessed 14 Mar. 2022.
29. Richard M. Nixon, '"Remarks at Longview, Texas'", 28 Oct. 1970, APP, https://www.presidency.ucsb.edu/documents/remarks-longview-texas, last accessed 14 Mar. 2022.
30. See, e.g., Nixon, 'Remarks on Arrival at Grand Forks, North Dakota'.
31. Richard Nixon, 'Remarks in Miami Beach, Florida', 27 Oct. 1970, APP, https://www.presidency.ucsb.edu/documents/remarks-miami-beach-florida, last accessed 14 Mar. 2022.
32. Memo, George Bell to Jim Keogh, 21 Sept. 1970, folder 'Black Silent Majority Committee', box 88, WHSF: SMOF – Charles W. Colson, NPLM; 'Form Black Silent Majority, Law, Order Group in D.C.', *Jet*, 29 Oct. 1970.
33. 'Form Black Silent Majority, Law, Order Group in D.C.'; memo, Robert Odle to Alex Butterfield, 25 Mar. 1970, folder 'Memoranda Received Jul thru Dec 1970', box 8, WHSF: SMOF – Butterfield, NPLM; memo, George Bell to Jim Keogh; Dean J. Kotlowski, *Nixon's Civil Rights: Politics, Principle, and Policy* (Cambridge, MA: Harvard University Press, 2001), pp. 176–8.
34. The use of the word 'astroturf' – a brand name for artificial grass – as a political idea was coined by Texas Senator Lloyd Bentsen in 1985 in response to insurance industry efforts to influence legislation before Congress. For more on the Nixon administration's own astroturf campaigns, see: Sarah Thelen, 'Mobilizing a Majority: Nixon's "Silent Majority" Speech and the Domestic Debate over Vietnam', *Journal of American Studies* 51 (2017): pp. 887–914; Sarah Thelen, 'Helping Them Along: Astroturf, Public Opinion, and Nixon's Vietnam War', *49th Parallel* 37 (2015): pp. 14–33;

Sarah Thelen, 'Give War a Chance: The Nixon Administration and Domestic Support for the Vietnam War, 1969–1973', PhD dissertation, American University, 2013.

35. 'Black Group Hits "Shabby Agitators"', *Philadelphia Tribune*, 17 Oct. 1970, p. 32.
36. William Raspberry, 'GOP Theme: Building, Not Burning', *Washington Post,* 14 Nov. 1970, p. A17.
37. Richard Nixon, 'Remarks at the Dedication of the Italian Community Center in Stamford, Connecticut', 12 Oct. 1970, APP, https://www.presidency.ucsb.edu/documents/remarks-the-dedication-the-italian-community-center-stamford-connecticut; memo, Charles Colson to H. R. Haldeman, 14 Sept. 1970, folder 'Nixon and Labor/Political', box 96, WHSF: SMOF – Colson, NPLM; Haldeman, *Haldeman Diaries*, pp. 191–2.
38. Memo, Charles Colson to Larry Higby, 22 Oct. 1970, folder 'President's Meeting with the Sons of Italy – September 11, 1970', box 21, WHSF: SMOF – Colson, NPLM; memo, Charles Colson to Hugh Sloan, 14 Sept. 1970, folder 'Meeting with Chicago Polish-American leaders – September 17, 1970', box 22; WHSF: SMOF – Colson, NPLM.
39. Memo, Charles Colson to Murray Chotiner, 11 July 1970, folder 'Jay Lovestone – AFL-CIO [3 of 3]', box 78, WHSF: SMOF – Colson, NPLM.
40. Memo, Charles Colson to H. R. Haldeman, 2 July 1970, p. 1, folder 'HRH-July-August 1970 – Staff Memos – Cole-D', box 61, WHSF: SMOF – Haldeman, NPLM.
41. See, e.g., Lisa McGirr, *Suburban Warriors: The Origins of the New American Right* (Princeton, NJ: Princeton University Press, 2001) and Gregory L. Schneider, *Cadres for Conservatism: Young Americans for Freedom and the Rise of the Contemporary Right* (New York: New York University Press, 1999).
42. For a sense of the Hard Hat views of Buckley and the 1970 race more broadly, see: Diana Lurie, 'Underneath the Hard Hats: A Political Symposium', *New York Magazine*, 2 Nov. 1970, in folder 'Labor Campaign [2 of 2]', box 77, WHSF: SMOF – Colson, NPLM.
43. Safire, *Before the Fall*, p. 319.
44. Ibid., p. 319.
45. Rick Perlstein, *Nixonland: The Rise of a President and the Fracturing of America* (London: Scribner, 2008), p. 530; Richard

Reeves, *President Nixon: Alone in the White House* (New York: Simon & Schuster, 2001), p. 268.
46. H. R. Haldeman, notes, 26 Sept. 1970, p. 3, folder 'H Notes–July–Sept '70 [7 Aug.–30 Sept. 1970] Part II', box 42, WHSF: SMOF – Haldeman, NPLM.
47. Haldeman, *Haldeman Diaries*, p. 205.
48. Haldeman, *Haldeman Diaries*, pp. 205–6; Nixon, *RN*, pp. 492–3; Safire, *Before the Fall*, pp. 327–33.
49. Nixon, *RN*, p. 492.
50. Haldeman, *Haldeman Diaries*, pp. 205–6.
51. Safire, *Before the Fall*, p. 333.
52. Richard Nixon, 'Remarks at Phoenix, Arizona', 31 Oct. 1970, APP, https://www.presidency.ucsb.edu/documents/remarks-phoenix-arizona, last accessed 14 Mar. 2022.
53. Haldeman, *Haldeman Diaries*, p. 206; Nixon, *RN*, p. 494; Safire, *Before the Fall*, p. 334.
54. Haldeman, *Haldeman Diaries*, p. 205.
55. Ibid., p. 207.
56. Nixon, *RN*, p. 494; Safire, *Before the Fall*, p. 337.
57. Safire, *Before the Fall*, p. 337.
58. Ibid.
59. Haldeman, *Haldeman Diaries*, p. 208.
60. Memo, Charles Colson to Ken Cole, 26 July 1971, folder 'Ken Cole [1971]', box 6, WHSF: SMOF – Colson, NPLM.
61. Memo, H. R. Haldeman to Charles Colson, 21 Nov. 1972, folder 'New American Majority', box 6, WHSF: SMOF – W. Richard Howard, NPLM; Charles Colson, Telephone Call Recommendation, 29 July 1972, folder 'Telephone Call Requests [2 of 2]', box 116, WHSF: SMOF – Colson, NPLM; Jefferson Cowie, *Stayin' Alive: The 1970s and the Last Days of the Working Class* (New York: New Press, 2010), p. 128.

10

'Democrats dominate': The Democratic Party in Congress and the Midterms of 1974 and 1978

Patrick Andelic

The 1970s are flanked by the most shattering defeats that the Democratic Party faced in any presidential elections in the post-war era. In 1972, the Democratic presidential nominee, George McGovern, lost forty-nine states to the incumbent president, Richard Nixon, a defeat more lopsided than any party had experienced in the twentieth century. Just eight short years later, in 1980, not only did Jimmy Carter become the first president to be defeated for re-election since Herbert Hoover, but the Democrats lost their majority in the Senate for the first time since the 1950s. Four years after that, in 1984, the Democrats chalked up a second forty-nine-state defeat, when Carter's former vice president Walter Mondale lost in a landslide to incumbent president Ronald Reagan. In histories of the post-war United States, these elections are often cited as stepping stones for the triumph of the New Right, as first Nixon and then Reagan solidified a Republican hegemony that would consign the Democratic Party to the political wilderness.[1]

Yet beneath those headline successes for the Republicans was another story of stubborn Democratic endurance in Congress. Nixon's 1972 landslide was remarkable for how short his coattails proved to be. Not only did the Republican Party fail to win either chamber of Congress, Democrats gained seats in the Senate. In 1984, in the midst of another landslide defeat for the party, Democrats held their lopsided House majorities and again gained seats in the Senate (although Republicans held the Senate majority they had won in 1980). Two years later, the Democrats would win back control of the Senate and seemingly resolidify their position on Capitol Hill. Indeed, by 1990, analysts were writing of the phenomenon of the 'permanent Democratic Congress'.[2]

In between those landmark elections for the coalescing New Right came a moment when the political realities of mid-century seemed to have reasserted themselves, with the Democratic Party enjoying a hegemony in Washington, DC, controlling both White House and Congress. Yet the relationship between Jimmy Carter's White House and the Democratic Congress was notoriously dysfunctional. Many historians have attributed this to Carter's shortcomings as a congressional manager.[3] However, the midterm elections of 1974 and 1978 are key to understanding why that relationship was so fractious and why congressional Democrats believed that they had a separate, even superior, mandate to that enjoyed by Carter.

In his landmark study of midterm elections, Andrew E. Busch categorises 1974 as a 'normal' midterm that produced no significant lasting effects and 1978 as a 'pre-aligning' midterm that played a role in Republican political successes over the following two decades.[4] The shifting control of the White House in the 1970s – from Nixon to Ford to Carter – means that few studies have viewed 1974 and 1978 as of a piece. From the perspective of Congress, however, these two midterms produced an essentially identical result: solid Democratic control of both House and Senate. They also took place during a period of unusual transformation in Congress, defined by institutional reforms that expanded the resources (committee positions, funding, and staff) available to individual congresspersons and a generational shift in Congress's membership, which in turn fed into growing spirit of rebellion against the 'imperial presidency'. Taken together, these two elections disrupt the idea that a presidential election resets national politics, with the president taking a new mandate that defines the politics of his or her administration.

'This is not just a victory, this is a mandate': the 1974 midterms

The early 1970s were marked by intensifying confrontation between the Democratic Congress and the Republican administrations of Richard Nixon and Gerald Ford. Nixon was the first president since 1849 to arrive in the White House without his party in control of either the House of Representatives or the Senate. Despite his efforts to construct a 'new American majority' in the 1970 and 1972 elections, the Democratic Party continued to hold their majorities in both chambers.[5] Although that divided government produced some substantial policy accomplishments, Nixon's abbreviated second term in particular saw a bitter tug of war over constitutional prerogatives.[6] Most of these emerged from Democratic frustration with what they saw as Nixon's usurping of congressional powers. There were two significant legislative monuments to that conflict. The first was the 1973 War Powers Act, passed over presidential veto, which limited the executive's power to wage overseas conflict, and required the president formally to seek authorisation from Congress in the event of any American military action.[7] The second was the Congressional Budget Control and Impoundment Act of 1974, which was passed to curb the 'impoundment' of congressionally appropriated funds and also established the Congressional Budget Office (CBO) to support the congressional budget-drafting process. These represented an assertion of congressional responsibility and capabilities in the face of what the Democratic majorities saw as Nixon's abuse of his executive powers.[8]

The struggle between Nixon and the Democratic Congress unfolded against the backdrop of the Watergate scandal, which climaxed with the president being forced to resign from office to avoid impeachment. Soon after his inauguration, Nixon's successor, Gerald Ford, sought a reconciliation with Congress. Ford, a former member of the House whose highest aspiration had once been to become Speaker, told a joint session of Congress only days after becoming president that 'part of my heart will always be here on Capitol Hill' and that he understood 'the co-equal role of the Congress in our constitutional process'. He told the assembled members that he did not want 'a honeymoon' with Congress, but rather 'a good marriage'.[9] As Ford had not even been on the Republican presidential ticket in 1972, he could claim no personal mandate from the voters in his dealings with Congress, unlike the more confrontational Nixon.

Ford continued to approach Congress with much more deference than Nixon had habitually shown. In October 1974, one month after he controversially granted his predecessor a 'full, free, and absolute' pardon, Ford appeared before a subcommittee of the House Judiciary Committee to defend his decision, becoming the first president to testify before Congress since Abraham Lincoln. And although Ford was received with all proper courtesies, the negotiations between the White House and the House Judiciary Committee in the weeks leading up to the hearings had been extensive. Subcommittee members had debated, at length, whether they ought to stand up when Ford entered the room. They eventually decided that they would not – because Congress was a co-equal branch of government and its members should behave that way.[10]

The pardon cast a pall over Ford's hopes for a rapprochement with Congress and badly damaged his public standing. 'Honeymoons do have to end,' remarked Washington senator Warren D. Magnuson in the days immediately afterwards.[11] Gallup polling suggested that the pardon had caused Ford's approval rating to fall from 71 to 49 per cent between mid-August and mid-September. Twenty-eight per cent of respondents said that the decision made them less likely to vote for Republican candidates.[12] Though public anger over the pardon would eventually dissipate, it was one more factor that worsened an already unfavourable political environment for Republicans as that year's midterms approached. The pardon pushed the Watergate scandal back into the headlines and denied the public catharsis. With the economy still weakened by the 1973 'Oil Shock' (when OPEC had imposed a temporary embargo on the United States and caused the price of oil to quadruple in a matter of months) and with inflation at 11 per cent, the Republican brand was in trouble. Just 18 per cent of the electorate was prepared to identify as Republicans.[13]

Privately, the Ford administration was braced for a heavy defeat. In memos, advisors tried to put a positive spin on the likely catastrophe, comparing it to the 'terrible bath' that Truman had undergone in the 1946 midterms before going on to win election in his own right two years later 'after settling in'.[14] They also prepared to reject any suggestion that the expected Democratic gains were a 'referendum' on Ford given the brevity of his tenure.[15] In public, Ford sought to limit the damage. On the stump, he warned of a 'runaway Congress' that might threaten the administration's anti-inflation programme and its foreign policy. He even suggested that an unchecked congressional Democratic Party might establish a 'legislative dictatorship'.[16]

However, on election day, the voters ignored these warnings. The Democratic Party scored its biggest wins in a decade, gaining forty-nine seats in the House of Representatives and four in the Senate. This enhanced the party's considerable majorities in both chambers, giving the Democrats 291 seats to the Republicans 144 in the House and 61–39 in the Senate. There were similarly lopsided gains in state contests. The Democrats won twenty-seven of the thirty-five gubernatorial races, representing a net gain of four governorships, including, as the *New York Times'* Christopher Lydon put it, the two 'giant anchors of national politics', New York and California.[17] the *New York Times* noted that the 'Democrats had trouble beating the averages only because they already held sizable majorities'.[18]

In the aftermath, Democratic Party officials claimed a mandate for the party and its policy priorities. Robert J. Keefe, the political director of the Democratic National Committee (DNC), claimed that there was 'a conservative trend in the country in terms of people's self-identification. But when you ask them about programs and candidates, they come down very liberal. People don't like the liberal label, but they like the substance behind it.'[19] DNC chair Robert Strauss boasted that the results showed that the party's coalition was being reconstituted: 'we've got the small businessman, the blue-collar worker and the farmer back voting Democratic.'[20]

'This is not just a victory, this is a mandate,' said the House Speaker Carl Albert soon after elections.[21] Robert Strauss told a National Press Club breakfast meeting that the election results represented 'mandated demand' for Congress to develop its own legislative agenda. The Democratic leadership in Congress, said Strauss, 'know they've got to move'.[22] Others within the party's wider coalition were more dismissive of those debates. 'I don't believe in this mandate stuff,' said George Meany, president of the American Federation of Labor and Congress of Industrial Organizations (AFL-CIO). 'A guy runs for office and gets elected. All of a sudden he's got a mandate. Two less votes and he's nothing.' For Meany, the bumper Democratic results were a reflection only of 'all the scandal and the collapsing economy'.[23]

Unsurprisingly, the Ford White House rejected the suggestion that the midterms were a popular rejection of the new executive. 'No one thinks this was a referendum on the President,' claimed White House press secretary Ron Nessen.[24] In his public statements following the election, Ford sought to repurpose the congressional 'mandate' for his own agenda. The 'number one issue' of the campaign had been inflation, the president claimed in his statement in response to the results: 'The mandate of the electorate places upon the next Congress a full measure of responsibility for resolving this problem.'[25] Ford reinforced that point in a message to Congress when it reconvened for the lame-duck session: 'I do not read any mandate in the recent election so clearly as the American people's concern about our economy and their urgent demand for fiscal restraint.'[26]

Before they had even taken their seats, the members of the Democratic class of 1974 had begun to draw considerable media attention. This was not only for the class's unusual size and distinctive features, but also for its apparent cohesion. They soon acquired a nickname – the 'Watergate Babies' – and were the subject of countless newspaper profiles.[27] While the media coverage sometimes overstated the class's homogeneity, the class's youth, relative political inexperience, relative diversity, and shared cultural sensibility were noteworthy commonalities.[28] The 94th Congress was the youngest since World War II. The average age of the House fell below fifty for the first time since 1945, and the number of House members under the age of forty almost doubled, from thirty-eight to seventy-eight.[29] There were similar changes afoot in the Senate, where eight of its eleven new members were under fifty.[30] Many of the new members had not followed a conventional political career path. Thirty-one of the new House Democrats had never held any political office before. The new congressman from Pennsylvania's 7th district,

Bob Edgar, claimed that he had 'looked up the word Democrat in the phone book' only a year before he was elected.[31] The number of African Americans and women in Congress increased, albeit slightly, with Frances Farenthold, chairwoman of the National Women's Political Caucus, dubbing 1974 'the year of the breakthrough for women'.[32] It was Tim Wirth, newly elected representative from Colorado, perhaps better than any other Watergate Baby, who encapsulated the generational and cultural shift that the class of '74 represented: 'JFK was our first vote, and we went through Vietnam. The others came of age during World War II and revered Ike. We are accustomed to television ... We're part of the supermarket age, the quick fix, and the fast shot.'[33] For all that this romanticised the Watergate Babies, and rather unfairly characterised their predecessors, it indicates the extent to which they shared both particular characteristics and a generational identity.

Soon after the elections, new Maryland congresswoman Gladys Noon Spellman was among those who called for the Watergate Babies to coordinate with each other in the 94th Congress: 'We can just be swallowed up and be one of hundreds or we can work together and have some clout.'[34] Initially, the incoming class seemed to have taken this to heart. Before the end of November, the freshmen had rented their own office near the Capitol and begun hiring staff.[35] They embraced the cause of congressional reform and resolved to use their superior numbers and organisation to pass sweeping changes to the committee system and precedents like seniority (the principle that committee chairmanships and other privileges should be allocated based on length of continuous service). The Watergate Babies invited committee chairs expecting to be reappointed to be quizzed in closed sessions in advance of the organisational caucus meeting to confirm leadership and committee chair positions.[36] When the caucus met, a number of committee chairs were dramatically removed from their positions, including Wilbur Mills, the long-serving and widely feared chair of the House Ways and Means Committee.[37]

These reforms strengthened the Democratic Party's coordinating bodies in Congress – the House Caucus and the

Senate Conference – at the expense of the committee system. Congressional Democrats could boast not only of increased majorities, but a rejuvenated mandate, as they faced in Ford an accidental president for whom no Americans had voted. 'I think the last election means the buck stops here,' Speaker Carl Albert told his members at the first House caucus meeting of the new Congress.[38] Indeed, there was speculation that Ford would not run for election in 1976 and that his protestations to the contrary were to prevent him from being seen as 'a lame-duck'.[39] Ford's White House was disturbed by the Democratic Congress's new purpose. 'It was a little startling to see how the Democrats marched in lock step,' said one presidential aide in early 1975.[40] Congressional Republicans echoed these concerns, with John Anderson of Illinois warning of 'the trend toward what . . . has [been] termed "congressional government".'[41]

However, the 94th Congress's accomplishments never matched those early hopes or fears, which only underscored the inherent challenges of Congress claiming any kind of mandate to supplant the president. While the Congress did enjoy some successes – such as rejecting military aid to South Vietnam and Cambodia, sought by the Ford administration – the Democratic majorities began to encounter difficulties within a matter of months.[42] In large part, this was due to Ford's enthusiastic use of his veto, blocking Democratic bills on a range of issues from employment relief to housing subsidies.[43] Despite these frustrations, the Democratic Congress's independent streak only widened over the remainder of the decade and became more noticeable with a Democrat in the White House, when most observers expected more comity between Pennsylvania Avenue and Capitol Hill.

'My chances for re-election don't depend on whether I snuggle up to the President': the 1978 midterms

The 1978 midterm elections took place in a political environment that was both radically different from and strikingly similar to that of four years earlier. The Democratic Party had resumed a hegemonic position in Washington politics, with its congressional majorities supplemented by the retaking of the White

House after Georgia governor Jimmy Carter won the 1976 election. Nonetheless, the relationship between the White House and Congress remained fundamentally antagonistic. This was, in large part, a result of those durable and pre-existing Democratic congressional majorities, whose members felt little gratitude to Carter and had no reason to attribute their political success to his coat-tails. As a result, they did not regard their mandate as being shared with the incoming president.

When Carter was inaugurated, 118 of the 289 Democrats in the House had been first elected in 1974 or 1976.[44] Of the Watergate Babies who sought re-election in 1976, all but two were returned to Congress, defying predictions that their election had been an aberration caused by the febrile political atmosphere of 1974. Most congressional Democrats did not feel they owed their victories to Carter. Indeed, the pollster Lou Harris estimated that almost three-quarters of Democrats in the House had run ahead of Carter in their districts.[45] On the campaign trail, Carter had promised to treat Congress as a co-equal branch and its members 'as though they were Presidents themselves'.[46] However, he also promised that if he had 'arguments' with Congress then he could 'take [his] case directly to the people': 'I can reach the consciousness of the average voter in a congressional district five times easier than a congressman as President.'[47] Carter's belief in his superior connection with the average voter would prove an ongoing source of tension with congressional members. This was of a piece with his broader political strategy. Before he was inaugurated, Carter's chief advisors urged him to avoid too close an association with the wider Democratic Party, and to preserve his distinct identity.[48]

Congressional Democrats were bullish at the beginning of Carter's term over the role they expected to play in his presidency. 'Give us a Democratic President, any Democrat,' Speaker Thomas P. 'Tip' O'Neill of Massachusetts told journalists, 'and we'll make him a great President.'[49] In the midst of the election for the new Senate Majority leader, Colorado senator and 'Watergate Baby' Gary Hart had suggested that in the 95th Congress the office would be 'a hollow log in which both sides leave messages', essentially a conduit between the White House and the Senate Democratic Conference.[50] However, for all the congressional party's self-assurance, there were no moves afoot to define a coherent legislative agenda that the president might be persuaded to embrace. Columnist Jack Germond wrote in January 1977 that 'when you ask a half-dozen of the most liberal Democrats in Congress what they want now that there is a Democrat in the White House, all you get are a lot of furrowed brows and thoughtful stares at the ceiling but no specifics'.[51] The expectation that the president would be the prime mover for any legislation remained overwhelming. However, congressional Democrats' sense of their own independent mandate meant that they had no intention of acting as a rubber stamp.

Despite Carter's campaign promises to approach Congress as an equal partner, his White House staff was soon attracting complaints from representatives and senators. Many of the complaints focused on his assistant for congressional relations, fellow Georgian Frank Moore. Members claimed that Moore did not consult them on appointments and policy issues, and even in some cases that their phone calls went unreturned. Presidential speechwriter James Fallows later described the congressional liaison office as 'structurally the weakest branch of the White House'.[52] Carter believed that the fact he was a Georgian, and that he had run an anti-Washington campaign, led the Washington press corps to look for signs of antagonism between him and Congress.[53] Nonetheless, there was genuine friction. Carter's fraught relationship with Congress reflected a feeling among Democrats that the president was neglecting, indeed was actively disdainful of, his role as party leader. It was not until June 1978, for instance, around seventeen months after assuming office, that Carter invited Democratic state chairmen and national committee chairs to the White House for a meeting.[54] New York congressman Benjamin Rosenthal noted that the Carter team 'ran against Washington, then became part of Washington, and were neither psychologically nor mechanically equipped to deal with that'.[55]

The 95th Congress was defined by a series of high-profile confrontations with Carter. In part, these were the consequence of the dysfunctional relationship between Carter and congressional Democrats. However, they also reflected deeper tensions between the White House and an increasingly assertive Congress. The first of these was the infamous 'water projects' controversy in early 1977, when Carter announced the cancellation of nineteen water projects which the administration deemed wasteful, unsafe, or environmentally damaging. Democrats in Congress responded with howls of outrage. Members were aggrieved not only at the loss of valuable infrastructure projects in their states, but also at the lack of White House consultation before the announcement.[56] Within months, Carter was forced to retreat on the issue.[57] Some observers praised Carter for his boldness. Columnist David Broder congratulated Carter for having 'turned the parochial congressional pork barrel into a national issue and broken up the game'.[58] However, the damage to the White House's relationship with Congress was severe and perhaps irreparable. Carter's Office of Management and Budget (OMB) director Bert Lance called it the president's 'worst political mistake', and one which 'doomed any hopes we had of developing a good, effective working relationship with Congress'.[59] In many respects, the episode revealed much about Carter's political style, which one friend, Warren Fortson, compared to a 'South Georgia turtle'. 'He doesn't go around the log. He just sticks his head in the middle and pushes and pushes until the log gives way.'[60] On this issue, the Democratic Congress was a log that would not give way.

As the 1978 midterm elections approached, the relations between Carter and Congress worsened. To a considerable extent, this was due to the administration's growing concern with inflation which often put it at odds with some in Congress. The president complained in his diary about congressional demands to increase spending.[61] Carter later reflected, 'I had the impression then and I haven't much changed it that Liberals at that time demand 100% and if you give them 95% they dwell on the 5%.'[62] Moreover, many congressional Democrats continued to resent Carter's political style and his tendency to try to circumvent Congress if he felt his agenda was being stalled. Just a few months into the Carter presidency, Vice President Walter Mondale's aide Bill Smith had suggested that relations with Congress might be improved if the president 'stopped threatening to go to the public'.[63] Few Democrats in Congress believed that their political prospects depended on Carter's political support. One north-eastern Democrat, who had won his seat in 1976 running fourteen points ahead of Carter, told the columnist Jack Anderson, 'My chances for re-election don't depend on whether I snuggle up to the president.'[64]

Nonetheless, the Carter White House hoped that the 1978 midterms might be an opportunity to build a better relationship with Congress. One congressional liaison aide, Jim Free, wrote to Frank Moore in May 1977 that 'the number one thing on Members' minds is their ultimate fate – re-election'. The Carter administration's inexperience in Washington meant that it had few favours to call in on Capitol Hill. Therefore, suggested Free, '[t]he best way to help Congressional relations is to systematically help Members with fund-raisers now and work on a plan to aid them in their campaigns.'[65] The administration threw itself into this effort. By polling day, there had been 1,100 campaign appearances involving Carter or a member of his family, Mondale or a member of his family, or a member of the Cabinet or White House staff.[66] Frank Moore was optimistic about the likely impact of the elections on the White House–congressional relations. The Carter administration, he noted, had made 'an extreme effort' to support Democratic candidates, and they expected that to pay off. 'And it's not just that we've got chits to cash in with them, but we know them better now and they know us better.'[67]

The results of the 1978 midterms gave the party few reasons to celebrate, as Democrats sustained a net loss of three seats in the Senate and fifteen in the House. In the Senate, several high-profile liberal Democrats went down to defeat against Republican challengers, including Iowa's Dick Clark and Colorado's Floyd Haskell. In an ominous sign of the collapse of the once solidly Democratic South, Mississippi returned its first ever elected Republican senator. Republicans won both Senate seats in the vice president's home state, Minnesota (in spite of an appearance by Carter in Duluth on the eve of polling day), including – in a result loaded with ominous symbolism – the seat that had been occupied by that pillar of post-war liberalism, Hubert Humphrey, until his death from bladder cancer in January 1978.[68] Of the twenty-eight candidates for the Senate and various governorships that Carter had stumped for in the last two months of the campaign, only twelve won their elections.[69] This only reinforced congressional Democrats' suspicions about the president's short coat-tails.

For many historians, the 1978 midterms heralded the arrival of a potent national conservative movement that would propel Reagan into office just two years later.[70] Conservatives exploited discontent over tax rates, government spending, and divisive foreign policy issues like the unpopular agreement to return the Panama Canal Zone to win votes for Republican candidates.[71] The recently founded National Conservative Political Action Committee (NCPAC), an independent conservative campaign entity, had targeted a slate of liberal Democrats and took credit for the defeat of high-profile candidates like Iowa's Dick Clark.[72] Other Republican-adjacent single-issue organisations, like anti-abortion right-to-life groups, claimed their share of the success and revealed a burgeoning grassroots movement for conservative issues.[73] 'In an overall sense,' the Republican National Committee chair Bill Brock told journalists, 'it's safe to say the Republican Party is back.'[74]

However, although the Democratic Party had endured net losses, the overall result was more mixed. The Democrats had retained control of the House and the Senate, with robust majorities in both chambers – 277–157 seats in the House and 58–41 in the Senate. Democratic candidates had also made gains, winning Senate seats in Michigan, Nebraska, New Jersey, and Oklahoma. In Massachusetts, Paul Tsongas, a Watergate Baby first elected to a House seat four years earlier, defeated Republican Edward Brooke (less happily this meant that the Senate lost its only African American member). David Broder suggested that, despite the changing of seats between liberal Democrats and conservative Republicans, the ideological balance of the Senate remained basically stable.[75]

As journalist Adam Clymer noted in his round-up ('Democrats Dominate' ran the headline), if the Republicans' haul of governorships and state legislatures suggested a party building for the future, 'most American voters rejected the [GOP]'s arguments of the moment and maintained their identification with the

Democratic Party at its recent high level.'[76] The Democrats, said one presidential aide, 'ended up in good shape'. The White House claimed that the results, and continued Democratic control of Congress, were a restatement of public confidence in the administration's agenda.[77] In particular, the results reinforced Carter's conviction that he had been elected to 'bring fiscal responsibility to the federal government'.[78] This interpretation of the presidential mandate would run counter to some Democrats in Congress who took different lessons from the elections. Those tensions would dramatically erupt when the Democrats gathered for their first party-wide convention since the 1976 election a month later.

Conclusion: 'the Democratic sponge'

When the Democrats gathered in Memphis, Tennessee, in December 1978 for their second quadrennial midterm convention, the party was in turmoil. The midterm conventions had been created only a few years earlier as part of a wider suite of party reforms that would enable more internal party democracy.[79] Many senior figures viewed them as a cumbersome liability. The first, in Kansas City in 1974, had been a more harmonious affair, in part because of the huge wins that Democrats scored in that year's midterms, and also because it had been aggressively stage-managed by then-DNC chair Robert Strauss.[80] With a Democrat in the White House, a fresh batch of midterm losses, and a much more disgruntled party, most expected the convention to be altogether more painful.

The president arrived in Memphis prepared for a confrontation with members of his own party. Carter's staff had urged him to be 'firm and blunt' with the assembled Democrats, urging them to support 'an austere budget and cuts in many popular programs' to control inflation. 'This is not a message all Democrats want to hear,' concluded communications director Gerald Rafshoon.[81] Some Democratic critics of the president despaired that they would be able to offer any real resistance. Connecticut representative Toby Moffett dismissed it as 'Meaningless Memphis'.[82] Another complained to a journalist that it would be 'a rah-rah, here-we-are type event, nothing more'.[83] However, others were more optimistic and dismissed the idea that the convention would be toothless. Maryland representative Barbara Mikulski told a women's caucus meeting, 'We're not gathering here in Memphis to sing a hallelujah chorus to Jimmy Carter.'[84]

The most dramatic confrontation came at a workshop on health insurance, where Massachusetts senator Edward Kennedy memorably exhorted his party to 'sail against the wind'. The Democrats could not, he said, 'afford to drift or lie at anchor' or 'heed the call of those who say it is time to furl the sail'. There could be, he said, 'few more divisive issues' than 'a Democratic policy of drastic slashes in the federal budget at the expense of the elderly, the poor, the black, the sick, the cities and the unemployed'. Though Kennedy's only direct mention of Carter in the speech was to praise his peace-making efforts in the Middle East, the implicit rejection of Carter's tight budget policy was obvious.[85] As Kennedy thumped the rostrum and recommitted himself to comprehensive national health insurance, the assembled Democrats roared their approval.

Kennedy's impassioned speech in Memphis has featured prominently in histories of his 1980 primary challenge to Carter, as the moment when the rivalry between the two crystallised and the Massachusetts senator fired the starting gun on his candidacy.[86] But it also reveals the extent to which the Democratic Party still felt some confidence in its majority status. This was not a party that felt chastened by the results of the most recent midterm elections and fearful of a Republican resurgence that might displace it. In retrospect, this may seem complacent, even hubristic, but it reveals the extent to which Democratic control of Congress had become a fact of political life in Washington. Elections seemed to be a biennial mechanism for determining the size of the Democratic majorities in the House and Senate.

This did not necessarily mean that the Democratic Party would be able to enact a specifically liberal agenda. The midterm convention ultimately rejected a liberal-backed resolution that would have exempted domestic welfare programmes from spending cuts, which enabled the White House to claim that the party had backed the president's agenda.[87] The policy direction and public philosophy of the Democratic Party seemed up for grabs.

However, the idea that the Democratic hegemony might disintegrate and the party be cast into the wilderness still seemed fanciful to many Democrats in the 1970s. Even some conservatives were resigned to the Democrats remaining the nation's majority party. One week before the 1978 midterms, conservative columnist George Will wrote fatalistically that the 'Democratic sponge' was 'too plastic and squishy to split, for which fact it should give thanks'. It was increasingly the case that 'the nation's two most important political parties are not the Democratic and Republican Parties, but the two wings of the Democratic Party'.[88]

Notes

This chapter draws in part on some material that appears, for a different purpose, in Patrick Andelic, *Donkey Work: Congressional Democrats in Conservative America, 1974–1994* (Lawrence, KS: University Press of Kansas, 2019).

1. See, e.g., Steven F. Hayward, *The Age of Reagan, 1964–1980* (Roseville, CA: Forum, 2001) and *The Age of Reagan: The Conservative Counterrevolution, 1980–89* (New York: Crown Forum, 2009); and Sean Wilentz, *The Age of Reagan: A History, 1974–2008* (New York: Harper, 2008).
2. Norman Ornstein wrote that 'the persistence of firm Democratic majorities in Congress', even as the party continued to lose the White House, was '[o]ne of the most enduring, puzzling, and contentious phenomena of modern American political life'. Norman Ornstein, 'The Permanent Democratic Congress', *Public Interest* 100 (Summer 1990): pp. 22–44 (quotation at p. 24).
3. Charles O. Jones, *The Trusteeship Presidency: Jimmy Carter and the United States Congress* (Baton Rouge, LA: University of Louisiana Press, 1988); John Dumbrell, *The Carter Presidency: A Re-evaluation* (Manchester: Manchester University Press, 1995), pp. 39–42.
4. Andrew Busch, *Horses in Midstream: US Midterm Elections and Their Consequences, 1894–1998* (Pittsburgh, PA: University of Pittsburgh Press, 1999), pp. 83, 106, 110.
5. See, e.g., Robert Mason, *Richard Nixon and the Quest for a New Majority* (Chapel Hill, NC: University of North Carolina Press, 2004), pp. 77–112.

6. David Mayhew notes that neither the Nixon nor Ford administrations have 'a reputation for legislative achievement', which he attributes to the White House–Congress relationship not following 'an appropriate script' of a victorious president winning an election and then claiming a mandate to push their agenda forward. The often productive 'creative disorder' of the Nixon and Ford era is overlooked because of its narrative unfamiliarity. David R. Mayhew, *Divided We Govern: Party Control, Lawmaking, and Investigations, 1946–1990* (New Haven, CT: Yale University Press, 1991), pp. 89, 91.
7. The act required the president to notify Congress within forty-eight hours of the deployment of American forces to any action, and then to seek further congressional authorisation within sixty days for that military action to continue. Richard L. Madden, 'House and Senate Override Veto by Nixon on Curb of War Powers; Backers of Bill Win 3-Year Fight', *New York Times*, 8 Nov. 1973.
8. 'Congress Gains Wide Budget Role', *New York Times*, 13 July 1974.
9. 'Transcript of President Ford's Address to Joint Session of Congress and the Nation', *New York Times*, 13 Aug. 1974.
10. Haynes Johnson, 'Ford's Historic Visit: Questions Remain,' *Washington Post*, 18 Oct. 1974; James M. Naughton, 'History Played Out on Familiar Stage', *New York Times*, 18 Oct. 1974.
11. Spencer Rich and Richard L. Lyons, 'Democrats Criticize Pardon', *Washington Post*, 10 Sept. 1974.
12. According to the *New York Times* write-up, '[t]he survey showed wide disapproval at least for the timing of the pardon, although there were indications that most of the persons questioned in the survey would not have opposed a pardon for the former President at a later time.' 'Support for Ford Declines Sharply', *New York Times*, 12 Sept. 1974.
13. Yanek Mieczkowski, *Gerald Ford and the Challenges of the 1970s* (Lexington, KY: University Press of Kentucky, 2005), p. 65.
14. Memo, Dean Burch to Gerald Ford, 4 Nov. 1974, Dean Burch Files, box 3, folder (Election Analysis, Nov. 1974), Gerald R. Ford Presidential Library (GFPL).
15. Memo, Fred Slight to Chuck Lichtenstein, 4 Nov. 1974, Dean Burch Files, box 3, folder (Election Analysis, Nov. 1974), GFPL.
16. As the *New York Times* noted, this meant that Democrats occupied thirty-six of fifty governors' mansions. Christopher Lydon, 'The Awful Arithmetic', *New York Times*, 21 Apr. 1974,

p. 213; Philip Shabecoff, 'Ford Warns G.O.P. on Rivals' Sweep', *New York Times*, 17 Oct. 1974; Philip Shabecoff, 'Ford Says a "Runaway Congress" Would Harm Peace', *New York Times*, 30 Oct. 1974.

17. Christopher Lydon, 'Democrats Gain 4 Governorships', *New York Times*, 7 Nov. 1974.
18. 'A Mandate to Do What?' *New York Times*, 10 Nov. 1974.
19. Christopher Lydon, 'Democrats Gain 4 Governorships,' *New York Times*, 7 Nov. 1974.
20. David S. Broder, 'Nationwide Sweep Nets 6 Governors, Over 30 in House', *Washington Post*, 6 Nov. 1974.
21. James M. Naughton, 'Democrats View Their Victory as Spur to Legislative Moves; Ford Asks Responsible Action,' *New York Times*, 7 Nov. 1974.
22. Richard L. Madden, 'Meany Says the Democrats Did Not Receive a Mandate', *New York Times*, 8 Nov. 1974.
23. Ibid.
24. 'Ford's Inclination to Run in '76 Intact', *Los Angeles Times*, 6 Nov. 1976.
25. 'Ford's Inclination to Run in '76 Intact', *Los Angeles Times*, 6 Nov. 1976.
26. Richard L. Lyons, 'Ford Welcomes Congress, Lists Essential Bills', *Washington Post*, 19 Nov. 1974.
27. Julian E. Zelizer, *On Capitol Hill: The Struggle to Reform Congress and Its Consequences* (Cambridge, UK: Cambridge University Press, 2004), p. 163.
28. Diane Granat, 'Whatever Happened to the Watergate Babies?' *Congressional Quarterly Weekly Report*, 3 Mar. 1984.
29. 'A Mandate to Do What?' *New York Times*, 10 Nov. 1974.
30. 'New Congress Is Youngest Since World War II', *Congressional Quarterly Almanac* 30 (1974): pp. 852–3.
31. Granat, 'Whatever Happened to the Watergate Babies?'.
32. 'New Congress Is Youngest Since World War II', *Congressional Quarterly Almanac.*
33. Sanford J. Ungar, 'Bleak House: Frustration on Capitol Hill', *Atlantic Monthly*, July 1977.
34. Stephen Green, 'New Members in House Planning for Bloc Voting', *Washington Post*, 30 Nov. 1974.
35. Granat, 'Whatever Happened to the Watergate Babies?'.
36. John Jacobs, *A Rage for Justice: The Passion and Politics of Phil Burton* (Berkeley, CA: University of California Press, 1995), p. 268.

37. For more on Mills's career, see Julian E. Zelizer, *Taxing America: Wilbur D. Mills, Congress, and the State, 1945–1975* (New York: Cambridge University Press, 2001).
38. Minutes of the Democratic Caucus for the Organization of the 94th Congress, 2 Dec. 1974, Papers of the House Democratic Caucus (HDC), Library of Congress (LOC), Manuscript Reading Room, box 4.
39. Rowland Evans and Robert Novak, 'Ford: Avoiding the Lame-Duck Label', *Washington Post*, 14 Nov. 1974.
40. 'Congressional Government: Can It Happen?' *Congressional Quarterly Weekly Report*, 28 June 1975.
41. Mary Russell, 'GOP Fears Return of "King Caucus" in House Next Year', *Washington Post*, 29 July 1974.
42. Hearings, Special Democratic Caucus for Consideration of Resolution Opposing Further Military Assistance to Cambodia and Vietnam, and Resolution Supporting the Emergency Employment Appropriations Act of 1975, 12 Mar. 1975, HDC Papers, LOC, box 6.
43. A. James Reichley, *Conservatives in an Age of Change: The Nixon and Ford Administrations* (Washington, DC: Brookings Institution, 1981), p. 323.
44. Jon Ward, *Camelot's End: The Democrats' Last Great Civil War* (New York: Twelve, 2020), p. 117.
45. David Nyhan, 'Carter, Congress Circling Warily', *Boston Globe*, 6 Feb. 1977.
46. Jack W. Germond, 'Congress and Carter: Who's in Charge?' *New York Times*, 30 Jan. 1977.
47. David Nyhan, 'Carter, Congress Circling Warily', *Boston Globe*, 6 Feb. 1977.
48. Memo from Stuart Eizentat, Walter F. Mondale, and Jack Watson to JC, 1976, Stuart Eizenstat Papers, LOC, box 130, folder 3.
49. David Nyhan, 'Carter, Congress Circling Warily', *Boston Globe*, 6 Feb. 1977.
50. Joseph Lelyveld, 'Liberals, Despite Humphrey Ties, Are Expected to Elect Byrd Today', *New York Times*, 4 Jan. 1977.
51. Jack W. Germond, 'Congress and Carter: Who's in Charge?' *New York Times*, 30 Jan. 1977.
52. Interview with James Fallows, 17 Sept. 1992, Stuart Eizenstat Papers, LOC, box 79, folder 1.
53. Second Interview with President Carter, 25 Oct. 1991, Stuart Eizenstat Papers, LOC, box 63, folder 8.

54. David S. Broder, 'A Neglected Democratic Party', *Washington Post*, 14 June 1978.
55. Martin Tolchin, 'Carter's Congress Lobbyist Battles Problems of Office', *New York Times*, 25 Feb. 1977.
56. Mercer Cross, 'Carter vs. Congress: At War over Water', *Congressional Quarterly Weekly Report*, 19 Mar. 1977, p. 481.
57. Edward Walsh, '$10 Billion Public Works Bill Is Signed', *Washington Post*, 9 Aug. 1977.
58. David S. Broder, 'Mapping Out the Carter–Congress Connection', *Washington Post*, 26 June 1977.
59. Jeffrey K. Stine, 'Environmental Policy during the Carter Administration', in Gary M. Fink and Hugh Davis Graham, eds, *The Carter Presidency: Policy Choices in the Post–New Deal Era* (Lawrence, KS: University Press of Kansas, 1998), p. 185.
60. Ward, *Camelot's End*, p. 115.
61. Jimmy Carter, *White House Diary* (New York: Farrar, Straus and Giroux, 2010), p. 165.
62. Second Interview with President Carter, 25 Oct. 1991, Stuart Eizenstat Papers, LOC, box 63, folder 8.
63. Emphasis as in original. Memo, Bill Smith to WFM, RE: Taking the President's Case to the People, March 21, 1977, Papers of Walter F. Mondale (WFM), Minnesota Historical Society (MNHS), box 153.L.20.2F.
64. Jack Anderson, 'An Optimistic President Faces a Mid-Term Test', *Washington Post*, 23 Apr. 1978.
65. Memo, Jim Free to Frank Moore, RE: Congressional Liaison, 23 May 1977, Jimmy Carter Presidential Library (JCPL), Office of the Congressional Liaison Files (OCL), folder 32, folder (House Memoranda, 2/24/77–11/10/80).
66. Jack Nelson, 'Carter Efforts in Behalf of Party to Pay Off with More Rapport with Congress', *Los Angeles Times*, 8 Nov. 1978.
67. Ibid.
68. Humphrey's death meant that both of Minnesota's Senate seats were contested in 1978, one in the regular cycle and one in a special election. Edward Walsh, 'Carter Performance on the Campaign Trail: 28 Tries and 12 Hits', *Washington Post*, 9 Nov. 1978.
69. Ibid.
70. Laura Kalman, *Right Star Rising: A New Politics, 1974–1980* (New York: W. W. Norton & Company, 2010), pp. 310–11; Dominic Sandbrook, *Mad as Hell: The Crisis of the 1970s and the*

Rise of the Populist Right (New York: Alfred A. Knopf, 2011), pp. 336–7.

71. John Herbers, 'Thunder on the Right Has Turned into an Insistent Rumble', *New York Times*, 4 June 1978.
72. Myra McPherson, 'The New Right Brigade', *Washington Post*, 10 Aug. 1980; 'The New Right Takes Aim', *Time*, 20 Aug. 1979.
73. John Herbers, 'Sweeping Right-to-Life Goals Set as Movement Gains New Power', *New York Times*, 27 Nov. 1978; Douglas E. Kneeland, 'Clark Defeat in Iowa Laid to Abortion Issue', *New York Times*, 13 Nov. 1978.
74. 'Brock Sees Gains as GOP Revival', *Los Angeles Times*, 8 Nov. 1978.
75. David S. Broder, 'That Shift in the Senate', *Washington Post*, 15 Nov. 1978.
76. Adam Clymer, 'Democrats Dominate', *New York Times*, 8 Nov. 1978.
77. Edward Walsh, 'Carter Performance on the Campaign Trail: 28 Tries and 12 Hits', *Washington Post*, 9 Nov. 1978.
78. 'The New Congress: A Small Step to the Right', *Congressional Quarterly Almanac* 34, (1978): pp. 3-B, 4-B; Jimmy Carter, *Keeping Faith: Memoirs of a President* (Fayetteville, AR: University of Arkansas Press, 1995), p. 77.
79. For a detailed account of the reform of the Democratic Party between 1968 and 1972, see Byron E. Shafer, *Quiet Revolution: The Struggle for the Democratic Party and the Shaping of Post-Reform Politics* (New York: Russell Sage Foundation, 1983).
80. Christopher Lydon, 'Strauss Symbol of Party Future', *New York Times*, 8 Dec. 1974.
81. Memo, Gerald Rafshoon to the President, RE: Mid-Term Speech, 29 Nov. 1978, folder 'Speeches – Memphis Speech File [CF 187]', Office of the Assistant to the President for Communications Files (OAPC), JCPL, box 61.
82. Mary McGrory, 'Midterm Gloom Among the Liberals', *Boston Globe*, 22 Nov. 1978.
83. Ibid.
84. Warren Weaver Jr, 'Democrats in Memphis: Of Birds, Sorghum, and Sincerity', *New York Times*, 9 Dec. 1978.
85. Edward M. Kennedy, Remarks at the Workshop on Health Care, Democratic National Committee, Mid-term Convention, Memphis, TN, 9 Dec. 1978, Adam Clymer Papers, John F. Kennedy Presidential Library (JFKPL), box 12.

86. See, e.g., Timothy Stanley, *Kennedy vs. Carter: The 1980 Battle for the Democratic Party's Soul* (Lawrence, KS: University Press of Kansas, 2010); Ward, *Camelot's End*, pp. 14–19.
87. David S. Broder, 'Democrats Back Carter on Budget', *Washington Post*, 11 Dec. 1978.
88. Will defined those two wings as the 'George McGovern-Walter Mondale-Dick Clark [liberal] wing' and 'the more moderate Sam Nunn-Ernest Hollings-Gary Hart wing'. George F. Will, 'Midterm Elections: Strange Politics', *Boston Globe*, 2 Nov. 1978.

11

The Favourite Son's Favourites: Ronald Reagan and the Presidential Home-State Effect in the 1982 Midterm Elections

Richard Johnson

American politics abounds with campaign folklore and truisms. One such aphorism is that popular candidates for high office generate a 'coat-tail' effect, whereby lower-tier candidates are boosted by the popularity of the candidate at the 'top of the ticket'.[1] Another axiom is that candidates for national office can benefit from a 'favourite son' (or daughter) effect, whereby voters give an additional boost in support to a candidate from their own state.[2] A third adage of US elections relates to those contests when the president's name is not on the ballot: midterm elections. A common theme in midterm election scholarship centres on the motif of 'over-correction' or 'balancing'. Voters who provided an electoral mandate to a presidential candidate then offset their choice two years later by voting for candidates of the opposition party.[3]

Scholars have studied the various configurations of these apparent laws of American politics at considerable length. No study has yet considered how these three maxims – (1) presidential coat-tails, (2) the favourite son effect, and (3) midterm election backlash – relate to each other. This is not surprising. Given that the president is not on the ballot in midterm elections, it is not immediately obvious that the presidential coat-tail or favourite son effect would apply. This chapter, however, posits that presidents have a 'ghost coat-tail effect' in these elections. The midterm election backlash theory implicitly embraces the idea that presidents have some effect on voting behaviour even in those elections in which they are not a candidate. This is well established, but no study has yet looked at how presidents' 'ghost' presence in a midterm election might play in their home state in particular. Is there some residual pride for the president that makes their home-state audience less inclined to 'punish' the president's party in the midterm elections? Can presidents use their personal ties to their home state as a means of assisting local candidates better than they can in the rest of the country?

This chapter explores the effect of a president's ghost coat-tails in midterm elections in the president's home state. It finds that in general, the evidence for such an effect is mixed. Sometimes the president's party did exceptionally well in the president's home state relative to the rest of the country, but at other times the effect was seemingly null or even negative. Different theories are discussed as to why this might be the case, chief among which is the strength of the connection between president and home state. Some presidents were strongly identified with their state and its local politics, especially those who had served as governors. US senators, while having had a statewide constituency, nonetheless spent most of their time in Washington. Other presidents were creatures of Washington long before they became president and had few durable ties to their home state. Their weaker personal identification with their home state might explain electors' weaker loyalty to them.

The chapter then moves on to explore an intriguing case of the presidential favourite son coat-tail effect in the 1982 midterm elections. In these elections, President Ronald Reagan's Republican Party lost a net of twenty-six seats in the House of Representatives and seven governorships to Democrats. Nationally, Democrats led the Republicans in the total popular vote by 11.8 per cent, one of the party's worst defeats in post–World War II history. Yet in seat terms the election losses were fewer than the national popular vote would imply.

The outcome was sunnier for President Reagan in his native California. The swing against Republicans was smaller than in the rest of the country in the House elections and virtually identical in that year's Senate contest. In the gubernatorial election, Republican candidate George Deukmejian improved his party's performance by 12.8 percentage points against a formidable Democratic nominee, Los Angeles mayor Tom Bradley. One close observer called the California governor race the Democrats' 'only major disappointment' that year.[4] This chapter highlights the 'ghost' presence of Ronald Reagan in the California elections, especially for the office which the former California governor once had held himself.[5]

The favourite son effect

Before parties reformed their presidential nomination procedures, the favourite son vote was an observable phenomenon at national party conventions.[6] State delegations boosted home-state candidates during presidential and vice-presidential roll call votes, even when the candidate was otherwise a lost cause, to signal local pride and call attention to local issues.[7] At a nominating convention, a favourite son was traditionally a no-hoper. However, this chapter takes a slightly more expansive view to refer to all national-level candidates who receive a boost from their native state.

Even after the Democratic Party's McGovern–Fraser reforms and similar changes were made in the Republican nomination process during the 1970s, the favourite son or daughter effect was detectable in presidential primaries.[8] In the 1988 Democratic primaries, the only state won by Senator Paul Simon was his home state of Illinois, which one opponent attributed to Illinoisans paying 'respects to a sitting senator'.[9] In 2004, Howard Dean, the former governor of Vermont, won a commanding victory in his home state's Democratic primary, in spite of having dropped out of the race two weeks earlier. In the 2016 Republican primaries, Ohio was the only state carried by its former governor John Kasich.

In general elections, home states tend to show extra loyalty to a local presidential nominee. Famously, the only state that Walter Mondale won in the 1984 presidential election was his home state of Minnesota. A notable exception was Al Gore's failure to carry his native Tennessee in the 2000 election, costing him the presidency. One might argue that Gore's linkages to

Tennessee were less robust than at first meets the eye. In spite of coming from a famous Tennessee family, Gore was born in Washington, DC, and spent most of his life there, including his boyhood when he was educated at the elite St Alban's School while his father was a US senator.

Every four years there is speculation as to whether the vice-presidential candidate can generate a favourite son or daughter effect for the ticket.[10] Campaign lore credits John F. Kennedy's selection of Texas senator Lyndon Johnson in 1960 with helping the Democrats win back the Lone Star State after the Republican Party's victories in the state in the previous two elections.[11] Overall, the evidence of state pride in vice-presidential candidates is less clear – in part because it is not evident that many people vote for a ticket based on the second-tier candidate.[12]

In presidential elections, the winning candidate almost always increases his party's vote share in his home state (Figure 11.1). Even presidents who lost ground in the national popular vote compared to their party's nominee four years earlier sometimes still gained support in their home state. In 1948, Harry Truman performed 3.8 points worse in the national popular vote than

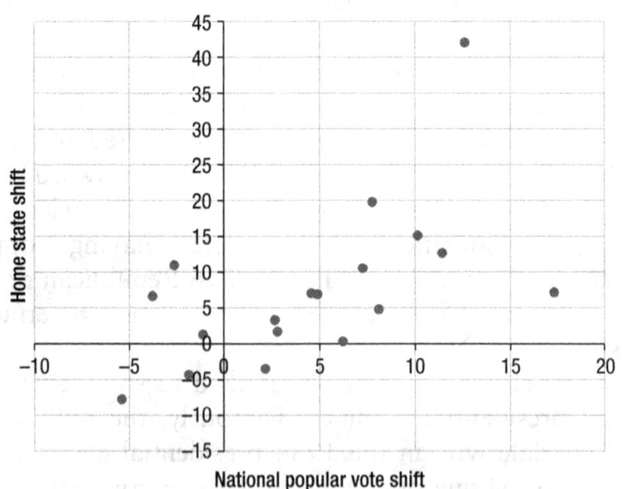

Figure 11.1 Percentage point shift in support for winning presidential candidate's party compared to four years earlier, 1948–2020

Franklin Roosevelt had four years earlier, but he outperformed Roosevelt in Missouri, Truman's home state, by 6.7 points. Bill Clinton underperformed Michael Dukakis's 1988 national popular vote result by 2.6 points, but Clinton did 11.0 points better than Dukakis in Arkansas.

The most successful favourite sons were both southern Democratic governors: Jimmy Carter and Bill Clinton, whose home-state affiliations were a powerful part of their political 'brand'. Carter, for instance, was famed for being a 'peanut farmer from Georgia'.[13] In 1972, Democrat George McGovern polled only 24.7 per cent of the vote in the southern state. Four years later, Jimmy Carter carried Georgia with 66.7 per cent, an astonishing 42.0 percentage point increase. It was Carter's best state in the election.[14] Additionally, Carter and Clinton were Democratic nominees at a time when southern states tended to vote Democratic in local contests but Republican in national elections. Having a local candidate on the national ticket appears to have stemmed this tide somewhat.[15] Another clear beneficiary of the favourite son effect was John F. Kennedy, whose distinctive Boston accent clearly marked the Massachusetts senator's local roots. In 1956, Democrat Adlai Stevenson won 40.4 per cent in the Bay State, losing it to Eisenhower. Four years later, Kennedy carried Massachusetts with 60.2 per cent of the vote.

In the post–World War II period, George H. W. Bush is the only winning presidential candidate who has failed to increase his party's showing in his home state (Texas). Bush's lukewarm performance is not surprising for a couple of reasons. First, Bush was very much a creature of Washington by the time he ran for president. He had served as Ronald Reagan's vice president for eight years. In the 1970s, he held roles which kept him out of Texas: ambassador to the United Nations and to China, director of the CIA, and national chair of the Republican Party. The last time that Bush was elected to office in Texas was in 1968, two decades before his run for the presidency. Two other candidates lost ground in their home states (Eisenhower in Kansas and Obama in Illinois), but only in their re-elections. They may have 'maxed out' their local support in their first election campaign.

Table 11.1 Favourite son effect in first successful presidential election, 1948–2016

President	State	Year	Relative home-state boost
Jimmy Carter	Georgia	1976	29.49
Bill Clinton	Arkansas	1992	13.62
John Kennedy	Massachusetts	1960	12.13
Harry Truman	Missouri	1948	10.54
Dwight Eisenhower	Kansas	1952	5.04
George W. Bush	Texas	2000	3.34
Barack Obama	Illinois	2008	2.50
Donald Trump	New York	2016	2.45
Richard Nixon	California	1968	2.13
Lyndon Johnson	Texas	1964	1.42
Ronald Reagan	California	1980	0.64
George H. W. Bush	Texas	1988	–2.26

Presidents' local 'star dust' in midterm elections

It is well established that the president's party nearly always suffers losses in midterm elections for congressional, senatorial, and other state offices.[16] This phenomenon seems particularly acute in presidents' second set of midterm elections in their sixth year in office.[17] There have been a handful of exceptions to the midterm backlash rule in recent electoral history. In 1998, as President Bill Clinton was undergoing an impeachment process for having lied about an affair, Clinton's Democratic Party gained four seats in the House of Representatives and held steady in the Senate. Four years later, Republican President George W. Bush defied the midterm backlash rule in the first set of federal elections since the 9/11 terrorist attacks, gaining eight House and two Senate seats, the first time a president had made gains in both chambers in a midterm election since Franklin Roosevelt's first term, as Iwan Morgan discusses in Chapter 4. There are no other examples of a two-chamber midterm election gain since the establishment of the Republicans and Democrats as the two main parties in 1860.

Americans orient their evaluation of lower-level candidates in part based on their assessment of the president.[18] This coat-tail effect is well documented in presidential election years. In 2016, a state's presidential pick was exactly predictive of its Senate choice's party affiliation. Yet, even in off-year elections, presidents tie their own success with that of their party. President Barack Obama frequently campaigned in midterm elections reminding supporters that, at least in spirit, he and his agenda were on the ballot.[19] Similarly, in the 2018 midterm elections, Donald Trump told supporters, 'I'm not on the ticket, but I am on the ticket, because this is also a referendum about me. I want you to vote. Pretend I'm on the ballot.'[20]

Given that voters seemingly respond more favourably to a home-state presidential candidate and given that many presidents argue that they are symbolically on the ballot even in midterm election years, it is worth exploring the extent to which the favourite son effect lingers in the midterm election cycle. The simplest way to determine a midterm favourite son effect is to compare the change in the support for the president's party in their home state and nationally across two elections. An increase in the party's support in the president's home state is not itself indicative of the favourite son effect. The boost must *outpace* the national swing. To keep election type constant, I compared the popular vote for House of Representatives elections in the year of the president's election and in their first midterm election. I then calculated the total votes cast for the president's party's House candidates in their home state across these two elections. I subtracted national swing from home state swing to calculate the favourite son effect. Using data from every midterm election since 1954, I find that on average, the president's party outperforms the national trend in the president's home state by 2.5 points.

However, it might be argued that the favourite son effect is partially concealed by this comparison between a presidential election year and an off-year election. I, therefore, also examined two proximate midterm election cycles. To draw this comparison, I compare the governor elections on either side of the presidential election. As it happens, every recent president's home state holds its governor's elections in even off-year elections (in midterm elections, that is), making the comparison across presidents straightforward. I find that on average the gubernatorial

Table 11.2 The favourite son effect in midterm elections

President	Party	Home state	First midterm	House (2-year)	Governor (4-year)
Dwight Eisenhower	R	Kansas	1954	–0.63	3.15
John Kennedy	D	Massachusetts	1962	–0.41	–1.73
Lyndon Johnson	D	Texas	1966	19.96	23.02
Richard Nixon	R	California	1970	–2.55	–1.22
Jimmy Carter	D	Georgia	1978	8.18	15.63
Ronald Reagan	R	California	1982	0.93	13.96
George H. W. Bush	R	Texas	1990	7.72	–4.25
Bill Clinton	D	Arkansas	1994	–6.30	10.82
George W. Bush	R	Texas	2002	1.94	–10.05
Barack Obama	D	Illinois	2010	–1.46	3.11
Donald Trump	R	New York	2018	–0.07	–2.04
			AVERAGE:	2.48	4.58

President's party performance in home state relative to national performance in House and gubernatorial elections at first midterm elections

candidate of the president's party performed 4.6 points better in their home state relative to national trends.

Some presidents seem better able to deliver the effect than others. Lyndon Johnson's and Jimmy Carter's home-state Democrats performed exceptionally well, compared to national trends, when they were in the White House. Ronald Reagan's California Republicans also outpolled national trends, especially in the gubernatorial election. For other presidents, the effect is not particularly strong. Indeed, California and New York appear to have revolted *even more* against their apparent favourite sons Richard Nixon and Donald Trump, respectively, than the country at large.

Of course, there are many other factors that explain why a president's party did better or worse in a set of House or gubernatorial elections. One set of candidates might be weak, while the comparator set might have been exceptionally strong. This chapter does not seek to assert a causal link; the data cannot definitively show the favourite son effect. However, they do demonstrate a modest pattern. I propose that a case study will help to illustrate the ways in which a president can sprinkle their 'star dust' on their home state and help boost their chosen candidates.

The 1982 midterm elections

Ronald Reagan entered the White House in 1981 with a deserved air of triumph. Reagan had secured a lopsided electoral college victory, winning forty-four states and 489 electoral college votes. Gaining twelve Senate seats off the Democrats, his Republican Party won control of the US Senate for the first time since 1952. An assassination attempt by John Hinckley on 30 March 1981 helped to prolong Reagan's honeymoon. In the six weeks to follow, Reagan's approval rating hovered at about 67 per cent. With an approval rating around 60 per cent throughout the summer of 1981 (Figure 11.2), Reagan was able to pass his budget through the Democratic-controlled House of Representatives thanks to southern Democratic support (217–211) in June. He then passed sweeping tax cuts in August by an even healthier margin of 238–195.[21]

Things were going so well in 1981 that conservative activist Phyllis Schlafly was even openly discussing the prospect of the Republicans winning control of the House of Representatives in 1982.[22] Schlafly's view was shared by many in the commentariat. On the one-year anniversary of his election, Reagan's approval was still over 50 per cent. One Democratic member of the House of Representatives, Eugene Atkinson, who represented Beaver County in industrial south-western Pennsylvania, crossed the aisle to become a Republican, anticipating the coming tide.[23] By the start of 1982, Democrats had grown highly pessimistic about their chances of retaking the Senate and worried about losing House seats to the Republicans. 'Panic is not too strong a word to describe it,' reflected the executive director of the Democratic Congressional Campaign Committee (DCCC) Martin Franks in April 1982.[24]

By the autumn of 1982, the picture looked very different. The United States was in the midst of a recession, experiencing its highest levels of post-war unemployment. The last jobs report before election day, issued on 8 October 1982, showed unemployment at 10.1 per cent, a forty-two-year high. Sixty-two per cent of Americans identified unemployment as the most serious problem facing America. The federal budget deficit was

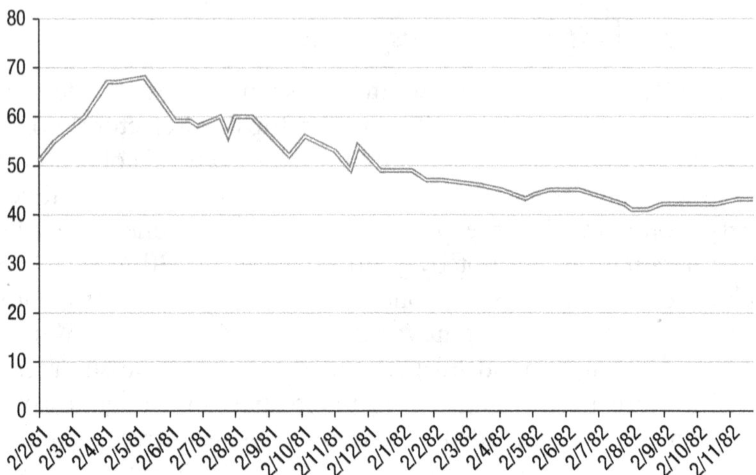

Figure 11.2 Ronald Reagan's approval rating (February 1981–November 1982)

growing. Congress had just overridden Reagan's veto of further spending. Reagan's budget for fiscal year 1983, submitted weeks before the 1982 midterms, was rejected almost as soon as it had been submitted to Congress.

The economic crisis cast a dark pall over the Republicans' electoral prospects. Political scientist Gary Jacobson said that conditions were 'ripe' for 'disaster'.[25] By his calculations, Republicans were on course to lose about fifty-eight House seats. Yet some polling experts cautioned that 1982 was not likely to be as bad for the Republicans as the 'fundamentals' suggested. Republican pollster Robert Teeter, president of Market Opinion Research, found that voters were showing a degree of 'patience' with President Reagan. His focus groups were telling him 'it took a while to get into this mess and it will take a long time to get out of it.'[26] Reagan's approval ratings gave some hint to this. Although Reagan's approval ratings had dipped, they remained stable in the low to mid-40s. This was relatively impressive given that millions of Americans were out of work. In contrast, Jimmy Carter's approval rating had been in the low to mid-30s in his final year in office when unemployment had been lower. Democratic consultant Peter Hart advised Democratic leaders that 1982 would be a 'midcourse correction' on the economy rather than a direct repudiation of Reagan.[27] Hart's voter research showed that 'they don't want to give up on Reagan'.[28] Voters were sceptical about Reaganomics but still liked the president for the most part.

Reagan, for his part, reinforced this narrative. His strategy had three components. First, he blamed the Democrats for the economic malaise. Four days after the catastrophic October jobs report, the president delivered a national televised address in which he blamed Congress and the previous administration for sinking the American economy with their profligate spending and short-term solutions. Reagan decried '[t]he pounding economic hangover America is suffering', and he solemnly intoned, 'the current recession is part of a long series – a series that hasn't stopped, because in the past, when the crunch came, too many in government resorted to quick fixes instead of getting to the root cause'. Second, Reagan argued that his strategy would take longer than past responses because he needed time to lay down the country's new economic foundations. Reagan urged patience with his economic plan because 'there's no single instant cure'. He assured viewers, 'the one big difference between the recovery America is headed for today and the shaky, temporary recoveries of the recent past [is] this one is built to last'. Third, Reagan maintained faith in his overall optimism about the direction of the country. Reagan assured Americans that his vision was consonant with middle America, vowing that his administration would 'stand for the values of hard work, thrift, commitment to family, and love of God that made this country so great and will make us great again'.[29]

It seems that Reagan was able to avoid being dragged down by the economic crisis in part because American voters trusted his overall analysis.[30] Robert Rowland and Rodger Payne argued that, 'The Teflon sheath that seems to surround Reagan comes from [his vision]. The American people haven't been concerned with the details of Reagan's policies because those details seem like mere quibbles when compared against Reagan's vision of the future.' Reagan had promised to restore American greatness, and voters believed that he was committed to this project. In words that are reminiscent of President Donald Trump's relationship with his core base of supporters, Rowland and Payne assessed that Reagan's supporters 'endorse the aims of the program and treat specific policies and appointments as unimportant details. Consequently, they let Reagan get away with errors that might destroy a different president.'[31]

Infrastructurally, the Republicans were also in better shape than the Democrats. The 'over-correction' effect in midterm elections is, partly, a self-fulfilling prophesy. Ambitious candidates of the president's party sometimes hold off from running in a midterm year, expecting their party to do poorly, whereas strong opposition party candidates see midterm elections as an easier door to push. Similarly, donors are reluctant to give money if they expect their party to lose anyway. In both respects, 1982 was different because of Reagan's successful first year as president. The Republicans recruited a strong raft of candidates and out-fundraised the Democrats considerably.[32] The political 'boom' year of 1981 had helped the Republicans cushion the 'bust' of 1982. The buoyancy of Reagan's first year – with Republicans' skilful passage of budget cuts and tax cuts, Democrats defecting to the GOP, and the warm glow of Reagan's remarkable recovery from an assassination attempt – helped the Republicans raise money and recruit strong candidates for the upcoming midterm elections. The Republican National Committee, the National Republican Congressional Committee and the National Republican Senatorial Committee together spent $19 million on Senate and House campaigns in 1982, whereas the Democratic equivalents spent only $3.4 million.[33] Republicans had pioneered an effective direct mail solicitation effort, drawing partly on the expertise of North Carolina Senator Jesse Helms's National Congressional Club, which had raised millions for conservative causes by sending out impassioned letters in the post asking for donations.[34] Of the money raised by the Republicans, 85 per cent came from individuals donating less than $500, with an average donation of $28.[35]

The Republican Party's popular vote defeat on 2 November 1982 was the third worst in a post-war midterm, exceeded only by Dwight Eisenhower in 1958 and Gerald Ford in 1974.

Eisenhower experienced a poor performance in his sixth year in office, in the midst of a recession and in the wake of the Soviet Union's launch of *Sputnik*. The most disastrous midterm elections for an incumbent party occurred in 1974, when the country punished the Republicans for the Watergate scandal, which had seen President Richard Nixon resign from office in disgrace less than three months before polling day.

In seat terms, however, election day 1982 was a vindication of the Republicans' superior targeting effort and President Reagan's effective appeals in 'Reagan Democrat' heartlands. Democrats failed to win back the Senate, and they won only about half as many House seats as they had been predicted, lower than the post–World War II average to that point. Reagan's popular vote deficit was the seventeenth worst in post-war midterm history, yet his losses were only the tenth worst (Table 11.3). The Republicans had defied the odds, bruised but not broken. Given the circumstances, Robert Rowland and Rodger Payne assessed, 'It is not at all clear that the Republicans lost the election.'[36]

The 1982 midterm elections in California

Today, California is known as the bastion of American liberalism. Hillary Clinton won the state in 2016 with a margin of 4.3 million (excess) votes over Donald Trump, bigger than her national popular vote margin of 2.9 million votes. Yet, in the mid-twentieth century, California was known more as the epicentre of American acquisitive culture, pleasure-seeking, and individualism. The Pulitzer Prize–winning author Wallace Stegner wrote in 1967, 'Like the rest of America, California is unformed, innovative, ahistorical, hedonistic, acquisitive, and energetic – only more so.'[37] Governor Ronald Reagan (1967–75) came to embody many of this state's attributes. Rick Perlstein reflects that, in California, Reagan was 'a hero. He was like them – a midwestern transplant, from small-town Illinois.' For suburban Californians, 'He almost belonged more to them than he did to Hollywood', with his emphasis on traditional values, patriotism, and 'rags to riches' success.[38] Reagan won statewide campaigns in California four times: twice as governor (1966 and

Table 11.3 Ranking of change in popular vote and change in House seats for president's party at midterm elections, 1946–2018

Year	President	Popular Vote Margin	Rank	House Seats	Rank
1978	Carter	9.7	1	−15	8
1962	Kennedy	5.3	2	–4	3
2002	G. W. Bush	4.8	3	8	1
1966	Johnson	2.7	4	–47	14
1950	Truman	0.7	5	–28	12
1998	Clinton	−1.1	6	5	2
1954	Eisenhower	–5.5	7	−18	9
2014	Obama	–5.7	8	−13	7
1994	Clinton	–6.8	9	–54	17
2010	Obama	–6.8	10	–63	19
1990	G. H. W. Bush	–7.8	11	–8	5
2006	G. W. Bush	–8	12	–27	11
1946	Truman	–8.5	13	–55	18
2018	Trump	–8.6	14	–42	13
1970	Nixon	–8.7	15	−12	6
1986	Reagan	–9.9	16	–5	4
1982	Reagan	−11.8	17	–26	10
1958	Eisenhower	−12.4	18	–48	15
1974	Ford	−16.8	19	–48	16

1970) and twice as president (1980 and 1984). In 1980, Ronald Reagan won his home state with 52.7 per cent of the vote, the highest of any Republican in post–New Deal American history. Reagan won all but three counties in the Golden State, and he was the last Republican to win the San Francisco Bay Area. Reagan loved California. He later confided privately in his final term as president, 'I don't mind confessing we [he and his wife, Nancy] live in a constant state of homesickness for California.'[39]

California hosted two major statewide contests in 1982. Democratic Governor Jerry Brown, whose father Pat Brown had lost the governorship to Ronald Reagan in 1966, was term-limited after eight years in office. His ambitions turned to the US Senate seat, which was to be left vacant by retiring Republican Senator H. I. Hayakawa. Brown won in a crowded Democratic primary field with 50.7 per cent of the vote, trouncing his nearest rival, writer Gore Vidal, who won only 15.1 per cent. In turn, Los Angeles's Democratic mayor Tom Bradley focused his attention on Brown's now-vacant seat. Bradley had served as a mayor of

Los Angeles since 1973, and commanded an impressive 85 per cent approval rating across the state.[40] As an African American, he would be the first Black governor elected in United States history. He won the Democratic nomination with 67 per cent of the vote.

The Republican nominees were both unostentatious characters. Pete Wilson, who had served as a popular, if softly spoken, mayor of San Diego since 1971, was chosen to take on Jerry Brown, whose approval ratings as governor were floundering. For governor, the Republicans were divided between two statewide elected officials: Mike Curb, the lieutenant governor, and George Deukmejian, the attorney general. The former was a young firebrand conservative, while Deukmejian, according to former Nixon aide Douglas Hallett, was 'generally perceived as a plodding, competent, and not very exciting wheel-horse'.[41] Curb had been running for governor since his election as lieutenant governor in 1978. He began the contest as the favourite and outspent Deukmejian, $3.1 million to $2.6 million. Curb criticised Deukmejian, who had previously been a state legislator, for being a career politician, but Deukmejian found a more effective line. His opposition research team discovered that Curb had not registered to vote until he was twenty-nine in 1973. This meant that Curb did not cast a ballot in either of the 1966 and 1970 California gubernatorial elections, in spite of being eligible to do so, when Ronald Reagan was on the ballot. Deukmejian ran television advertisements questioning Curb's loyalty to the Republican Party and Ronald Reagan. Deukmejian said to camera in one of them, 'Curb has a lot of nerve attacking me when he didn't care enough about our state or nation to vote. He says he for eight years he was too busy – too busy to vote for Ronald Reagan.'[42] Deukmejian won the nomination in an 'upset' victory, 51 per cent to 45 per cent. In the general election, Deukmejian hired Bill Roberts and Stuart Spencer to run his campaign, the same men who worked on the activist actor's successful gubernatorial campaign in 1966. Behind the scenes, Deukmejian had been working to ensure that he held favour with the Reagan administration. In April 1982, he met privately with Ed Meese, counsellor to President Reagan.[43]

Shortly after winning the Republican nomination, Deukmejian and his family flew to Washington, at the recommendation of Ed Rollins, director of the Office of Political Affairs, to have a family photograph taken with President Reagan in the Oval Office.[44]

Reagan provided key infrastructural support for Pete Wilson and George Deukmejian, especially in terms of fundraising. California is a highly resource-intensive state due to its population and expensive media markets. Wilson spent nearly $7 million, the highest of any candidate in the 1982 midterms. Brown spent $5.2 million, making the combined costs of the California governor's race the most expensive in the country.[45] For his part, Reagan spoke at fundraising dinners for the candidates, often tying in such events with the time he spent at his Santa Ynez ranch where he frequently retreated as president. For example, Reagan spent eleven consecutive days in August 1982 at his ranch. At one fundraiser for Wilson, a cowboy-themed dinner attended by 1,600 supporters, Reagan raised $1 million ($2.6 million in 2020 dollars).[46]

Contrary to what the midterm backlash thesis might presume, Pete Wilson placed President Reagan at the centre of his campaign. He declared, 'The year 1982 is not just another election year because Jerry Brown will be a walking referendum on Ronald Reagan's policies – policies which I support and which Jerry Brown opposed.'[47] White House political strategist Ed Rollins was reported to have singled out the California Senate race as 'the White House's top priority', with Wilson described as 'getting royal treatment as the White House's favorite Senate candidate'.[48] A CBS News report on 23 August 1982 confirmed the framing of the California Senate election around Reagan, calling it 'a home state Senate race' and referring to 'efforts to link Wilson to Mr. Reagan's personal popularity'.[49]

In the gubernatorial race, George Deukmejian similarly did not shy away from his associations with Ronald Reagan. In a lengthy *Los Angeles Times* feature, Deukmejian was asked to name his hero. He replied, 'Ronald Reagan.'[50] Reagan made clear that he took special interest in the California governor race, having done the job himself for eight years. At an event for Deukmejian in Los Angeles in August 1982, Reagan reflected, 'You can't have held that job in Sacramento [governor] for this great state, so unique in all the countries of all the world, without having a lifetime feeling of proprietorship for it.'[51]

The Democratic candidates also did not campaign visibly against Ronald Reagan. Democratic Senate candidate Jerry Brown invited Reagan supporters to vote for him, telling an interviewer, 'I believe even people who support the President would be well-advised to consider voting for me as their senator because I provide a balance – a spur – to keep Mr. Reagan on the right track.'[52] A *San Francisco Examiner* reporter observed that, even when Brown critiqued an unfair US economy, 'he never mentions the president' except 'by implication'.[53]

Likewise, Tom Bradley rarely took aim at Reagan directly. Bradley's internal campaign polls 'showed many of his supporters expressed approval of President Reagan', according to his biographers J. Gregory Payne and Scott Ratzan.[54] Consequently, Bradley did not draw sharp lines against Reagan on policy. On immigration, Bradley said that he did 'not quarrel with the Reagan administration proposals'.[55] The *San Jose News* even ran a headline asking, 'Is Tom Bradley a Democrat?' Its heated editorial steamed, 'thanks to Ronald Reagan' there was no 'comparable liberal, Democratic Party line coming from Bradley'.[56] In fact, Reagan was not the target of a specific attack advertisement produced by the Bradley campaign. In the months before his announcement, Bradley was even more effusive to the former Republican governor, declaring 13 January 1981 'Ronald Reagan Day' in the city of Los Angeles.[57]

For all of Reagan's personal popularity, the Golden State had not escaped the dim economic conditions. Notably, however, many of the protests were focused on Reaganomics, as an economic theory, rather than on Reagan personally. At a talk given by Reagan's budget director David Stockman in Fresno in July 1982, protestors wheeled around a giant wooden horse with the label 'Reaganomics is a Trojan Horse'.[58] An October *Los Angeles Times* poll showed that, while many of Pete Wilson's supporters were motivated by personal animosity towards the

Table 11.4 California statewide results, 1982

	National US House	California US House	Governor	Senate
D	55.2% (+4.7)	50.3% (+5.5)	48.1% (–7.95)	44.8% (–2.1)
R	43.4% (–4.5)	47.5% (–3.7)	49.3% (+12.8)	51.4% (+1.3)

eccentric Governor Jerry Brown, 'much of Brown's support comes from voters opposed to President Reagan's economic policies'.[59]

In the end, while Reagan's 'star dust' was clearly a factor in California, it was not enough to overcome the background economic factors entirely. California gained two House of Representatives seats from the 1980 Census, growing from forty-three to forty-five members of Congress. Under the new district boundaries, admittedly drawn by Democrats in the state legislature, Republicans lost three seats while Democrats gained five. The statewide elections were cheerier for Reagan (see Table 11.4). Pete Wilson secured a commanding victory over the unpopular Jerry Brown. George Deukmejian eked out a narrow victory over Tom Bradley, an unexpected win, with polls having suggested that Bradley was set to become the country's first elected Black governor. After his victory, Reagan sent Deukmejian a congratulatory letter, the drafts of which are held in the Reagan Presidential Library. The first draft, likely written by a member of White House staff, concluded, 'With so many Democrats in Sacramento these days, you have your work cut out for you. But you know where you can get some sympathy.' Reagan crossed out the final line and jotted down a more humorous finish, 'But there's this other fella in Washington who has a similar "challenge" so you know where you can get a little sympathy any time you need it!'[60]

Other factors

Ultimately, the results of the 1982 midterms provide a mixed picture to the idea that the incumbent in the White House can provide a local boost in midterm elections. It could be argued that

California voters had already 'corrected' for Reaganism when they elected Jerry Brown as Reagan's gubernatorial successor in the 1970s. But Brown's controversial state judicial appointments, criminal justice policies, and flawed personal image guided Californians to support challenger Pete Wilson.

Similarly, the role of race in the Bradley–Deukmejian contest cannot be overlooked. Bradley attempted to pioneer a 'deracialised' strategy, highlighting his credentials on 'law and order' as a former police officer. He adopted the slogan, 'He doesn't make a lot of noise. He just gets things done', to deflect from perceived concerns about Black militancy. Bradley's campaign was virtually absent in the state's traditional minority and liberal activist bastions, preferring to focus resources in more conservative parts of the state. Bishop H. H. Brookins, a leading figure in the Los Angeles Black community, argued that Bradley had taken the Black community for granted. He told Gregory Payne and Scott Ratzan, 'He ignored the black community, and they didn't feel the fire for the campaign; consequently they didn't vote.'[61] Even Republican strategist Bill Roberts agreed: 'A lot more could have been done in the black community; the Mayor was not aggressive enough.'[62] Ultimately, Bradley's efforts to downplay his racial symbolism may have had the unexpected effect of depressing minority turnout while failing to achieve sufficient support from suburban, white voters.

Additionally, major statewide referendums had unexpected implications for that year's midterm election turnouts. In 1982, nine states (Arizona, California, Massachusetts, Michigan, Montana, New Jersey, North Dakota, Oregon, and Rhode Island) and a host of cities held referendums on whether the US should declare a freeze on the production of nuclear weapons. Obviously, such a provision was a symbolic measure, given that state and local governments have little influence over nuclear arms policy. But together the states (and large cities which also held referendums, like Chicago and Philadelphia) comprised one-third of the US population, making it the biggest same-day referendum on a single issue in US history.

In California, Governor Jerry Brown, a supporter of the freeze, saw an opportunity to differentiate himself on an emotive policy from ban opponent Pete Wilson. Brown ran an advertisement reminiscent of Lyndon Johnson's infamous 'Daisy' advert of 1964, implying that a vote for Pete Wilson would lead to nuclear Armageddon. The advert included three high-profile Brown endorsers – Los Angeles Dodgers player Ron Cey, composer Leonard Bernstein, and actress Candice Bergen. Cey said, 'I want to keep on playing baseball.' Bernstein said, 'I want to go on making music.' Bergen said, 'I want to keep on doing it all.' All of a sudden, the screen was filled with a fiery mushroom cloud, and a little boy could be heard pleading, 'I want to go on living!' The advert finished sternly, 'Pete Wilson opposes the nuclear arms freeze. Jerry Brown supports it. Vote for your life. Elect Jerry Brown to the US Senate.'[63] Wilson denounced the advertisement as 'character assassination' and defended himself: 'I don't think I am Mayor Strangelove trying to blow up the world.'[64] The nuclear freeze referendum passed in California (52–48 per cent), but Brown lost to Wilson (51–45 per cent).

The long-time California Republican consultant Stuart Spencer (correctly) predicted that conservative turnout from a handgun initiative would outweigh any liberal turnout driven by the nuclear freeze vote. Proposition 15 was designed to restrict handgun ownership by requiring all handguns to be registered with the Department of Justice, with the aim of then placing a cap on the number of handguns which could be registered in the state. The proposal was rejected by 62.7 per cent of voters. The National Rifle Association (NRA) and gun manufacturers were estimated to have spent around $6 million to defeat the initiative.[65] It is believed that the referendum drove turnout among gun owners who would not normally vote. One pollster, Mervin Field, had estimated that 38 per cent of voters would be gun owners, but the exit poll revealed that 48 per cent of those who had voted owned guns.

Conclusion

According to long-standing scholarly consensus, midterm elections are referendums on the incumbent president.[66] The scale of the president's defeat is usually said to depend on his approval rating and the economy. If the president wins his election in a landslide, his party is expected to sustain significant losses in the next midterm elections. Based on this political science, as the sheen of Reagan's exceptional first year wore off, commentators were expecting a midterm election which 'portended a Republican disaster of major proportions'.[67] In the end, the Republicans sustained losses, but they were not as bad as many commentators expected. In part, the Republicans overperformed because of their superior campaign infrastructure to the Democrats. Republicans' national campaign was better coordinated; they had a large campaign war-chest; they had recruited a strong set of candidates.

The 'rhetorical magic' of President Reagan may have helped to mitigate the worst political effects of the economic recession and record-high unemployment that characterised his second year in office.[68] As leading contemporary pollsters observed, 1982 was a referendum on the economy but not Reagan himself, who remained reasonably popular given the circumstances. *The Wall Street Journal*'s Al Hunt captured the mood, writing that many voters were reluctant not to give Reagan a chance. 'Thus it was hard to determine whether Reagan was a plus or minus for many of the GOP candidates.'[69]

There were no such questions in Ronald Reagan's home state of California. All four top-tier statewide candidates – Republicans and Democrats – went to considerable lengths to cleave to the president's positive reputation. Reagan appeared with reasonable frequency on the campaign trail, not least because he was a California voter himself. Such was his magnetism that he was able to fundraise $1 million in one night for Senate candidate Pete Wilson, nearly equivalent to the total median spend of a winning Senate candidate in 1982. Even if a causal effect cannot be definitively demonstrated with the data presented, there is little doubt that the celebrity presence of the home-state hero and favourite son Ronald Reagan was perceived by *all candidates* to be someone with whom they wanted to be associated.

This chapter, therefore, suggests that a favourite son president can make an impact in midterm elections. Presidents can sprinkle 'star dust' on their state's electorate, but they cannot cause voters to overlook important background factors, such as the condition of the economy, entirely. Moreover, a favourite son president can provide other resources, especially fundraising prowess, in expensive home-state contests. In California in 1982, the Republican statewide candidates ran *towards* the favourite son in the White House, clearly believing him to be a benefit rather than a liability, contrary to the conventional wisdom about midterm elections.

Notes

I would like to thank Jialing (Cindy) Liu for her generous assistance in helping me gather the statistical data on congressional, senatorial, and gubernatorial elections. This chapter draws on archival research conducted at the Ronald Reagan Presidential Library and the Mayor Tom Bradley Archives at UCLA. My thanks to the helpful and friendly archivists at both locations.

1. Charles Press, 'Voting Statistics and Presidential Coattails', *American Political Science Review* 52 (1958): pp. 1041–50; John Ferejohn and Randall Calvert, 'Presidential Coattails in Historical Perspective', *American Journal of Political Science* 28 (1984): pp. 127–46; James Campbell and Joe Sumners, 'Presidential Coattails in Senate Elections', *American Political Science Review* 84 (1990): pp. 513–24; Jeffrey Mondak and Carl McCurley, 'Cognitive Efficiency and the Congressional Vote: The Psychology of Coattail Voting', *Political Research Quarterly* 47 (1994): pp. 151–75; Gregory Fleming, 'Presidential Coattails in Open-Seat Elections', *Legislative Studies Quarterly* 20 (1995): pp. 197–211; Franco Mattei and Joshua Glasgow, 'Presidential Coattails, Incumbency Advantage, and Open Seats: A district-level analysis of the 1976–2000 US House Elections', *Electoral Studies* 24 (2005): pp. 619–41; David Broockman, 'Do Congressional Candidates Have Reverse Coattails? Evidence from a Regression Discontinuity Design', *Political Analysis* 17 (2009): pp. 418–34.
2. Michael S. Lewis-Beck and Tom W. Rice, 'Localism in Presidential Elections: The Home State Advantage', *American Journal of Political Science* 27 (1983): pp. 548–6; Hanes Walton, *The Native Son Presidential Candidate: The Carter Vote in Georgia*

(New York: Praeger, 1992); Hanes Walton, *Re-Election: William Jefferson Clinton as a Native-Son Presidential Candidate* (New York: Columbia University Press, 2000); Franklin G. Mixon and J. Matthew Tyrone, 'The "Home Grown" Presidency: Empirical Evidence on Localism in Presidential Voting, 1972–2000', *Applied Economics* 36 (2004): pp. 1745–9.

3. Barbara Hinckley, 'Interpreting House Midterm Elections: Toward a Measurement of the In-Party's Expected Loss of Seats', *American Political Science Review* 61 (1967): pp. 694–700; James Campbell, 'Explaining Presidential Losses in Midterm Congressional Elections', *Journal of Politics* 47 (1985): pp. 1140–57; Alan Abramowitz, Albert Cover, and Helmut Norpoth, 'The President's Party in Midterm Elections: Going from Bad to Worse', *American Journal of Political Science* 30 (1986): pp. 562–76; Bruce Oppenheimer, James Stimson, and Richard Waterman, 'Interpreting US Congressional Elections: The Exposure Thesis', *Legislative Studies Quarterly* 11 (1986): pp. 227–47; Robert Erikson, 'The Puzzle of Midterm Loss', *Journal of Politics* 50 (1988): pp. 1011–29; Richard Born, 'Surge and Decline: Negative Voting and the Midterm Loss Phenomenon', *American Journal of Political Science* 34 (1990): pp. 615–45; Alberto Alesina and Howard Rosenthal, *Partisan Politics, Divided Government, and the Economy* (Cambridge: Cambridge University Press, 1995); Jamie L. Carson and Aaron A. Hitefield, 'Donald Trump, Nationalization, and the 2018 Midterm Elections', *The Forum* 16 (2018): pp. 495–513.
4. Albert Hunt, 'National Politics and the 1982 Campaign', in Norman J. Ornstein and Thomas E. Mann, eds, *The American Elections of 1982* (Washington, DC: American Enterprise Institute, 1983), p. 40.
5. Jeffrey Cohen ('Presidential Referendum Effects in the 2006 Midterm Elections', *Presidential Studies Quarterly* 37, 3 [2007]: pp. 545–57) found, perhaps surprisingly, that George W. Bush's approval ratings had a stronger impact on gubernatorial than senatorial races in the 2006 midterm elections.
6. Svend Petersen, 'Arkansas's Favorite Son', *Arkansas Historical Quarterly* 3 (1944): pp. 137–46; William G. Carleton, 'The Revolution in the Presidential Nominating Convention', *Political Science Quarterly* 72 (1957): pp. 224–40; James Prude, 'Williams Gibbs McAdoo and the Democratic National Convention of 1924', *Journal of Southern History* 38 (1972): pp. 621–8; Brent Tarter, 'A Flier on the National Scene: Harry F. Byrd's Favorite-Son

Presidential Candidacy of 1932', *Virginia Magazine of History and Biography* 82 (1974): pp. 282–305.

7. Hanes Walton, Pearl Dowe, and Josephine Allen, *Remaking the Democratic Party: Lyndon Johnson as a Native Son Presidential Candidate* (Ann Arbor, MI: University of Michigan Press, 2016).
8. Jeffrey Walz and John Comer, 'State Responses to National Democratic Party Reform', *Political Research Quarterly* 52 (1999): pp. 189–208.
9. 'Simon Win Clouds Democratic Race', *Lawrence Journal-World*, 16 Mar. 1988.
10. Christopher Devine and Kyle Kopko, *The VP Advantage: How Running Mates Influence Home State Voting in Presidential Elections* (Manchester: Manchester University Press, 2016).
11. Guy Land, 'John F. Kennedy's Southern Strategy, 1956–1960', *North Carolina Historical Review* 56 (1979): pp. 41–63.
12. David Schultz, 'Unconventional Wisdom and Presidential Politics: The Myth of Convention Locations and Favorite-Son Vice Presidents', *PS: Political Science & Politics* 49, 3 (July 2016): pp. 420–5.
13. Alette Hill, 'The Carter Campaign in Retrospect: Decoding the Cartoons', *Semiotica* 23 (1978): pp. 307–32; Douglas Brinkley, 'A Time for Reckoning: Jimmy Carter and the Cult of Kinfolk', *Presidential Studies Quarterly* 29 (1999): pp. 778–98.
14. Phinizy Spalding, 'Georgia and the Election of Jimmy Carter', *Georgia Historical Quarterly* 61 (1977), p. 18.
15. Walton, *The Native Son Presidential Candidate*; Walton, *Reelection.*
16. Hinckley, 'Interpreting House Midterm Elections'; Samuel Kernell, 'Presidential Popularity and Negative Voting: An Alternative Explanation of the Midterm Congressional Decline in a President's Party', *American Political Science Review* 71 (1977): pp. 44–66; James Campbell, 'The Presidential Surge and Its Midterm Decline in Congressional Elections, 1868–1988', *Journal of Politics* 53 (1991): pp. 448–87; Alesina and Rosenthal, *Partisan Politics, Divided Government, and the Economy*; Stephen Nicholson and Gary Segura, 'Midterm Elections and Divided Government: An Information-Driven Theory of Electoral Volatility', *Political Research Quarterly* 52 (1999): pp. 609–30.
17. Abramowitz et al., 'President's Party in Midterm Elections'.
18. James Campbell, *The Presidential Pulse of Congressional Elections* (Lexington, KY: University of Kentucky Press, 1993), Sidney

Milkis, 'The President as a Partisan Actor', in Jeffrey Stonecash, ed., *New Directions in American Political Parties* (New York: Routledge, 2010).

19. Peter Wallsten, 'Obama to Blacks: Vote like I'm on the ballot', *Wall Street Journal*, 26 Oct. 2010.
20. Ashley Parker and Josh Dawsey, 'I am on the ticket: Trump Seeks to Make the Election about Him', *Washington Post*, 18 Oct. 2018.
21. Stephen Skowronek, *The Politics Presidents Make: Leadership from John Adams to George Bush* (Cambridge, MA: Belknap Press, 1993), p. 423.
22. Phyllis Schlafly, 'Conservative Government in Our Future?' *Oshkosh Northwestern*, 29 July 1981.
23. Kathy Kiely, 'Atkinson Eases into Republican Fold', *Pittsburgh Press*, 15 Oct. 1981.
24. 'Campaign Costs up Sharply in 1982', *New York Times*, 3 Apr. 1983.
25. Gary Jacobson, 'Party Organization and the Distribution of Campaign Resources: Republicans and Democrats in 1982', *Political Science Quarterly* 100 (1985–6): pp. 603–23 (quotation at p. 613).
26. Hunt, 'National Politics', p. 29.
27. Hunt, 'National Politics', p. 18.
28. Ibid., p. 29.
29. Ronald Reagan, 'Address to the Nation on the Economy', 13 Oct. 1982 (Reagan Presidential Library).
30. The six-month lag effect in retrospective economic evaluations evaluated by Michael Lewis-Beck and Tom Rice ('Forecasting Presidential Elections', *Political Behavior* 6 (1984): pp. 9–21) was not likely to have shielded Reagan on its own because the economy was already hitting the rails in the summer of 1981.
31. Robert Rowland and Rodger Payne, 'The Context-Embeddedness of Political Discourse: A Re-Evaluation of Reagan's Rhetoric in the 1982 Midterm Election Campaign', *Presidential Studies Quarterly* 14 (1984): pp. 500–11 (quotation at p. 508).
32. Jacobson, 'Party Organization'.
33. Ibid., p. 609.
34. Frank Csongas, 'Conservative PACs Top Fund-raiser List', *Tampa Bay Times*, 3 Oct. 1982.
35. Jacobson, 'Party Organization', p. 610.
36. Rowland and Payne, 'Context-Embeddedness of Political Discourse', p. 503.

37. Jackson Benson, *Wallace Sanger: His Life and Work* (Omaha, NE: University of Nebraska Press, 1996), p. 316.
38. Rick Perlstein, *Before the Storm: Barry Goldwater and the Unmaking of the American Consensus* (New York: Hill & Wang, 2001), p. 124.
39. Letter from Ronald Reagan to George Deukmejian, 27 Jan. 1987 (4692 CI002, Reagan Presidential Library).
40. Mid-March 1981 *Los Angeles Times* poll.
41. Douglas Hallett, 'California's First Conservative Governor', *Law Policy Review* (Winter 1984): p. 62.
42. J. Gregory Payne and Scott Ratzan, *Tom Bradley: The Impossible Dream* (Santa Monica, CA: Roundtable Publishing, 1986), p. 235.
43. Letter from George Deukmejian to Ed Meese, 6 Apr. 1982 (FG006-01, White House Office, 070700-070999, Reagan Presidential Library).
44. Schedule Proposal from Ed Rollins to Gregory Newell, 18 June 1982 (PR007-01, 086000-087999, Reagan Presidential Library).
45. 'Campaign Costs Soar as Median Spending for Senate Hits $1.7 Million'. *New York Times*, 3 Apr. 1983.
46. 'Wilson Belts Reagan at BBQ', *The Lompoc Record*, 24 Aug. 1982.
47. 'Campaign 82', *Sacramento Bee*, 8 Mar. 1982.
48. 'Wilson sweeps into capital', *Los Angeles Times*, 2 July 1982.
49. https://www.youtube.com/watch?v=ugohlGQSkCs.
50. Nancy Skelton, 'A Cautious Man Counters a Dull Image', *Los Angeles Times*, 18 Oct. 1982.
51. Remarks of the President, Reception for George Deukmejian, 24 Aug. 1982 (08/24/1982, #2910, box 37, Reagan Library).
52. danieljbmitchell, 'Reagan Supports Wilson for California US Senator in 1982', YouTube, n.d., https://www.youtube.com/watch?v=ugohlGQSkCs, last accessed 15 May 2022.
53. W. E. Barnes, 'Super Campaign Manager Adds a Homey Touch', *San Francisco Examiner*, 11 Oct. 1982.
54. Payne and Ratzan, *Tom Bradley*, p. 239.
55. 'Campaign Press Releases, 1981–1982', box 597, folder 2 (Bradley Archives, UCLA).
56. 'Is Tom Bradley a Democrat?', *San Jose News*, 1 Oct. 1982.
57. Payne and Ratzan, *Tom Bradley*.
58. 'Stockman's Talk in Fresno Draws a Trojan Horse', *Fresno Bee*, 13 July 1982.

59. 'Poll Says Deukmejian Cutting Bradley's Lead, Brown Trailing Wilson', *Los Angeles Times*, Oct. 1982.
60. Letter from Ronald Reagan to George Deukmejian, Dec. 1982 (Reagan Library).
61. Payne and Ratzan, *Tom Bradley*, p. 281.
62. Ibid.
63. Jay Matthews, 'The Nuclear Freeze Issue', *Washington Post*, 1 Oct. 1982.
64. 'Nuclear freeze issue still carries some punch', *South Florida Sun Sentinel,* 5 Oct. 1982.
65. 'Gun Control', *Washington Post*, 14 Nov. 1982.
66. Gerald Kramer, 'Short-Term Fluctuations in US Voting Behavior', *American Political Science Review* 71 (1971): pp. 131–43; Edward Tufte, 'Determinants of Outcomes of Midterm Congressional Elections', *American Political Science Review* 69 (1975): pp. 812–26.
67. Gary C. Jacobson and Samuel Kernell, 'Strategy and Choice in the 1982 Congressional Elections', *PS* 15, 3 (Summer 1982): pp. 423–30 (quotation at p. 423).
68. Beth Ingold and Theodore Windt, 'Trying to Stay the Course: President Reagan's Rhetoric during the 1982 Election', *Presidential Studies Quarterly* 14 (1984): pp. 87–97.
69. Hunt, 'National Politics', p. 38.

12

The 1986 Midterms: The End of the Reagan Revolution?

Joe Ryan-Hume

As the sun set on 4 November 1986, retiring House Speaker Thomas P. 'Tip' O'Neill (D-MA) triumphantly declared to the press that the midterm election results had produced one clear message: 'If there was a Reagan Revolution, it's over.'[1] While Democratic politicians had tried to claim this at earlier points in the decade, Reagan had framed the 1986 midterms as a pivotal ideological contest to protect the revolution, presenting the election to the public as a decision 'whether to hand the government back to the liberals or to move forward with the conservative agenda into the 1990s'.[2] He had campaigned across the country, hoping to make the midterms a national referendum and recast them as a replay of 1980, the year that Reagan – and the Republicans – clinched the presidency and the Senate, and made decisive gains in the House. Moreover, Reagan believed he was in a strong position going into the midterms – following a landslide victory in the 1984 presidential elections, he entered 1986 with historically high levels of support (66 per cent in a *Washington Post*–ABC News pre-election poll) and the economy was finishing its third year of unbroken growth.[3]

Nevertheless, to many political commentators' surprise, the Republicans suffered heavy congressional losses on election day. Although seat losses in the House were, at five, not particularly damaging, the Democrats' gains left them with a large majority there (258–177). More significantly, a net loss of eight seats in the Senate returned the majority back to the Democrats (by a margin of 55–45). With the Democrats now in full control of the legislative branch for the first time during his presidency, the Reagan Revolution seemed to be stalling. The Republican class of 1980 witnessed seven of its twelve freshman senators lose their re-election bids, a development the *New York Times* noted was an indication that the power of Reagan and his revolutionary guard 'had crested and fallen back'.[4] Moreover, scratch at the surface of Reagan's landslide re-election in the 1984 elections and it is evident that the revolution was already in jeopardy. Indeed, despite the lopsided presidential race, Reagan's coat-tails were clipped on election day – the Democrats retained a commanding majority in the House and gained two seats in the Senate, though the Republicans remained in control of the chamber. Even Reagan's chief of staff, James Baker, acknowledged after the election that 'it was a victory for [Reagan] personally, but I'm not sitting here claiming it's a big mandate.'[5] Still, few had predicted the sweep of the Senate in 1986, with the election proving particularly significant because it shored up Democratic strength in the South and West – two areas the Democratic Party was increasingly pivoting towards – and showed that self-described liberals could win in a number of close contests despite the Republicans' substantial advantage in money and technology.[6]

To be sure, divided government had characterised the political environment in the 1980s, with Reagan facing a Congress partially – and now fully – controlled by the opposition during his presidency.[7] But with the Democratic Party losing much of its conservative wing as the decade progressed – with members either switching party or updating their approach to suit changing demographics – Congress was now considerably more liberal as a result of these midterm elections, which spelled trouble for the revolution. By detailing the story of grassroots organising behind the midterm election, this chapter reveals how liberals developed sophisticated mobilisation strategies to energise key voting groups to turn out at the polls in increased numbers on election day, particularly women and racial minorities. It highlights how in an era of supposed conservative ascendancy, these liberal voters provided the winning margins in enough contests to hand full control of Capitol Hill to the Democrats, reordering the balance of power on Pennsylvania Avenue.

Moreover, as will be discussed, the midterm elections had far-reaching consequences as well, particularly as liberals were now in a position to place significant checks and balances on Reagan and his eponymous revolution through congressional action. Indeed, the new liberal majority in Congress went on to pass several key bills that it favoured, defeat one of Reagan's nominees to the US Supreme Court, and block most of his conservative agenda in the final two years of his presidency, ensuring that Reagan's legislative success rate was the lowest for a president since *Congressional Quarterly* began tracking the data in 1953.[8] By showcasing the strength of the liberal coalition at the time, particularly the emerging power of women and minority voters, not only does this chapter explore the impact of the 1986 midterms on Reagan's mandate, but, through doing so, it offers a wider reassessment of the Reagan years that challenges the predominant historiographical view of this period as one of liberal decline and conservative triumph.[9] Speaker O'Neill's assessment that the revolution was over may have been slightly premature, but what is clear is that the midterm elections reordered its parameters.

The 1986 midterms: signs of an emerging liberal coalition

As an anti-government crusade that was decades in the making, the Reagan Revolution had a long arc. In many ways, it represented the apogee of a conservative backlash to the Great Society, which utilised government to expand opportunity and promote equality through programmatic means in the 1960s. This backlash was also fuelled by emerging social and cultural issues, particularly those concerning race and gender, and the contemporaneous rise of assorted movements clamouring for political recognition in the 1960s and 1970s, which led the Republican and Democratic parties to assume more polarised stances on a myriad of issues, including civil rights, abortion, and welfare. Crucially, by the 1980s liberal groups seeking to represent women and minorities, such as the National Organization for Women (NOW) and the Leadership Conference on Civil Rights (Leadership Conference), were increasingly professionalising their approach to party politics and demanding more than simply political recognition. And in seeking a suitable political vehicle to resist the revolution, they were also becoming more entrenched than ever within the internal politics of the Democratic Party as the decade progressed.[10]

Moreover, with the Reagan Revolution signalling the Republican Party's conservative transformation to the public, particularly evident when the party dropped its support for the Equal Rights Amendment (ERA), embraced anti-abortion legislation and welfare state retrenchment, and escalated tensions with the Soviet Union through ramping up defence spending at the start of the decade, gender started to correlate with partisan preference and election outcomes in enough contests to give credence to the belief that women were emerging as a more liberal voting 'bloc' under Reagan. This became known as the 'gender gap', a term coined in the early 1980s to refer to the electoral phenomenon of women voting for the Republican Party in significantly lower proportions than men for the first time in history.[11] A Reagan administration report warned in 1982, for example, that women were '. . . now emerging considerably more liberal and Democratic than men.'[12] Indeed, large proportions of women would move towards the Democratic banner as the decade progressed, albeit with differing levels of enthusiasm disaggregated across demographic subgroups, such as race and age.[13] And, in many ways, these women were driven there by the political environment created under Reagan and his revolution. Throughout the decade, evidence demonstrated that the disproportionate impact of Reagan's welfare state retrenchment created the so-called 'feminization of poverty' and the Republican Party's stance on issues such as the ERA, abortion, and affirmative action drove aspects of the gender gap across the country. By 1986, the gender gap had essentially emerged as a structural feature of US politics.

Still, despite these organisational and demographic developments, the prospect for liberal recovery appeared bleak prior to the 1986 midterm elections. Walter Mondale's landslide defeat in the 1984 presidential election precipitated the establishment of the Democratic Leadership Council (DLC) in 1985, with the purpose of shifting the Democrats rightwards.[14] Meanwhile, in

Congress, liberals struggled to pass the Civil Rights Restoration Act, legislation designed to broaden the scope of earlier civil rights laws and tackle discrimination based on gender, race, age, and disability. Fast-forward to 1987, however, and the political outlook for liberals was quite different. Indeed, the 1986 midterm elections changed the calculus. After intense organising, liberals mobilised turnout, particularly among women and minorities, to help secure full control of Congress for the first time in the 1980s. As many political commentators argued, these electoral victories undermined the notion that the Democratic Party had to move right to be competitive.[15] And by winning back control of Congress, the liberal community now had enough support to pass the Civil Rights Restoration Act.

To be sure, the Democrats elected to the Senate that year ran the ideological gamut. On the liberal side, former House members Barbara Mikulski (D-MD) and Tim Wirth (D-CO) had cumulative vote ratings of 89 per cent and 86 per cent, respectively, from the liberal group Americans for Democratic Action (ADA), while Richard Shelby (D-AL) and John Breaux (D-LA) scored a lowly 15 per cent and 17 per cent respectively.[16] Still, instead of moving rightwards, a majority of the Democrats elected that year had focused broadly on liberal campaign issues, albeit to varying degrees. With Democrats focused on advocating redistributionist economic policies, expanding civil rights legislation, and protecting access to abortion, rather than offering 'Republican-light' platforms, the outcome led *Boston Globe* journalist Martin Nolan to describe the election as a 'defeat for Me-Tooism'.[17] Moreover, the constituencies that helped elect these new legislators were part of a newly emerging liberal coalition: women, minorities, and young professionals. Together, they sent Reagan a powerful wake-up call on election day that it was not 'Morning in America' for them.

In the Colorado Senate race, for example, which featured two contenders whose ideological differences were as 'clear and sharp as Venetian glass', according to the *Christian Science Monitor*, these constituencies tipped the liberal candidate over the edge.[18] The contest between Tim Wirth and Republican Ken Kramer was thought to be a precursor to the 1988 presidential campaign, where a Reaganite Republican and a new-style liberal (or neoliberal) Democrat were likely to emerge as the parties' standard-bearers.[19] Colorado, a conservative-to-moderate state where the Republicans held an iron grip on the legislature, had voted only once for a Democratic presidential candidate since 1952. However, as part of a new breed of legislator to emerge out of the Watergate imbroglio in the early 1970s, Wirth was a 'neoliberal', advocating a leaner but more activist form of government and seeking to update liberalism to account for the rise of identity-based politics.[20] He carefully calibrated the way he espoused his liberalism to the electorate, focusing on broad-based issues such as jobs and clean water while targeting the inequities at the heart of Reaganism. This 'progressive pragmatist' approach, mirrored by many of his Democratic colleagues, enabled him to attract enough support to win by a margin of 1 percentage point – 49–48 per cent.[21] Alongside minorities and young professionals, Wirth relied heavily on women to provide his slim margin of victory (despite winning by only 1 percentage point overall, Wirth finished with a 5 per cent gender gap advantage over his rival).[22]

Significantly, a gender gap emerged in every statewide contest that year, appearing in all forty-two senatorial and gubernatorial races.[23] Indeed, in 1986, the *New York Times* confirmed that women were now reliably 'more liberal and more Democratic' than the opposite sex. One poll, for example, found that, while men were evenly split in their support for both parties, women were now 'solidly Democratic'.[24] According to NOW, more than any other single factor, women's votes accounted for the Democrats recapturing the Senate in 1986; the Democrats that were elected each received less than 50 per cent of men's votes, but won because they secured 50 per cent or more of the women's vote.[25] By using Census Bureau data to suggest that six million more women than men voted in 1986, NOW also pointed to the growing strength of the women's vote and the importance of mobilising turnout to ensure maximum impact of the gender gap.[26]

Moreover, with the raison d'être of the Reagan Revolution being 'limited government', it was particularly damaging that these midterms demonstrated how women were now 'more likely than men to support candidates with an activist view of government against candidates who think government is too big' – a clear philosophical preference that favoured the Democrats.[27] But it was not simply enough to support male candidates anymore, with 1986 also witnessing 'a particularly dramatic increase', according to NOW, in the number of women who ran for statewide office themselves (sixty women ran in 1986, three times the number of 1984).[28] Notably, these women candidates gained their support from the other demographic strands of the emerging liberal coalition – younger people, professionals, and minority constituencies.[29] It was this support that provided the winning margin for Barbara Mikulski, who was the first Democratic woman to win election to the Senate without having previously been appointed to fill an unexpired term. With Mikulski's election representing yet another crack in the figurative glass ceiling, NOW's president, Eleanor Smeal, described 1986 as a 'historically significant' year for women in politics.[30] Evidently, the liberal counter-revolution was advancing.

Crucially, NOW and similar membership organisations, such as the Leadership Conference, had helped fuel these gains by developing effective mobilisation strategies and working behind the scenes to support and fund these victories. Indeed, following the Mondale defeat, with Geraldine Ferraro as the Democratic vice-presidential nominee, NOW re-evaluated its political strategy and decided to shift focus away from the top of the Democratic ticket and expand its efforts to elect more women at all levels of government. The 1986 midterms became its primary target. NOW launched a new campaign, 'The Feminization of Power', which aimed to 'flood the ticket . . . from top to bottom' and challenge the conventional notion that only a slow, incremental approach would result in success.[31] This was still an ideologically driven operation, however – the goal was not simply to elect more women, but to elect more liberal ones. Eleanor Smeal acknowledged as much when, in 1987, she launched a concomitant political organisation, 'The Feminist Majority Foundation', in an effort to build on the success of the 1986 midterms and recruit and support as many liberal women as possible.[32] Others joined the cause, too, including Ferraro herself, who in 1985 formed a political fundraising committee that concentrated on getting liberal women elected to Congress in 1986. That year, Ferraro's committee focused its efforts on ten female candidates for Congress, eight of whom were elected.[33]

Alongside the rising power of the women's vote and its impact on Reagan's political mandate, demographic shifts in the South were also an important aspect of the 1986 midterms, demonstrating to a host of southern Democrats that they could not possibly hope to win election without attracting significant support from the more liberal-leaning constituencies in their regions. In particular, with southern whites continuing to defect to the Republicans, minority voters were becoming increasingly central to the Democratic Party's electoral fortunes in the once-solid South, often providing the margin of victory in close races. Former Governor Terry Sanford, who had previous ties to the Democratic Leadership Council (DLC) and was now running for the Senate seat in North Carolina, tackled this by enlisting Reverend Jesse Jackson to ease tensions with minority communities during the campaign.[34]

Moreover, as part of an even wider effort to harness the power of the minority vote and stymie the Reagan Revolution, liberal groups also started stressing to voters that control of Congress would determine the shape of policy and politics for the rest of the decade. As the *New York Times* pointed out, liberals, particularly those in civil rights organisations, argued that the election would 'determine whether the Civil Rights Restoration Act, bills to create jobs and other measures favoured by blacks are passed.'[35] Moreover, because nominees for the federal judiciary are subject to Senate confirmation, civil rights advocates claimed that only a Democrat-controlled Senate could act as 'a bulwark against attempts to appoint right-wing conservatives'.[36] Indeed, given the fact that the two principal Senate committees that dealt with these issues were chaired by staunch conservatives – Senator Orrin Hatch of Utah (Labor and Human Resources Committee) and Senator Strom Thurmond of South Carolina (Judiciary Committee) – liberals argued that regaining the Senate would give them the power to set and control the flow of legislation and structure the judicial confirmation process. Only months earlier, Reagan had been able to get the Supreme Court's most conservative justice, William Rehnquist, confirmed as chief justice, despite vocal opposition from liberals both on and off the committee.[37] Thus, liberals set out to convince voters that the stakes were particularly high in 1986.

In the end, according to the Joint Center for Political Studies, minority voters provided the edge in six Senate races (Alabama, Georgia, Louisiana, North Carolina, Nevada, and California – where the Democratic candidates each received less than 50 per cent of the white vote) and helped boost the Democratic margins in the two other contests (Maryland and Florida).[38] But the question became whether these newly elected Democrats would be responsive to minority voter interests. Immediate signs suggested that the new officials would – Senator John Breaux (D-LA), for example, quickly pledged to remember that 'he could never have won without the black vote' (he had attracted nearly 90 per cent of the Black vote, as compared to 40 per cent of the white vote).[39]

Clearly, despite attempts to push the Democratic Party rightwards after 1984, particularly those by the DLC, the 1986 midterms demonstrated the voting power of the party's more liberal-leaning constituencies and showcased the extent to which some of the DLC's most loyal adherents would be increasingly forced to juggle efforts to advance the organisation's cause with respecting the changing electoral dynamics of their regions. Some, like Alabama's Shelby, would eventually switch party as a result while others, like North Carolina's Sanford, would compile a more liberal voting record as the decade progressed. Still, in a more immediate sense, the voting strength of these liberal-leaning constituencies and the results of the 1986 midterms would have an important impact on the direction of policy in Reagan's America. During the campaign, Reagan had pleaded with voters not to make him a 'six-year President'; instead, they handed the nation's legislative machinery over to his opponents.[40]

Stalling the revolution: the impact of the 1986 midterms

In the immediate aftermath, the midterm elections provided a significant boost to the coalition seeking passage of the Civil

Rights Restoration Act. The Restoration Act was designed as corrective legislation to expand the power of anti-discrimination measures and civil rights statutes following a Supreme Court ruling in 1984. That year, the court ruled in favour of Grove City College, a little-known conservative educational outpost in Pennsylvania that had refused to sign a federal compliance form mandating anti-discrimination measures. During its defence, the college pointed to its historic tradition of rejecting state and federal assistance in an effort to preserve its institutional autonomy and protect its conservative principles. However, the college had enrolled students who received government-sponsored grants, which triggered the application of Title IX of the 1972 Education Amendments – designed to tackle gender discrimination in education – and the requirement to sign the compliance form.[41] Nevertheless, the Supreme Court ruled that the receipt and use of federal grants '[did] not trigger institution-wide coverage under Title IX', and that the college was only liable to such regulations at the specific entry point of federal funds – which, in the college's case, was the financial aid/admissions department.[42] Though the ruling only affected Grove City's admissions department, it had implications far beyond the college grounds since the 'program-specific' interpretation logically threatened a host of similar civil rights statutes.[43]

The Reagan administration and the conservative movement supported this ruling and, according to the Leadership Conference, 'vigorously opposed' the Civil Rights Restoration Act, claiming that it was liberal smokescreen for a vast expansion of federal power.[44] When opposing the Equal Rights Amendment (ERA) earlier in the decade, Reagan had argued that he preferred a statute-by-statute revision of laws to eliminate discrimination and enshrine equality. Given that the Civil Rights Restoration Act did just that, NOW questioned the sincerity of Reagan's argument: 'it is peculiar that Reagan has not come out strongly in favour of the proposed legislation – legislation that makes clarifying changes in existing statutes.'[45] Nevertheless, Reagan and his supporters staked out defensive positions and the bill was defeated in the Republican-controlled Senate, an action for which Senator Edward Kennedy (D-MA) chastised his colleagues.

'Shame on this body . . . we are tucking discrimination under the mattress,' Kennedy said.[46]

Determined to pass this crucial legislation, liberals shifted their focus to winning back Democratic control of Congress, thus ensuring more liberal voices on key committees to change the fate of the bill. NOW, for example, claimed they were going to tie the Civil Rights Restoration Act directly to the 1986 elections in an organising effort that would 'make the extension campaign for the ERA look small'.[47] This effort proved successful as not only did the arrival of more Democratic senators provide new allies, but by winning back the Senate, liberals secured control over the all-important Labor and Human Resources Committee, with the bill's most ardent supporter, Senator Kennedy, taking over the chairmanship. As NOW noted, the change in control of the Senate 'from Reaganite Republicans to liberal Democrats has enhanced significantly the prospects for passage of the Civil Rights Restoration Act'.[48] Evidently, with this new mandate for passage seemingly delivered, the policy landscape had shifted significantly as a result of the midterm elections, thereby checking Reagan's power to defeat or delay it.

Therefore, given this new political environment, the coalition pursued a fast-track strategy, believing that the bill had received an adequate amount of scrutiny over the years.[49] Within a few months, passage seemed inevitable; by June 1987, the bill had been reported out of committee by a 12–4 vote (with all weakening amendments defeated by a 2–1 margin) and over seventy senators supported it.[50] According to the Leadership Conference's executive director, Ralph Neas, this showed the importance of shifting the power balance in the Senate: 'Now you see what happens when you have a civil rights champion in charge.'[51] However, just as they were preparing for victory, the coalition's calculus changed abruptly when Supreme Court Justice Lewis Powell unexpectedly announced his retirement from the bench, opening a vacancy on the court. Crucially, Powell was seen as the moderate 'swing vote' on the court – he had voted with liberal justices on a variety of issues in the past, and decisively, in his last two terms on the court, he had cast the deciding vote in rejecting positions of the Reagan administration in cases involving affirmative action and abortion.[52] Thus, with the balance of the court now in jeopardy, this relegated and delayed consideration of the Civil Rights Restoration Act as the coalition agreed to throw everything behind the effort to stop Reagan achieving confirmation of a staunch conservative nominee.[53]

Indeed, having already successfully nominated two justices to the Supreme Court – Sandra Day O'Connor in 1981 and Antonin Scalia in 1986, the latter at the same time he named William Rehnquist as chief justice – Reagan was determined to use the vacant seat to ensure his conservative philosophy would outlast his administration. As Reagan's attorney general Edwin Meese claimed, the administration aimed 'to institutionalise the Reagan Revolution so it can't be set aside no matter what happens in future presidential elections'.[54] Moreover, the timing of Powell's retirement also gifted Reagan a much-needed opening to reinvigorate his administration, which was caught in the maelstrom of scandal at the time. Breaking the same month as the midterm elections, the Iran–Contra scandal was a complicated affair that eventually revealed the details of a covert and potentially impeachable operation conducted at the White House. As the nation would discover, not only had his administration violated an arms embargo with Iran under the pretext of securing the release of American hostages, but the president had also circumvented a congressional amendment to use the proceeds from such sales to fund anti-communist rebels in Nicaragua covertly.[55]

Therefore, in a combined effort to revitalise his presidency and cement his legacy, Reagan nominated Judge Robert Bork, an accomplished federal appeals court judge in Washington, DC, and a leading conservative legal theorist, who was considered a doyen of the Right at the time.[56] More than any other qualified candidate Reagan could have nominated, Bork was a symbol of Reagan's conservative campaign, an intellectual crusader for the Reagan Revolution. In what many saw as an effort to tilt the court's ideological balance in the president's favour, Reagan's choice galvanised the emergence of a coordinated grassroots movement to block the appointment. Liberal groups, such as NOW and the Leadership Conference, worked closely with a network of elected liberal officials, including Senator Kennedy, to mobilise opposition elements across the country and form a solid phalanx to 'Block Bork'.[57] Here, securing control of Congress in the midterms proved pivotal as liberals were able dictate the structure of proceedings and use their newfound prowess on Capitol Hill to block his appointment.

Facing a tough Senate vote, Bork's elevation to the bench demanded Republican unity and Democratic defections. At the beginning of his presidency, Reagan was able to convince southern Democrats to support his conservative agenda, but by 1987 the situation was different. As noted, losses in the 1986 midterms had given the Senate majority – and therefore control over the confirmation machinery – back to the Democrats. Moreover, five freshman southern senators had owed their margin of victory to minority voters that year, and numerous others facing re-election fights in upcoming years were conscious of the reservations in the region.[58] Aware of these shifting political considerations, the liberal movement placed heavy pressure on southern Democrats to oppose the nomination, sending a clear signal that significant political costs were associated with a vote for Bork. Speaking on behalf of the 'Block Bork' coalition, Reverend Joseph Lowery of the Southern Christian Leadership Conference powerfully told these Democrats, 'The people who support Bork will forget how you vote, but we will never forget.'[59] In the end, the southern bloc opposed Bork, which former Texas congresswoman Barbara Jordan argued was a reflection of the 'growing political strength of the region's black voters, empowered by the very civil rights laws and Supreme Court decisions which Bork had opposed'.[60]

Following months of intense conflict across the ideological divide, the Judiciary Committee voted nine to five against Bork's appointment on 6 October and the full Senate rejected him by 58–42 on 23 October after Bork refused to withdraw – the largest number of votes ever cast against a nominee for associate justice.[61] With a new mandate to check Reagan following the 1986 midterms, liberal activist groups outside of Congress had effectively joined hands with liberal officials within to paint a picture of Bork as a threat to civil rights and civil liberties and to help convince moderate senators to vote against confirmation.

To do so, the liberal opposition engaged in an effective public relations campaign that moved beyond the realm of classic left-wing tactics, utilising Madison Avenue–style advertising techniques to communicate their message directly to the people and control the narrative presented in the media – the most powerful example of this being the so-called 'Gregory Peck ad'.[62] A clear case of grassroots democracy in action, the 'Block Bork' campaign strategically and successfully navigated the court of public opinion to politicise the nomination and worked closely with the new majority in Congress to defeat Reagan's nominee.

In many ways the contest over the Bork nomination became more than simply a vote for or against Robert Bork; it represented a referendum on the Reagan Revolution as a whole. Bork's constitutional theories, if carried to their logical conclusion, threatened to break down the legal barriers blocking the implementation of conservative approaches to a host of issues, including abortion and affirmative action. And by confirming Bork, Reagan would have decidedly tilted the court rightwards and ensured his agenda far outlasted his administration. In the Reagan era, liberals viewed the Supreme Court as a last bastion for the defence of hard-won civil rights and social justice battles of the previous decades, and scored a major symbolic victory in defeating Bork. Moreover, the nominee eventually confirmed in Bork's stead, Judge Anthony Kennedy, proved more liberal on precisely the issues – sexuality, civil rights – that Bork's critics emphasised in their attacks. While ideologically conservative, Kennedy's expansive view of constitutional rights was sufficient enough at the time to placate most of the liberal groups who fought against Bork – only NOW seriously opposed him.[63]

In an immediate sense, the Bork campaign also reinforced to the Democratic Party that their more left-leaning constituencies still held significant political leverage, despite the continued pressure from the DLC to shift the party rightwards. According to the *Washington Post*'s Mary McGrory, for example, liberal voting groups, previously derided as 'special interest groups', were now being discussed in Democratic circles as 'constituencies' once again. 'Blocking Bork', McGrory wrote, demonstrated that 'liberal issues still sell'.[64] This verdict was immediately confirmed when the liberal coalition, empowered by the 1986 midterms and energised by the Bork battle, quickly refocused attention on the Civil Rights Restoration Act, writing to legislators across Congress to lobby for swift passage.[65]

Within weeks of Kennedy being confirmed to the Supreme Court, both the House (315–98) and the Senate (75–14) had passed the Civil Rights Restoration Act by wide margins, and the liberal coalition was now writing to the president to urge him not to veto it: 'A presidential veto of a bill to end federal funding of discrimination would leave a terrible and lasting stain on your presidency.'[66] Despite this, and warnings from Republicans that a veto would damage their election prospects in 1988, Reagan became the first president in 122 years to veto a civil rights bill (the nation's first civil rights law had passed in 1866 over a presidential veto).[67] Reagan argued that the bill would unjustifiably extend federal government power over the decisions and affairs of private organisations. 'The truth is, this legislation isn't a civil rights bill . . . It would force court-ordered social engineers into every corner of American society,' Reagan said. 'I won't cave to the demagoguery of those who cloak a big government power grab in the mantle of civil rights.'[68]

In response, liberals lobbied hard for senators and representatives, including those on the Republican side, to override the veto. On 22 March, the Senate voted 73–24 (all Democrats present voted in favour, with a 21–24 split for the Republicans) and the House voted 292–133 (House Democrats split 240–10, while the Republicans voted 52–123) to do so.[69] Kennedy claimed passage sent an unequivocal message that the nation rejected Reagan's 'narrow view of civil rights'.[70] Certainly, by reaffirming past civil rights statutes, its passage was a repudiation of the Reagan administration's approach. Not only did it restore the traditional practice of denying federal funds to discriminatory institutions, but it broadened protection for women, minorities, the elderly, and disabled citizens – all key Democratic constituencies. Following this success, the liberal coalition pushed Congress to legislate in another area where discrimination was rampant: housing. With eventual passage of the Fair Housing Act of 1988, the Leadership Conference claimed that these victories represented 'the most significant and dramatic improvement in civil rights laws in two decades', and were an indication that, despite 'fierce opposition', the 1980s would be remembered 'as an era of reaffirmation of our civil rights laws and remedies'.[71]

As a direct result of the 1986 midterm elections, in the final two years of Reagan's presidency, a liberal majority in Congress pushed through a number of key bills, defeated Bork's Supreme Court nomination, and proved robust enough to block most of Reagan's conservative agenda, ensuring that his legislative success rate was 43.5 per cent in 1987 and 40.6 per cent in 1988 – the lowest rates for a president since *Congressional Quarterly* began tracking in 1953.[72] According to the Leadership Conference's report card, 'while the Reagan administration continued to compile the worst civil rights record of any administration . . . the 100th Congress was one of the most successful and productive Congresses in our nation's history.'[73] Republicans had actually anticipated this, recognising the importance of the midterms for Reagan's mandate. As Republican pollster Richard Wirthlin noted at the start of 1986, for example, if Reagan was left without leverage in either chamber of Congress, 'the president will be very much on the defensive in 1987–88 and he doesn't play well on defense'.[74] This argument proved prescient, as the midterm results forced Reagan to operate in a more hostile political environment and delivered a significant setback to his eponymous revolution.

Farewell to the revolution?

Speaker O'Neill used the 1986 midterm results as an opportunity to administer last rites to the Reagan Revolution. However, rather than representing a premature epitaph for the revolution, the 1986 midterms signalled more of a course correction. Throughout the 1980s, Reagan's actions forced the emergence of a coordinated liberal counter-movement and spurred the development of politically sophisticated coalitions, with groups such as NOW and the Leadership Conference, as demonstrated, strategically building and refining coalition-based politics. In doing so, these liberal groups established direct ties with officeholders and increasingly moved in a partisan direction, forming strong institutional links with the Democratic Party as a result. By the middle of the decade, these groups had convinced enough voters that a Democratic-controlled Congress was necessary to check the excesses of Reagan and the conservative movement he led.

With the Democrats securing control of Congress, and with several senators owing their elections to liberal constituencies in 1986, liberals were able to gain significant concessions and counter the administration's conservative policies over the final two years of Reagan's presidency. The Bork defeat and the passage of two significant pieces of civil rights legislation exemplify this point. While each of these developments alone represent a substantial – and not necessarily predicable – victory, taken together they demonstrate the extent to which liberals, both within and outside the Democratic Party, had strengthened their political position by Reagan's second term. By modernising their political operations, honing their coalition-building processes, and updating their approach, liberals had clearly developed strategies in Reagan's shadow to mobilise their supporters and compete – successfully at times – with conservatives in the political arena. The 1986 midterms reflected a pivotal moment in the Reagan era, demonstrating just two years after Reagan's landslide victory that, while voters may have accepted some of its underlining principles, they still endorsed an activist role for government. Rather than a teleological view that overemphasises the binary relationship between liberalism's decline and conservatism's rise, the 1986 midterms show the extent to which the Reagan era was a far more complex and nuanced political era. Voters had heard Reagan's pleas to 'stay the course' but responded by altering the political journey of the nation, steering it in a more liberal direction and adjusting the balance of power in Reagan's America.

Notes

1. Quoted in E. J. Dionne, 'Democrats Rejoice at 55–45 Senate Margin but Still Seek Agenda to Counter Reagan', *New York Times*, 6 Nov. 1986.

2. Ronald Reagan, 'Remarks at the Annual Dinner of the Conservative Political Action Conference', 30 Jan. 1986, The American Presidency Project, https://www.presidency.ucsb.edu/node/254254, accessed 3 Aug. 2020.
3. Poll cited in David S. Broder, '1986 Stakes Unusually High for Midterm Election Year', *Washington Post*, 2 Jan. 1986.
4. Anthony Lewis, 'The End Begins', *New York Times*, 6 Nov. 1986.
5. Quoted in William Schneider, 'Half a Realignment: Why the Voters Rejected the Democrats', *New Republic*, 3 Dec. 1984.
6. 'Shifting power: 1981–1993', *Guide to Congress*, 7th edn, vol. 1 (Washington, DC: CQ Press, 2013), pp. 145–53. As both a political approach and a philosophical viewpoint, liberalism is a particularly elusive term. However, while it may not be systematic or logically coherent on every count, some key traits can be identified for the purposes of definition. Generally, liberals favour the use of government action to expand opportunity and achieve a greater degree of social and political equality through legislative and programmatic remedies; these views stand in contrast to conservatism and its emphasis on individualism, limited government, and market-based solutions to assure economic and political freedom.
7. Richard S. Conley, *The Presidency, Congress, and Divided Government: A Postwar Assessment* (College Station, TX: Texas A&M University Press, 2003), pp. 126–41.
8. Mark Willen, 'Congress Overrides Reagan's Grove City Veto', *Congressional Quarterly Weekly Report*, 26 Mar. 1988, folder 3, box 28, Leadership Conference on Civil Rights Records (LCCR Records), Manuscript Division, Library of Congress, Washington, DC, pp. 774–6.
9. See, among others, Gil Troy, *Morning in America: How Ronald Reagan Invented the 1980s*, (Princeton, NJ: Princeton University Press: 2007); Donald T. Critchlow, *The Conservative Ascendancy: How the GOP Right Made Political History* (Cambridge, MA: Harvard University Press, 2007); and Jeffrey Bloodworth, *Losing the Center: The Decline of American Liberalism, 1968–1992* (Lexington, KY: University Press of Kentucky, 2013). To be sure, there have been some recent, vital contributions to the historiography that offer a more nuanced appraisal. Timothy Stanley, *Kennedy vs. Carter: The 1980 Battle for the Democratic Party's Soul* (Lawrence, KS: University Press of Kansas, 2010); Lily Geismer, *Don't Blame Us: Suburban Liberals and the Transformation*

of the Democratic Party (Princeton, NJ: Princeton University Press, 2014); and Patrick Andelic, *Donkey Work: Congressional Democrats in Conservative America, 1974–1994* (Lawrence, KS: University Press of Kansas, 2019).

10. See Joe Ryan-Hume, 'The National Organization for Women and the Democratic Party in Reagan's America', *The Historical Journal* (June 2020), https://doi.org/10.1017/S0018246X20000175.
11. While gender differences in presidential voting had occurred in the past, the margins generally favoured the Republican Party instead; more women than men voted for Richard Nixon in 1960 (2 per cent) and Gerald Ford in 1976 (3 per cent), for example. Still, while the gender gap represented a significant breakthrough for the female vote, it is important to note that male voting patterns were also becoming more partisan, and thus more influential as well. For historic Gallup data, see Lydia Saad, 'Big Gender Gap Distinguishes Election 2000', 22 May 2000, https://news.gallup.com/poll/2884/Big-Gender-Gap-Distinguishes-Election-2000.aspx, accessed 24 Mar. 2021; and Henry C. Kenski, 'The Gender Factor in a Changing Electorate', in Carol M. Mueller, ed., *The Politics of the Gender Gap: The Social Construction of Political Influence* (Newbury Park, CA: SAGE, 1988), pp. 49–53; for contemporary data, see the Center for the American Women and Politics (CAWP), 'The Gender Gap: Fact Sheet', https://cawp.rutgers.edu/sites/default/files/resources/ggpresvote.pdf, accessed 24 Mar. 2021.
12. Lee Atwater, '"The Gender Gap": A Postelection Assessment', 23 Nov. 1982, in Julian E. Zelizer and Meg Jacobs, eds, *Conservatives in Power: The Reagan Years, 1981–1989 – A Brief History with Documents* (Boston, MA: Bedford/St. Martin's, 2011), pp. 114–17.
13. Evidently, the gender gap is a multifaceted, multicausal phenomenon, and data consistently illustrates that women are not a monolithic voting bloc. Across a majority of demographic indicators, women are more likely than men to report voting for Democratic candidates. However, this ranges significantly, particularly when delineated across marital status, education, and income, for example. For more information, see Kenski, 'The Gender Factor', pp. 49–53; and CAWP, 'The Gender Gap: Presidential Vote Choice', https://cawp.rutgers.edu/gender-gap-presvote, accessed 29 Mar. 2021.
14. See Kenneth S. Baer, *Reinventing Democrats: The Politics of Liberalism from Reagan to Clinton* (Lawrence, KS: University Press of Kansas, 2000).

15. Martin F. Nolan, 'An Election Defeat for Me-Tooism', *Boston Globe*, 17 Nov. 1986.
16. These figures are cumulative for Reagan's presidency. Paul Taylor, 'Senate to Have 55 Democrats', *Washington Post*, 6 Nov. 1986.
17. Nolan, 'Me-Tooism'.
18. Scott Armstrong, 'Race for US Senate Seat in Colorado an Ideological Tug of War', *Christian Science Monitor*, 23 Oct. 1986.
19. Ibid. The label 'neoliberal' was often used to describe the younger political class that emerged after the Watergate affair in the 1970s, who sought to recalibrate liberalism for a period of economic strain and update its approach to account for the rise of assorted civil rights movements. A common 'neoliberal' expression was that 'the solutions of the thirties will not solve the problems of the eighties' but, for all their scepticism, these newer-style liberals remained deeply committed to the ameliorative capacities of government and strongly supportive of egalitarianism and social justice. For a contemporary account, see Randall Rothenberg, *The Neoliberals: Creating the New American Politics* (New York: Simon and Schuster, 1984).
20. Rothenberg, *The Neoliberals*.
21. Armstrong, 'Race for US Senate Seat'.
22. Based on CBS/New York Times Polls, NOW Report, 'Women and Politics, Election '88', July 1988, folder 13, box 370, [Collection MC666], National Organization for Women Records (NOW Records), Schlesinger Library, Cambridge, MA, p. 6.
23. All but three of these gaps were pro-Democratic, with the three pro-Republican ones being moderate-to-liberal Republicans such as Senator Bob Packwood (R-OR). Ibid, p. 6.
24. Men split their party preference (45 per cent Democratic, 45 per cent Republican), whereas women were firmly in favour of the Democrats (50 per cent Democratic, 40 per cent Republican). Adam Clymer, 'Polls Suggest Women Support Democrats in '86 Races', *New York Times*, 11 May 1986; NOW 1988 Election Booklet, July 1988, folder 13, box 370, [MC666], NOW Records, p. 8.
25. Ellie Smeal, Memo to NOW Leadership, 17 Dec. 1986, folder 1, box 203, [MC496], NOW Records, p. 4.
26. NOW Report, 'Women and Politics, Election '88', July 1988, folder 13, box 370, [MC666], NOW Records, p. 1; The Center for American Women and Politics (CAWP) has the figure closer to five

million. 'Gender Differences in Voter Turnout', *CAWP*, 16 Sept. 2019, https://cawp.rutgers.edu/sites/default/files/resources/genderdiff.pdf, accessed 3 Aug. 2020.

27. 'Women and Politics', p. 18.
28. Ibid., p. 15.
29. The voters least likely to support women candidates are consistent with this liberal/conservative demographic divide – older voters, people in small towns or rural areas, those in blue-collar jobs or with lower levels of formal education, and voters in the South. Ibid., pp. 15–18.
30. Eleanor Smeal, 'Women Candidates Win Incremental – Yet Significant', *The Eleanor Smeal Report (ESR)*, Vol. 4, No. 10, 10 Nov. 1986, Eleanor Smeal Reports (Smeal Reports), Schlesinger Library, Cambridge, MA, p. 3.
31. 'Elect Women for a Change' 1992 Organizing Packet, NOW/PAC, July 1992, folder 8, box 330, [MC496], NOW Records.
32. Eleanor Smeal, 'Feminization of Power Campaign Launched', *ESR*, Vol. 5, No. 6, 23 Oct. 1987, Smeal Reports, 1.
33. According to Ferraro, 'my candidacy can't be just a footnote . . . Each point is a step in the historical process. Someday, this nation will elect a woman president.' Quoted in Sam Roberts, 'A History Maker Recalls the Door That She Opened', *New York Times*, 18 July 1988.
34. Lena Williams, 'Black Vote Courted in South', *New York Times*, 19 Oct. 1986.
35. Quoted in Williams, 'Black Vote'.
36. Ibid.
37. Benjamin L. Hooks, 'Statement of LCCR Opposing the Confirmation of William H. Rehnquist to Be Chief Justice', 28 July 1986, folder 7, box 61, LCCR Records; Press Release, 'NOW Opposes Rehnquist Nomination', 28 July 1986, folder 33, box 114, [MC496], NOW Records; Joseph L. Rauh Jr, 'Rehnquist: Not a Sure Thing', *Washington Post*, 28 July 1986.
38. Linda F. Williams, '1986 Elections: Major Implications for Black Politics', *Focus* 14.11/12 (Nov.–Dec. 1986): p. 5.
39. Quoted in Ibid., p. 6.
40. Dionne, 'Democrats Rejoice'.
41. Nadine Cohodas, 'Grove City Rights Bill Shelved by Senate', *Congressional Quarterly Weekly Report*, 3 Oct. 1984, folder 5, box 26, LCCR Records.
42. *Grove City College v. Bell,* 465 US555 (1984).

43. Title IX had been modelled after Title VI of the 1964 Civil Rights Act, which prohibited discrimination on the basis of race, colour, and national origin in programmes/activities receiving federal assistance; Section 504 of the 1973 Rehabilitation Act, prohibiting discrimination on the basis of disability, and the Age Discrimination Act of 1975 adopted the same model.
44. 'Dear Senator' Letter, LCCR, 2 Aug. 1984, folder 4, box 26, LCCR Records.
45. Judy Goldsmith, 'Testimony before Education and Labor Committee & Judiciary Committee', 21 May 1984, folder 28, box 201, [MC496], NOW Records, p. 7.
46. Quoted in Helen Dewar, 'Senate Votes to End Rights Debate', *Washington Post*, 30 Sept. 1984.
47. Quoted in Beverly Beyette, 'NOW Election Means New Activist Course'. *Los Angeles Times*, 22 July 1985.
48. Memo to NOW Leadership, 'Year in Review', 17 Dec. 1986, folder 1, box 203, [MC496], NOW Records, p. 6.
49. The coalition also raised the fact that fourteen former high-ranking officials from the Johnson, Nixon, Ford, and Carter administrations had testified on behalf of the CRRA. Ralph Neas, 'Enact the CRRA Now', 21 Apr. 1987, folder 1, box 28, LCCR Records.
50. 'Dear Senator Letter', LCCR, 11 June 1987, folder 2, box 28, LCCR Records.
51. Quoted in Lena Williams, 'Panel Approves a Key Measure to Battle Bias', *New York Times*, 21 May 1987.
52. John C. Jeffries, *Justice Lewis F. Powell Jr.: A Biography* (New York: Fordham University Press, 2001).
53. LCCR Memo, 'Notes on Bork Book', [undated], folder 5, box 55, LCCR Records; '"Grove City" Bill Delayed by Battle over Bork', *Congressional Quarterly Almanac*, 43rd edn (Washington, DC: Congressional Quarterly, 1988).
54. Quoted in David M. O'Brien, 'Federal Judgeships in Retrospect', in W. Elliot Brownlee and Hugh Davis Graham, eds, *The Reagan Presidency: Pragmatic Conservatism and Its Legacies* (Lawrence, KS: University Press of Kansas, 2003), p. 327.
55. See Doug Rossinow, *The Reagan Era: A History of the 1980s* (New York: Columbia University Press, 2015), pp. 181–200.
56. For a detailed account of the nomination, see Ethan Bronner, *Battle for Justice: How the Bork Nomination Shook America* (1989; New York: Union Square Press, 2007).

57. Senate Democratic Whip Alan Cranston (D-CA) urged mobilising a strong liberal coalition to stop an 'ideological court coup' by Reagan. 'Senate Press Release', 29 June 1987, folder 2, box 58, LCCR Records.
58. Robin Toner, 'Saying No to Bork, Southern Democrats Echo Black Voters', *New York Times*, 8 Oct. 1987.
59. Quoted in Michael Pertschuk and Wendy Schaetzel, *The People Rising: The Campaign Against the Bork Nomination* (New York: Thunder's Mouth, 1989), p. 78.
60. Barbara Jordan, 'Robert Bork: The Continuing Controversy, The Lasting Lessons', [undated], folder 8, box 1, Michael Pertschuk Papers, Manuscript Division, Library of Congress, Washington, DC, p. 7.
61. The split was along partisan lines – fifty-two of fifty-six Democrats voted against, and forty of forty-six Republicans voted for confirmation.
62. As Arthur Klopp, president of the liberal group People for the American Way, noted '. . . [we've] started using mass media and moving away from the old-fashioned politics of confrontation . . . the right wing is losing its grip.' Quoted in Ethan Bonner, 'Passing Judgment', *Boston Globe* magazine, 27 Aug.1989.
63. Molly Yard, 'Testimony before the Senate Judiciary Committee', 16 Dec. 1987, folder 26, box 114, [MC496], NOW Records.
64. Mary McGrory, 'Democratic Unity and Disarray', *Washington Post*, 8 Oct. 1987.
65. 'Dear Senator Letter', LCCR, 20 Jan. 1988, folder 2, box 28, LCCR Records.
66. LCCR Letter to Ronald Reagan, 8 Mar. 1988, folder 2, box 28, LCCR Records.
67. Republican Senator Rudy Boschwitz, for example, pleaded directly to the president: 'I implore you to sign the bill.' Rudy Boschwitz, 'Letter to Ronald Reagan', 3 Mar. 1988, folder 2, box 28, LCCR Records.
68. Quoted in Helen Dewar, 'Congress Overrides Civil Rights Law Veto', *Washington Post*, 23 Mar. 1988.
69. Ralph Neas, 'Congress Acts to Prohibit the Federal Funding of Discrimination', 2 Apr. 1988, folder 2, box 28, LCCR Records.
70. Quoted in Nadine Cohodas, 'Senate Passes Civil Rights Bill That Rolls Back Abortion Rules', *Congressional Quarterly Press*, 30 Jan. 1988, folder 3, box 28, LCCR Records, p. 215.

71. Ralph Neas, 'LCCR Hails the Enactment of the Fair Housing Law', 13 Sept. 1988, folder 10, box 42, LCCR Records; Ralph Neas, 'The Civil Rights Legacy of the Reagan Presidency: Forcing the Nation to Refight Battles Won Long Ago', LCCR Memo, Oct. 1989, folder 2, box 10, LCCR Records.
72. Willen, 'Congress Overrides Reagan's Grove City Veto'.
73. Neas, 'Civil Rights Legacy'.
74. Quoted in Broder, '1986 Stakes'.

Index

EU representative:
Easy Access System Europe
Mustamäe tee 50, 10621 Tallinn, Estonia
Gpsr.requests@easproject.com

www.ingramcontent.com/pod-product-compliance
Lightning Source LLC
Chambersburg PA
CBHW071730270326
41928CB00013B/2624

* 9 7 8 1 4 7 4 4 7 8 1 9 9 *